Exploring Society

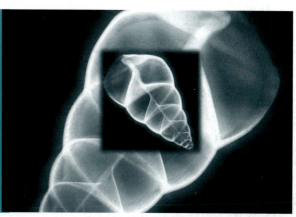

Sociology for
New Zealand students

Gregor McLennan, Allanah Ryan and Paul Spoonley

Dedicated to the memory of our colleague and friend, Nicola Armstrong

Your comments on this book are welcome at
feedback@pearsoned.co.nz

Pearson Education New Zealand Limited
46 Hillside Road, Auckland 10
New Zealand

Associated companies throughout the world

© Pearson Education New Zealand Limited 2000

ISBN 0 582 73943 8

All rights reserved. No part of this publication may be reproduced, stored in a retrieval system, or transmitted, in any form or by any means, electronic, mechanical, photocopying, recording, or otherwise, without the prior permission of the publisher.

Produced by Pearson Education New Zealand Limited
Printed in Malaysia
Typeset in Palatino

We use paper from sustainable forestry

Contents

Preface v

Acknowledgements vi

1   The sociological imagination: insights, themes and skills 1

2   The story of sociology I: enter sociology 17

3   The story of sociology II: from classical to contemporary 38

4   Gender, sexuality and identity 59

5   Family life 77

6   Education 96

7   Work and economic life 116

8   Stratification and class 137

9   Politics, state and nation 156

10   The city and city life 172

11   Racism and ethnicity 191 –

12   Health, illness and medical power 211

13   Deviance and crime 232

14   Social movements 251

15   Sport and leisure 271

16   The story of sociology III: from the past to the post 289

References 306

Index 319

Preface

There are several useful and interesting introductory-level sociology textbooks available to students today. Why offer another one? Our response to this perfectly valid question is threefold. Firstly, textbooks are often written as if the place, culture and politics of the teachers and students of the academic subject matter are irrelevant or of secondary importance. We do not hold this view, and would like to begin to overcome the customary division in our tertiary institutions whereby courses on 'sociological principles' on the one hand and courses on 'New Zealand society' on the other exist in isolation from one another. This book is neither a sociology introduction as such, nor a course on New Zealand society, but a sociology *for New Zealand students.*

Secondly, the book is designed to work through some important sub-areas of sociological analysis – health, social divisions, gender, etc. – through the filter of some running *themes* and *tools.* Too often, people doing sociology experience the subject as 'just one darned thing after another' – 'health', followed by 'sex', followed by 'class' and so on. To go beyond this familiar blockage, we have identified three main threads or themes of analysis which ensure continuity and cumulative learning. The themes are 'the social and the personal', 'the local and the global', and 'differences and divisions'. These pairings of terms are guaranteed to give us a handle on just about any debate and research finding in sociology today, and indeed the study of society is as much about grasping the significance of these themes as it is about absorbing information on particular substantive topics.

We have also singled out two traditional and inescapable general tools for enhancing our studies – *theorising* and concrete *investigation.* How do we conceptualise a particular event, process or belief? What theoretical debates and assumptions are relevant to the way we understand it? This is the theoretical dimension of sociological study. But sociology is not philosophy: answers to sociological questions cannot be resolved just in the head, that is, in the realm of ideas alone. Rather, concepts and theories must be accompanied by a process of research, or in simple terms, by finding out. Sociologists must always want to *know more* about their society, and whilst they cannot do this without theoretical ideas, those ideas cannot survive without relevant information about the events, processes and ideas that are being considered.

Thirdly, we have tried to make the book suitable for courses in the New Zealand tertiary system, which generally covers a period of 12–14 teaching weeks in a semester format. To that end, we have avoided producing a huge doormat of a text, yet have allowed some room for choice of focus by both teacher and student. Not only that; we have constructed the book in a fairly 'teacherly' way, with each topic being framed according to the set menu of themes and tools. However, since there is a risk here of 'recipe' presentation, each topic-oriented chapter has an insert written by a prominent New Zealand sociologist. Often punchy or argumentative in style, and showing how the general issue under discussion can be exemplified, debated and made to come alive, these inserts give the text diversity and breadth. In fact, they are consciously intended to showcase the thoughts of a range of people working in our sociological centres, and to remind us that whether in teaching, researching or theorising, sociology is a politically relevant and challenging pursuit. We hope that this variety of ingredients makes the book a little bit different – and that the sociological community in Aotearoa/New Zealand as a whole might come to see it as a shared project and resource.

Acknowledgements

We would like to acknowledge the help of Heather Hodgetts, School of Sociology and Women's Studies, and Viv McGuire, College of Humanities and Social Sciences, Massey University, for their help in producing this book.

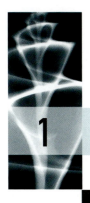

1 The sociological imagination: insights, themes and skills

Chapter aims

- to introduce some of the key features of sociology;
- to introduce the three core themes that will be used throughout the book;
- to discuss briefly the roles that theorising and research play in developing sociological knowledge.

Introduction

This chapter addresses three main tasks. The first is to say a few things about sociology – about what it is, about how it is best done, and about what you can do with it in your own lives. Secondly, we need to discuss the *core themes* that we have chosen to be running threads throughout the book. We see these themes not only as interesting ideas in their own right, but as a way of getting a 'handle' on the wide range of material covered in this book, and in the study of sociology more generally. Thirdly, we want to introduce the two main characteristic – and indispensable – skills of sociological inquiry, namely *theorising* and *researching*. In fact, we will concentrate on the role of theory in what sociologists do and how they think – not necessarily because theorising is more important than research (where research basically means 'finding out'), but more because theorising is sometimes perceived by starting students as being something that is quite difficult. Our view is that there is absolutely no reason for anyone to be afraid of doing theory, and that, in fact, theorising (and discussing competing theoretical perspectives) is actually one of the most enjoyable and rewarding aspects of the sociological endeavour. Ultimately, it is interesting theoretical speculation that results in true *insight*.

Why study sociology?

What is your own personal answer or answers to this basic question? There are many and various reasons for wanting to study sociology. Here are some possibilities, with a comment on each.

- Sociology can be of use in developing a *career.*
  We would not wish to convey the impression that there are plenty of jobs around for sociologists – job availability obviously depends greatly on the state of the labour market at any given time and also on the prevalent ideology of what it means to have employable skills. Even so, sociology has come to be recognised as providing the kind of *analytical* and *research* skills that are particularly suited for careers in state sector policy departments, the education system, the media, and commercial organisations which engage in research or survey activities. Sociology provides the kind of critical perspective that enhances work in 'people-centred' professions such as journalism, nursing, social work, teaching, personnel and human resources management. Sociology is also a great stimulus to engage in important informal areas of endeavour, such as community work, voluntary work, the churches, political parties and other campaigning social movements.
- Sociology helps us understand our own situation and helps in our personal *self-development.*
  For people who have just left school, sociology provides a deeper understanding of the contemporary social world and our place within it than do many other disciplines. For older students, sociology proves to be an invaluable way of giving formal shape to the rich practical knowledge that they have already acquired in real life. Sociology helps us understand real life experiences better, and often challenges the 'common-sense' assumptions that we hold – sometimes with liberating results. Whether we are relatively young or rather more mature, sociology helps us develop as critical and reflective selves.
- Sociology helps us understand the situation of *other people.*
  Sociology is about self-development. However, some people take to it precisely to *get away* from their own situation, problems and experiences. They want to know about *other people's* perspectives and issues; they want to develop a broader picture of the world as they have come to know it. Sociology enables us to do this.
- Sociology helps us to develop ideas which might *change* our societies and institutions for the better.
  A memorable slogan of one of the founding fathers of sociology, Karl Marx, was that to date, the philosophers have only *interpreted* the world; the point, however, is to *change* it. In a sense, understanding ourselves, understanding other people and getting the bigger picture is of limited value unless we also try in some way to connect them to social practice. Sociology constantly forces us to think about whose side we are on; what the way forward is; what we should be doing to change things for the better.

What sociology is

In his widely used international textbook on sociology, Anthony Giddens describes our subject in the following way:

> Sociology is the study of human social life, groups and societies. It is a dazzling and compelling enterprise, having as its subject matter our own behaviour as social beings. The scope of sociology is extremely wide, ranging from the analysis of passing encounters between individuals in the street up to the investigation of global social processes.
>
> (Giddens, 1997: 2)

This is as good a general definition as there is. First of all, it signals the fact that sociology is an academic, and in some ways a scientific discipline: like other sciences, sociology takes a distinctive subject matter for analysis. That subject matter is assumed to represent an independent and complex reality, and our analysis of it is assumed to produce knowledge of it, rather than merely whimsical or subjective opinion.

But Giddens's definition clearly also refers to the subjective side of social analysis. Sociology is 'dazzling' and 'compelling' to us – whether or not we can say it produces correct knowledge as such. And the 'scope of sociology is extremely wide' – so wide in fact that a multitude of topic areas can be covered, and a multitude of points of view can be debated. In sociology, nothing is ruled out and no views, not even scientific views, are sacred. So whilst sociologists do strive to ensure that their analytical and research work is as thorough – and in that sense as impartial – as it can be, sociology is the study of social relations undertaken from the points of view of people who operate from within those social relations. Sociology is the search of people who feel the *need to know* about their own and other societies. Sociology cannot, then, ever be a wholly objective enterprise, and indeed sociologists would argue that no human investigation, including science itself, can be wholly objective, if that phrase is taken as meaning an aspiration to a 'God's-eye view' of the world. Such a view is simply not available, and that means that there is considerable scope in sociology for intellectual debate and moral commitment.

One often hears the popular saying, 'the facts speak for themselves'. But in fact they don't: facts always have to be *interpreted* to take on any significance for us at all. Accordingly, in sociology, there is a necessity not only to ensure that all factual data are reliable, but also to let the inquiring *imagination* run free. Thus one of the key catch-phrases of introductory sociology emphasises the importance of *'the sociological imagination'*. The originator of this phrase was C. Wright Mills, an American sociologist working in the 1950s, whose message still speaks to us today. Mills describes the promise of sociology as 'the capacity to range from the most impersonal and remote transformations to the most intimate features of the human self – and to see the relations between the two' (Mills, 1959: 7). In this connection, Mills emphasises that what we often experience as private troubles in life – unemployment perhaps, or relationship difficulties, or personal apathy – should more appropriately be seen as public issues, things to be debated and researched. It was sociology's great task, Mills thought, to explore the interface between private troubles and public issues, and he went on to outline three key general steps in developing a more general sociological picture of contemporary social life (Mills, 1959: 6–7):

1   What is the structure of this particular society as a whole? What are its essential components, and how are they related to one another? How does this society differ from other varieties of social order? Within it, what is the meaning of any particular feature for its continuance and for its change?
2   Where does this society stand in human history? What are its characteristic ways of history making?
3   What varieties of men and women now prevail in this society and in this period? And what varieties are coming to prevail? In what ways are they selected and formed, liberated and repressed, made sensitive and blunted?

The three themes of the book

As mentioned in the preface, we believe that our learning in a subject like sociology is made more coherent and efficient if there are some keynote *themes* running through the programme of study. The three themes we have chosen are of intrinsic sociological interest, and indeed can readily be seen as variants on the main points that emerged in the discussion of Mills's 'sociological imagination'. In addition, the themes also provide a convenient handle for discussing just about any particular topic area in this book – and beyond.

The social and the personal

This theme is our version of Mills's contrast between personal troubles and public issues. It can be explained like this. We are all unique individuals. We have our own names, and nobody else's. We are our parents' children and nobody else's. We have our peculiar daily routines and practices; our own social, political and sexual preferences; and our very own emotions and thoughts. Nobody else in the whole world does things or thinks things quite like we do. Each of us is a separate person and we live our own *personal lives.* Sociologists would not deny these obvious truths. And yet, for sociologists, there is something very misleading about them, because as individuals we are profoundly shaped by, and live our lives within, an essentially *social setting.* We are our parents' children, for sure, but those parents are themselves inevitably parents of a certain social type – they may be white or black, Pakeha or Maori, middle class or working class, together or divorced, heterosexual or homosexual,

1 The sociological imagination: insights, themes and skills 5

employed or unemployed, country folk or townies, Americans or New Zealanders. These social traits actually make us what we are; and they are social rather than individual characteristics. Of course, the particular combination of traits that make up our particular 'selves' does distinguish us from many other people. But not as much as we sometimes think, because those traits themselves are usually general features of our society, applying to very many individuals, households and groups.

As individuals, we take on and reproduce **social roles** – as fathers, mothers, lovers, students, workers, etc. It is impossible to be lovers, for example, without negotiating in our most intimate encounters some very general and society-wide assumptions and expectations about sexuality, masculinity and femininity. Similarly, it is impossible to be a parent without taking on board many authority roles that are not so much freely chosen by us as imposed upon us by the current norms and structures of the society in which we live. As workers, our choice to work all day so as to be paid whatever we are paid is not a choice freely made: living in a capitalist society, we have to work according to goals and wages and products that are determined by firms that operate in the 'free market' economy. And inevitably, as workers of a certain type – printers, housewives (or househusbands), dockers, secretaries, computer programmers, teachers – we become accustomed to running our lives in this way, to living according to certain income standards and social expectations, to talking and behaving at work in a certain way, to splitting our work lives and the rest of our lives in a certain way, to becoming skilled at some things and useless at other things, to giving lots of time to some activities and none at all to others. In short, our working lives, largely constructed for us by the society in which we live, become a core part of our personal **identity**. And the same is true of the kind of more general 'peer groups' we belong to, the residential areas we inhabit, and the leisure circles that are available to us.

> **Social roles** are the expectations and attributes associated with social positions such as teacher, mother, father, worker, etc.

It is precisely because our social roles, practices and situations become an intrinsic part of our personal identities, often, that when they alter in a significant way, we experience an identity crisis or sense of loss. The experience of unemployment has been like this for many people – perhaps most obviously for many men, since in the past men have more single-mindedly than women associated the meaning of their lives with their paid work roles.

> **Identity** refers to the distinctive characteristics of persons (or groups).

> We were raised on work up here. I find myself even now thinking it's time to get up, and I put my feet out of bed, grab my trousers before I remember that I don't have to go. Then you get back in bed, and you're glad you're not late; till it dawns on you you'll never have to get up early again … You don't realise what it means to you … You feel as if your whole life is crumbling, You feel devalued out of work; you feel your age, you feel you have less to offer. Instead of feeling you're getting richer in experience, you feel something is being taken away from you.

(Seabrook, 1982: 109, 122–123)

The power of social reality over individual experience can be demonstrated by real life examples such as the above, and also in other ways. In a famous American experiment conducted by Zimbardo et. al. (1990), researchers asked approximately seventy college students to participate in a prison scenario, in which – by the toss of a coin – some were to play guards and some to play inmates. The author summarises:

> At the end of only six days we had to close down our mock prison because what we saw was frightening. It was no longer apparent to most of the subjects (or to us) where reality ended and their roles began. The majority had indeed become prisoners or guards, no longer able to clearly differentiate between role playing and self. There were dramatic changes in virtually every aspect of their behaviour, thinking and feeling.

> (Zimbardo et al., 1990: 177)

Finally, on this first theme, it is worth pointing out that the very idea of 'the personal' as something that might be firmly contrasted with 'the social' is quite a *culturally specific notion*. The idea of an individual self, inside each of us, as it were, fending off the influence of outside society, is very much a product of modern industrial, Western, liberal society. In ancient Greece, and in many tribal societies, both past and present (also in some aspects of Maori society), the individual simply does not have this precious, separate status. In those cultures, the individual is seen as being an intrinsic part of the society, since the society in a very positive sense gives the individual the collective resources, traditions and values without which a meaningful life could not be led. The point here is not necessarily to devalue individualism as a particular belief system: it is simply to point our that individualism *is* just one particular belief system, and not something that is part of a changeless human nature, as the Western tradition of thought has tended to assume.

In addressing the theme of 'the social and the personal', then, (a) we are keen to highlight the strong and varied influence of social situations and meanings on our sense of personal identity, and (b) we want you to be sensitive to the culturally variable ways in which 'self and society' are imagined in different groups or societies.

The local and the global

This theme deals with aspects of C. Wright Mills's advice that we have to look at how the social world is *changing* over time. It appears as if the modern social world has become more global than ever in the period since Mills wrote: we seem to live in an increasingly *interconnected world*. This is a world in which certain distinctive social relations prevail (such as capitalism, i.e. the buying and selling of goods for profit on the free market). But it is also a society which *changes*, both historically and geographically, and sometimes these changes are very dramatic. For example, only ten or twelve years ago it was almost unthinkable to the generation of people brought up through forty years of Cold War between the capitalist, liberal West and the state socialist societies of the Soviet Union and Eastern Europe, that the social system of the latter nations would crumble as dramatically as it did in 1989 and in the 1990s.

A useful way of looking at the most recent phases in the **globalisation** of modern society is to think of what the American sociologist George Ritzer has termed 'the McDonaldisation of society' (Ritzer, 1993). McDonald's was founded as a family restaurant in Pasadena, California, in 1937, and it was not until the mid-1950s that it was transformed into a franchised business, and was gradually 'cloned' throughout the USA and subsequently throughout the world. By 1991, McDonald's had 13 000 outlets in a great many countries, with a total sales turnover of $6.8 billion. In China, the biggest McDonald's in the world (seating for 700) opened in April 1992, recording 40 000 customers on its first day. In Moscow – the previous heartland of the Communist world – there is a McDonald's which is staffed by over 1200 young people, who, like their counterparts everywhere else are paid low wages for fast, intense, but basic service.

Globalisation refers to the increasing interdependence between societies on a worldwide basis.

Where is *this* McDonald's?

However, it is not only these bare economic facts of global spread that we should dwell on. Nor are we talking only about the firm called McDonald's – we could just as easily be talking about the 'K-Martisation' or 'Coke-isation' of society. The point is also to look at the way in which a common *culture of consumption* is being created across the globe, touching not only on the way work is organised, but also on

8 Exploring Society

> Rationalisation is the process by which all aspects of human action become subject to calculation, measurement and control.

the way we shop, eat and interact, and even on the way we think. McDonaldisation creates a model and an image of society itself in quite a broad sense. It encourages the reaction that this is the way things must go, and that this way is accessible, affordable, and good. Ritzer himself wants to say that, very generally, McDonaldisation graphically illustrates the process of **rationalisation** that the classical sociologist Max Weber identified as one of the central tendencies of modern industrial society – a social dynamic that increasingly requires things (and people) to be standardised, calculable, and disciplined into a common way of life. Think about it this way:

- McDonaldisation is a way of organising economic firms – the model of cheap and efficient work organisation now prevails in the consumption industries worldwide.
- McDonaldisation in fact represents an increasing emphasis on consumption and services as the leading socio-economic sector (as opposed to manufacturing, production, materials extraction, or public service).
- McDonaldisation represents a model for *privatising* all the very different types of consumer provision, whether in the private or public sector – there are, for instance, areas that were previously in the public domain of health that are now private, operated by firms with names like 'McDentist' and 'McDoctor'.
- McDonaldisation has transformed patterns of *leisure* activities. Its outlets have become places for the expression of youth culture and its existence has materially affected typical family routines (daily meals, birthday parties, indoor parks).
- It has transformed our built-up environment and daily aesthetic experience: the shopping malls in which McDonald's restaurants can be found are almost identical, whether they be in Pasadena, Inverness, Palmerston North or Moscow.
- McDonaldisation encourages a global sense of virtual reality, so that you identify a mega-capitalist firm whose goal is to make profits with a friendly, family figure such as Ronald McDonald. In a 1986 poll of young American children, for example, 96% of the participants successfully identified the figure of Ronald – he was second only to Santa Claus. Images of Ronald are everywhere, and walking, waving Ronald puppets can be seen sponsoring sand-castle competitions, awarding educational grants, telling us that McDonald's cares for the environment by recycling and by no longer cutting down rain forests to grow the feed that fattens the cattle that supply the burgers. Ronald is a larger-than-life figure, but he is certainly a social personality, contributing to images of economic well-being, leisure satisfaction, social expectations and public morality.

Food for thought indeed. And yet for all our awareness of the increasing salience of 'the global' – actually, precisely *because* of this – people throughout the world seem at the same time to be more aware of 'local' identities and issues. We can hardly begin to conceptualise the local except in the context of the global; and yet it is the local which has become most meaningful to us in many ways. Our place of origin or domicile, our neighbourhood quality of life, the state of our immediate environment, our national and regional identities, the richness of our indigenous cultures, the importance of our own little piece of history and humanity, our friendships, iwi, families and networks – all these things have taken on an immediacy and value worth thinking through and worth fighting for. And this had happened at the very same time as the world has gone seriously global at the end of the twentieth century.

Differences and divisions

Sociologists are interested in social groups, their place in the social structure, their interrelationships and their particular experiences and self-images. In any society there is a range of social groups. Very few societies, if any, have been (or are) homogeneous in the sense of containing only one type of group. In traditional societies, there are elders and youngsters, hunters and gatherers, shamans and laypersons. In feudal societies, there are lords and serfs, clergy and flock, artisans and courtiers. In modern societies, there are workers and bosses, high-tech and low-tech specialists, town dwellers and countryfolk, migrants and indigenous peoples … and so on. One can differentiate almost endlessly between social groups, and it is easy to list some of the main different social groups in New Zealand society today: Pakeha and Maori, rich and poor, employed and unemployed, men and women, urban and rural, heterosexual and homosexual, educated and under-educated, old and young, able-bodied and disabled, nuclear families and other households … and so on. Of course, such group differences are in one sense just part of the rich tapestry of modern life, and sociologists obviously are interested in describing these. But sociologists want to go further than this: they are interested in describing and *explaining* why social *differences* between people frequently turn into social divisions. The force of the concept of social division is that differences are perceived and experienced not just as interesting *variations*, but as *inequalities* between people. When people are divided, they not only 'differ', but they see their group interests as being fundamentally opposed to those of other groups. Because of this, they seek either to impose or to resist a situation of systematic inequality which may develop as a result of such opposed group interests and positions.

Let us take, for example, the social difference between homosexuals and heterosexuals. An enlightened view of this difference would be that there are interesting diversities of sexual preference amongst people – some are 'straight' and some are 'gay' – but there is no right or wrong about the issue, since all people have an equal place in a democratic and humane society. But, of course, reality is not so simple. For one thing, not all societies are democratic anyway, and there is a brutal history of intolerance towards homosexuals in undemocratic societies. And even in liberal democracies, the dominant group and the dominant attitude have been firmly heterosexual. As a result, throughout history homosexuals have suffered, either from a social stigma, or even persecution and discrimination. In spite of some important changes in liberal societies, this is still the situation – broadly speaking – today, although the emphasis has perhaps moved from discrimination to stigma. Now, because the heterosexual tendency is dominant in most modern societies, and because it sees itself as being more 'natural', an interesting *difference* amongst *people* has turned into fixed and unequal *division* of interest and advantage amongst social *groups*.

There is a similar situation in respect of ethnic, cultural, age and class differences. The fascinating and unique coexistence of Pakeha and Maori groups in Aotearoa/New Zealand, for example, in which there are many rich differences of custom and value to appreciate, is in fact the product of a history of group and cultural struggle. In spite of the rhetoric of partnership in the nation's heritage, that history has been one in which the dominant Pakeha group/culture has subordinated and exploited the indigenous Maori group. In today's atmosphere, where there is considerable effort to try to regain a sense of mutual respect and tolerance, those efforts will not be successful as long as the long-standing social inequalities between these two cultural groups are ignored or denied. On all the indicators of social well-being – employment, income levels, educational attainment, state of physical and mental health – Maori are considerably worse off than Pakeha New Zealanders. Currently, and for the foreseeable future, social differences are overlain by material inequalities and social division between these ethnic groups.

In each of the topic chapters you will come across one or other of the three guiding themes. Try to work with them, figure them out, apply them, not only in the reading of this book, but in your assimilation of information and news, and in your conversations and arguments with others.

The skills of sociological enquiry: researching and theorising

Sociology is the understanding of social events, processes and relationships. It tries to get in touch with the reality that is represented in the media, amongst politicians, or in everyday common sense. That may sound a little abstract and academic, but don't jump to conclusions: what we as sociologists wish to understand and help explain is not abstract or boring at all, nor is the task of gaining that understanding. Let's take as a module for showing the skills of sociology one of the most extensive and dramatic urban upheavals of recent times, namely the Los Angeles (LA) riots of 1992. Many people died in the riots, many businesses and buildings were burned to the ground, and several very graphic scenes of violence, anger and looting were beamed into living rooms all around the world as the media story unfolded.

1 The sociological imagination: insights, themes and skills 11

The Los Angeles riots of 1992: 'criminal' riot or 'social disorder' or 'urban uprising' or 'political rebellion'?

Photo: New Zealand Picture Library

Indeed, in many ways, the LA riot could be seen as a media event. The initial incident which triggered the disorder, the beating by police of an African-American man, Rodney King, was caught on a personal video camera by a passer-by. This clip was then represented on the main TV networks, and tension mounted in the streets. The trial of the officers involved was shown on TV, and the riots were begun by people standing outside TV shops in their LA neighbourhoods. A surge of shock and anger developed when the white police officers were seen to be acquitted. We know about this because more TV cameras were filming people watching the TV trial of the case about an event first caught on video. Thereafter, nightly scenes of the blazing, violent events were represented to the world at large (sparking off some related rioting in other US cities), and throughout the whole process from the initial incident to the sombre aftermath, a huge sequence of experts, protagonists and ordinary people were wheeled in front of the viewers to give an account of their own feelings, views and proposed remedies. In the process, several different **representations** not only of the LA rebellion, but also of the entire state of the nation in America were given, all orchestrated into a relatively coherent overall picture by the main media channels – a representation of competing representations! The events were real, but the representations and their impact, in their own right, were very real too. The questions which then confront the sociologist are, firstly, can we come to some kind of overall understanding of the social reality that is filtered and shaped by the dominant forms of representation? If we decide we

Representations are the re-presentations of actions, beliefs, events and things through the media.

cannot achieve such a 'privileged' account, the next question is: have all the perspectives in such a complex and disturbing event as this been properly attested and explored? In other words, even if sociologists cannot exactly 'get to' the reality behind the various representations of social events, they can help ensure that the public is exposed to the full range of competing or supplementary representations.

Finding out

Understanding the LA unrest involves coming to terms with a lot of hard facts: the numbers of people dead or wounded, the numbers arrested, the figures for property damage. There is also the need to find out about the full range of representations mentioned above. How did the police see it, how did the President see it, how did the shopkeepers see it, how did the black youth see it? Was there a Latino point of view that was different from that of black people? Were any white people involved? Was there a discrepancy between the accounts of African-American and Korean-American people? Did Americans generally think that the trial of the officers who beat Rodney King was fair? In addition to these facts relating to the events and to perspective, there are important background facts into which sociologists must enquire: what were the trends in income and employment levels amongst African-Americans in LA in the period leading up to the disturbances? Were the drop-out and truancy rates in schools increasing? What is the evidence of prior police racism or heavy-handedness? Does the record show that US justice is fair to black Americans? Do black Americans think they get fair justice? What does a comparison between the situations and views of black, Latino and Korean people in LA reveal?

You can see here that sociologists have plenty to find out about the context of the LA riots, and *finding out* is as good and user-friendly a phrase as any to describe the process of *sociological research*. Something occurs in society, and it seems of great significance, so sociologists devise ideas about and methods of *finding out more* about the event and the situation in which it occurred. There are different ways of finding out – different research methods. For example, if we want to know how many people died in the LA disturbances, or what property was destroyed, or what the extent of previous social deprivation was, we can collect and work through the relevant *documentary sources* (death certificates, police statistics, fire department damage assessment reports, school records, employment statistics, indices of housing and living standards). If we want to know what various groups of people *thought* about what happened and its significance, we could go and talk to them in order to get an inside view. However, we can't talk to everyone, so we might design a questionnaire that a large number of people might fill in and return to us. This would give us a substantial amount of information, allowing us to draw conclusions about aggregate views and attitudes. We might, on the other hand, want to get hold of more detailed, intimate information, and so might try to get involved for a considerable amount of time in just one of the local communities, getting to know some people fairly well, and discussing with them at length their life history, their community characteristics, their attitudes to authority, their hopes and fears. This kind of in-depth personal exchange, designed to develop in the sociologist a close-up feel for a particular way of life is sometimes referred to as *ethnography*.

If we wanted to try to understand the pressures the police feel under in situations such as the LA riots, we might temporarily join up with the police, or follow them around, to try to get a sense of their motivations and perceptions – and even to just find out what they do on the streets. This kind of research is sometimes known as *participant observation*. If we wanted to know *how often* items of news and comment on the riots appeared in the media, and the coloration of editorial opinion, we might collect all the relevant newspapers for the period and work out the column inches devoted to the subject, as compared with other subjects. We could then work out a scale of measurement to summarise the editorial values of the main papers towards the events. We could do a similar exercise on the importance of the events in terms of TV-time (this involves what is called *content analysis*).We would also want to give attention to the subtle ways in which the images and words that were published in the media to represent the riots – perhaps unintentionally – led to a particular political or moral interpretation. This kind of research is more qualitative and interpretative, working on the meanings of the main 'texts' which feature the riots and their significance. Such texts would include statements, interviews, reports, images, commentaries, testimonies, and the interpretations of these textual meanings is sometimes known as the *semiotics* of sociological research.

'Finding out' is thus a multi-dimensional and indispensable part of the sociologist's task, and we find out by using various research methods. Essentially, no one method is any better or worse than any other: everything depends on what it is that you want to find out. If you want to know what it was really like growing up as a woman in Timaru during World War II, for example, a life history methodology is more likely to be appropriate than a survey questionnaire. On the other hand, if you are interested in something quite specific, such as whether young wartime mothers also did stints of paid and unpaid work to help the war effort (and if the official employment statistics do not already show this), a targeted mass questionnaire sent to all women born between 1910 and 1925, and currently living in Timaru might be of real value. How much value will depend, of course, on the response rate – you do not actually know whether your target population really does include the people who took part in the activities about which you want to find out more.

Theorising

Finding out is indispensable in sociology. But it is by no means the only issue. Take the simple question, 'What happened?' For example, 'What happened in Los Angeles in 1992?' This question cannot be satisfactorily answered only by 'finding out', even if our finding out about various perspectives, facts and experiences is as thorough as it possibly can be. The reason for this is that questions such as 'What happened?' are not *factual* questions as such, or at least they are *not only* factual questions. They are *theoretical* questions too. For example, was what happened in LA a criminal riot, or perhaps a case of social disorder? Perhaps an urban uprising? Or a political rebellion? You may not have noticed, but we have already used variants of each of these terms in our casual descriptions of the LA topic for discussion. Yet the use of such terms is not at all a casual or merely descriptive matter, for the terms are distinctively different theoretical terms; and the use of one term and not another can give us very different explanation sketches of the whole 1992 phenomenon. They give us different big pictures of the events, and a different political coloration too. For example, to see the events as an uprising would appear to bestow participants with a sense of justice and rational action, whereas the term 'riot' has the connotation of spontaneous, perhaps criminal and possibly even pointless disorder.

The facts will never really tell us whether one such evaluative term is more correct than another. The facts, as we noted before, simply do not speak for themselves. Another useful slogan in this respect is that of the famous French physicist Henri Poincaré, who once said that 'an accumulation of facts is no more science than a pile of bricks is a house'. In short, all finding out is done within, and requires to be made sense of by, a framework of theoretical *interpretation*. Not only do theories about what sort of thing happened and why it happened *supplement* factual findings, they actually *precede* the gathering of evidence, for it is only in the light of theoretical **hypotheses** (e.g. 'It was a social uprising') that it even makes sense to go hunting for certain types of evidence (e.g. statistics of black urban deprivation). The word *hypothesis* is useful here because it signals that the theory that we have in mind is not fixed in stone from the outset, nor is it necessarily a *fully developed* and complex explanatory framework. **Theories** in this sense can be quite simple and straightforward, and they can be modified by the evidence they help uncover. 'Rioting will tend to occur when levels of disadvantage amongst large minority communities are high, and when there is a strongly felt sense of being marginalised.' This is a not-too-complex theoretical hypothesis which prompts certain research investigations and helps us explain important 'goings on' like the events in 1992 in LA. This kind of hypothesis and research could then be extended into a full-scale theoretical perspective on all aspects of racial and social disadvantage in modern capitalist societies – a theoretical perspective not only on particular events but on the social system as a whole.

Hypotheses are propositions put forward for empirical testing.

Theories are bodies of ideas that attempt to explain in a general way why things happen as they do. Theorising involves **abstracting** an explanation from the particular features of a situation.

What, then, is theory? Theory comes into play whenever we wish to *explain* something. Theory thus involves developing concepts and arguments which answer *'why' questions* ('Why did that happen?' 'Why is there racism?') and *'what' questions* ('What sort of social phenomenon is a "riot"?' 'What type of social system is the current free-market-based economy in New Zealand?'). Theory is indispensable for getting us to think about the deep significance of the things that we find interesting and important: theory involves **abstracting** from the countless particular features of a situation and developing **concepts** which allow us to generalise sufficiently to get a big picture of our field of interest.

Theories consist of various concepts, coherently related. Concepts are abstract ideas, but don't get the impression that because they are abstract, concepts bear no relation to the concrete terms of our everyday lives. On the contrary, all usage of *language* automatically involves using abstract terms to refer to concrete things. For example, the term *dog* is a concept – it refers to the abstract general properties of 'doghood' and not to any specific individual canine beast. Also, the words we use to abstract from concrete particular things like individual dogs actually bear no relation to the real things themselves: the concept *dog* does not bark! All language, then – everyday language as well as scientific language – involves the use of general concepts to enable us to abstract and classify things into types. The LA riots had very many unique features, but we can generalise certain social features out of that situation, so that what went on in LA resembles, in certain ways, what happened in LA in 1965 (the Watts riots/ uprising), and many other modern urban disturbances. It could even be compared in some ways with the events in Paris in 1789 (the storming of the Bastille), which sparked off the first great social revolution of modern times – the French Revolution.

Theorising is about abstraction, but it is by no means merely academic. People who would never dream of saying that they engage in sociological theory often do just that. For example, people speculate (theorise) about the causes (explanation) of their marriage break-downs. Did they split up because of his depression after becoming unemployed? Was it because he spent more time with his mates than with his wife? Perhaps it was that sociology course which stimulated her into wanting a more serious form of intellectual engagement than he could offer her, seeing that he was the type of bloke who expected a wife to cook and sew for him? These are all theoretical hypotheses which can lead to satisfactory explanations of the events and trends in question. And that is what theorising is all about: gaining insights, figuring out situations, seeking out explanations, framing hypotheses, understanding the particular in terms of the general (and vice versa).

> **Concepts** are abstract ideas that refer to the general properties of chosen aspects of social life. For example, the concept of 'riot' does not include details about specific riots, but allows us to make some general statements about how to understand the phenomenon of riots.

Conclusion

We hope that this brief introduction to the 'dazzling and compelling enterprise of sociology' has whetted your appetite for what is to come. This text will introduce you to the study of sociology through examining a number of substantive topics, exploring a variety of theoretical perspectives, and organising all of this using three key sociological themes. The following two chapters, however, throw you right into the heart of sociological theory as it has developed from the late nineteenth century to the present.

Study questions

1.1 Think about an aspect of social life that concerns you (it might be youth suicide, unemployment, your child's education, health care, domestic violence, leisure, etc.). Taking each of the three themes: the social and the personal; the local and the global, and differences and divisions, outline some of the questions a sociologist might bring to the social issue you have chosen.

1.2 How would you begin finding out about the social issue identified in question 1.1? Which research methods would provide you with answers that are relevant to your questions?

1.3 What kinds of theoretical issues (e.g. hypotheses and concepts) will form part of the sociological enquiry you have begun in questions 1.1 and 1.2?

Further reading

Abbott, P. and Wallace, C. (1997) *An Introduction to Sociology: Feminist Perspectives*, 2nd ed. Routledge, London.

Babbie, E. (1995) *The Practice of Social Research*, 7th ed. Wadsworth, Belmont, Ca.

Bauman, Z. (1990) *Thinking Sociologically: An Introduction for Everyone*. Blackwell, Oxford.

Giddens, A. (ed.). (1992) *Human Societies: An Introductory Reader in Sociology*. Polity Press, Cambridge.

Giddens, A. (1997) *Sociology*, 3rd ed. Polity Press, Cambridge.

Harvey, L. and MacDonald, M. (1993) *Doing Sociology: A Practical Introduction*. Macmillan, Basingstoke.

Marshall, G. (1990) *In Praise of Sociology*. Unwin Hyman, London.

Mills, C. Wright (1959) *The Sociological Imagination*. Oxford University Press, Oxford.

Willis, E. (1999) *The Sociological Quest: An Introduction to the Study of Social Life*, 3rd ed. Allen and Unwin, St. Leonards.

2 The story of sociology I: enter sociology

Chapter aims

- to locate the formation of sociology in relation to the development of modernity;
- to outline the features of social evolutionism in early sociological theory;
- to discuss the key features of the classical sociological theories of Marx, Durkheim and Weber.

Introduction

The three chapters (Chapters 2, 3 and 16) which deal with the development and character of sociology as an intellectual discipline are rather different from the other topic discussions, being best thought of as resources that you can draw on – and reflect upon, whenever you feel motivated to do so – as you work through the rest of the book. They provide the kind of preliminary sketch of the history of sociology which is indispensable for any proper understanding of the sociological traditions and their future potential. We emphasise at the outset that there is no single definitive way of understanding the history of sociology: what is presented here is a 'story-line', just one possibly interesting way of journeying through the history of the thinkers and paradigms that have defined what sociology is up to now. Also, as a first approximation, the account we provide is very much indebted to other surveys of sociology, such as those listed in the 'further reading' suggestions at the end of the chapters. It is also important to remember that the history of sociology tends to get written as the history of sociological theory, and that this overview is no exception to that rule, even though there are good reasons for *not* favouring social theory in that way. Most practising sociologists, for example, are not theorists as such – or at least not exclusively so. Having said that, to concentrate on sociological ideas does provide a convenient and popular way of grasping sociology's various origins, episodes, and characters, and, importantly, its degree of relevance to the culture, politics, and society of Aotearoa/New Zealand.

Sociology as understanding modernity

Sociology came into being as an intellectual response to the rapidly changing social world of late eighteenth- and early nineteenth-century Europe. In many ways, the basic features of that world are still with us today, and the label frequently given to the whole period from that time until round about now is **modernity**. There is, in fact, a great debate going on about whether, at the end of one century and the beginning of another, we are still inside the period of 'modernity', or whether we have actually exited it and have come out into a new period or social type: **postmodernity**. Some say we have, some say we haven't, and others say we are probably balancing on the edges of each, as if collectively bestriding two gigantic tectonic plates.

What is meant by 'modernity' in these big debates? Modernity, roughly speaking, means the kind of society that is:

- secular rather than religious;
- capitalist, rather than feudal, or slave-based, or socialist in economic structure;
- industrial rather than pre- or post-industrial;
- based on the nation-state form of rule;
- dynamically mobile rather than 'static';
- individualistic rather than based on traditional tribes or castes;
- urban rather than rural;
- democratic in political ideology;
- a mass society, in terms of access to basic goods and rights.

Part of the reason for talking about the 'story' of sociology rather than the 'facts' of sociology's development is that in using such terms as *modernity* and *postmodernity*, we are reconstructing a history by attaching a theoretical label to it. In so doing, we are classifying and 'ordering' our subject matter – in this case sociology itself – in a certain way. 'Modernity' is thus a way of looking at the facts: 'modernity' and 'postmodernity' are *interpretative constructs*, and like all concepts in social science, they are open to debate, revision, and replacement.

The onset of modernity can usefully be viewed in terms of three revolutions:

- the industrial revolution (1780–1840) = *socio-economic* revolution;
- the French revolution (1789–1804) = *political* revolution;
- the Enlightenment (1730s–1800) = *cultural* revolution.

Many sociologists would say that it was the industrial revolution that most profoundly introduced the typical social structure of modern societies, and that the impact of the new factories, capitalist markets and urbanisation cannot be underestimated. According to the great historian Eric Hobsbawm (1969: 13), the industrial revolution 'marks the most fundamental transformation of human life in the history of the world recorded in written documents'. And yet for many years this momentous episode had a very narrow basis in just one industry, cotton manufacturing, in just one part (Lancashire) of just one country (England).

Modernity refers to the modes of social life which emerged in Europe from around the later eighteenth century and which have now become more or less global.

Postmodernity refers to the modes of social life that have developed in late twentieth-century societies. Postmodern society is said to be characterised by post-industrialism, 'virtual reality', media saturation and a general sense of disconnectedness.

But soon the imagery and the reality of the new urban industrial capitalist landscape of factories, mills, mines and closely packed tenement housing came to spread rapidly and to dominate people's lives and thoughts. The new social environment of early capitalist industry was dynamic but squalid, threatening yet lucrative.

Socio-economic revolution, however, could probably not have happened without the 'help' of the other two revolutionary processes. The cultural revolution known as the European Enlightenment, prior to industrialisation, had rapidly altered people's mind-sets, and without this intellectual reorientation, the notable entrepreneurial and 'rational' attitudes of the new capitalist industrialists may not have developed. Similarly – from where we are now – it is almost impossible to imagine a typical framework for modern capitalist and democratic development outside the liberal democratic ideologies which emerged during the French revolution ('Liberty, Equality, Fraternity!'). That Revolution brought about a pathbreaking role model: the first modern **nation-state**. We take the nation-state for granted in so many ways nowadays – we even probably think of **society** itself as coterminous with our nation-states or 'countries'. But nation-states, like capitalism and industrialism, are relative newcomers in historical terms, and their arrival first in Europe and then around the world was partly due to the impact of the French Revolution in creating the first modern nation.

Nation-state is a form of state associated with the modern world in which governments have power over a given territorial space.

Society refers to the organisation of people and groups into a collectivity.

The enlightenment inheritance

The cultural revolution known as the Enlightenment was a quintessentially 'idealist' phenomenon; that is, it was believed that the right sort of *ideas* – especially those of reason, science and progress – could produce a more rational and free society. As sociologists, though, we should see the Enlightenment not only as a set of ideas, but also as a *social movement*. The second half of the eighteenth century in Europe was the period during which a new and hugely enlarged 'public sphere' of learning, discussion and 'applied' thinking began to emerge; when salons and coffee houses, libraries and journals, academies, Royal Societies, newspapers and public lectures suddenly thrived, breaking through the old system in which the production and dissemination of ideas had depended on the sponsorship of individual aristocrats. In that context, educated people became excited by, committed to, and organised into the new scientific possibilities of the age – remedies for plagues and diseases, improvements to agricultural methods, inventions of industrial machines for the production of new wealth, and systematic accounts of the development of society itself. Knowledge produced human progress, it was believed, and knowledge itself could not progress without a wholesale re-examination of (mainly religiously inspired) received authority. In the sentiments of the great Scottish philosopher, David Hume, whatever could not be demonstrated by either pure logic or empirical demonstration, should be 'committed to the flames'. In this spirit, many people felt that intellectual and moral liberation was being achieved very rapidly – often at the expense of religious and parochial authority – after centuries of 'darkness'.

Whilst forming a very powerful cluster of ideas, the Enlightenment world view contained some contradictory elements that are worth noting, for in many ways these intellectual and moral tensions are still at the forefront of debate in social philosophy today.

Rationalism and empiricism

Rationalism is a top-down theory of how human knowledge occurs. It holds that our previous prejudices and self-interests can be 'corrected' if we rigorously put them under the microscope of pure reason. In terms of social theory, the rationalist view would be that we can aspire to an 'objective' account of what the core structures of any society are at a given time, and how society has developed as a whole over time. Empiricism, by contrast, is the view that nothing can be established by reason alone, and that careful empirical observation can often surprise and offend our sense of reason as well as refute some ingrained beliefs. Science, then, including the science of society, is not so much about the speculations of theorists; rather it is the painstaking accumulation of facts and observations. In a nutshell, rationalism says: 'Work it out!' Empiricism says: 'Look and see'.

Universalism and relativism

The Enlighteners were extremely broad-minded, given their time and class background. They were remarkably unwilling to take anything for granted in their study of human society. The Enlightenment thus represents the first modern movement to express a *relativistic* impulse: social interaction and values, it was thought, must be understood as relative to the particular circumstances and cultures of the society under investigation. At the same time, Enlightenment thinkers certainly also believed that their own world view, expressing as it did a powerful faith in reason, science, and progress, was ultimately a universally valid programme for all of humanity.

The West and the rest

The 'place' of the Enlightenment was Europe, and its writers, whilst they tried valiantly to comprehend other cultures on an 'equal' basis, nevertheless prided themselves on the level of civilisation that was achievable in the West. They clearly believed that although it was no Utopia, the emerging commercial society of Europe was more advanced than the supposedly 'primitive' societies that were increasingly coming to its attention through many so-called voyages of 'discovery'. As the anthropological reports from these explorations (e.g. Captain Cook's) came in, so the exploration and mapping of human society in general was constructed. Inevitably, it was felt that, although tribal or 'savage' societies were admirable and 'noble' in many ways, they *would* eventually have to become like Europe in order to advance and develop. Because intellectual exploration was linked closely to the political and economic process of **colonialism**, there is an underlying assumption of Western superiority in Enlightenment thinking, though this did not always have an overt racist bias as such.

Colonialism is the historical process by which Western societies have occupied and exploited other territories and societies.

Men and women

The Enlightenment claimed to speak for all humanity, and one of its catchphrases came from the poet Alexander Pope: 'the proper study of Mankind is Man'. But of course, to epitomise the Enlightenment in this way is immediately to pose the question, where do *women* come into the picture? The answer is that they don't, very much. There were many women involved in the social movement of the Enlightenment, and these women were highly intellectual. But they tended to play the roles of the wives and mistresses of the more renowned male thinkers, or as the hostesses of the salons where lots of exciting discussions between the men, and sometimes the women, took place. Now it could well be that male bias has served to obscure or downplay women's prominent role in the Enlightenment, and that there were more women, and more important women thinkers, around and active than male history-writing has allowed for. Certainly, Mary Wollstonecraft (1759–1797), for one, has been steadily 'upgraded' over time into a thinker of the highest order, and other women writers and thinkers are being 'rediscovered' all the time. So it is no longer possible just to assume that women were not at the forefront of intellectual activity. Yet Wollstonecraft's remarkable *A Vindication of the Rights of Women* shows the author being caught between, on the one hand, having to sound as 'rational' as a man in making the case for the extension to women of recently achieved male rights of freedom and equality, and, on the other hand, seeking to appeal 'emotionally' against the injustices women suffer. Wollstonecraft was also one of the first and most eloquent writers to argue that the very split between rational argument and public life on the one hand, and the emotional life and domestic/parenting values on the other, was a divisive and unreasonable one – yet the men of the Enlightenment were as guilty of accepting that split as other men, and indeed, legitimated it all by prizing 'rationality' above everything else. Later the Romantic reaction against the dominance of rationality in the Enlightenment to some extent challenged this spurious division between head and heart, and between public and personal responsibilities, but the Enlightenment ideology remained powerful, and has only in our own day been seriously contested, largely through the renewed impact of feminist ideas and politics.

Social evolutionism

We tend to talk about the Enlightenment in the eighteenth century as a Europe-wide phenomenon, but it was primarily centred in just two milieux – Paris and Edinburgh/Glasgow – and the role of Scottish culture and thought in the formation of sociology has been neglected until recently. The Scottish Highlands had been cleared of its indigenous people by the English in the 1740s to make way for commercial stock rearing; the towns of the central lowland belt were thriving centres of the new world trade generated by colonialism and mercantilism; shipbuilding and the new industries of iron, steel and coal took off sharply in the third quarter of the century, and the Scottish education system was more systematic and available to a greater proportion of the general population than anywhere else at the time. During the Enlightenment period, Edinburgh – the 'Athens of the North' – quickly established itself as an advanced financial, legal and commercial centre. In this context of practical, educated, and busy people (men), the world of commerce and capital began to thrive, and the typical contradictions of modern society also came to the fore – divisions between rich and poor, urban and rural, the central state or government and the wider civil society, and between scientific knowledge and rough common sense.

In this context, a group of Scottish writers emerged as the founders of an historically-grounded sociology. Adam Ferguson and John Millar, for example, tried to develop an overview theory of how societies develop, combined with a consciousness of the typical social tensions that their advanced commercial society contained. According to their 'stageist' theory of history, there are four main stages in the process of social development or societal evolution. The first is the hunter-gatherer stage, which is followed by pastoral (shepherd) society, which leads to settled agricultural civilisations, and finally the modern polished world of industry and commerce. Each of these stages was seen as a necessary and (on the whole) beneficial phase through which 'mankind' had to pass.

The four stages theory was formulated as a result of the cosmopolitan theorists having unprecedented access to missionary and 'discoverer' reports of non-European societies elsewhere in the world. As the conservative sage Edmund Burke put it, 'the great map of Mankind is unrolled at once, and there is no state or gradation of barbarism, and no mode of refinement which we have not at the same moment under our view; the very different civility of Persia and Abyssinia; the erratic manners of Tartary and of Arabia; the savage state of North America and of New Zealand' (quoted in Meek, 1976: 173). The Scottish school speculated that there had to be a necessary element of inevitable progress which led human society from a state of relatively simple and 'primitive' tribal existence to 'advanced' commercial civilisation. At the same time, Millar and Ferguson accepted that progress was neither smooth nor desirable in every respect. They were aware of the *contradictions* of historical progress, of the clash between rich and poor people, between rich and poor nations, and they worried about the fact that, if progress was 'inevitable', this appeared to leave little room for human agency and political choice.

Finally, the Scots organised their thinking about the logic of historical epochs around the concept of *the mode of subsistence* – the way in which social groups produced their food and shelter. You can see this in the very phrasing of the four stages – hunting/gathering, stock rearing, agricultural produce, and the commercial trading of the necessities of life. This gave the thinking of the Scottish school a definite 'materialist' dimension which was very new and very insightful. Karl Marx, further down the track, would develop this idea by theorising social development in terms of *the mode of economic production*.

Sociology thus came to life as a debate about the 'good' and 'bad' consequences of the three revolutions, and about how 'universal' Western social development really was. The more complex and dynamic forms of social life generated by the new industrial and commercial society created a sense of decisive contrast between the 'old' traditional ways and the 'new' era unfolding in nineteenth-century Europe. A little later than the Scots writers, Henri Saint-Simon (1760–1835), for example, expressed an acceptance of, and *excitement* about, the new industrialised society. Saint-Simon argued that the future of humanity rested on the shoulders of the new 'productive classes' of **industrial society** – the enlightened entrepreneurs, the rational administrators and scientific 'experts', and the new working classes based around productive and systematic factory labour processes. Worried by the disorder and individualism of the French revolutionary period, and wanting to apply a scientific 'map' to the fast-changing world in evidence, Saint-Simon envisaged society as having a logical and ethical basis of its own – outside of the clutches of the 'state' as such. Society was to be seen as ideally consisting of an autonomous and healthy interrelationship between the new productive classes; as being a collective endeavour in which co-operation and consensus in the industrial workplace could form the seed of a new religion of humanity. The expert, knowledgeable administrators and workers of the new industrial system would together develop the kind of social consensus that would make obsolete the need for both political governors and anarchic individuals.

> Industrial societies are characterised by large-scale production processes in which machine production is dominant, and most of the labour force works in industrial production.

Auguste Comte (1798–1857) and Herbert Spencer (1820–1903) shared much of Saint-Simon's generally 'progressivist' outlook, but their theories were developed in a much more systematic and lengthy way – they introduced the first major treatises of sociological understanding, and indeed it was Comte who coined the term *sociology*. We should not be fooled by Comte's obsession with making sociology a 'science', indeed *the* science, because his own intellectual project was clearly an ideologically driven one. Comte believed vehemently that the basis of *social* order was *intellectual* order, and that progress in the science of sociology could be the precondition for coherence and stability in the wider society. Comte's thought was a continuation, in some ways, of Enlightenment rationalism, but he was frightened of the anarchic consequences of the other revolutions of the time, such as rapid industrialisation and rampant individualism. He thus wanted sociology to help form new sorts of solidarity now that those of the traditional world had passed.

Comte developed a theory around three stages of social development, but unlike that of the Scots – Comte also had a weaker grasp of social contradictions than they – this was an 'idealist' rather than a 'materialist' vision of history. Comte held that the development of the human mind was governed by a certain pattern, and that this pattern could be found in any number of phenomena, from the course of human history as a whole to the course of each individual's life, to the way that any particular event is structured (including his own episodes of psychic breakdown). First of all, there is the 'theological' stage, in which we seek to know how things originated and why they exist in terms of the authority and will of supernatural forces/deities; then there is the 'metaphysical' stage, in which general abstract principles dominate our consciousness (nature, the people, freedom, etc.); finally, there is the most desired and complete stage of all, the 'positive' stage, one in which knowledge is attained through general laws which explain the facts of specific phenomena. This type of rational knowledge would enable us to create and sustain the rational society, where action is always taken in accordance with controlled scientific understanding, not through primitive faith in gods or an abstract metaphysics of static forces.

In addition to this overarching positivist manifesto for sociology and society, Comte introduced a methodological distinction between 'social statics' and 'social dynamics'. In order to look at society at any given time, Comte argued, you have to engage in social statics: you take a 'slice' of time (rather like a natural scientist taking a slice of material) and you analyse its 'structure'. In the case of sociology, part of the static material examined is 'human nature' – basic tendencies and capacities that are always present, but which cannot be taken for granted. The other parts of 'statics' are those elements or levels of society that are consistently present but whose content may vary enormously – Comte is thinking here of the use of language, the family, religion, property forms, and the division of labour. At the same time, Comte was well aware that social statics must be complemented by social dynamics, and by this he meant the logic of social change – how his 'elements' get transformed over time, especially in accordance with his three-stages model.

Herbert Spencer, like Comte, made a distinction between social statics and social dynamics. Unlike Comte, though, he developed a theory of the 'elements' of any given society that used the notion of a societal system being divided into *sub-systems*. Spencer argued that any society could be analysed according to a division between its regulating (political/military) sub-system, its sustaining (economic) sub-system, and its distributing (social policy) sub-system. This is a useful way of conceptualising

social structure, and seems rather more up to date than Comte's references to family, religion and so on. Again, like Comte, Spencer saw sociology as the culmination of the scientific enterprise. In his book, *Principles*, for example, Spencer spends many hundreds of pages going through the fundamental logic and subject matter of a range of different sciences before he turns his attention, at last, to the principles of sociology. His thinking on the general issue of scientific knowledge and its effects was widely regarded as authoritative in Victorian Britain.

> Social structure refers to the enduring, orderly and patterned relationships that organise social life.

The next overlap between Comte and Spencer was the latter's acceptance of a 'stageist' theory of history. However, Spencer felt that there were really only two main stages, the 'militant' and the 'industrial', and here we see a very common refrain in many classical sociologists, namely the division between a traditional, rural-based, religious and authority-oriented society and a modern, urban-industrial, secular and liberal-democratic form of society. Comte himself, indeed, thought that his own second stage, the metaphysical-juridical form of society, was really a long 'transitional' phase between his other two phases, so in this respect the divergence is only superficial anyway.

There are two general methodological contributions of Spencer's that are worth highlighting. He insisted on seeing social change not so much as progress (Comte was already convinced of this) but more specifically as *evolution*, so that, like other forms of life, social phenomena should be seen as developing and adapting in a patterned way. The argument seems to be that society is not just *like* a biological organism, society *is* an organism of a certain type, that is, a higher form of life that reveals its own objective principles of growth, and a complex interdependence of its component, functional elements. Spencer basically sees structural adaptation as beginning merely 'additively'; that is, where simple social units (individuals, villages, etc.) grow until a point of population crisis is created which makes necessary a move out of the relatively simple form of life, and into a more *complex* form of life. Thereupon, a new equilibrium is reached under new structural principles, until things once again begin to multiply beyond the structure's capacity, and a further critical transition to a new principle of organisation is demanded. And the more developed a social organisation becomes, the more heterogeneous and *multidimensional* become the relations between its various parts. With this advancing complexity also comes greater *coherence* in the general principles of organisation.

Secondly, Spencer regarded society in what later became known as a 'structural-functionalist' manner. That is, he saw the different parts or sub-systems of societies as functionally inter-related and mutually interdependent phenomena. Like any organism, societies had structural principles of operation which translated themselves into the way in which each part 'functioned' for the whole. Thus, for example, we might want to say that the education system of a society 'functions' to fulfil the needs of the economic (sustaining) sub-system of the society as a whole, because you cannot really examine the logic of any one of the parts without working out its structural and functional relationship with other parts (economy, politics, culture, etc.). Many other sociologists since Spencer have adopted this kind of 'structural-functional' perspective, and are therefore indebted to him, even though their political and social views might diverge greatly from his.

How are we to summarise the contributions of these 'first founders' of sociology? In some ways, the ideas of the Scottish school, Saint-Simon, Comte and Spencer seem terribly old-fashioned and out of date. They also seem to some critics to be embarrassingly 'scientistic' – that is, obsessed with the (impossible) idea that sociology is a science which is just like, and complementary to, the sciences of the natural world. The consensus in sociology since the 1960s has probably been that sociology cannot be a science, at least in that sense, and that societies do not evolve in the way that living organisms do. Consequently, evolutionist frameworks in sociology are generally regarded as disreputable.

- They seem excessively deterministic and 'inevitabilist' – as if the whole of social history has a goal and drive which is beyond the influence of actual human beings.
- They seem excessively abstract – the key terms in these large-scale theories are grand notions like Mankind, Civil Society, the Human Mind, and so on. Today, we are more inclined to theorise about actual social groups and particular societies.
- Society is not thought by many people today to be like an organism.
- Evolutionary theories cannot shake off the *Eurocentric* cast of mind which produced them. All these thinkers were fascinated by the reports of American 'savages', and they were united in seeing the European West as representing the 'highest' level of civilisation, a social stage/ state to which 'lower' level societies would inevitably, in due course, 'progress'.

In defence of evolutionism, it should be said that we probably cannot understand the great changes in human society, or confront the biggest questions, without some sense of why it was that society of Type X gave rise to/adapted to/changed into society of Type Y. Why has war not only persisted, but increased in intensity and destruction, in the supposedly 'advanced' civilisations of the late twentieth and early twenty-first centuries? Why is heterosexuality still dominant – but also, why has its dominance been eroded somewhat? What has led Communist societies to turn into Capitalist societies in recent historical times? Why is nationalism so rampant? All these sorts of issue seem to require answers about how the logic of a certain type of society at a certain stage of development results in a loss of equilibrium, an increase in societal complexity, and a move towards a new/transformed type of stability.

Also, it is important to remember that it is only 'vulgar' evolutionism that sees progress as completely inevitable and that sees development/ evolution as necessarily entailing progress, morally and politically speaking. Darwin's theory of evolution, we should note, says very little about necessary progress; it does not say anything about how things will inevitably turn out, whether for good or ill. But somehow, it is assumed (wrongly) that social evolutionism must always be a matter of inevitabilism and perfectionism – humanity moving steadily onwards towards a higher, better state of being.

Even Spencer's notion that all things develop according to a sequence of how simple units join into a complex structure that has a balance and equilibrium for a time before either dissolving altogether or passing into another sort of equilibrium, has something going for it in social terms. Think, for example, of how a sports team or work unit or friendship network comes together out of separate past existences, establishes a way of fusing together and then in due course either begins to break up, or perhaps moves on again to a new type of equilibrium.

The classical period: Marx, Durkheim and Weber

Interestingly, the first founders mentioned above – Saint-Simon, Comte, Spencer – were slightly 'crazed' individuals. They felt themselves isolated from the current orthodoxies of the day, they felt little need to engage with other theories, works or theorists of the time, and their work is generally obsessive and dogmatic. There is thus a definite feeling amongst sociologists today that the classical work of Karl Marx (1818–1883), Emile Durkheim (1858–1917) and Max Weber (1864–1920) shows a more rounded form of intellectual individuality – though these people too experienced considerable personal turmoil. In addition, whilst it is true that all three of these men were engaged deeply in issues of evolutionary theorising, they all had a much greater sense of the contradictions of 'progress', and a profound awareness of the waste, oppression and brutality which accompanied the 'progress' represented by the maturing industrial capitalist civilisation in which they lived. Civilisation, Comte announced, has 'under every aspect, made constant progress', but this would be an impossible sentiment for Marx, Durkheim or Weber. Finally, the latter were not, as the earlier writers were, simply philosophical speculators. The classical sociologists did of course have, as their primary goal, the need to 'crack', theoretically, the 'code' of modern social development, but they based their big ideas on painstaking research into the state of public health, working conditions, suicide, corporate and economic growth, ancient and modern history, anthropological reports, and so on.

There are four main dimensions of the sociological 'big pictures' constructed by the classical sociological authors, and these allow us to produce some interesting comparisons and contrasts. These (always inter-related) dimensions are:

1   *social change*: the way the theorist understands the development of society over time and in historical context;
2   *social structure*: the dissection of the primary social elements at any given time;

Epistemology refers to the methods by which sociologists establish that their knowledge is accurate or 'real'.

Ontology refers to the propositions we have about 'reality' and the nature of existence.

Mode of production refers to how societies organise the production and reproduction of their material basis. For Marx modes of production were distinguished by how they generated and appropriated economic surplus.

Class was defined by Marx in relation to the ownership of capital. According to Marx, the population could be divided into two main classes, those who owned and controlled the means of production, and those who sold their labour power.

Class consciousness refers to awareness of one's 'objective' class situation, especially working-class self-awareness.

3   *philosophical underpinnings*: the way in which sociologists justify their work in terms of what they think *knowledge* is (= **epistemology**), and in terms of the fundamental nature of social existence (= **ontology**);
4   The *ideological-political assumptions* or implications of the theories.

Karl Marx

Marx saw the development of history as a sequence of **modes of production**. This idea refers to how societies organise the production and reproduction of their material basis, and crucial for Marx is the contention that modes of production are distinguished from one another by the ways in which the economic surplus is generated and 'appropriated'. Marx argued that **class** inequalities and conflicts between socio-economic classes had characterised all known human history, and that these were, in turn, crucially connected to the basic social division between the direct producers of economic goods and the (minority) social strata – the dominant or ruling classes – who 'expropriated' for their own class whatever surplus arose. The fact of class division and surplus appropriation is common throughout history, according to Marx, but each of the modes of production generates a specific set of 'relations of production', meaning different types of wealth generation and different legal and social forms for their respective labouring and appropriating classes. Thus, Marx identified an *ancient or slave* mode of production in classical Greece and Rome, where the ruling class directly owned the means of production *and* the human labourers themselves, and where the large-scale slave-based cultivation of the land was central to wealth production. He also defined a *feudal* mode of production, in which the labour was also primarily land-based but this time on a smaller scale, and in which the labourers were not directly owned by the landowning ruling class. Rather, the peasants worked the fields for their own subsistence, in addition to which they delivered an obligatory extra amount (whether in kind, or in service, or in money terms) to the feudal lord.

Marx believed that history was essentially dynamic, that it could not be held 'frozen' according to the rules of any particular mode of production as long as it was based on profound class exploitation. Accordingly, he maintained that there would be tendencies within each mode to gradually intensify technological and social contradictions. He also held that **class consciousness** and the levels of class conflict would intensify, along with social contradictions, until a combination of 'objective' and 'subjective' factors would result in a revolutionary breakthrough into another type of society and mode of production altogether. That is what happened when the ancient civilisations broke down into the period of the Dark Ages, and Western society resurfaced on very different – feudal – socio-economic lines. In turn, Marx argued, feudalism gradually developed its own technological and social contradictions, reaching a point at which capitalism dramatically bounces onto the world stage.

Applying this general way of understanding history – known as *historical materialism* – to the capitalist society of his own day, Marx defined capitalism as the generalised production of all commodities or goods for sale on the market, including, uniquely, labour power itself. That is to say, in a capitalist system, workers have to sell their talents and abilities on the open market to employers, who pay cash for the use of that labour power. Notice that we say labour power here, not actual labour, because what the capitalist is buying is the *potential* of the labourer to produce a flexible range of output, not always a given fixed amount. And this in turn is related to the capitalist's need to vary the intensity of work according to circumstances, if maximum feasible profit levels are going to sustained. Those circumstances, Marx saw, crucially included a dynamic of monopoly and competition amongst rival capitalist firms. Such competition encouraged the maximum intensification of labour – in factories, mines, etc. – within the available forms of technology, but it also encouraged the introduction of ever-new forms of labour-saving technologies, periodically and cumulatively causing bouts of unemployment and 'restructuring'.

Generally, Marx saw capitalism as governed by strong intrinsic tendencies: the growth of larger and larger conglomerate firms; a higher and higher dependence of capital on labour-shedding technology; a more and more massified or under-employed working class; and more generally, attendant social problems and unrest that was sure to escalate. As for human consciousness and political protest, Marx's argument was that capital itself was nothing other than 'congealed' human labour, that is, the 'dead' result of the workers' 'live' labour, which is, for its part, sold like any other commodity on the open market. Marx believed that this state of affairs represented a generalised and growing process of **alienation** for the working class, an alienation of workers from the product of their own labour, from the creative process of labour itself, from fellow workers, and indeed from the inherent potential within the human species to find creative expression and fulfilment in work. The products of the labour process under capitalism, Marx argued, become reified or thing-like, taking on a life of their own as disembodied commodities trading in the capitalist marketplace. Even so, Marx depicted capitalism as a socio-economic system prone to irrational and accentuated swings of boom and bust, contradictions between monopoly and competition, and between miserable unemployment and the liberating potential of science and knowledge. In these circumstances, he hoped, a consciousness would grow amongst the ever-broadening working class (proletariat) that it could defend its own interests through collective workplace struggle; and that it then would come to the understanding that the whole mode of production is a contradictory and alienating social totality. The 'subjective' understanding of the proletariat thus comes into line with the 'objective' fact that the problems of capitalism can only be 'solved' by its replacement with a more rational and non-exploitative socio-economic system. This is where Marx envisages a 'revolutionary' change occurring,

Alienation is a process through which workers lose control over their labour and the products of that labour.

whether through rapid and violent political action, or by means of a more quasi-evolutionary process (Marxists have argued about which it is to be ever since).

Marx, then, developed a powerful theory of historical materialism to explain social change, and he saw the specific social changes of his day constituted not as 'modernity' *per se*, but as *capitalism*. In terms of his analytical framework for analysing any particular society, Marx sought to identify socio-economic *class* and *class struggle* as the key to sociological understanding, themselves underpinned by the thesis that in any mode of production, there is always a dynamically developing set of contradictions between the social relations of production (class/ownership relations) and the productive forces (the potential of socially applied science and technology). As for his politico-ideological assumptions, it is important to remember that Marx saw himself not as a sociologist but as a revolutionary, convinced of the wastefulness and unfairness of capitalism in human terms and, at the same time, of its inherently *transitory* nature as an historical phenomenon. Conscious that a state of 'primitive communism' reigned amongst relatively egalitarian tribal societies, some in the very recent past, he passionately sought to contribute to the creation of an 'advanced' communist society, which accepted the creativity-enhancing powers of modern science, but which sought to collectively, democratically and non-exploitatively utilise the latter to the benefit and self-fulfilment of all. In line with this 'utopian' motivation for his 'objective' theorising, Marx was an activist in the socialist and trade union movements of his day, advocating support amongst workers for initiatives which seemed to take things forward, and often vehemently opposing campaigns and ideas, however well meant, which seemed to Marx a regressive or merely reformist socialist tactic.

In terms of his methodological or philosophical beliefs, Marx could be said to have adhered to a *dialectical materialist* ontology and a *scientific realist* epistemology. The first of these labels, *dialectical materialism*, indicates Marx's view that the social world was dynamic and material in character. That is, whereas some previous materialist philosophers saw things as they are in the world as being essentially separate, simple and static, Marx saw them as connected, contradictory and dynamic. Instead of *things*, Marx was interested in *relationships*. However, Marx was a 'materialist' and not an 'idealist' – he felt that although reality was an on-going process and not a fixed entity, he saw that process as still being very much to do with real, concrete existences in the social world, which itself had to be seen as a part of the wider physical universe. This view sets Marx firmly against previous philosophers such as Georg W.F. Hegel. Although Hegel also held to a dynamic and process-based ontology, everything was ultimately to be conceived, in Hegel's view, as the expression of the development of what he termed the Absolute Idea – that which intellectually and spiritually encompasses everything else.

2 The story of sociology I: enter sociology 31

Turning now to *scientific realism*, in the case of Marx, this refers to the view that some kind of 'objective' knowledge of social and natural reality is achievable, and that it can be put to good use in controlling the forces of nature and society that have up to the present proved to be obstacles to human progress. Natural science, for Marx, was not the same as social science. Unlike the former, the latter could not use experiments as its main methodology; social science had to develop systematic concepts instead, and use these to heighten and guide the business of observation and evidence-sifting. Marx thought that the 'power of abstraction' was central to uncovering the innermost secrets and structure of concrete reality as lived and experienced. Accordingly, Marx felt that his own theory of capitalism got to the essence of the real dynamic of modern social reality by pointing out its underlying workings and essential principles of operation. Armed with that understanding, we could then better explain and understand innumerable concrete aspects of surface life in capitalist society, and what ultimately governs the activities of most people within it, most of the time.

This contrast between the deep structures of social life (often hidden from view) and surface events and phenomena (which often seem most immediate to us as social actors in everyday life) is central to all 'realist' thinking in the social sciences, and it certainly shaped much of Marx's substantive theorising. Marx had a tendency to polemicise against all sorts of ideological illusions, whether in common sense or in academic theory, because he felt that these ideas remained at the level of surface reality only, leaving the deeper reality hidden from view. And to remain superficial in this way, Marx held, was to actually bolster the existing social status quo – capitalism. Thus, for example, he thought that liberal doctrine of 'equality before the law' was an ideological illusion in this sense, because it mistook a surface appearance of capitalist society (formal rights for everyone, rich or poor) for the deeper reality (capitalism as a systematically exploitative and unequal social system).

Emile Durkheim

When it comes to Durkheim and Weber, we are dealing with the generation which established sociology as an academic subject. Marx was more of an activist than an academic, a prophet rather than a scholar pure and simple. By the time Durkheim and Weber have completed their thoughts on modernity, the latter has been thoroughly bedded in as a social and cultural system, whereas Marx was active during a formative rather than a settled period of capitalist modernity. In Durkheim, we are dealing with someone who accepts the legitimacy of nation-states and of a world system made up of nation-states, someone for whom social life is a complex series of institutions, each necessarily having its own level of operation and its own valid **norms**. Thus, for example, Durkheim was concerned to legitimate the specific role and values of sociology as a profession; indeed he felt that the conduct of professional associations

Norms are the socially accepted ways of behaving in a given situation.

Division of labour involves the division of the production process into specialised tasks. For Durkheim, the division of labour is related to social integration in societies.

Social solidarity refers to the form of social integration in societies.

Collective consciousness is the external normative order which coerces members of a group to behave and think in certain ways.

served as a model for the political progress of society as a whole. Generally, Durkheim has a more positive sense of the necessity and benefits of modern capitalist society, and whilst he fervently disliked the kind of rampant individualism that capitalism seemed to have introduced, he felt that society could be reformed without the need for revolution. Marx, of course, would have been rather scathing about this kind of petit-bourgeois ethical stance in the face of deeper, more turbulent forces.

For Durkheim, the key notion in understanding the logic of social change is not so much class struggle or capitalist development but the more technical idea of the **division of labour**, and the fundamental starting point in this regard is to draw a strong contrast between traditional and modern societies. In traditional – or tribal, or segmental – societies, Durkheim says, a very simple form of the division of labour exists, with what specialist roles there are taking shape within the fundamental family (kin, clan) groups, which themselves are all uniformly structured. Durkheim labels the form of social consciousness or **social solidarity** that goes along with a simple social structure and division of labour, as 'mechanical'. This is because, in traditional society, the form of labour, life and experience is essentially very similar, homogeneous even, right across all groups. People know their roles and places, they are firm in their common allegiances to authority, their belief in supernatural forces, deities and totems, and their transference of these roles and world views to their children is utterly fixed, automatic and accepted. The 'primitive' division of labour and the form of collective consciousness that goes along with it are, then, 'mechanical' – taken for granted and reproduced unproblematically by all units.

However, such a rigid form of society, in Durkheim's perspective, cannot respond very well to changing conditions in the social and natural environment. It is a static organisational form which quickly confronts serious survival challenges in times of either scarcity or population growth. These types of gradual evolutionary pressure – and here you can see Durkheim's debt to the social evolutionism of Spencer and Comte – lead, possibly inevitably, to the development of more 'modern', that is, more complex and robust, forms of labour and solidarity. Durkheim thus contrasts *mechanical solidarity* with *organic solidarity*, emphasising how, under an 'advanced' division of labour, more and more specialisms develop and people become at one and the same time more individualised and yet also more interdependent. According to Durkheim, this process of social differentiation – ever-increasing specialisation and individuation – is an intrinsic feature of modern society, and one which in principle produces greater human freedom, knowledge and mutual respect. In principle, therefore, it is a good thing.

Durkheim's understanding of the key structures of society was that they were not principally materialist, in contrast to that of Marx. Rather, Durkheim examined social structure in terms of the forms of **collective consciousness**, and ultimately saw social reality as having morality and religion at its heart. Even when the 'collective effervescence' of ostensibly religious ceremonials seem outdated, he thought, society puts *civic* rituals in their place, thus preserving the fundamental feature of all social bonding, which is to invest some social beliefs and phenomena with a *sacred* aura, and categorise others as essentially *profane*. So even when Durkheim is looking at the changing forms of the division of labour and the rise of specific occupational groups, he is looking at these in terms of how they reflect deeper-level *symbolic* changes in the moral structure of society; its ability or inability to reach Durkheim's personal ideal: a quasi-religious sense of social integration together with the encouragement of true, responsible individuality.

As regards the philosophical underpinnings for Durkheim's work, ontologically he was an idealist, in the sense that moral facts, not material conditions, were more basic or essential to the nature of social life. But, unlike philosophers such as Hegel, Durkheim was a social idealist – he believed not in the ideas in individual minds, or in the Absolute Spirit as an a-social abstraction, but rather in the bonding power of collective identity. He felt that all belief systems were really about the power of the social bond. Religions were about society, deep down, and society was essentially religious – even if modern worship took unfamiliar forms – like the worship of science itself, which can be seen as serving as a replacement for established religions.

Epistemologically, Durkheim has been described as a 'positivist', though the exact meaning of this term is much debated in the social sciences. Certainly, Durkheim thought that sociology could be a positive science in its own right, since it dealt with entities and realities (above all 'society' itself) which were beyond the reach of other disciplines such as psychology or human biology. Moreover, the reality of social relations and norms could be 'objectively' perceived, Durkheim thought, through rigorous attention to the collective 'facts' of social life – statistical measures of, for example, suicide or secularisation. Famously, he invited his readers to *think of social facts as 'things'* – real forces that had a strong 'external' influence on individuals. Durkheim thought that these kinds of social fact had as 'brute' an existence as any other solid reality, and the first condition of scientific sociology was therefore to accurately observe and understand the distinctive nature of social conditions and how they might change over time.

All of this merits the description of 'positivism', because positivism can be read as a doctrine which gives a special place to the accurate *observation of empirical facts* in scientific enquiry, and positivism also holds that the scientific *method* is basically the same right across the very different types of scientific investigation – physics, biology, sociology, and so on. In fact, like Spencer, Durkheim tends to see society as a *social organism*, evolving progressively if not always smoothly; functioning healthily when everything is well integrated and mutually supportive, but behaving 'pathologically' when those supportive functions are disrupted. Having said that, Durkheim strongly believed that sociology's specific object of enquiry was collective moral phenomena, and these have almost nothing to do with the laws of physics and biology. Moreover, they are not observable as such on the surface of society. In a sense, the 'facts' of suicide told us nothing of sociological importance until Durkheim put his interpretative framework to work on them, a framework that itself could hardly be said to be free from particular values and preferences. So in those ways he was not really a positivist as that label is sometimes understood.

In politics, Durkheim was a social reformist. He was a strong supporter of the French Third Republic, and thought that through education, socialisation and a rich array of ceremonial rituals, the twin threats to modernity – selfish individualism and revolutionary socialist collectivism – could be avoided. Coping with social 'strain' was partly a matter of liberal tolerance and state-led reforms, but partly it was a matter of replacing the older collective allegiances of church and class with new, stable and fulfilling ones. In particular, Durkheim thought that the growth of the occupational cultures and loyalties typical of the *professions* would provide this new sort of bonding, perhaps in a parallel way to the medieval guilds for artisans, apprentices and master craftsmen.

Max Weber

Weber saw the development of modern society neither as the progressive, if difficult, march of organic solidarity (Durkheim) nor as class conflict within the capitalist socio-economic system (Marx). Weber certainly felt that capitalism was a powerful material reality, and that it generated important forms of collective consciousness. But what he thought was distinctive about modernity was the particular form of **rationality** that accompanied capitalism, the way of thinking and calculating social life that was typical of the modern era. Weber felt that the 'material' and scientific potential to develop capitalism had existed to some extent in other civilisations, for example China, but the power of the top-heavy administrative bureaucracy in Imperial China, he argued, had stifled the emergence of individual initiative and an entrepreneurial spirit. In early modern Europe, by contrast, the unique appearance of ascetic Protestant sects – Calvinists, Methodists, etc. – served as a springboard for 'capitalistic' business practices and the kind of rational calculation about means and ends that industrial society requires in order to thrive. A crucial doctrine, Weber thought, was the Calvinist belief that one's place in heaven or hell was already predetermined, and so the individual's fate was directly in God's hands, not mediated by one's role in any established Church. Whilst one could not affect God's judgement on these matters, the *signs* of one's fate were thought to be present, to some extent, in the 'good works' and 'industry' one performed in the real world. This religious doctrine, Weber argued, provided the motivation for individuals to act entrepreneurially in the world, creating wealth and contributing productively to the collective good.

The establishment of capitalism saw the complete triumph of 'formal' rationality, that is, the kind of thinking that is more about how you get

Rationality, in the modern world, is characterised by efficiency, calculability and accountability.

2 The story of sociology I: enter sociology **35**

from A to B than whether that route or destination has moral virtue in itself. Efficiency, calculability, accountability – these are the generic social qualities which Weber saw as outstripping their religious context. The whole modern world, Weber thought, was becoming relentlessly and increasingly subject to modes of calculation, specialisation, and bureaucratisation, such that the form of rationality was taking on a life of its own, outside all 'content' or specific human values. Bureaucratic rationality – the obsession with efficiency, order and administration – had gradually conquered individualism and religion alike as ethical systems, and indeed Weber felt the world was becoming progressively more 'disenchanted' in the face of such rationality: society had lost its sense of spirituality and magic, as more and more areas of life had become routinised and monitored for calculability. We face, he thought, the prospect of living within an 'iron cage' of bureaucratic rationality. Ironically, the age of the individual capitalist entrepreneur, having broken free of medieval or oriental administrative constraint, had gradually led to another kind of nightmare – the administered, endlessly rule-governed and disenchanted modern society.

Weber did not really have a precise theory of society or social structure, in the way that both Marx and Durkheim did. Certainly, he offered his thoughts on the capitalist mentality to counter 'vulgar Marxist' emphasis on the pure economics of capitalist development; but rather than producing another 'master plan' of explanation, Weber preferred a *multi-factorial* approach to the study of social life. In other words, he saw capitalism, and modern society generally, as having many important but different dimensions, some of which were material, some cultural. Similarly, he opposed Marxism's focus on social *class* as the single most important determinant of people's position and beliefs. Weber did not reject class altogether, but felt that it had to be supplemented by a range of other things, such as **social status** and people's political identifications. Weber was always happy to accept, as Marx and Durkheim were not, that social life was very complex; so complex, in fact, that perhaps no definitive picture of its structure or logic could be established. He felt that there were many ways of explaining inequality and power – for example, through various practices of **social closure**. Certainly, capitalists and bourgeois groups exclude workers, but some workers have ways of excluding other workers on grounds of status or perhaps ethnicity, etc. The Weberian sociologist therefore cannot justify favouring any particular way of analysing society or the role of any particular group within it.

Weber's view of social knowledge, his epistemology, was that we gain insight by constructing 'ideal type' concepts, such as capitalism, protestantism, and so on, and by looking at social reality through the 'lenses' of those interpretative concepts. We use these ideal types for purposes of research and argument, but we cannot, according to Weber, claim that any single ideal type – or any combination of them – uniquely *reflects* the social reality 'out there'. That reality always escapes any attempt to understand it. Weber was not too worried by this, because he was not

> **Social status** is one element of Weber's understanding of social stratification. Status refers to the relative position of people in a publicly recognised hierarchy of social worth.

> **Social closure** is the means by which groups seek to restrict access to rewards to members of their own group.

a philosophical realist – he did not believe we could ever really know what the deep structure of social reality was like, 'in itself'. This view of his – that reality exists but that we can never ultimately know what it is like because our concepts help *construct* our view of it – is sometimes known as 'neo-Kantian', after the Enlightenment thinker Immanuel Kant, who held a similar view about our understanding of the physical world of nature.

Weber believed that sociology could in some sense be value-free, and to an extent 'scientific'. Sociologists must learn to put their own values to one side in examining problems and ideal types, he thought. Yet this is not a completely convincing expectation, coming from Weber, for it was he more than the other classical sociologists who insisted that society was not an 'objective' totality, waiting to be observed and scientifically theorised. Rather, social reality was quite different from the natural world, Weber held, in that *social action* is uniquely concerned with the *meanings* that people give to their actions and situations. Sociology, cannot, as Durkheim seemed to recommend, make progress simply by treating social significance as *external* to individual actors, as disembodied social facts. On the contrary, for Weber it is only by accepting that social significance is 'internal' to meaningful action that sociology as an interpretative science can get off the ground at all.

Weber's sociology could be described as 'abstentionist' or even 'pessimistic' when compared to the more 'positive' and 'positivist' Marx and Durkheim. This reflects his politics in key respects, for Weber was rather pessimistic about the way things were going in liberal society as well as in social science. As mentioned before, he envisaged the last drop of 'magic' being squeezed out of social life by the forward march of administrative rationality. And socialism, he argued, far from being an alternative to this, was simply another variant of it. Increasingly, Weber felt that some kind of 'charismatic' solution to the dead hand of rationalisation might emerge, even though his own theory made it unlikely that this could happen. Weber was a democrat, a liberal and a nationalist, but his moral pessimism and inclination towards charismatic politics meant that democracy and liberalism played 'second fiddle' to his German nationalism towards the end of his life.

Theorist	Social change	Structure	Epistemology	Ideology/Politics
Marx	Capitalism	Class	Realism	Revolutionary socialism
Durkheim	Organic solidarity	Collective consciousness	Positivism	Liberal reformism
Weber	Rationalisation	Class + status + party	Neo-Kantianism	Liberal pessimism

Table 2.1

Conclusion

In this chapter you have been introduced to the earliest developments of sociological theory. The social evolutionists, as well as Marx, Weber and Durkheim, all produced a 'big story', about society – in particular focusing on the nature of social change and the social structures that organise social life. These theories have also been compared in relation to their philosophical and ideological/political assumptions. In the following chapter we turn to sociology as it has developed throughout the twentieth century.

? Study questions

2.1 What do sociologists mean by the term *modernity*?

2.2 What are the main elements of social evolutionism?

2.3 According to Marx, what is social class and what role does it play in society?

2.4 Outline Durkheim's concept of the division of labour and discuss its role in social change.

2.5 What does Weber mean by 'rationalisation'? Why was he critical of this force in modern societies?

Further reading

Craib, I. (1997) *Classical Sociological Theory*. Oxford University Press, Oxford.

Hall, S. and Gieben, B. (eds). (1992) *Formations of Modernity*. Polity Press, Cambridge.

Hawthorn, G. (1987) *Enlightenment and Despair: A History of Social Theory*, 2nd ed. Cambridge University Press, Cambridge.

Hobsbawm, E.J. (1969) *Industry and Empire*. Pelican, Harmondsworth.

Hobsbawm, E.J. (1977) *The Age of Revolution*. Abacus, London.

Hughes, J.A., Martin, P.J., Sharrock, W.W. (1995) *Understanding Classical Sociology*. Sage, London.

Lemert, C. (1993) *Social Theory: The Multicultural and Classic Readings*. Westview Press, Boulder, Col.

McIntosh, I. (1997) *Classical Sociological Theory: A Reader*. Edinburgh University Press, Edinburgh.

Meek, R. (1976) *Social Science and the Ignoble Savage*. Cambridge University Press, Cambridge.

Ritzer, G. (1996) *Classical Sociological Theory*, 2nd ed. McGraw Hill, New York.

Swingewood, A. (1991) *A Short History of Sociological Thought*, 2nd ed. Macmillan, Basingstoke.

Sydie, R.A. (1987) *Natural Women, Cultured Men: A Feminist Perspective on Sociological Theory*. Open University Press, Milton Keynes.

3 The story of sociology II: from classical to contemporary

Chapter aims

- to outline the concerns of sociological writers at the turn of the nineteenth century;
- to outline the growing influence of American contributions to sociology, and in particular to focus on the challenges of feminist and black American writers;
- to discuss the mid-century dominance of American sociology in general and Talcott Parsons in particular;
- to describe the variety of sociological approaches in the latter part of the century and the development of a pluralism of theoretical understanding.

Introduction

The previous chapter introduced you to the beginnings of sociology in nineteenth-century Europe. Here we turn our attention to further developments around the turn of the century, and in twentieth-century America. Whereas the classical sociological theorists focused on 'big stories', twentieth-century writers have been concerned to analyse the more everyday and micro-elements of social life. In addition, the analysis of racism and gender inequalities have been incorporated increasingly into sociological theory at the insistence of feminist and black writers.

The first '*fin de siècle*'

During the 1890s in Europe, some of the great works of modern sociology were written, and some of its key figures emerged. But during that decade, and increasingly through to World War I (1914–1918), the dream of progress and enlightenment which had previously guided sociology lost some of its appeal. Weber, we saw, had a complex view of how society operated – it can be said that he lacked a definite 'theory' of society, unless this was the 'iron cage' vision of modern bureaucracy. But this latter was as much an expression of his personal and political pessimism as it was a theoretical doctrine as such. Weber was not entirely comfortable with

3 The story of sociology II: from classical to contemporary **39**

modernity, though he saw little alternative but to accept Western liberal capitalism. This reflected something of the intellectual climate of the time, which in the 1890s became much more self-consciously complex and sophisticated than had been the case in previous decades. Sociologists and others, instead of being fixated on single-story accounts of human progress, began to focus on smaller-scale thinking, and on the particularities of culture and consciousness. The period also saw the emergence of 'oppositional' strands within social thought, manifesting themselves not only as a stronger Marxist political challenge, but also as feminist ideas and significant black American inroads into European/ Eurocentric thought.

One sociologist whose work and influence is still being rediscovered today was Georg Simmel (1858–1918), a contemporary and friend of Weber's. Simmel's sociology was very different from that of the other 'classical' writers. Simmel was sceptical about the way in which society as a whole was theorised by people like Marx and Durkheim. Instead, Simmel developed what he called 'formal' sociology – ways of thinking about the *form* that social interaction takes in *particular role-situations*. For example, whatever the 'content' or 'setting' of interaction between two people might be – it might be a discussion about art in a café, or it might be a chat during breaktime at work – the form of that two-way interaction (a 'dyad') is fundamentally altered, and very *different* forms of power, authority and trust emerge, when a third person joins the conversation or situation (a 'triad'). Simmel looked at other general forms of 'sociality' too: co-operation, sociability, conflict, subordination, and so on.

In a related field, Simmel wanted to explore the kind of social experience and behaviour that occurred whenever recognised social *roles* or *types* were being acted out. The kinds of role he was interested in were not so much the classic social identities of industrial society – capitalist, worker, poor person, bureaucrat, etc. – but again referred to phenomena that could occur almost anywhere in modern life. For example, Simmel was interested in what happened to a group when someone comes into it as a *'stranger'* from outside. He was intrigued by the changing reaction to people when they become identified as a *'gambler'* or a *'waster'*. You can immediately think of a whole series of possible investigations along these lines: the confidante, the supervisor, busybody, informer, know-all, know-nothing, lover, mediator, and so on. This kind of sociology of people's experience, mutual reaction, and strategy within specified cultural situations was a quite new line of thought, and it led to a growing 'micro-sociological' emphasis within the sociological tradition, as compared with the 'macro' concerns of the other classic sociologists. Aspects of what might be considered to be social psychology ('how do I feel now that he has just joined our table?') became, thanks to Simmel, part of the central business of sociological understanding.

It wasn't that Simmel exactly lacked concern about the larger structure of society – he wrote a major treatise on the role of money within the capitalist system, for example. But even in that treatise his angle was to

40 Exploring Society

Consumption includes the purchase and use of goods and services.

Urbanisation refers to the growth in the proportion of people in a population living in towns and cities.

Anomie is a situation in which norms cease to have a hold over individuals.

Feminist sociology attempts to explain these disadvantages in terms of the patriarchal nature of societies.

think through the social roles, experiences and emotions created by the universality of money as a medium and a goal in modern life. Similarly, he saw during his own time how 'macro' patterns of social **consumption** were becoming as important as, if not more than, the *production* of goods and roles; dwelling, for example, on the nature and contradictions of *fashion* as a social phenomenon. Finally, by way of illustration of his sociology of the 'forms' of social life, Simmel perfectly understood the need to see **urbanisation** as a major 'structural' feature of industrial society; but he approached this, once again, through the typical sorts of feeling and cultural style that differentiate our sense of living in the modern metropolis from living in the country. Thus, he wrote about how things seem less permanent, more fleeting and moving in the modern city; about how there is an effervescence and heightened immediacy about even such an everyday event as crossing a busy street, compared with previous ways of life. Living in the city means that other people come flitting in and out of our experience, sometimes in useful impersonal roles (banker, police, etc.), sometimes conveying a curiously combined atmosphere of excitement and danger (e.g. in the presence of crowds). To Simmel, we still had to theorise about society, but the purpose of theory was to sharpen our perception of the quality of experience of modern life and the dynamics of interpersonal relationships.

At the *fin de siècle* (century's end), the main impulse within sociology was to investigate and understand the relationship between 'objective' social forces and personal experience. Durkheim's **anomie** and Marx's 'alienation' had already underlined this, of course, but as the work of Simmel shows, those earlier notions were still extremely abstract, and tended to deal with the plight of modern 'man' in general rather than with that of very specific social groups. From the 1890s onwards, sociological debate opened up again to a range of styles of thought and empirical concerns, in which differences of experience and group life within society as a whole were as important as what was happening to the social totality seen as one big unit.

The work of Charlotte Perkins Gilman (1860–1935) is particularly important in registering the power and urgency of **feminist** ideas, directly confronting the inequalities in the respective conditions of men and women as distinct modern social groups. Mary Wollstonecraft, at the end of the previous century, had argued strongly that the rights of 'man' had not (yet) been conceived by the Enlightenment thinkers as the rights of everyone, and that by advocating their extension to women, social and political thought could become truly 'universal'. Wollstonecraft was enlightening the (male) Enlighteners, drawing sharp attention to the inconsistencies and hypocrisies in any view of human or 'universal' democratic rights which excluded women as full and equal social participants. Part of Wollstonecraft's argument raised the whole issue of domestic responsibilities and the exploitation of women by men within the home/family, but this remained an underdeveloped aspect of debate until Gilman and others tackled it again head-on.

Like Wollstonecraft, Gilman's revolutionary arguments were couched in terms that sought to improve and make more consistent the mainstream/malestream world-view of the day, which in Gilman's case was a progressive social evolutionism. How can it be, she asked, that when society is well-placed in so many ways to make significant human progress, it reveals a 'backward' trait which is characteristic of no other animal species, namely, the utter economic dependence of the female upon the male? Holding, with Marx, that economic relations were crucial to social structure and human freedom alike, Gilman systematically worked through all the possible arguments and excuses for the lack of women's independence in economic and public life in the 'advanced' modern world.

Her point was twofold. First of all, women were exploited and undervalued. No matter how much men might speak of 'valuing' women's contributions to economic and social life, or of men and women being equal (if different) 'partners' in life, the truth was that women's work was grossly unrewarded in economic terms. Even if we could succeed in converting the various indirect 'returns' that wives do get within the modern patriarchal family into monetary values, these would not, even remotely, equate to the value of the women's labour that has been invested. Moreover, Gilman believed that by keeping women in this position of dependence, men were allowed to monopolise the wider public sphere of work and politics and to thereby seek self-aggrandisement, stunting the creative and self-actualising potential of women as social beings – and indeed of men as well. These completely artificial 'separate spheres' for men and women, together with the relations of dependence and monetary monopoly that usually go with the division are then expressed and reproduced in all forms of socialisation, and in basic ideological conceptions of what the very 'essence' of manhood and womanhood is.

These profound sociological propositions led Gilman to a fundamental re-think of how people live in the modern world. Why do we live in separate nuclear families, why can't there be more collective and rational ways of organising domestic labour, education, home life and economic activity, she demanded to know. With great consistency and commitment, Gilman went on herself to explore and advocate practical alternatives to the prevailing 'sexuo-economic' structures. In addition to a range of substantial sociological and utopian works, Gilman also wrote a novel about the breakdown and illness she had suffered a little earlier in her life, one which poignantly and alarmingly portrayed her problems, caused by her role as a wife trapped in the home and patronised by her husband, who was preoccupied with his professional life in the public sphere.

W.E.B. du Bois (1868–1963) and Anna Julia Cooper (1858–1964) were prominent African-American thinkers and activists, bringing to the classical sociological tradition the previously ignored experiences of slave and post-slave conditions in the rapidly modernising USA. Indeed, the whole question of **ethnicity** and **racism**, whilst still largely kept

> **Ethnicity** as a social marker occurs when groups share a particular history, a set of cultural practices and institutions, and are conscious of having a shared identity as a result.

> **Racism** involves attributing characteristics of inferiority to individuals on the basis of certain physical 'racial' characteristics.

'marginalised' within the sociological mainstream, became a significant counterpoint from then on. These were sociologists, who, once again, from a situation of exclusion and unorthodoxy, immersed themselves in the ideas of the European tradition and defended it up to a point. Cooper began her studies of society by reading Comte and Spencer, and completed her journey by attaining a doctorate at the Sorbonne in Paris at the age of sixty-five. Du Bois took himself off to Germany for two years to study European philosophy before undertaking his Harvard doctorate, and throughout his life maintained a global presence and network. Both figures expressed a deep commitment to the ideas of enlightenment and progress, justice and freedom, but they insisted that these principles were being corrupted, not fulfilled, in a modern society which would not face up to the racism and oppression at its heart.

How did it feel to be a black person in America, simultaneously included by the nation's liberal principles, and made an 'outcast' and a 'stranger' by its racist practices? How did it feel to be a sociologist and activist, inspired by European ideas but conscious that the ideas did not match the reality, and that one's own personal experience was marginalised in the culture? Du Bois addressed these burning questions in terms of his concept of 'double consciousness'. Within one self and one (black) body, he reflected, there were two souls, at times fighting for supremacy, at times desperate for harmonious reconciliation. But more complicated still, for Du Bois, was the fact that, as a 'Negro', one was compelled to see oneself through the eyes of the dominant culture, producing a tense amalgam of self-stigma, defiance and double-sidedness. Anna Julia Cooper had a related sense of the deep dilemmas and ambivalences that characterised black identity, particularly perhaps the problematic identity and 'belongingness' of black intellectuals. However, in her case, the question of gender roles cross-cuts the 'racial' dilemma. Thus Cooper describes how her own personal uncertainty reflects social relations more generally in a situation where she has to choose between going into the railway station waiting room marked 'for Colored People' and taking the door marked 'for Ladies'.

From Europe to America

With the catastrophic European war of 1914–1918, and the subsequent inter-war depression and the rise of political tyranny and extremism, the dream of orderly continuous progress was shattered. The 'new' and positive elements in modern society seemed to be moving across the Atlantic, to the economically booming and culturally upbeat American setting. Sociology followed, in spirit and then in bodily numbers, as many European intellectuals sought to escape fascism by emigrating to the USA. There were accompanying shifts in sociological bearings. The change towards more 'micro-sociological' concerns was one of these. The understanding of *personal identity* rather than *structural constraints* seemed in keeping with the driving message of America's young capitalism: that

3 The story of sociology II: from classical to contemporary **43**

individuals can achieve what they want, given sufficient determination to succeed. The American sociologists of the early twentieth century took on board not only Spencer's sense of evolutionary development, but also his ideological emphasis on individual self-interest as the positive motivation for social adaptation. It was thus held to be part of 'structural' social development itself that 'structural constraints' were *less* determining of interaction than once they had been. The pragmatic question facing Western civilisation was how, systematically, to encourage mobility and diversity amongst individuals and social groups, while at the same time coping in a realistic but piecemeal way with the *social problems* inevitably thrown up by such a go-ahead and 'melting-pot' society.

Spencer was joined by Simmel as a major influence on sociological work in the USA, and their ideas in turn were blended with the ideas of William James, the doyen of American philosophical and psychological pragmatism. *Pragmatism* in this context meant taking a back seat on 'ultimate' philosophical questions such as the meaning of life, the nature of world history, and the search for absolute truth, and concentrating instead on how meanings and worlds are constructed on a 'local' basis, in the here-and-now. Charles Cooley was one sociologist who developed this socio-psychological orientation with his notion that we are all 'looking-glass selves': we imagine ourselves largely according to how we think *others* see us. And the angle of the looking glass changes – we may be ultra-sensitive to our cowardly traits in the presence of a brave person, or think of ourselves as 'dumb' when seen in the mirror of the clever person, and so on. Another soundbite of the time was that 'if men define situations as real, they are real in their consequences'. In other words, 'society' does not pre-exist our own subjective and intersubjective construction of it: we literally *create* society in and through mutual definitions of our situations.

Most influential of all in the attempt to grasp social selfhood was George Herbert Mead (1863–1931), who founded what was later labelled the 'symbolic interactionist' tradition in sociology through his teaching at the University of Chicago, the foremost location of sociological renewal in the first thirty years of the twentieth century. Mead argued that it is the use of *language as a symbolic medium* that distinguishes human interaction from that of other animals, and that meanings are actively created in and through interaction with the other person(s), not *prior* to that interaction. When we talk together, we always simultaneously put ourselves in the place of the other as well as expressing 'ourselves'. The social self is thus uniquely positioned as both the subject and object of consciousness. We anticipate certain responses from the other person, assuming a shared understanding, and we work towards confirming that shared understanding as acting, co-operative beings. Even when we are conducting an 'internal' dialogue, trying to think of what it is that we think, we are, according to Mead, engaged in an interpretative process between the 'Me' (the part of me that others see) and the 'I' (the part of myself that reflects on how I am seen by others).

Symbolic interactionism is a theoretical approach which focuses on the role of language and symbols in the production of human interaction.

Micro-sociology refers to sociological approaches which focus on small-scale and face-to-face interactions.

Mead went further still, accepting that the 'Me' is a social role in key respects, one that is formed through many processes of socialisation, the result of innumerable situations of social interaction. In this way, we become conscious of how society has formed us, and of what society expects of us. Mead termed this socialised part of the interactive self the 'generalised Other' – the presence of *social norms* within each of us. For example, we learn to see the reactions and influences of our particular parents (or friends, or Church minister) as representing the role of parents (or peer groups, or the Church) in general in this type of society.

After Mead, **symbolic interactionism** developed a number of different currents. Some 'Chicago school' advocates felt that its essence lay in a socio-psychological interpretative analysis of particular situations, believing that you couldn't usefully generalise beyond what Mead had said about the meanings of interactions. Rather, you had to take it situation by situation, adopting a very 'qualitative' approach to sociological understanding. Others (e.g. the 'Iowa school') felt that the prevalence of social meanings, even in particular situations, could be *measured and generalised* in a systematic and quantitative way, for example through responses to questionnaires. Perhaps most important of all, the impact of the symbolic sociology of Mead and others was to fully establish **micro-sociology** as a going concern, such that 'society' itself is to be seen as a constructed, negotiated reality reproduced and altered on an everyday basis by individuals. By the same token, society is not to be seen, in the 'classical' manner, as a thing-like general abstraction, having its own laws of motion like some strange planetary object.

The 'Chicago school' era of sociology was not only concerned with individual identity as constructed through social interaction but also with social problems, which of course in places like Chicago would have been plain for all to see. The rapid growth of American cities and the almost 'natural' way in which the new metropolis grew generated a spread of very different social 'zones' and subgroups – business zones, shopping zones, middle-class residential streets, distinct ethno-cultural districts, 'underclass' domains, and so on. The rapid growth of American corporations and heavy industry brought into being a large, solid and militant labour movement. The egalitarian liberal ideology of the New West allowed marginalised groups – women, African-Americans, European immigrants – to at least stake a *claim* to be fully included in the upwardly mobile society. The social conflict, deprivation, strikes, racist violence, and various other sorts of backlash reactions that resulted from these developments invited both understanding and a response (social policy, welfare). Such 'problems' were seen by the American mainstream (including sociology) as things that were troubling, but that could be realistically responded to by a steadfast reforming impulse, whether this remedial action be funded by the state or through religious or other private charity action. Some sociologists were prominent in the churches, and sociologists were certainly the beneficiaries of some of this reform-oriented funding. As a result, the previous dominance of sociological *theory* within

3 The story of sociology II: from classical to contemporary 45

the discipline gave way to a rather different and more 'relevant' professional identity: sociologists were people who undertook empirical research projects designed to identify and help solve the social problems which characterised the new 'ecology' of cities and group life.

Whilst the focus of this aspect of Chicago sociology was rather different from the more philosophical speculations of Mead and others on the nature of the self, there was a broad consensus that the best way to look at group experience as well as individual selfhood was as a matter of shared meanings, and that the paramount task was to work pragmatically and co-operatively to ensure that shared solutions could be generated around 'local' situations. That is why, although Chicago sociologists were dealing with the effects of a rapidly developed capitalism, and although phenomena like the zoning of cities and the sprouting of new occupational groupings – including the expanding profession of sociology itself – had a definite 'structural' logic to them, the sociological understanding of the day generally avoided seeing these features in terms of the social system as a whole, or in terms of a specific ideology such as 'capitalism'. Sociology in these times was a matter of solid empirical research – closely related to informed journalism (some sociologists of the day had been journalists) – and pragmatic problem-solving.

The reforming ambience of American thought in the first half of the twentieth century is also interestingly captured in the role which **feminism** and feminists played in sociological debate. Indeed, the extensive sociological network that has been termed 'the women of Chicago' was probably more activist and radical than that of the Chicago School men. The Chicago women shared the same broadly social evolutionary and 'progressivist' world-view, but their work was centred *outside* university circles, in community projects and reforming campaigns of various kinds, in which context it was felt that sociological knowledge and personal experience could most usefully be brought together. The leading figure in this feminist political sociology was Jane Addams (1860–1935), whose interactionist perspective highlighted the fusion, within social experience, of 'rational' and 'emotional' elements, and whose political motivation was to insist that the mission of modern democracy could not be fulfilled unless it was fully *socialised*, that is, given a firm grounding in a more equal, participative and inclusive society. Democracy for Addams and the women of Chicago, was not the 'formal' matter of legal rights and voting at elections, but rather the 'hands-on', on-going business of people working responsively for and with one another in all spheres of life – in the family, in education, in their neighbourhoods.

> **Feminism** refers to the set of ideas that argue that women are systematically disadvantaged.

Talcott Parsons and the mid-century consensus

During the period we have just looked at, sociology had become, perhaps for the first time, an established (male) profession, attuned to considerations of modern social selfhood, oriented towards social problems, and increasingly skilled at large-scale empirical research.

However, the turbulent condition of Western society disallowed any new, confident sociological 'big picture' prior to the 1940s. Only then was the tide of Nazism and fascism in Europe beginning to be turned; only then were the economic depression and the crisis of capitalism being significantly reversed (largely through the boom of the wartime economy); and only then did the very notion of 'society' begin to seem legitimate once again, after decades of quite extraordinary *state dominance* within the fabric of civil society. As the major nation least affected by outright political tyranny and capitalist depression, the USA increased its domination in sociology just as it became supreme in global politics, especially after its extraordinary economic success during and immediately after the war. With Nazism defeated in World War II, the survival of liberal capitalist society as the supposed emblem of the 'good side' of modernity could openly be celebrated. This was especially true in the face of the continuing threat to it of 'state socialism' as led by the Soviet Union after twenty years of Stalinist repression. And just as with the Cold War that existed between these two political systems, so in academic life there was a cold war between those ideas fundamentally critical of liberal capitalism and those basically supportive of it.

If American sociology continued to dominate, its intellectual style changed dramatically, a change embodied above all in the figure of Talcott Parsons (1902–1979). Parsons was a man with a mission. He felt that the pragmatism and empiricism of the Chicago-era sociology had gone too far, and that it was time for another dose of 'grand theory'. Parsons felt that to accomplish this, there had to be a new synthesis of the analytical foundations of sociology, and this in turn required a fresh appreciation of the European tradition. Parsons's 'reading' of the sociological classics was inevitably selective, and it was clearly oriented towards his own quite affirmative views of modern society. Though he was not exactly complacent about social problems and group conflicts, Parsons has been described as the first great sociological theorist to be fundamentally comfortable with 'high modernity', understood as liberal capitalist society in its new post-war phase of technology-driven prosperity. His work achieved a kind of dominant position within sociology for around twenty years. Partly, this was due to the tremendous determination with which Parsons pursued his synthesising efforts, bringing together the old and the new, the social and the personal, social structure and social action, the theoretical and the political in an impressive way. Partly it was because he reconstructed the image of a basically benign, well-integrated modern society, where the achieving individual was guided by, and reproduced, the governing 'norms' of Western life. Finally, it was because Parsons's rather peculiar mode of theorising increasingly fitted the idea of what social science should look like in a computer-led technological culture – his work is curiously impersonal in tone, and full of stipulated definitions, symbols, box and flow diagrams, feedback loops, systems and sub-systems. Though the content of Parsons' theories strongly featured the human attachment to

3 The story of sociology II: from classical to contemporary 47

(liberal) norms and values, the way he established this priority was very much in the manner of a white-coated scientific technician. A brave new sociology for a cybernetic (American-led) world.

Parsons defended again the centrality of *theory* to sociology. Social problems, individual identity, empirical research: none of these, he felt, could be coherently characterised without theory coming first, creating the interpretative framework without which no empirical topic makes any real sense. He then reviewed the contributions of Durkheim and Weber especially (he excluded Marx as a great sociologist), arguing that whilst these giants were building up towards a proper 'theory of social action', they never quite delivered it, and the task remained to be completed. This focus on action, and of *'voluntary'* action at that, reflects Parsons's debt to Weber, and also his acceptance of liberal individualism, helping to explain his relatively low assessment of Marx's contribution. But Parsons's individualism was not of the self-interested sort – he opposed the 'utilitarian' notion that the goals of individuals were simply material and self-seeking. Like Durkheim, Parsons saw the goals and actions of agents as strongly shaped by social *norms and values*, but unlike Durkheim, he did not see norms and values as externally constraining, in a coercive fashion. Norms and values, for Parsons, were an *aspect* of a total action situation, not a separate reality, and so in his view not even Durkheim had achieved the proper synthesis between norms and motives, individual and society.

Parsons saw what he called the 'unit act' as the microcosm or elementary particle of all social action. Abstractly conceived, this is the situation in which an agent selects specific goals according to the means available to achieve them, and in negotiation with the normative values attaching to those goals and means in the wider culture. Writ large, Parsons sees all social systems and sub-systems as similarly situated: they are goal-directed structures which have adaptational needs, which are motivated by a commitment to prevailing norms and which are kept in line by social controls. Thus Parsons conceived the 'total action system' as comprising the human physiological system (adaptation), the personality system (individual motivation), the social system (roles and positions), and the cultural system (symbolic resources, the arts, human expression, etc.). But the very same 'code' can be used to unlock the secrets of smaller systems within larger systems. Within the total action system, for example, you have the social system which itself is subdivided into four: the adaptational sub-system (the economy, roughly); the goal attainment sub-system (politics); the integrative sub-system (recognised social controls – the law, police, etc.), and the cultural-ideological sub-system (the socialisation process, symbolic ways of generating commitment to social values, etc.).

Parsons thought you could just keep going with this 'Chinese Box' or 'Russian Doll' model, so that, for example, within the social control sub-sub-system of action you could analyse the law, say, as having its own four prerequisites to fulfil. The legal system, after all, has to have an 'adaptive' sub-system of its own – economic resources, ways of responding to external realities in order to survive, physical premises and institutions, which may all have to change with the times, and so on. And it also has to have its own internal processes of decision making and hierarchy with which to formulate its objectives (its goal-attainment sub-system). The law also needs to have formal and informal controls over its members – through professional associations, rules and penalties for the conduct of law firms, etc. (i.e. its integration sub-system). Finally, the 'pattern maintenance' sub-system of law, to use Parsons's favourite term for the building of cultural and normative commitment to the integration and goals of the wider society, might be secured through training lawyers (and others) into a law-revering belief systems, with appropriate notions of 'rights' and 'duties' and 'lawbreaking', etc. You could go on even further: take law firms as an important part of the integration and pattern maintenance sub-systems of the law. Law firms themselves have to have resources, and have needs which ensure that they survive by adapting to changing environmental conditions – perhaps by growing in size or switching brand identity from one branch of the law to another. They need their own internal authorities and political decision-making processes – senior and junior partners for example. Law firms need explicit rules and sanctions for their members' behaviour – how much can an individual lawyer earn on the side, for example? And they need to find ways of stimulating and sustaining value commitment of members to 'the firm' – training sessions, office parties, emphasis on noble cases won, and so on.

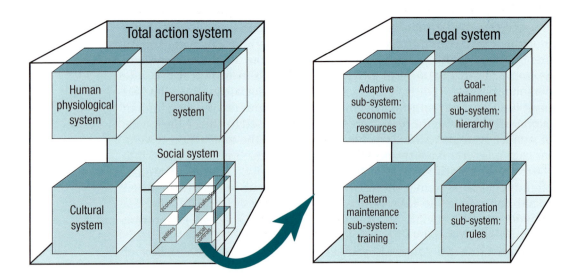

Figure 3.1 The 'Chinese Box' model of systems and sub-systems

3 The story of sociology II: from classical to contemporary 49

These interlocking examples indicate why, although he confessed himself to be an 'incurable theorist', Parsons passionately believed that his general theory could strongly guide empirical research programmes which would 'tap into' every nook and cranny of the social system, showing at every level how institutions were organised according to their omnipresent 'functional prerequisites' i.e. adaptation, goal attainment, integration and pattern maintenance. Many of Parsons's followers applied his insights into a whole range of very particular aspects of modern American society. To other sociologists, the kind of 'structural-functional' framework articulated by Parsons seemed at least sufficiently 'advanced' for them to regard the theoretical scene as settled for a while, so that they could press on with other 'advances' of the day, notably sophisticated empirical surveys of mass social behaviour and attitudes.

By the mid-1960s, however, Parsons's brand of sociology had been attacked from all possible angles. It was accused of being both too abstract, and yet too empiricist. It was accused of being too complex, and accused of being too simplistic. Parsons was attacked for having forgotten about *dis*equilibrium and *dys*functionality and social change in his obsession to theorise equilibrium and functionality and social integration. He was thought to be too 'idealist' in terms of his ontological emphasis on the existence and power of collective *norms* and *values*. He was berated for creating a vision of 'conformist man', for underestimating the prevalence of social conflict and for exaggerating the power of socialisation. He was charged with committing a grave inconsistency, having started with a *voluntarist* theory of action and ended up with an impersonal, abstract, all-powerful social system in which concrete human beings seemed like nothing more than functional cogs or cyphers.

Parsons was no fool. He was not wholly uncritical of capitalism and liberalism; he did not believe he had completely forgotten about social change and conflict and material inequalities. Indeed, the structural-functionalist perspective generally was shown convincingly by Robert Merton in particular to be capable of incorporating several of the 'critical' points made against it. Despite this, it is not really 'unfair' that Parsons's theories came to grief when they did, because his work, in some sense, certainly reflected the attainment of a new, apparently stable capitalist and liberal order – stable in relation to the turbulent recent past, more normatively secure in a sense than the Communist societies, and above all optimistic in its prospect of continued growth and social integration. This was the era of the belief in the emerging 'affluent' Western society, the 'you've-never-had-it-so-good' days. Parsons clearly shared some of those assumptions, and seeing that he was the most systematic of theorists in and for those times, it was not surprising that his star waned dramatically when the 1960s' moment of protest and conflict crashed on to the scene.

From the sixties to the nineties

Though Parsons was by no means uncontroversial in his heyday, the kind of dominance exercised by American sociology, and the kind of leading role taken by structural functionalism within American sociology at the time, has not occurred since. The period from the 1960s to the 1990s is marked by overlap and succession amongst a range of different perspectives or 'paradigms' in sociology, leading to the claim frequently heard today that, for better or for worse, sociology is a 'multi-paradigm' discipline, a subject in which you agree to disagree, rather than a potentially unified science with an established set of concepts and contents.

After Parsons, sociology undoubtedly became more radical politically, recruiting in the late 1960s and 1970s large numbers of critically-minded staff and students in the USA and Europe, and beginning to spread its subversive message – challenge 'common sense', challenge the ruling elites! – well outside its normal cultural heartland. This was the time of disillusionment with the Cold War and the West's vested interest in its continuation, which was seen as driven by the 'military-industrial complex' of profit-making corporations and Establishment conspiracies against democracy from within. The Vietnam War turned much of middle-class American youth against its parent culture; serious urban uprisings amongst African-American groups broke out, along with white reaction to that. The end of colonialism was approaching as many states in the 'Third World' began to assert their right to economic and political independence and cultural autonomy. Sociologists were not asking, with Parsons, how society worked and what the secret of cultural integration was, but rather, against Parsons and other cautious professionals: whose side are we on?

> **Conflict theory** asserts, contrary to consensus theorists, that social order is a precarious thing.

Structural functionalism was challenged, on the radical political side, first of all by a strand of work known as **conflict theory**, then by **neo-Marxism**. Conflict theory asserted that the assumption of Parsons and others that society tended towards integration and a *consensus* of values was wrong: on the contrary, a historical perspective and an empirical eye on the present showed social order to be a precarious thing, with considerable dispute over fundamental beliefs. Society was seen as divided into a plurality of groups and sub-cultures, rather than as a homogeneous populace, all members of which shared the same 'Dream'. However, conflict theory itself was soon felt to be over-generalised. In place of consensus as the magic key to analysis, we now had 'conflict', but critics thought this all-purpose idea of conflict extremely vague, and in its own way misleading, since conflict could not be seen to be any more 'obviously' operating than consensus. Marxists in particular argued that you have to do more than just say that there is always a plurality of conflicting groups; you have to say *which* groups are powerful or oppressed, and you have to analyse such divisions in terms of the conflictual structural logic of the modern capitalist system.

> **Neo-Marxist** theorists use Marxist analysis; however, they extend this to include the role of culture and consumption within modern society.

The apparently greater rigour of Marxism in filling out exactly what 'social conflict' meant found widespread favour through the 1970s, despite the continuing shadow cast by undemocratic Communist Party states governing in the name of Marxist thought. Some of the newly academicised Marxists, or neo-Marxists, or 'Western Marxists' as they have been labelled, conducted their own critiques of Stalinism and state control. Their work also emphasised, far more than did old-style Marxism, the importance of *culture* and *consciousness* within modern society. The roles of politics and the state, too, were increasingly deemed to be 'relatively autonomous' from the dictates of the capitalist economy or the capitalist 'ruling class'. In other words, though capitalism might still provide the 'logic' of the global economic system, just how it 'rules' – in either politics or culture – was felt by neo-Marxists to be an open and complex question. Accordingly, neo-Marxists made important contributions to the general sociological study of culture and ideology, politics and philosophy, in that although these were placed within the overall framework of capitalist society, they were, to a certain extent, understood as 'arenas of contestation'. As neo-Marxists also came to take on board the concerns of movements of colour and feminism, they quite subtly argued that these 'arenas' too were (a) *influenced* by considerations of capitalism and social class, but (b) not, ultimately, *reducible* to class and capital.

Through the 1980s a pincer movement took place which led to a sharp decline in the position of Marxism within academic sociological rankings. From one side – a more conservative side – came **exchange theory** or *rational choice theory* as it is sometimes termed. This tradition has a long pedigree, going back to the 'utilitarianism' that both Marx and Parsons felt had no place at all within sociology, since it more or less disregarded the question of the influence of collective norms and values. This is because, in exchange theory, social interaction is basically understood in 'behaviourist' terms as a transaction between people which carries various *costs and benefits* to the participating individual. If one type of behaviour seems to be rewarded and reinforced by others, causing us to be materially or emotionally better off, then we will probably take that course of action or adopt that way of behaving. If the result of the overall exchange seems adverse, causing us deprivation or disapproval, then we will probably refrain from doing it again if we can. This sort of interpretation of social exchange does not have to be limited to the domain of individual psychology; it can be extended to the strategies and actions of *social groups* and structural roles too.

In terms of groups, for example, you can see class conflict or ethnic exclusion as forms of 'game playing' or 'profit seeking'. In situations of limited resources and group competition – and what else, after all, is social interaction all about? – there will inevitably be various attempts, whether conscious or not, by people in certain situations, to engage in short-term gains, long-term advantages, trade-offs, and compromises in such a way as to strengthen their own position, status or material rewards. Because

Exchange theory argues that social interactions should be understood in 'behaviourist' terms as transactions between individuals which carry various costs and benefits to the participating individual.

of his emphasis on cultural norms and his obsession with inventing obscure labels for countless theoretical boxes, Parsons simply forgot how powerful this kind of 'instrumentalist' approach to social explanation is, and how relatively easy it is to observe social behaviour from that point of view. Our focus can be on individuals, certainly, but corporations, trade unions, churches, governments, states, and all manner of social movements and institutions can be conceptualised and observed in the same sort of way, i.e. as game-players and benefit seekers.

Some 'rational choice' theorists have tried to go further still, to embrace not only individual motivation and group advantage, but also social structure and cultural norms. After all, 'rationality' is not purely about material self-interest – people all the time do things which are oriented around what they believe in. We could still be acting according to a net calculus of profit and loss, even when the coinage of the profit is in terms of the success of our ideas and beliefs. Similarly, people's understanding of the situations they are in, and of how they might best improve those situations, generally allows for the probable impact of the prevailing social structures and cultural belief systems. In this way, the exchange and rational choice perspectives have broadened out from their initial 'individualist' and 'behaviourist' bases to try to cover many of the things that other sociologists would see as crucial for a full understanding of social interaction.

Rational choice theory was obviously more individualistic than the structural approach to society of neo-Marxists, but the notion of the material interests of individuals and groups was one point of overlap. However, the notion of material interest, especially if it includes strategies for strengthening positions of social *power*, is not as obvious a concept as it looks. It was perhaps feminism above all, during the 1970s and 1980s, which blurred the boundary in sociology between the idea of power on the one hand and material gain on the other. Feminist sociology bombarded the sociological male establishment – including Marxism – with the accusation that it had simply ignored the question of women's material and cultural subordination, and that in doing so, sociology had actually contributed to **patriarchal** conceptions and practices. In the feminist view the 'mainstream' was really nothing less than the 'malestream', given that such an extraordinarily basic and obvious 'structural' feature of society as male domination, through all classes and ethnicities, was so often and so conveniently overlooked.

Initially, the feminist critique was directed towards exposing this erasure of women, and of gender relations more generally, from social history and from the history of the social sciences themselves. More substantively, feminist concepts of the social structure of modernity were developed, *either* in conjunction with Marxist theories to produce ideas about the 'dual system' operation of class and gender; *or*, in politically-inspired separation from all malestream trends, the focus would be on modes of patriarchy as specifically male relations of ruling, thus arming feminist sociologists with a fully 'alternative' structural sociology which

> **Patriarchy** is a concept used by feminist theorists to refer to the structured nature of men's domination of women.

3 The story of sociology II: from classical to contemporary **53**

could be used to generate all manner of empirical research, theoretical debate and critique.

Approaches such as Marxism and feminism thoroughly opposed previous functionalist models of sociological analysis, but in a certain sense, this opposition was mainly ideological. Marxism and feminism, in the forms they took in the 1970s at least, were certainly structuralist in inspiration, and indeed functionalist too. Both saw the modern social system as a complex totality governed by interrelationships between sub-systems – for example, economic relations, politics, and culture. And like Parsons, but giving very different motive forces, Marxists and feminists singled out special principles of societal integration and cohesiveness – those around class and capital for Marxists, those around patriarchy and gender for feminists. These core social relations and values were seen as what makes the modern social (capitalist, patriarchal) system work as it does. These surprising parallels between Parsons and more radical alternatives played a part in the revival of a 'neo-functionalist' current in the 1980s, which sought to rehabilitate the most general aspects of Parsons's project, but minus the capitalist 'apologetics'. At the same time, however, the very idea of a clearly structured social totality – whether it be driven by liberal norms, class interest or patriarchal power – came under increasing fire. Such schemes, it was felt, were always in the end 'reductionist', despite all efforts by clever Marxists and feminists to inject their paradigm with motivational complexity and the 'relative autonomy' of sub-systems of action. Reductionism here means that just about everything is seen as boiling down, in the end, to a question of class, or gender (or advantage-seeking behaviour, in the case of exchange theory). But what if individual and groups meanings are far more pluralistic than these theories allow, and what if social structure as a whole has little of the 'crushing' quality that structuralist theorists always imply it has? Two major lines of thought have developed in the post-war period which want to take sociology decisively beyond its 'structuralist' and 'reductionist' tendencies.

One very broad line of thinking follows on from the 'symbolic interactionism' of the earlier period, but takes the latter to new levels of observation and theory. This is the 'micro-sociological' tradition – in reality comprising several very different ways of conceiving everyday interaction. The micro-sociologists share the idea that social structures are nothing more than what is created in face-to-face interaction on an everyday basis. Parsons, Marxists and feminists, they would say, are all guilty of reifying society – making it a thing-like entity which has the effect of somehow manipulating human agents as if they have no control over what they do. Micro-sociologists do, however, wish to retain the idea of social order; it's just that this order is something that requires constant redefinition according to the nature and perception of interaction. The order we perceive is actually quite a precarious thing, the result of a vector of situational meanings and behaviours.

Total institutions are those situations where individuals are cut off from the wider society for an appreciable period of time, and where people lead an enclosed form of life.

Ethnomethodology is a sociological perspective which focuses on identifying the means by which lay actors construct their everyday worlds.

Structuralism is a theoretical approach which attempts to identify the structures or unconscious symbolic codes shaping social life.

Different strands of microsociology have taken this insight in different directions. Symbolic interactionism continues, for example, to have many adherents, but there are newer influences too. Erving Goffman (1922–1982), for example, introduced a dramaturgical sociological perspective in which interaction is seen as an extended acting metaphor. All the world is a stage, but so are each of its component situations, and we, as actors, go through our scripted roles, often improvising. Sometimes what we do and say is 'front-stage' and explicit, sometimes it is 'back-stage' and covert. We have 'front' regions and 'back' regions in our interactive strategies; we 'save face', 'front up', 'play to the crowd' and so on. Goffman developed an engaging way of using these general ideas without their ever becoming so intrusively theoretical that they take our attention away from the engaging social dramas he was keen to describe. Goffman was particularly interested in the dynamics of conformity and subversion in what he termed **total institutions** – asylums, hospitals, prisons, etc.

Goffman presented the colourful corners of the world as places where people knew a lot about what was going on, and played up to that, sure of their instinct about what could be 'taken for granted'. **Ethnomethodology** is a micro-sociological perspective which sees social order and interaction at the humblest level as a much trickier business. Drawing initially on influences from the philosophical currents of existentialism and phenomenology, ethnomethodologists have tried to get us to see the wonder and danger in reproducing *any* social 'world'. Even such 'ordinary' events as telephone conversations, or buying things in shops for the listed price have been highlighted by ethnomethodologists as social situations in which the dynamics of social confirmation are very basic, yet extremely complex too and easily undermined. We take a lot for granted (for example, I assume that you will say 'hello' when you pick up the phone, or that the customer will actually pay the stated price for a given brand of toothpaste), but how exactly do these things 'work'? (We take turns to speak; I understand the role of money in making our meeting in your shop a successful one.) And how easily can things get out of hand? (What if I refuse to take my turn in the phone exchange; or offer another price for the toothpaste?) Conversations, exchanges, rituals, and personal dependencies: there are myriad things like this going on every day, say the ethnomethodologists, things which are fascinating and sometimes very tense. If sociologists are going to study social integration and conflict, this is perhaps where they should start.

Another type of reaction against 'structural' macro-sociology became known as post-structuralism. Structuralism (without the post) was for its own part something more than just large-scale thinking about the nature of society – Durkheim and Weber had done that, but they could not really be called structuralist. **Structuralism** was the idea that society worked as a *total system of meanings*, and that to understand this theoretically, there had to be a kind of abstract 'code' to unlock its secret. Think of how language works, the structuralists suggested. Language is a system of meanings which is settled by convention – the meaning of *black* depends on it being, amongst other things, *not white*. The meaning of *father* is logically bound up with what it means to be a *son* or *daughter*. There are several relatively simple binary codes and conventions which reveal the way in which a language works as an interrelated totality. As language users, we have to inherit and learn these general codes if we are to reproduce them successfully. We can, of course, improvise to some extent, but not to the point of gibberish: all our utterances and marks must make sense within the total language matrix, and affirm it as we learn how to inhabit it properly, and thus reproduce the whole system.

In sociological structuralism, we are invited to see society and all its connections as if they operated like a language. All the meanings that are reproduced in society are systematically interconnected, each of our social improvisations can be understood as part of the overall logic of the codes learnt. And in social theory, we can try to unravel the relationships between social meanings: at the simplest level, not only father–son but also capitalist–worker, husband–wife, old–young, Western–Eastern, in-group–out-group, and so on. Put that way, structuralism is more a style of theorising about the total social structure than it is a particular theory about which social relations are most important. You could have a Marxist structuralism and a feminist structuralism, for example. Fashionable as it was as a sophisticated way of understanding the workings of social structures and social meanings, through the 1980s structuralism was eclipsed by post-structuralism.

Post-structuralism is the view that what structuralism and other 'grand theories' take for granted should be radically questioned. The point is not to revert to *pre*-structuralist social theories, for undoubtedly structuralism provided about the best effort there could be to grasp the social totality. For example, structuralism taught us to see social interactions as meanings, 'texts' rather than outright material realities. But structuralism failed to follow through its own logic – namely that 'society' itself is a 'text', the product of the meanings we tentatively assign to it in our discourse around it. For post-structuralists, the whole set of assumptions highlighted by structuralism, and so central to *all* social theory – i.e. that we can articulate what society 'really' is, what its key meanings are, how the structure relates to the lives and identities of its component groups and individuals – all this must be abandoned as a misguided project.

Post-structuralists argue that no social meanings are ever 'stable'; that discourses do not 'belong' to their authors; that there are very many different types of discourse; that no particular social 'meanings' can be definitively 'privileged' over others, whether these be the discourses of ordinary social agents or sociological theorists. It follows, therefore, that the role of post-structuralist social theorists is firstly to be *critical* of all claims to have unearthed the 'secret' of how society really works. Such claims need to be *'deconstructed'* for their pretentious absolutism and essentialism, it is insisted. (*Absolutism* = asserting the single, all-powerful truth; *essentialism* = showing us the true underlying essence of how things

> Post-structuralist theorists are critical of structuralism because they argue that the social world is not as stable as structuralists assume it is. Rather than attempting to 'uncover' underlying structures, social theorists should be 'deconstructing' the reality that we take to be stable.

are.) After so many failed attempts to find the 'God's-eye view' of social life, post-structuralists feel that, for a change, to see things as fragmented and deconstructed can be no bad thing.

Social thought at the second *fin de siècle*

At the end of the twentieth century (and the situation is not unlike that of one hundred years previously), an awareness of complexity and plurality characterises sociological thought. We now live, many feel, in a world of unprecedented complexity, cultural diversity and risk. In that context, what is the role of sociology and social theory? After two centuries of effort, no acceptable 'big picture' that is adequate on its own has emerged. Indeed, in today's multi-perspectival and multi-cultural world, there are more and more *small* 'big pictures' around, just as society itself is strewn with innumerable ways of classifying people, things and different forms of social interaction. Who is any longer to say, then, which of these *small* 'big pictures' is any more valid than any other? In response to this situation, some sociologists have fully embraced the new pluralism and absence of simple answers, suggesting that sociologists could try for a change to stop their pronouncing and legislating for people's lives, and move over into a more humble and 'dialogic' way of operating. Sociology could start down this new humble path, for example, by owning up to its notable failure so far to comprehend some major social forces in people's lives, such as *sexuality* and *emotion*.

Other sociologists feel that sociology does continue to offer strong leads and insights, even if no new 'consensus' has emerged. This line of thinking would contend that the world is perhaps *not* as perplexing as some make out. There is a very clear pattern of globalisation going on, for example, and it is still not too difficult to discern both at the 'local' and the 'global' levels what the chief sources of social division and integration are. In terms of general ideas, defenders of modern sociology would note that although a theorist like Parsons may have been wrong about just about everything else, he was right in trying to synthesise the sort of 'dualisms' that almost every new large-scale social theory seems to rediscover (whatever it says about its own radical novelty): 'the micro' and 'the macro' levels of analysis, the dimensions of social structure and individual human agency, statics and dynamics, material life and ideology, and so on. Each new generation of sociologists advertises its own 'adequate' solution to these dualisms, only for later theorists to accuse their predecessor of, in practice, favouring either the 'action' or the 'structure' side of things. Nevertheless, all these efforts at 'synthesis' do produce a kind of 'progress' in sociological thinking, it could be said, such that in the post-war period talented authors like Anthony Giddens, Pierre Bourdieu, Dorothy Smith and Jeffrey Alexander have come up with interesting theoretical syntheses of previous positions, upon which to base further research and argument.

A third line of thought would be that sociology should avoid both the helplessness of post-sociological thinking and the waffly generality of theoretical synthesising in the abstract. Perhaps altogether too much effort is being put into trying to resolve unresolvable questions, what is needed is possibly a strong dose of problem-solving within quite specific empirical topic areas. Sociologists do actually, by now, know quite a lot about some empirical dimensions of social life, and they should give priority to developing further research projects of that kind, bringing in wider theories only where these seem to illuminate the particular projects.

As we move into the twenty-first century, therefore, sociologists hold a variety of views in theory and politics. For some, 'progress' represents a full acceptance of diversity and even fragmentation within sociology, as elsewhere in post-modern life. Perhaps we even need to welcome *the end* of sociological thought as we have known it. After all, what is the difference between sociology, cultural studies, women's studies, anthropology, and other types of commentary on the globalising, multi-cultural society that we are engaged in? For others, sociology still represents a more 'disciplined' and 'structural' approach to society as a whole, and for them, future progress will mean attaining greater consensus within the social sciences, and perhaps a more positive attitude on the part of sociologists themselves.

Conclusion

Some of the most influential sociological theories have been outlined in this and the previous two chapters. Our approach has been to give very broad definitions and a sweeping overview of sociological concepts, themes and theories. While this approach has the advantage of covering a wide range of material quickly, its obvious drawback is a lack of detailed discussion of the intricacy and complexity of sociological analysis. In the following chapters some of this lack of detail will be addressed as we turn to the substantive topics that have provided the research focus for contemporary sociology.

Study questions

3.1 In what ways is Simmel's approach to sociology different from the 'classical' works of Marx, Durkheim and Weber?

3.2 What contributions did writers such as Gilman and Du Bois make to early twentieth-century sociology?

3.3 What is the basic premise of Mead's symbolic interactionist perspective?

3.4 Outline Parsons's theory of structural functionalism. What are some of the drawbacks of his approach?

3.5 What does 'micro-sociology' contribute to our understandings of social life?

Further reading

Alexander, J.C. (1987) *Sociological Theory Since 1945*. Hutchinson, London.

Callinicos, A. (1999) *Social Theory: An Historical Introduction*. Polity Press, Cambridge.

Craib, I. (1992) *Modern Social Theory: From Parsons to Habermas*, 2nd ed. Harvester Wheatsheaf, Hemel Hempstead.

Hall, S., Held, D. and McGrew, A. (eds). (1992) *Modernity and Its Futures*. Polity Press, Cambridge.

Layder, D. (1994) *Understanding Social Theory*. Sage, London.

Lemert, C. (1993) *Social Theory: The Multicultural and Classic Readings*. Westview Press, Boulder, Col.

Lengermann, P.M. and Niebrugge, J. (1996) Early Women Sociologists and Classical Sociological Theory: 1830–1930. In Ritzer, G. (ed.) *Classical Sociological Theory*. McGraw Hill, New York.

May, T. (1996) *Situating Social Theory*. Milton Keynes, Open University Press.

Ritzer, G. (1996) *Modern Sociological Theory*, 4th ed. McGraw Hill, New York.

Scott, J. (1995) *Sociological Theory: Contemporary Debates*. Aldershot, Edward Elgar.

Tietjens Meyers, D. (1997) *Feminist Social Thought: A Reader*. Routledge, London.

4 Gender, sexuality and identity

Chapter aims

- to discuss some of the ways in which gender and sexuality are socially constructed;
- to outline the connections between gender, sexuality and power; particularly in relation to sexual harassment and rape;
- to demonstrate the connection between globalisation and the notion of 'the body beautiful'.

 ## Introduction

This chapter examines some of the ways in which gender and sexuality are linked to personal identity. Each of us has a sense of our self which is fundamentally connected to being male or female, being heterosexual or homosexual. These aspects of personal identity do not come to us from biology but can be explained in relation to social processes – socialisation and the social construction of each category. In addition, we examine how gender differences are not neutral in their effects, but are connected to systematic forms of power which we refer to as patriarchal relations. In general, men have more social power than women. This power is manifested in a number of different ways, but at its most unsubtle it takes the form of sexual violence. Finally, we explore how large-scale global processes, such as the way in which food is now produced and distributed, can have an effect at the level of the individual body through such things as eating disorders.

Women, men, sex and difference

Bodily and sexual difference as a marker of the differences between men and women

That men and women are different appears to be a self-evident truth. The photo above captures one element of this 'truth' in which bodily difference becomes a marker for other more profound differences (in terms of sexuality, work, emotions, power and so on). While it is clear that male and female bodies do differ in several important respects, it is also true that they share a greater number of similarities. These similarities, however, are largely ignored in favour of focusing on the *differences* that exist between male and female bodies. This marking of each and every individual as a male or female person begins at birth (or sometimes even prior to birth) where the very first observation that is made of the newborn child is whether it is a girl or a boy. The assignment of gender, given in response to sighting either one set of sexual organs or another, will come to have profound consequences for the newborn child. Gender assignment will shape the child's life in a myriad of ways, influencing the clothes it wears, the sports it plays, the education it receives, the kind of job it will have, its income level, the illnesses it will suffer – perhaps it will even help explain how he or she will die.

However, at this stage of its life there is nothing that can be said with certainty about the newborn's tastes, desires, aptitude, intelligence, emotions, or social skills. The newborn is in all important respects an asocial being, with no consciousness of a self-identity or understanding of its place in the world. Any identity associated with the newborn baby only comes via others, for example in terms of a name and position within a pre-existing set of social relationships (of family, whanau, iwi and so on). While the newborn lacks a *consciousness* of its own identity, other people will be beginning the lifelong process of marking and reinforcing the gender of this new human being.

What this suggests is that it is possible to make a distinction between 'sex', (i.e. the physical characteristics of males and females), and 'gender' (i.e. the social attributes of men as masculine and women as feminine). While it would be understandable to view sexual difference as a dichotomy in which one is *either* male *or* female, this does not account for those individuals who are born with mixed sexual characteristics. An 'intersexed' person might have the external genitalia of a male but have a female chromosomal structure. Other combinations of physical and chromosomal characteristics are also possible. While there are several biological variations of sex, other than unambiguously male and unambiguously female, most cultures only allow for two socially sanctioned genders. We must be *either* masculine *or* feminine. We do not tolerate very well people who blur the distinction between being a man and being a woman. An indication of this is that intersexed individuals are always assigned one or other gender at birth, Through surgery and socialisation they are 'shaped' into individuals with the 'appropriate' gender characteristics.

The initial assignment of gender is only the first step in producing masculine and feminine individuals. The sociologist Harold Garfinkel argued that we should understand gender as something that has to be *accomplished*. That is, in order for us to recognise ourselves and be recognised by others as people of a certain gender, we have to 'do' certain things which embody the social characteristics associated with masculinity or femininity. From this perspective, then, gender has very little to do with nature, but is a cultural artefact. As babies and young children, we are shaped by the work that others do on our behalf. For example, one way that gender difference is marked in Western cultures, at an everyday level, is through dressing boys and girls in different colours: pink for girls and blue for boys. Many people might look askance at parents who dress their boys in pink and girls in blue (though it is probably seen as less of a deviation for girls to be dressed in blue than the other way around – demonstrating that masculinity is perhaps more socially valued than femininity: it is preferable to be seen possessing masculine characteristics than the more undervalued feminine ones.) We seem to believe that there is some kind of natural affinity between certain colours and each of the genders. However, the association of blue for boys, pink for girls is a fairly recent one. Before World War I it was not uncommon for boys to wear pink, which the promotional literature of the time called 'a stronger, more decided colour'. Girls wore blue which was understood to be 'delicate' and 'dainty' (Garber, 1992: 1).

Even tissue boxes are gendered!

While this example might seem trivial, it illustrates two points about gender. Firstly, the significance we place on differentiating between humans on the basis of gender. We do this in most settings. Often it makes little sense to do so but we persist in the belief that the *differences* between the genders must be of more significance than the *similarities*. Although there is now a vast amount of research into 'psychological sex differences'; the main finding is that there is an overwhelming degree of psychological *similarity* between women and men. Where there are clear-cut differences between men as a group and women as a group they are few and confined to restricted areas. What is more usual are some small 'differences-on-average' that occur in the context of a very large *overlapping* of the distributions of men and women (Connell, 1987: 170). Secondly, many of these seemingly 'natural' differences are in fact constructions of the social world. There is after all nothing in the wave length of light that we call 'pink' that links it naturally to girls.

It is clear then that the reality of gender difference is all around us but how do we explain why male and female babies come to be masculine and feminine beings who are so different in temperament, social skills, income level, propensity to violence and so on? Common sense arguments tend to rely on the notion that biology explains the differences between men and women. It is argued that because men and women have different biological make-ups – anatomically, chromosomally and hormonally – it should be no surprise that they end up doing different things and having different experiences of the world. In contrast to this view, sociologists maintain that many of the so-called 'natural' differences between women and men are the result of various social processes that shape the newborn child from an ungendered human being into a boy or girl. We are not born possessing all the appropriate characteristics of our gender. Rather we are *socialised* into them through practices that occur in the family, school and indeed most social situations. **Gender socialisation** describes a process by which we learn to take up the socially approved characteristics of the gender we were assigned at birth. Through socialisation we learn to adopt the appropriate gender *roles* and gender *identity.* Gender role refers to the different *behaviours* that are associated with men and women. For example, in the family women tend to be responsible for housework and child care, while men's gender role is organised around paid work and the public world. Gender identity refers to the way that men and women *feel* about themselves.

An important and interconnected aspect of gendered identity involves **sexuality**. The photograph on p. 60 displays a common representation of the female body as being sexual, desirable, passive and available. Men's bodies are much less likely to be represented in this way and, where they are depicted as sexual, the meanings of that sexuality are rather different, connected as they are to power, control, and activity. These two dominant representations of masculine and feminine sexuality are constructed as a matching pair in which heterosexuality is deemed the normal and natural outcome of the sexual difference between male and female bodies. In the following contribution, Allison Kirkman discusses how the seemingly natural practice of heterosexuality, and therefore the deviant and unnatural practice of homosexuality, are in fact social constructions.

> **Gender socialisation** refers to the process by which individuals learn the appropriate behaviour associated with their gender.

> **Sexuality** is a broad term referring to sexual practices, identities and desires. Sociologists take these things to be an outcome of culture rather than nature.

Becoming sexual: heterosex as 'natural' and 'normal'

Allison Kirkman

'I think I was gay at five or before … things always seemed different to me; well they didn't seem to be fitting in with other people's way of doing things.'

These words from an interview with a 30-year-old Pakeha woman about her sexual identity and religious beliefs illustrates one of the ways in which we come to see our sexual identities. In this case, the woman suggests that she knew that she was different from a very young age. While there were a number of women in this study who felt the same way, there were other women who believed that becoming sexual was something that was open to change and their individual sexuality was not fixed at any particular time.

How do we become 'sexual', and how do we become other than 'heterosexual'? These questions are closely related to what it means to become male and female. The codes of female sexuality, however, are different from the codes for male sexuality, and within both male and female sexualities there are a number of ways in which sexuality could be expressed. However, for many of us our first contact with ideas about sexuality is based on what is 'natural' and it is what is natural which determines what is considered 'normal'. In our society we should 'naturally' and 'normally' be heterosexual. How do we know this? While there may be many ways of 'becoming sexual' in our society, heterosexuality is the social **institution** through which this process is mediated. 'Male' and 'female' as indicators of complementary and natural pairings infiltrate every aspect of our lives (right down to the labelling of the interlocking parts of nuts and bolts – that which is either the male or female part). Young women and men in New Zealand grow up expecting to become a part of a heterosexual pair – and being female, in particular, used to mean both getting married and having children. While getting married may now not be part of the equation, there is still an expectation that women and men will become 'coupled' and that children will eventuate from that couple.

> Institutions refer to social practices that are regularly repeated, that are sanctioned and that are maintained by social norms.

We become aware of these cultural expectations when controversies about sexual behaviour enter the public arena. Two such controversies in the recent past are briefly examined here: what has been termed 'the Parker–Hulme case' and the debate surrounding homosexual law reform.

The first example which has been part of on-going discourses about sexuality is 'the Parker–Hulme case', a case which has represented lesbians as either mad or bad. In 1954, Juliet Hulme, then aged 15, and Pauline Parker, aged 16, killed Honora Parker, Pauline's mother, in Victoria Park in Christchurch. This murder became the subject of a sensational trial, followed by a continual resurfacing of articles on the case up to the present day. There have been other occasions in New Zealand when women labelled 'lesbian' have received media scrutiny but the accounts about Pauline Parker and Juliet Hulme have been the most revisited, and widely known. Julie Glamuzina and Alison Laurie wrote an account from a lesbian feminist perspective in 1992, and the case was used by a criminologist, Greg Newbold, to open his discussion on women and deviance. After describing the event, he writes 'Thus ended one of the most bizarre episodes in criminal history, a case in which the intrigues of love, madness, and a hint of the occult provided all the ingredients of a Hitchcock thriller' (Newbold, 1992: 43). However, the case has also had a more public viewing in the form of a stage play, *Daughters of Heaven* written by Michelanne Forster and performed at the Court Theatre in Christchurch and Downstage in Wellington in 1992. Peter Jackson's movie *Heavenly Creatures* ensured that even more people became aware of the Parker–Hulme case. A number of times over the years, journalists have speculated in the popular media about where these women were living, but it was only in 1995 that Juliet Hulme was finally 'uncovered' by journalists in a small village in Scotland, living as a successful crime fiction writer called Ann Perry. In 1997 the *New Zealand Women's Weekly* tracked down Pauline Parker living in a small English village. This focus on the lives of Pauline Parker and Juliet Hulme has ensured that debates about being lesbian have remained within the public domain, regardless of whether either Juliet Hulme or Pauline Parker could correctly be viewed in this light.

The second case which reminds us of cultural expectations about sexuality are times of homosexual law reform. In 1974 and again in 1985 the issue of homosexual law reform caused sexuality to become a topic of everyday discussion, and also polarised views about sexual behaviour. Homosexual law reform was aimed at decriminalising male homosexual acts – female homosexual acts have never been illegal in New Zealand, something which reflects the way the New Zealand law originated from the English legal system. (The most frequent explanation for the anomaly is that Queen Victoria did not believe sexual activity was possible between women and hence it was felt that there was no need to legislate against such acts.) The 1985–1986 homosexual law reform bill consists of two parts: Part I (decriminalisation of male homosexual acts), and Part II (anti-discrimination against gay men and lesbians). Part I received the greatest publicity and was the only section passed into law in 1986. Part II was incorporated into an amendment to the Human Rights Act and passed in 1993.

In both 1974 and 1985 many of the submissions to the Select Committee included opposition from religious organisations to the bills. The groups which made up the New Christian Right condemned homosexuality as a sin. In 1985 the main Christian opposition came in the form of a petition, entitled 'For God, For Family, For Country', organised by two conservative evangelical churchmen, Keith Hay and Barry Reed. In their submission they claimed that 'this Bill will encourage the breakdown of the family unit by legalising sodomy'. At the other end of the tolerance continuum the Wellington Inner City Ministry in its submission to the Select Committee argued that 'beyond the need for procreation, our sexuality can be seen to foster God's purposes by celebrating our need for others and their need for us. Our lives are shaped by those who love us and those who refuse to love us.'

However, many national church organisations did not hold such liberal views. The Catholic Church was primarily concerned with the need for procreation, while also endorsing the view of some Protestant denominations that the problem lay not with individual homosexual people but was whether they chose to engage in homosexual acts or not. That is, the sin attaches to the act and not the person. The basis for this position is one of biological determinism – the cause of the homosexuality is something innate in the individual and therefore something for which the individual cannot be held responsible. The more fundamentalist churches disagreed with the decriminalising of homosexual acts – they contended that homosexuality is not a natural behaviour; that it is a learned behaviour and therefore is something which can be changed or a 'pattern which can be broken'. Groups such as Exodus, Rock of Life and Lion of Judah were founded on this premise and aimed to promote the 'conversion' of homosexual behaviour into heterosexual behaviour.

During the 1985 campaign a new focus was HIV/AIDS. The risk to public health rather than the risk to morality became central to the debate and demonstrated a move from religious discourses to medical discourses in defining deviance. But despite this focus, and while the criminalisation of gay men was the reason for the law reform, the public debate on homosexuality had consequences for both women and men. The effect of an event like this campaign was a heightened anxiety about exposure for those gay men and lesbian women who were 'passing' as heterosexual, because it moved the topic of homosexuality into an everyday context. To return to the words of the woman speaking at the beginning of this piece: 'I felt frightened at that time because even though the bill was intended to give greater freedom, it brought people under scrutiny, and it was like stirring up a hornet's nest. It was reminding people that we were out there'. This reminder of the presence of gay and lesbian people in our society alerts us to that which is deviant, and in doing so highlights heterosexuality as the behaviour which is expected in our culture.

Young women growing up in New Zealand today still encounter many conflicting messages about sexuality and how to be female. On the one hand they have been told that 'girls can do anything' through a well-known media campaign, but on the other hand the decisions they make about how they become sexual continue to be mediated within a heterosexual framework. In 1996, when The New Zealand Family Planning Association published two pamphlets for secondary school boys and girls, the pamphlet for girls called *Sisters* received attention from some sections of the community because it included lesbianism as an option for women. Members of the New Christian Right criticised this aspect of the publication in particular; and so while the stories of Pauline Parker and Juliet Hulme, or the accounts of the homosexual law reform campaign may not have much impact on young women and men growing up in the 1990s, the overall societal message remains unchanged – the desired and 'normal' way to be male and female is to be heterosexual.

Questions

Having read Allison Kirkman's discussion try to answer the following questions:

1   How have homosexuality and deviance come to be linked in public discourse?
2   What effects might this link have on how people think about homosexuality?
3   What does Allison Kirkman mean when she says that heterosexuality is a 'social institution'?
4   What is the wider social significance for lesbian women of the popular media attention to the Parker–Hulme murder?

The social and the personal: the social construction of sexuality

Kirkman has drawn our attention to some important elements in the social construction of sexuality. Now we will explore in more detail some of the ways in which the categories of *homosexuality* and *heterosexuality* have come to be linked to personal identity. Firstly, though, let us return to the notion that heterosexuality is 'normal' and 'natural' and that homosexuality is 'abnormal' and 'unnatural'. It may well be the case that homosexuality is not the norm (in terms of being the most common form of sexuality); however, the fact that a category is a minority one does not in itself justify the view that such category is 'unnatural'. The view that homosexuality is 'unnatural' rests on a belief that the only kind of 'natural' sex is that which can potentially lead to procreation. Further support for the idea that homosexuality is unnatural is drawn from the belief that homosexual behaviour does not exist amongst animals. Firstly, it should be said that there are numerous examples of such activity among animals. But perhaps more importantly we might want to argue that humans, because we create and use *culture*, are sufficiently distinct from animals that an argument based on biology ignores crucial elements of what it means to be human. We do not find 'artists' amongst animals but this does not lead to the assumption that artistic activity is unnatural. By pursuing this general line of critique, sociologists are not arguing that the biological realm of life is completely irrelevant (we cannot, for example, ignore the fact that the experience of sexual arousal is a very different bodily experience for men and women). However, it is often the case that appeals to 'nature' are not innocent, but form part of an *ideological* strategy. **Ideology** refers to sets of ideas that help us to make sense of social life, and that tend to legitimise power relations in society. In the realm of sexuality, appeals to nature are used to support the view that heterosexuality is universal and unquestionable and as such it hides the ways in which heterosexuality, as much as homosexuality, is socially constructed.

Just as sociologists see gender difference as being primarily the outcome of social rather than natural biological processes, so too we see sexuality as shaped by culture. Evidence of this cultural element of sexuality is to be found in the various ways in which different cultures express sexuality through sanctioning with whom, when, where and how it is permissible to have sex. In Western societies heterosexuality and homosexuality are seen as mutually exclusive categories, in which individuals are either one or the other; however, this way of linking sexual practice and identity is in fact relatively recent in historical terms and does not characterise all cultural expressions of sexuality. For example, among the Sambia (a Papua New Guinean tribe) all men take part in 'ritualised homosexuality' as part of the initiation into manhood. In this culture semen, which is considered an essential part of masculinity, must

> **Ideology** refers to sets of ideas that help us to make sense of social life and that tend to legitimise power relations in society.

be ingested by boy initiates in order for them to become 'real men'. So for a period of some years, boys and young adult men take part in sexual practices (fellatio, but not anal intercourse) that in Western culture would be called 'homosexual'. These men, however, go through this ritualised homosexual practice in order to become the *heterosexually* active and aggressive masculine beings that are appropriate in their culture. Among the Sambia, homosexuality is not the expression of a *desire* (in terms of sexual attraction for the sake of pleasure), nor the expression of an 'identity' (as a kind of person who wants to live his life relating sexually only to men). 'Homosexuality' in Sambia society is a *practice*, confined to a particular period of the life span, for the express purpose of initiating boys into the proper Sambian form of masculinity. In the sense then that we all live our sexual lives *within* particular cultures, we come to express our sexuality in culturally defined terms rather than in a purely individual way. We are the creatures of our cultures. So a Sambian man would be perplexed by the notion of 'gay identity' that is found in Western societies, just as we find the notion of an age-specific homosexuality unusual.

What this example demonstrates is that the general category of sexuality, what Jeffrey Weeks has referred to as a 'fictive unity', actually involves three rather different elements. Firstly, we can identify *sexual practice* which refers to the acts that take place between individuals when they have sex (broadly speaking, which body parts are placed where). Secondly, *sexual desire* (or attraction) refers to the feeling of wanting certain kinds of sexual activity and the kind of person with whom we want to have that activity. When this desire relates to the gender of the other person it is sometimes referred to as 'sexual orientation'. When we desire a person of the same gender we talk of homosexual desire; when the person is of the other gender we talk of heterosexual desire. It is also possible to desire particular kinds of sexual activity (for example sadomasochistic practice) or to have a desire for a more or less passive (or active) role in sexual practice. Thirdly, where aspects of our sexual practice or desire come to play a key role in how we think of ourselves as sexual people, we can talk of *sexual identity*. In contemporary Western culture, sexual identity is typically organised in relation to the gender of the person we feel attracted to. In this sense there are people who *are* homosexual, heterosexual, or bisexual (where both men and women are found to be sexually attractive and individuals consciously see themselves as, in some way, pursuing both forms of attraction). While sexual identity organised on the basis of 'sexual orientation' is common, there are also some people for whom another form of sexual identification is equally or more important (for example, sadomasochism). These three aspects of sexuality do not always line up with each other in any one individual. To illustrate, it is possible for a woman to desire sex with another woman, but to be married to a man. Her sexual identity, as publicly expressed, may be heterosexual (she may not even think of herself as lesbian); her sexual practice is heterosexual but her desire is homosexual.

This sociological way of thinking about sexuality cuts across some commonsense ideas we have about the essential and fixed nature of our own sexual personas. We each of us *live*, in our daily existence, as men and women, gay, lesbian, bisexual, 'straight'. It may be disturbing to have this existence placed under the harsh light of sociological analysis. For most of us, our gendered and sexual identities feel very much like fundamental and 'natural' parts of our selves. They seem very 'personal'. These identities do not feel 'socially constructed' and we may want to resist such an analysis because it seems to destabilise our view of our selves. In a sense that is part of the task of sociology – to shake up our taken-for-granted assumptions about how the world works and to explain that what seems personal has its source in the social world of culture, institutions, organisations, and socialisation. The process is sometimes challenging, even disturbing, but nonetheless it is essential for the development of self-reflexive sociologists who are equally prepared to look at their own selves and attitudes, as they are to study the social world of which we are a part.

At this point you might be thinking to yourself that your sexuality doesn't feel particularly socially constructed, and that you would have difficulty shifting the focus of your desire onto a person of your own – or the other – sex (as the case may be). Let us take that issue and look at it in some greater depth. To begin with, it is useful to differentiate between two levels of analysis:

1   the social construction of sexual practice and identity at the level of cultural norms and values; and
2   the shaping of relatively 'asexual' infants into children, adolescents and adults with particular sexual desires.

Taking the first point, cultural norms and values provide the *environment* in which broad patterns of sexuality are organised. One way of exploring this is to study changes that have occurred over time in the way that the gendered nature of heterosexuality has been socially constructed. While there continues to be a differentiation made between male and female sexuality, and between how men and women should relate to one another in heterosexual relations, there have been major changes in the ways that female sexuality is perceived in Western culture. One example of this is the change from seeing women as relatively passive, possessing little desire of their own, to more contemporary ideas which emphasise an active female sexuality. Similarly, the cultural meanings in Western societies associated with homosexuality have shifted over the years, so that it is now less stigmatised than was once the case. This change is reflected in the language attached to people with homosexual identities who are no longer thought of as 'inverts' or 'perverts' but rather more positively as 'gay'.

This broad level of the social construction of sexuality is perhaps easier to grasp and less threatening than the view that there is a *social process* (rather than biology or a personal essence) by which individuals become beings with sexual desires and identities engaging in particular sexual practices. We tend to believe that through our sexual lives we express a sexuality that is a 'natural' part of us. The idea that sexuality is 'natural' is reinforced by the work of some scientists who have tried to identify particular genes or parts of the brain that determine sexual 'orientation' (i.e. attraction to a particular gender). Many sociologists are critical of this kind of research because it tends to confuse issues of desire, identity and practice. Some sociologists are happy to accept that there may be a biological component to feelings of desire and attraction, while others are more sceptical about this. One argument suggests that feelings of sexual desire are related to early, and largely unconscious, experiences of love, dependence and connection with one's primary caregivers (i.e. mothers, fathers, grandparents, foster parents). This approach is broadly psychoanalytic, relying as it does on an understanding of the *unconscious*. Having said this, it is not at all easy to identify exactly how our desires and attraction to particular kinds of people have been shaped early in life. For the time being this remains a mysterious process that the discipline of sociology is rather poorly equipped to examine.

Even if we accept that our individual sexual desires and identities are socially constructed this does not mean that it is easy to change these desires on an individual basis (just as it is difficult to change our gendered identities). Individual sexuality is not 'like a new outfit plucked from the closet at whim' (Vance, 1989: 16). We have little conscious control over sexual desire. However, there does seem to be some *variability* in the extent to which individuals can change their sexual desires and identities. For some people an initial preference for particular kinds of sexual activity with a person of a specific gender does not change. It feels solid and 'natural' and does not change over a lifetime. For others sexual desire and identity are more changeable and open to experimentation.

Differences and divisions: men, women, sex and violence

A clear theme that has developed in the discussion so far is the way in which gender and sexuality are interconnected. We cannot understand the social nature of sexuality without paying attention to its gendered character. This is as true of homosexuality as it is of heterosexuality. For both categories of sexual expression there are clear gender differences in terms of what is considered sexually appropriate behaviour. In homosexual practice and identity there is no gender difference *within* the relationship; however, gay men and lesbian women have very different experiences of sexual relationships, identity, practice and desire. Moreover, the regulation of gay men and lesbians has been quite different. Lesbian sex has not been the focus of law in Western societies (although it has still been regulated through informal norms, discrimination and violence). On the other hand, homosexual activity between men has been – and in some countries still is – illegal. Similarly, gender difference is also connected with unequal power relations through which men have generally fared better than women. Difference, then, is a matter not simply of *distinctions* between people but also of *inequalities*.

The inequalities that exist between men and women have long been a focus of **feminism**. In the late eighteenth century, feminists such as Mary Wollstonecraft were drawing attention to women's unequal status in relation to men. Recent feminist sociological theorising has examined the systematic inequalities that seem to exist between men and women in almost every sphere of social life. For example, in New Zealand, women's total weekly earnings are, on average, only 73.4% of that of men (Statistics New Zealand, 1996). Women are clustered in the lower status and lower paying jobs. They tend to have less authority and power than men in employment, organisations and politics. Even though women typically live longer than men, they tend to experience worse health throughout their lifetime than men. Women often face sexual and domestic violence from men – this rarely occurs the other way around.

Feminists have argued that there is a *pattern* to these, and other social and power relations, in which men are favoured at women's expense. This pattern of male dominance is *patriarchal* in that we can observe in a number of different social relations (e.g. between husband and wife, or father and daughter, or male boss and female secretary), and organisational structures (e.g. the workplace, state and so on) a dynamic in which women are systematically disadvantaged in some way. Patriarchal relations clearly involve the organisation and exercise of masculine power. A basic but useful starting definition of power is provided by Giddens: 'the ability of individuals, or members of a group, to achieve aims or further interests that they hold' (Giddens, 1997: 584). Much of the organisation of men's dominance in the social world is accomplished through non-violent, and non-sexual, forms of power (some of these will be discussed in following chapters). However, here we want to explore the connections that have been made in many contemporary Western societies between masculinity, sexuality, power and violence.

The view that there is an understandable (if not accepted) connection between men, sex and power partly rests on a set of ideological assumptions about the differing sexual natures of men and women. An example of this is what is sometimes called the 'sexual double standard'. This is firmly entrenched so that sexual permissiveness on the part of men is more tolerantly accepted than similar permissiveness on the part of women. This is reflected in the fact that there are far more words used of women who have sex outside what is deemed culturally acceptable (e.g. slut, whore, tramp) than are available to describe men who are sexually 'promiscuous'. There is really no masculine equivalent of 'slut'. Instead, men might be considered to be 'studs' – a name that does not have the negative connotations that are associated with 'slut' – in fact, to be a 'stud' is positively valued among many men and some women.

This kind of view is used in a variety of settings to regulate women's lives; for example, it may be connected to the experience of sexual harassment at work. This is one means by which men seek to maintain

> **Feminism** refers to the set of ideas that argue that women are systematically disadvantaged. Feminist sociology attempts to explain these disadvantages in terms of the patriarchal nature of societies.

their control of the work space. Harassment of women workers is often considered commonplace and hardly noteworthy. It occurs in a variety of subtle and not-so-subtle ways and is often passed off as a 'bit of good fun'. The ability of men to define sexual harassment in this way testifies to their power to assert the authority and 'naturalness' of a particular definition of male and female sexuality. Men's right to judge women on the basis of their sexual attractiveness, and to initiate sexual contact, is taken for granted as part of the normal play of heterosexuality. Indeed, it is often difficult for sexual harassment to be taken seriously because 'normal' male sexual behaviour is assumed to involve aspects of coercion (though they may not be explicitly defined as such). For example, think about the common belief that when a woman says 'no' she really means 'yes'. It then becomes a man's job to 'persuade' her that she does after all want to have sex with him. There is also an assumption that women's bodies are available to be looked at, commented on and touched in a way that men's bodies are not. Look back to the photo at the beginning of this chapter to see how men's and women's bodies are typically *represented* differently in the media. This kind of representation is very common. While there are now more images of the scantily-clad man, these are nowhere as common, nor do they have the same kind of meaning for men, as the sexualising of the female body has for women.

One of the effects of sexual harassment is that is a means of disciplining and controlling women workers by 'keeping them in their place'. By defining women in relation to their sexuality it is possible for men in positions of authority to affirm their control over the working environment and to subordinate women workers. Sexual harassment is often used in occupations that are traditionally 'male'. It is one way to marginalise and sometimes eliminate women from these jobs.

While sexual harassment is still often viewed as a minor exercise of male power, rape is increasingly being recognised as unacceptable. Sociologists reject the notion that men have a *biological* imperative to rape, bash or sexually harass women. Some **sociobiologists** have argued that male biology (in particular the hormone testosterone) predisposes men to violence. This argument fails to account for those cultures in which men are not violent. For example, in Western Sumatra there is a very low, almost negligible incidence of rape compared with countries like the United States and New Zealand. Sumatran men do not have less testosterone than the 'Kiwi bloke', so an explanation for violence must address other issues. One useful way to understand male violence is to examine the social meanings and attributes of masculinity. The fact that it is overwhelmingly men who rape women, and not vice versa, can be related to the way in which masculinity, and not femininity, is associated with power, dominance and toughness. Moreover, male sexuality is constructed around themes of conquest, control and mastery of the situation. Men initiate sex, women respond. These beliefs about different masculine and feminine forms of sexuality have developed over time and are related to culture. There is enough variation across both history

Sociobiology seeks to explain the social organisation of humans with reference to biological characteristics such as genes and hormones.

and culture to suggest that these are social rather than biological constructions.

While not all women are raped, some feminists have argued that fear of rape affects all women. This fear contributes to the limitation of women's access to certain, usually public, spaces. If a woman is raped at 3 am on her way home from a nightclub it may be suggested that she was foolish to be out so late. Rarely is it argued that it is men rather than women who should limit their activities. Calls for a curfew of males after 11 pm would be met with outrage.

The discussion so far has focused on the sexual regulation of women and the general argument that heterosexuality benefits men more than it does women. However, there are costs for some men in having to achieve some of the standards of performance, and being in charge, that are associated with particular versions of masculine sexuality. Being a 'stud' does not come naturally and may take a great deal of work. It may also involve the repression of other desires (e.g. the desire to be passive, to be held, to be the 'beloved') in order for men to meet the standards of masculinity. While these costs may be apparent for some men, they are generally less profound and debilitating than women's experience of the exercise of male power. In this respect, then, it does seem appropriate to talk about the patriarchal nature of gender and sexual relations.

The local and the global: the body beautiful

Much of the discussion to this point has emphasised the importance of trying to understand gender difference and sexuality as these exist at any one point in time. However, as suggested in Chapter 1, the sociological enterprise is concerned as much with social changes over time as with a single snapshot of societies and their social relations. In this respect then, it is important to explore the ways in which gendered and sexual relations have varied historically. While we can see that much of the history of Western societies has been characterised by patriarchal relations, the ways in which these relations have been organised have changed substantially over time. One dimension of this can be illustrated by examining how much of what we understand about men, women and sexuality is organised in relation to our bodies. As mentioned earlier, the very first observation made of the newborn baby's body is what kind of genitals it has. Cultures then build upon this bodily difference very specific ideas about the 'natures' (sexual, emotional, working, physical, etc.) of men and women. Cultural definitions of what are deemed to be the appropriate and desirable masculine and feminine bodies have shifted over time. For example, the contemporary Western ideal of female beauty that involves a slender body-type, is in fact a relatively recent one. Throughout most of history a rather more fleshy body was desirable because it symbolised ready access to food and therefore wealth. Up until the mid-nineteenth century, thinness was generally seen as a sign of poverty, but around this time being slender emerged as a desirable characteristic among many middle-class groups in Western societies.

While there have always been cultural norms about what is deemed beautiful, the effect of these norms on people's lives, particularly in the case of women, has been variable. In modern societies where the body has become a project to be worked on, the consequences of not fitting the dominant view of what is desirable are more profound than at a time when bodies were seen neither as malleable to change, nor as being a key component of personal identity and self-worth. The connections between feelings of self-worth and a certain body shape are particularly marked for women. Many feminists have argued that models, with their thin, tall and 'perfect' bodies, provide an unrealistic guideline about how women should look. The poster produced by 'The Body Shop', highlights this point.

'There are 3 billion women who don't look like supermodels and only 8 who do.'

It can be argued that contemporary ideals of female beauty and thinness have contributed to the existence of eating disorders in Western societies. These disorders are unheard of where lack of food is a real problem. However, they are increasingly an issue in societies like New Zealand. An explanation for this form of illness can be found by turning to the interconnections between patriarchy and global capitalism. As Giddens (1997) has argued, it is possible to locate the development of eating disorders such as anorexia nervosa and bulimia in terms of the globalisation of food production. At first glance this might seem like an unlikely place to look for an explanation for eating disorders which appear to be a manifestation of individual and personal psychology. Nonetheless, an explanation for the development of eating disorders amongst a growing number of women and some men (about 10% of anorexics are men) must turn to the way in which diet is now a matter of choice and anxiety for us in a way that was almost unknown before the middle of this century. Firstly, we now live in a world where most kinds of food are available to us all year round. Thanks to the development of new forms of refrigeration, food can now be stored for long periods, and with the use of container transportation food can be delivered from one side of the world to the other with ease. This gives us the ability to choose from a vast range of foods. At the same time as this variety of foods has become increasingly available, we are also being told to watch our dietary intake – too much fat is bad for us; we should eat more carbohydrate; we need to eat more fresh fruit and vegetables, and so on. In addition, the abundance of food available to us means that:

> we are able for the first time to design our bodies in relation to our lifestyle habits (jogging, aerobics) and what we eat. Eating disorders have their origins in the opportunities, but also the profound strains and tensions this situation produces.
>
> (Giddens, 1997: 119)

These tensions are particularly marked for women whose self-esteem is much more closely linked to how their bodies look than is that of men.

The connections described above between relatively large-scale global processes and local expressions of life can also be explored in relation to the way in which Western ideals of beauty have come to be seen as defining beauty for all women – the Western image of beauty is coming to be seen as a 'universal' model that can be applied to all women. Certainly, events such as the Miss World and Miss Universe 'pageants' constantly reinforce the idea that a very narrow range of physical body types and facial characteristics are worthy of the accolade of 'most beautiful'.

Conclusion

The sociological analysis that we have begun in this chapter has only scratched the surface in terms of identifying the many ways in which gender and sexuality inform all aspects of social life. We have examined how both gender and sexuality should be thought of as 'social constructions' rather than elements of 'nature'. The differences that are said to exist between men and women, and between homosexuals and heterosexuals, should be understood as creations of culture and power, rather than fiats of biology. These arguments will be developed further in several of the chapters that follow, since it is difficult to examine any sociological issue without looking at the way in which gender relations help structure it, and are in turn structured by it.

Study questions

4.1 Define gender socialisation and identify elements of this process in your own upbringing and/or in that of your children.

4.2 Why do sociologists argue that sexuality is socially constructed? Provide examples of this social construction.

4.3 How do gender, sexuality and patriarchal relations interact to produce sexual harassment and rape?

4.4 How can globalisation be linked to the growing numbers of anorexic women in Western societies?

Further reading

Abbot, P. and Wallace, C. (1997) *An Introduction to Sociology: Feminist Perspectives*, 2nd ed. Routledge, London.

Connell, R.W. (1987) *Gender and Power*. Allen and Unwin, Sydney.

Du Plessis, R. and Alice, L. (eds). (1998), *Feminist Thought in Aotearoa/New Zealand: Corrections and Differences*. Oxford University Press, Auckland.

James, B. and Saville-Smith, K. (1994) *Gender, Culture and Power: Challenging New Zealand's Gendered Culture*, 2nd ed. Oxford University Press, Oxford.

Weeks, J. (1986) *Sexuality*. Ellis Horwood/Tavistock Publications, London.

5 Family life

Chapter aims

- to define *the family* and to briefly explore several sociological perspectives on the family;
- to examine the historical development of 'affective individualism' and its role in the construction of marital relationships;
- to examine gendered divisions in the family;
- to discuss the role of neo-liberal ideas in the relationship between the state and the family.

 Introduction

This chapter takes the family unit as its focus. The **family** is viewed as an institution that can be examined both in connection to its relationship with the 'outside world', and relative to its internal processes – i.e. what happens within the family. Several sociological perspectives take the family as their focus, and here we examine the differences between the functionalist, Marxist and feminist perspectives on the role that the family plays in society, as well as exploring what symbolic interactionism can tell us about the internal dynamics of family life. The modern experience of family life has come to include expectations about intimacy. Unfortunately, these expectations and experiences exist alongside the sobering facts about domestic violence, sexual abuse and women's lack of equality within the family. This disjunction between intimacy and inequality is an overarching theme for our discussion here. We close the chapter by briefly exploring the increasing trend of liberal democratic governments to argue that the family unit should take more responsibility for the provision of health, education and welfare.

Family refers to a group of people who are related to each other by blood ties, marriage or adoption. Families usually form economic units and are responsible for the upbringing of children.

Families: definitions and theoretical perspectives

While we might commonly talk about families as if we knew to whom or to what we were referring, there is in fact a good deal more confusion about just who is to count as family, and what we mean by this term. This section therefore explores some definitions of family, briefly examines the role of families within **kinship**, and outlines four sociological approaches to understanding the form and function of families in contemporary Western societies.

It might be useful to begin by distinguishing between households and families. While a household may be a family, and family members may live together in one household, these terms are neither mutually exclusive nor indeed do they mean the same thing. We can take the household to be a 'spatial' category referring to the co-habitation of individuals (who may or may not be related) within the same place. On the other hand, 'family' refers very broadly to a group of persons tied together by kinship. Shared kinship usually implies ties of 'blood' or marriage (although in many contemporary societies de facto relationships, whether heterosexual or same sex, may also be recognised as legitimate). Families are part of a broader set of kin relations that set out the obligations and responsibilities that should exist between individuals and groups. In pre-modern and traditional societies, kinship systems form a significant part of the whole structure and organisation of society. In such societies the obligations between kin are central to the distribution of food, wealth, status and power between families and individuals. This is less typical for most modern societies where family members have far lower expectations of their extended kin. In Aotearoa/New Zealand, this is particularly true of Pakeha families; however, in Maori and Pacific Island communities, broad kin relations are still very important aspects of social organisation.

For Maori, kin relations existing within whanau (a broader group than family), hapu (a grouping of related whanau connected to a common marae) and iwi (tribe) are still important organising principles of Maori social and political life. All of these aspects of kinship rely on descent from a named, founding ancestor. While Maori live within family household forms similar to those of Pakeha, they are also part of a broader set of whanau relations which, while not directly concerned with daily living, involve considerable co-operative action between related individuals. The reciprocal and shared nature of this action is clear in Donna Durie-Hall's identification of the four functions of the whanau as 'providing mutual moral and economic support, sharing the raising of children, sharing the care of taonga, and gathering to mark major events in members' lives, especially deaths' (Durie-Hall, 1993: 68).

As individuals we have little difficulty in identifying who are members of our immediate families. For good or ill, we have rich and meaningful relationships with these people and we are clear about who are insiders and who are outsiders. However, sociologists have not found it so easy

> **Kinship** refers to links between individuals on the basis of blood ties, marriage or adoption. Kin relations extend beyond the institutions of the family and marriage.

to define the family in such a way that it encapsulates the diversity of relationships and household forms that people claim to be 'family'. For example, an early definition of the family argues that it is:

> a social group characterised by common residence, economic co-operation, and reproduction. It includes adults of both sexes, at least two of whom maintain a socially approved sexual relationship, and one or more children, own or adopted, of the sexually cohabiting adults.
>
> (Murdock, 1949: 1)

This definition was an attempt to encompass all the diverse ways in which various societies (he studied 250) organise close kin relations. Murdock concluded that the family is a universal institution that is found everywhere, from small-scale hunter-gatherer societies through to large-scale complex industrial societies. Nevertheless this claim has been challenged by other writers who point to both cross-cultural and contemporary Western examples of family forms in which one or more of the characteristics identified by Murdock are not present.

For example, the anthropologist Kathleen Gough used the example of the kin relations within the Nayar of Kerala in Southern India to demonstrate that families could exist outside Murdock's definition. In this society girls, before reaching puberty, would engage in a form of ritual marriage with a Nayar man. However these *tali-rites* did not require the cohabitation of the couple and carried only one obligation: the wife was expected to attend her husband's funeral and mourn his death. More significant relationships for both men and women were called *sandbanham*. After puberty women who had taken part in the tali-rite would take a number of sandbanham husbands of the same or higher caste. These men, who typically spent most of their time away from their villages, would periodically visit their wives. At these times the men would arrive at their wives' houses after the evening meal, have sexual intercourse with them and leave the next day before breakfast. These multiple relationships are very unlike our modern notion of marriage. They were not lifelong unions and the husbands had no responsibility for their offspring. The principle economic unit therefore was not based upon a 'sexually approved adult relationship' but on a grouping of brothers, sisters, the sisters' children and their daughters' children. While Murdock's definition clearly does not include societies like the Nayar, it can still be argued that some kind of 'family' existed in this society.

Contemporary examples of household forms that do not fit Murdock's definition include the female-headed families, common in many low-income black communities in the United Sates, West Indies and parts of Central America. It has been argued that these 'matrifocal' families are a well-organised social group that represents a positive adaptation to poverty. By being free of a husband, the mother is able to have a number of casual relationships that may provide her and her children with financial support. She also maintains close connections with relatives who can give both emotional and economic support. Other family forms not accounted for by Murdock's definition include lesbian and gay relationships. As these relationships have come to be more accepted within many societies, families based around gay couples and their children also provide a challenge to Murdock's definition of the family. These cross-cultural and contemporary exceptions to the norm suggest that any definition of the family must be sufficiently broad to include a wide range of domestic arrangements.

While it might not be very productive to try and establish a definition of the family that can encompass *all* of the ways in which mating, sexuality, gender and age can be organised, sociologists are still concerned with examining how, in any particular society, families play a central role in social life. In this respect the family can be seen to play an important role as an institution that fulfils certain 'functions' within society. Here the emphasis is less on *intra*-family relations than on the relationship *between* the family and society. An early exploration of this issue is found in Talcott Parsons's (1959) work. While Parsons based his theory on a study of American society, he argued that in all industrial societies there is a functional relationship between the nuclear family and the economic system. This relationship is assumed to be beneficial both for individuals, and for society in general, because it helps to maintain social stability.

According to Parsons, the nuclear family has two basic functions. One is to socialise children into the appropriate values and norms of society. In particular, two central features of American culture, independence and achievement motivation, should become part of the child's personality. The second function is the stabilisation of the adult personality through marriage. This relationship was expected to provide emotional stability for the married couple as they experience the stresses of everyday life. For Parsons then, there is a close connection between the *form* of the nuclear family and the *function* that it performs for society. In industrialised societies, the economy requires a labour force that is specialised, geographically mobile and emotionally stable. Because the nuclear family has taken on the roles that used to be associated with broader kin relations, it can now detach itself more readily from the obligations of kin. This means that the family is freer to move to where labour is needed. From the functionalist perspective then, the nuclear family is seen as the appropriate family form for complex industrialised societies. Parsons is largely uncritical of these societies, taking them for granted as part of an evolutionary form of social progress. However, not all sociologists have seen the relationship between the family and society as so benign. For example, the *structuralist* approaches of Marxists and feminists, while still concerned with the functions that families perform, focus on the way that particular family forms are implicated in capitalist and patriarchal *power relations*.

In general, Marxists believe that the family is an institution principally concerned with upholding the values and structure of capitalist society.

An early Marxist view of the family is to be found in Engels's book *The Origin of the Family, Private Property and the State* (1884). Through an analysis of the historical development of the family, Engels argued that as the mode of production changed, so too did the family. The monogamous nuclear family that is now prevalent in capitalist societies developed with the growth of private property and the emergence of the state. Monogamous marriage came to be protected by the state because it was seen as a means for the smooth operation of the inheritance of private property from men to their sons. The monogamous nature of the family helped fathers to be sure of the paternity of any offspring who would become heirs to the property. More recently, Marxist perspectives on the family have emphasised the family's role in 'reproducing' a productive workforce. This reproduction of labour occurs both literally, through the procreation of new workers, as well as through women's domestic labour which ensures that workers are prepared for each day's work at no cost to the employer.

Feminist sociologists have turned their attention to how the family produces and reinforces men's power. The previous chapter touched briefly on violence by men against women – much of this occurs in the family. Feminists argue that in addition to this extreme use of male power, the family is structured in such a way that women are systematically disadvantaged. In particular, the organisation of labour between men and women in the family benefits men. For example, in *Familiar Exploitation,* Delphy and Leonard (1992) argue that the family operates as a system in which men take the role of head of the household and women and children take on dependent positions. The male head of the household is primarily responsible for decision making and for providing the main wage income. The division of labour within the family is gendered and women are expected to do the bulk of the domestic labour as well as provide sexual and reproductive services. Women are also expected to care for the young, elderly and sick family members. Feminists argue that these differences in domestic roles between men and women lead to women receiving fewer of the material benefits of family life than men. They have less power to make household decisions, they cannot participate equally in the workforce, and they have less leisure time than men.

Symbolic interactionists have taken a different view from both the functionalist perspective on the family and the structural approach of Marxists and feminists. While symbolic interactionists do not deny the macro and structural relationships that exist between families and societies, they turn their attention to the *processes* that are involved in developing parental and marital behaviours and identities. Rather than seeing mother, father, son and daughter roles as pre-existing and given structures, that are adopted quite unproblematically, interactionists focus on the meanings and lived experience associated with these roles and explore how roles within the family are constructed through *interaction.* For example, in *Mothers and Fathers,* Kathryn Backett (1982) examines how couples seek to achieve a sense of acting in the same reality through engaging in a continuous process of negotiation. From this perspective, the roles of mother and father are rather different from the static model used by functionalists which assumes that family members can easily identify and take up the norms associated with the roles of mother, father, child, husband, wife and so on. Backett argues that parental roles are much more problematic and subject to a constant process of construction and negotiation between the parents.

The social and the personal: familial relationships and identities

What does it mean to be a member of a family? For the most part this seems a unique, natural and largely unquestioned aspect of our lives. Yet there are certain pervasive social beliefs that shape personal views about what makes a good mother or father, about how sons and daughters should behave, and about what kinds of relationship should exist between husbands and wives. In this section we explore the historical development of marital relationships (in particular through the ideology of individualism), and the way in which parental relationships are socially constructed through lived experience.

One of the most pervasive and significant expectations associated with families is that of intimacy. We expect our parents, children, and partners to be loving and supportive. The private home is assumed to be a sanctuary from the harsh realities of the outside public world. Unfortunately these 'dreams of intimacy' are not always met. Violence against children and women, sexual abuse, neglect and exploitation are also common within families. In many respects, then, we can think of the family as having a 'double life' where both intimacy and exploitation exist – sometimes side by side (Bittman and Pixley, 1997).

The expectation that the family should provide our most satisfying experiences of intimacy is connected to the relatively recent development – in the last three hundred years or so – the family as a private realm. This expectation was not present in the pre-industrial family which was primarily an institution concerned with the subsistence of family members. At that time, families were sites of production; marriages were mainly considered to be economic bargains and children were seen as further labour to help increase family wealth. In contrast to this, modern families have become more preoccupied with consumption than with production; marriages and partnerships are entered into for reasons of love; and children are viewed as treasured individuals. An explanation for these changes can be found in the twin forces of capitalism and industrialisation. In particular, these social structures led to the privatisation of the family and the separation of the home and workplace. The development of industrial capitalism contributed to the idea that the family is a realm of privacy and respite from the rigours of the public world of work. At the same time, the privatisation of the family has increased the emphasis that is placed on the *personal life* of individuals within their families. Eli Zaretsky argues that the impersonal marketplace:

> generated new needs – for trust, intimacy and self-knowledge, for example – which intensified the weight of meaning attached to the personal relations of the family. The organisation of production around alienated labour encouraged the creation of a separate sphere of life in which personal relations were pursued as ends in themselves.
>
> (Zaretsky, 1976: 66)

The separation of home and work and the privatisation of the family contributed to the development of an ideology of **affective individualism** (Bittman and Pixley, 1997) that reshaped the expectations we have come to have of family life. While this ideology intensifies the *desire* for intimacy, at the same time it works against its *realisation*.

In relation to marital relationships, affective individualism has emphasised the intimate and romantic nature of married love between two 'equal' individuals. In this context, marriage became a more private institution separate from the concerns and interference of kin groups and the larger community. While we are now quite comfortable with the idea that married couples should feel a form of romantic love for each other, this is in fact a fairly recent set of ideas and practices. For much of Western history, there was no expectation that romantic love would be an automatic part of marriage. Indeed, romantic love was associated with 'courtly' love, and with its adulterous relationships between men and women of high status. At this time, marriages were more likely to be formed for economic reasons than for love. Women were therefore typically seen as *economic resources*, for the labour they could perform in poor families, and for the alliances they made possible between rich households. This pattern of marriage began to alter as home and work became increasingly separate realms of social life.

Prior to the advent of industrial capitalism, families were important sites for subsistence production. That is, they were the place where food, fuel, shelter and clothing were produced for family members. While markets did exist at this time they were much less important than they are in today's world in the provision of the basic necessities of life. With the shift from the feudal mode of production to capitalist and industrial society, the market took on a greater role as the main way in which economic activity was organised. The household was no longer the main site for the production of goods required by family members. The shift to capitalist markets required a pool of property-less labourers whose main source of income was their ability to sell their labour. As a result of this change, workers were 'freed' from the older relationships that had existed between serfs and their masters. However, the freedom to work outside these older relationships also brought with it the freedom to starve. Whereas in feudal relationships the welfare of workers was of concern to their masters, under the new forms of market relations workers became

Affective individualism refers to an expectation of intimacy between individuals within institutions such as the family.

interchangeable commodities. Competition was therefore increased and labourers had to search outside their old communities for work. In this context, tight family ties became an encumbrance and individualism took root as a powerful ideology that served the interests of capitalism.

An ideology of individualism contributes to the idea that men and women are not only free in the labour market, but are also free to make other kinds of contracts as they see fit. As Bittman and Pixley argue:

> the intrinsic structure of both romantic mate choice and the market are essentially similar, based on the idea of free and equal autonomous individuals spontaneously following their own interest. Henceforth women must appear the equal of men. Likewise, marriage is justified as the result of a process of coincidence of romantic interest in much the same way as market transactions of buyer and seller. Marriage itself takes on the character of a contractual relationship.
>
> (Bittman and Pixley, 1997: 61)

However, just as individualism is an ideology which obscures the social bonds that still shape our lives, so too the idea of the marriage contract between equals ignores the inequalities that exist between men and women – a theme that we turn to in the next section.

The historical construction of affective individualism has also shaped the construction of parental relationships and the value placed on children. In particular, there has been increasing emphasis on the mother-child bond as being important for the child's physical, mental and emotional development. More recently still, the role of the father has come to be extolled as being central to a stable and happy family life. However, at the level of lived experience, 'being' a mother or a father involves very different kinds of parenting identities and practices. Men and women seem to have quite different orientations to how they care for and love their children. We have already suggested that the symbolic interactionist perspective might have something to say about how these identities and practices are constructed and negotiated between parents. However, some writers have pointed out that such a perspective cannot account for the *depth* of feelings that are associated with being a mother or a father.

Psychoanalysis is a psychological perspective which focuses on the workings of the unconscious mind.

It is here that the **psychoanalytic** perspective offers another level of analysis that is difficult to capture through sociology. In her book, *The Reproduction of Mothering* (1978), Nancy Chodorow describes the different ways in which children and mothers interact. Chodorow builds on the psychoanalytic recognition that children construct a sense of a separate and autonomous self-identity through the process of separating from their mother. For girls this is a less fragmented experience than for boys. While girls seek autonomy from their mother they do not separate themselves entirely and so an identification with their mothers as women is still important. Mothers contribute to this process by treating their daughters as similar to themselves while sons are seen as being different from the mother. Boys are therefore pushed towards differentiating themselves from femininity. These different experiences of mothering contribute to women developing a 'self-in-relation' (as they share a closer relationship with their mother) while men develop a sense of self that tends to deny relatedness. These different forms of gendered self-identity can also be related to the parenting roles that men and women take on in later life. Women typically find it much easier to take on a caring role than men. The father role is less connected to intimate and everyday forms of parenting because men have a more strongly differentiated sense of self that incorporates unconscious needs to be separate from others.

This psychoanalytical approach provides an interesting insight to one level of the differentiation between mothering and fathering roles. However, it is also important to examine how individual men and women *work with* the social expectations associated with motherhood and fatherhood. Lupton and Barclay (1997) draw together a number of studies that illustrate men's and women's different orientations to parenting. In particular, they highlight 'the importance of dominant *meanings and discourses* circulating in relation to how "good" motherhood and fatherhood are defined and practiced' (Lupton and Barclay, 1997: 58 – emphasis added). For example, Martha McMahon's (1995) study of Canadian parents illustrated some of the ways in which motherhood and fatherhood are very different parental practices. Women typically see being a mother as central to achieving an appropriate feminine sense of self. The strong loving feelings that women have about their children are seen as evidence of femininity. On the other hand, men do not see fatherhood as expressive of masculinity. Men's tendency to compartmentalise and separate parts of themselves in relation to their children was seen by women in the study as evidence that while fathers might well be involved and responsible parents this was a qualitatively different experience from what it is to feel and think as mothers do. Another interview study of couples identified clearly differentiated roles for men and women (Walzer, 1996).

> The mothers in this study tended to talk about mothering as involving worrying about the child, feeling primarily responsible for her or him, seeking and implementing information and advice on child care and feeling that the child's behaviour and welfare were directly attributable to them as 'good' or 'bad' mothers. In contrast, the fathers were less likely to discuss these processes as part of their role, and even argued, for example, that their partners 'worried too much' about the child. Walzer argues that a father may be perceived as a 'good' father in the absence of such mental labour, but the same could not be said of mothers.
>
> (Lupton and Barclay, 1997: 58)

We hope that what this discussion will have highlighted is that the way in which any individual comes to experience being a mother or father is related to a complex interaction of historical, psychoanalytic and sociological processes.

Differences and divisions: domestic labour and the control of household income

The expectation of intimacy outlined in the previous section contributes to the view that families will work in the interests of all their members. However, as we have already argued, the notion of the family's double life alerts us to the existence of inequality alongside intimacy. In particular, gender is an important social division that shapes the different tasks and experiences of men and women. This is often expressed in largely unquestioned ways, for example through the acceptance by both men and women of the 'naturalness' of different domestic roles based on gender. This section examines the division of domestic labour as well as how, and by whom, household income is controlled.

Housework is an area of family life that is sometimes trivialised as being of little social significance. Certainly, it was not considered to be an important part of sociological study until relatively recently. However, the pioneering work of Ann Oakley, in her book *The Sociology of Housework* (1974) established that housework was a significant form of *work*, and not just something that women did in the home as a way of filling in an otherwise empty day. While domestic labour may be largely unrecognised *as* work, and is therefore seen as having little social value, it is now increasingly being recognised as a major contributor to national economies (Waring, 1988). While this recognition might be growing amongst some social scientists, it would be true to say that the work that is done – overwhelmingly by women – in the home is still undervalued and, moreover, is a source of inequality between men and women. An Australian Time Use Survey has found that on average men do only about 30% of all household work, with women doing the remainder (ABS, 1994, cited in Bittman and Pixley, 1997). While this figure is derived from aggregated data it is still startling to learn that even where women also work in the full-time paid workforce they still do vastly more housework than men.

Not only is there a difference in the amount of housework done by women and men; the following table from the Australian Time Use Survey illustrates that there is a very clear gendered division of domestic labour. Men and women do very different tasks in the home. It is interesting to note that in general women have a greater role in those tasks that are daily, repetitive and invisible while men partake in forms of domestic labour that need to be done less frequently and that are not so readily 'undone'.

Activity	Women's share %	Men's share %
Laundry, ironing and clothes care	89	11
Physical care of (own) children	84	16
Other housework (cleaning)	82	18
Food preparation and clean up	75	25
Care of other children	75	25
Shopping	61	39
Play with (own) children	60	40
Household management	56	44
Gardening, pool and pet care	42	58
Home maintenance and car care	17	83

Source: Australian Bureau of Statistics. (1994) *How Australians use their time*. ABS, Canberra.

Table 5.1 Australian women's and men's shares in selected unpaid work tasks, 1992

It would be pleasing to think that some of this inequality in the distribution of tasks had decreased in recent years – certainly some advertising for household cleaners and appliances now incorporate images of men alongside women. However, the real changes that have occurred are minimal. For example, while the Australian studies show a change in the amount of time men spent in cooking between the 1974 and 1987 survey (an increase of about an hour on average) there appears to have been no change between the 1987 and 1992 surveys, and still men lag behind women.

Another area of domestic life which has the potential to lead to inequalities between men and women is the control of household income. Jan Pahl's (1989) study of British couples discovered four main ways in which household income was managed. In the 'whole wage system' one partner manages all the household income. This is often the woman, especially if the income is low. In the 'allowance system' the main breadwinner hands over an amount of money for housekeeping. The third system involves pooling of income and then joint management of that pool of money. Finally, a system of independent money management was the least common method and involved both partners managing their own income. Each of these means of managing money has its own form of inequality. For example, while women might manage all of the income in a poor household, they might not actually receive the whole wage in the first place, as men may keep some of their income for their own leisure spending. In the pooled, joint management system, women, more often than men, have to justify their spending, especially on personal items. Where women might well be in charge of the day-to-day management of money this does not necessarily equate with overall financial control. More typically, men retain control over major financial decisions. Other inequalities enter where, for example in dual earning households, women's income is used on expenditure for things like childcare, a second car and paying for domestic help. These forms of spending that are necessary where both parents work, are seen as 'a charge on *women's* earning, rather than on household income' (Brannen and Moss, 1987: 82).

While gender is clearly a major social division that shapes the management and control of household income, other cultural features may also be relevant. For example, in Maori families money earned within the family may not be thought of as the sole preserve of the immediate family but as part of a wider whanau resource. In a recent New Zealand study, Robin Fleming has also argued that male control of money in Maori families was less common than among Pakeha families. She argued that 'money management was not as integral a part of the relationship as it was for the Pakeha couples. This is not to say that men do not exercise power and control in Maori couples; only that authority in the relationship is not necessarily expressed through the control and management of money' (Fleming, 1997: 67).

Many studies of the control of household income have identified a tension that exists between the contemporary promises of intimacy and greater domestic equality, and the continuing theme of inequality within the family. In the following contribution, Vivienne Elizabeth approaches this question through a discussion of methods of money management used by couples committed to an ideal of equality. What becomes clear is that there are significant structural forces that make it difficult for men and women to attain the equality they desire in the distribution of monetary resources within relationships.

Let what is mine be mine, and what is yours be yours

Vivienne Elizabeth

When I began living with my former partner, many moons ago, I was determined not to replicate the inequalities of my parents' marriage which I attributed to my mother's financial dependence on my father. This sentiment led to me vociferously rejecting the mantle of marriage: my identity was not going to be compromised by becoming somebody's 'wife'. Just as significantly, I was committed to being financially autonomous: I was not going to rely on another's goodwill to determine my access to money, nor feel obliged to provide sexual favours.

At the time, my partner and I 'initiated' a system of managing our finances – independent money management (IMM) – that years later I discovered in use by other couples (see Fleming and Easting, 1994). In fact, cohabitees are the most frequent users of this style of money management (Glezer and Mills, 1991; Pahl, 1989). Like pooling and income splitting systems, IMM is often used by couples who wish to maintain personal autonomy and avoid relations of financial dependency. Although the ultimate agenda of these three systems may be similar, the ethos underpinning each system tends to be different. Pooling is associated with the principles of sharing and partnership, whereas the focus of IMM is on independence and autonomy to the extent, in some case, of repudiating the idea that heterosexual couples form an economic unit. Income splitting (a system where splitting the combined incomes of both partners precedes independent management) represents an attempt to incorporate both of these orientations – independence, sharing and partnership – within one practice.

As a practice, IMM has become increasingly common (perhaps because of its resemblance to the financial practices of many flatting households) although relatively ignored by sociologists. However, IMM may not be all that it is cracked up to be. The position of 'wives' as financial dependants has already received a great deal of critical attention. But new practices like IMM, that represent attempted solutions, should also be subjected to critical scrutiny. Does the pursuit of independence and autonomy through IMM facilitate the establishment of egalitarian heterosexual relations? Or does it, in certain circumstances, allow for the continued exercise of power within heterosexual relationships, albeit in slightly different ways? Before addressing these issues I want to outline briefly how the system itself operates.

Independent money management is distinguished by several features. IMM relies on both parties having an independent income. This can be threatened at crucial junctures by the birth of a child, undertaking full-time education or training, or unemployment. The state, with very few exceptions, treats co-residing heterosexual couples as if they were married and pays benefits and student allowances accordingly. Within IMM, control over income resides with the person who earns it: what is hers remains hers and what is his remains his. IMM thereby entrenches a principle – earner control of financial resources – that has served to legitimate male dominance within allowance systems, and contradicts the sharing edict of pooling arrangements and undermines the sense of entitlement that this system is supposed to engender. Each person contributes a portion of his or her income to those expenses that are judged to be joint, like rent, food, telephone and electricity; individual control is retained over whatever is left. A method for each party to pay for his or her share of expenses is necessary. This method varies between couples using IMM, and can even be quite ad hoc. Some couples use a kitty. Other couples divide up their joint bills between them so that each pays a set range of bills. Still others operate by periodically balancing how much each person has spent recently.

Regardless of the exact method chosen, the basic premise between the division of joint expenses tends to be the notion of a fifty-fifty split. This point is made explicit in the extract that appears below. Like other extracts in this piece, it comes from an interview I carried out as part of my doctoral research on the use of cohabitation as a practice to resist the conventions of marriage (Elizabeth, 1997). Although the financial arrangements of the cohabitees in my studies varied, IMM was in common use. Richard, Tanya, Louise, and Kirstie were amongst those who used this system:

> *Richard:* We share fairly much fifty-fifty. I'll get the groceries or she will get the groceries. We take turn about. And it is not a hundred per cent equitable, but I mean what is? As long as neither of us take advantage of the other. We just make sure it works out fairly equitably. And Lisa sometimes keeps accounts and I keep accounts sometimes. But they are not good accounts. It is just a way of making sure that it is kept equitable.

Equality is generally understood, by the cohabitees in my research who used IMM, to entail the payment of the same amount towards their joint expenses. Where both members of a couple earn roughly the same amount, the major difficulty arising from this stipulation is often one of logistics: how do you keep track of who paid for what, and when?

Yet the use of fifty-fifty split can, where incomes are quite different, result in one partner paying a much higher proportion of his or her income towards the couple's joint expenses, whilst also having far less money to spend on personal needs after dues have been paid. This partner, in the New Zealand context where women's average weekly earnings are still less than 80% of the male average, is much more likely to be female than male. Under these circumstances, the use of IMM simply transports the inequalities of a gendered labour market into the domestic environment.

The inequities associated with this outcome exposes the difficulties of using 'sameness' as the basis upon which equality is pursued (Scott, 1988). When 'sameness' is used as the standard, important differences can easily remain hidden from view. This may mean, in the specific case of IMM, that the constraining effects of a variation in the size of one's spending pool are unrecognised, or – even worse – viewed as 'fair'. Countering equity, as Scott argues, requires an attentiveness to difference. With respect to the practice of IMM, the achievement of financial equality may necessitate the use of variable contributions to joint expenses in order to leave each partner with a comparable personal pool.

Challenged about the possibility that the use of fifty-fifty contributions might not produce equality, one of the women I spoke with responded in the following manner:

> *Vivienne*: Can you imagine a context in which paying fifty-fifty wouldn't translate into equality?
> *Louise:* Yes, if you were doing it with everything. Say you had a joint cheque account and anything that either of you wanted to buy, you bought out of that, you could end up in some real arguments. 'What did you spend money on that for?'

As Louise suggests, equality, in the context of IMM, is linked to control. Specifically, equality means equal power to determine how money is used, rather than the more usual equal access to equal amounts of money. Within

IMM, equality hinges on the preservation of a domain of autonomy free from struggles for the power to define what constitutes proper expenditure. This domain of autonomy is established through the retention of individual control over one's own income.

The issue of equality is thus conceptualised as a question of financial independence, of being able to determine freely how one spends one's money:

> *Kirstie:* I want to pay my obligations to the communal expenses, but then I don't want to be called to account for whether I spend my money on cigarettes, or magazines, or cups of coffee, or lunch. I don't want to have to explain.

The advantage of retaining individual ownership and control of financial resources is that one of the most repugnant features of financial dependency, the need to ask and seek approval for money to cover personal purchases, is removed.

It is ironic, therefore, that a strategy enacted to avoid the negative repercussions of financial dependency actually establishes the potential, through its adherence to the idea of earner control, for dependencies to emerge in other guises. If one lacks a legitimate claim on the income of the other, it may be very difficult to initiate going out for dinner or to the movies, the purchase of new household items, even fixing the car, if you are unable to pay for these yourself:

> *Kirstie:* ... I wouldn't ask someone to go and see something and then assume they are going to pay. Whoever thinks of it, pays. Like if I say, 'Let's go and do such-and-such,' it is my shout. Or if Matthew says it, it is his shout.

It this situation, faced with the limitations imposed by the size of your personal income, instigating action can be entirely dependent on the co-operation and financial support of the other. This dependency may be most poignantly felt in the realm of personal needs, when financial assistance (by way of a gift or repayable loan) between partners may be required in order for these needs to be met.

Questions

Vivienne Elizabeth begins her discussion by saying that in a previous relationship she entered into a system of independent money management because she thought it would help her to be financially independent. By answering the following questions, you should be able to discuss why she now believes that IMM may actually contribute to the exercise of power in heterosexual relationships.

1   How do broader patterns of gender relations affect the ability of women to earn an independent income?

2   How does the 50/50 splitting of joint expenses lead to inequalities within relationships?
3   What does Vivienne Elizabeth mean when she says that 'the use of IMM simply transports the inequalities of a gendered labour market into the domestic environment'?
4   In what ways might the tension that exists in the case of heterosexual couples between autonomy and equality in systems of IMM be the same, or different, in gay and lesbian relationships?

The local and the global: the state, neo-liberalism and family responsibility

In modern societies the family has increasingly come under the purview of the state. In particular, the development of the welfare state during this century has seen the state taking on responsibilities (for the care of the elderly, children, the unemployed and so on), that had previously been shouldered by kin. This provision of social security reflected the belief that 'the state had a responsibility to respond to the needs of these groups to ensure that they had sufficient income to "belong and participate"' (Cheyne, O'Brien and Belgrave, 1997: 182). Whether this relationship between the state and individuals is beneficial for families has been a source of debate for those on the left, the right and for feminists. For example, Marxist sociologists such as Christopher Lasch have argued that the capitalist state, with the related growth of professional welfare and health experts, has all but destroyed the privacy and intimacy of families. Feminists have identified various ways in which the state has supported a patriarchal nuclear family with its male breadwinner and dependent women and children. However, it is the concerns espoused by the 'new right' that are becoming increasingly influential across industrialised capitalist societies. These concerns have been taken on board by many governments, where the focus is now less on how the *state* can support the family but on identifying the responsibilities that *individuals and families* have in looking after themselves and their needs for health, education, income support and so on. This neo-liberal agenda has come to be increasingly important in New Zealand since the mid-1980s. Indeed, sociologists from other countries recognise how the National Government of the early 1990s 'acquired the dubious status of being the first government in modern times to oversee the creation of what has been described as the first "post-welfare society"' (Rodger, 1996: 118). In this type of society, state provision for health, social security, and education are being steadily whittled away. This section explores how the ideology of **neo-liberalism** has come to define a particular view of the relationship between the state and the family, and of their respective responsibilities.

Neo-liberalism refers to the view that the state has become too large in recent years and that a shift back to markets, economic efficiency, competition and choice is an appropriate response to the crisis of the welfare state.

Neo-liberalism includes an emphasis on **economic rationalism** with its belief that the market provides the best means for allocating resources efficiently. Such a view leads to policies of privatisation and the cutting back of government responsibilities. In this context, the state tends to treat families as if they were entities free to make their own choices. 'If the wrong choices are made, then the family (or the unhappy family member) has only itself to blame. These normative expectations leave us all feeling that any trouble stems from personal inadequacies, even failures' (Bittman and Pixley, 1997: 212). Here it is assumed that the family can make decisions as if it were a rational economic actor, making choices from a range of options offered by the market. The rational choice theory that underlies this kind of view assumes that actors are defined by self-interest and that those who make the most rational decisions are those who have no responsibilities or obligations. Choice is seen as being a series of equal preferences rather than as involving difficult decisions about social obligations. This, of course, ignores the reality that for many individuals there is no choice about the familial obligations that we are caught up in. Who has the ability to say 'today I will exercise my other preferences and refrain from feeding this helpless child or looking after this ageing person'? (Bittman and Pixley, 1997: 213).

> **Economic rationalism** includes the belief that the market provides the best means for allocating resources efficiently (see also pp. 135 and 199).

In Aotearoa/New Zealand one expression of economic rationalism is seen in the 1997/8 Coalition Government's *Code of Social and Family Responsibility*. This public discussion document (Department of Social Welfare, 1998) illustrates an increasing trend by liberal democratic states to remove themselves from key areas of welfare. Although the rhetoric of the Code included reference to both government and family responsibility, the over-riding emphasis was on families and individuals taking more responsibility while the state takes less.

The *Code* identified eleven issues, each with associated expectations.

1 Looking after our children
   Parents should love, care for, support and protect their children.
2 Pregnancy care
   Pregnant women will protect their own and their babies' health with the support of their partners. They will begin regular visits to a doctor or midwife *early* in pregnancy.
3 Keeping children healthy
   Parents will do all they can to keep their children healthy. They will make use of free health checks and immunisations, and seek early advice and treatment for sick or injured children.
4 Learning for the under-5s
   Parents will do all they can to help their children learn from the time they're born.
5 Getting children to school ready to learn
   Parents will take responsibility for seeing that their children are well prepared for school, and attend every day, ready to learn.

6 Young offenders
Children must not break the law. Parents will take responsibility for bringing their children up to be law-abiding members of society. When children do offend, families, communities and government agencies will work together to prevent re-offending.

7 Sharing parenthood
Parents will love and care for their children, support them financially and, where possible, share the parenting responsibilities, even when they are not living together.

8 Training and learning for employment
People will take responsibility for developing the skills and knowledge they need to help them get a job, or take on a new job.

9 Work obligations and income support
People receiving income support will seek full-time or part-time work (where appropriate), or take steps to improve their chances of getting a job.

10 Managing money
People will manage their money to meet the basic needs of themselves and their families.

11 Keeping ourselves healthy
People will do all they can to keep themselves physically and mentally healthy.

It would be hard not to be in favour of these issues and expectations. However, the document assumes that individuals and families, as rational economic actors, will act in their own self-interest, and be able simply to make a positive choice in favour of these options. As we have already suggested, this assumption ignores the fact that choices are not simple equal preferences but may involve weighing up a variety of social obligations. Moreover, an emphasis on individual and family responsibility conforms to a dominant theme of modernity which emphasises that the rational actions of *individuals* are the most significant features of social life. In contrast to this view, sociologists point to the fact that modern individuals do not act independently of their wider social relationships and social context. Rather, we are all embedded within societies that are characterised by an extremely high degree of *interdependence*. Individuals are always dependent, in various ways, on a whole range of other people and groups of people, and there are significant social organisations and processes that are distant from us but that nevertheless shape our lives. For example, with the best will in the world it may be difficult for some unemployed people to find a job in the context of large-scale structural changes to the economy and the structure of the labour market. The recognition that distant and 'global' social relations have an impact at the local and lived level of individual families certainly goes against the grain of neo-liberalism and forces us to query its logic.

Conclusion

The experience of family life is at once one of intimacy, but also of inequality. We have vast expectations of our family members that we do not have of our friends or workmates. Yet even when these expectations are not always met, we continue in the belief that our families will provide us with support when we need it. Rather than taking for granted this faith in the family, sociologists believe it is worthy of analysis. Here we have outlined some of the historical developments in modern capitalist industrial societies that have contributed to the ideology of affective individualism that lies at the heart of the modern family. This ideology is a powerful one; however, it exists alongside a gendered division within the family in which women tend to be disadvantaged relative to men. Finally, we have examined how the family has come to be understood as a unit having certain responsibilities that once were viewed as belonging to the state.

? Study questions

5.1 What role has the ideology of affective individualism played in the social construction of modern marital relationships?

5.2 What do studies of the control of household income tell us about gender power in the family?

5.3 Look back over the expectations set out in the *Code of Social and Family Responsibility* and give a sociological account of why it might be difficult for families to meet these expectations.

Further reading

Adair, V. and Dixon, R. (eds). (1998) *The Family in Aotearoa New Zealand*. Addison Wesley Longman, Auckland.

Bittman, M. and Pixley, J. (1997) *The Double Life of the Family: Myth, Hope and Experience*. Allen and Unwin, St Leonards, NSW.

Gittens, D. (1993) *The Family in Question: Changing Households and Familiar Ideologies*, 2nd ed. Macmillan, Basingstoke and London.

Muncie, J., Wetherall, M., Dallos, R. and Cochrane, A. (eds). (1995) *Understanding the Family*. Sage, London.

6 Education

Chapter aims

- to introduce functionalist, Marxist and feminist theories on the relationship between schooling and society;
- to critically examine the role of intelligence in school achievement;
- to explain the role of the school in the reproduction of class inequalities;
- to discuss some of the ways in which education is being affected by the development of new information technologies.

Introduction

In this chapter we explore the role that education plays in society. For functionalist sociologists, the schooling system is relatively benign, beneficial even, as it contributes to the overall smooth running of society. However, other sociologists have identified the ways in which schools benefit some groups rather than others. We examine the issue of school attainment – a concern for most parents who want their children to do well. The commonsense view explains high school achievement in terms of personal attributes such as intelligence and hard work; however, sociological explanations focus on social processes involved in schooling. Most sociologists point to the role of schools in the reproduction of inequality, rather than their being a mechanism for social mobility. Finally we explore the changing world of global information technologies and the way they are changing some features of education.

Schooling and society

In modern societies there is an expectation that every child will receive a basic formal education that will prepare him or her for the world of work.

Most children spend six hours a day, five days a week, in buildings that are specially designated for the purpose of teaching. In secondary schools students move from room to room as they study different subjects. Teachers are kept busy providing information and exercises designed to promote learning. This learning is assessed through a range of tests and formal end-of-year state examinations. And, at the end of this process, students are thought to have been educated, to have been given the skills that will equip them for the world of work. We have come to take for granted that all of this activity is what counts *as* education. However, the provision of this kind of specialised mass schooling is a relatively recent historical development.

In Western Europe this formal education system was established in the nineteenth century, once the processes of industrialisation and urbanisation were well under way. The growth of both cities and industrial capitalism contributed to the development of new occupations and work patterns. These forms of work required new, more complex skills that were not readily passed from parent to child as had been the norm in earlier, agriculturally-based feudal societies. In such societies it had been possible for all important knowledge to be transmitted from one generation to the next through the processes of socialisation and direct instruction that happened within the family and community life. The formal education that occurred earlier than the nineteenth century was provided only for the wealthy, or for those who were destined to join the clergy. In the feudal social context education, in the modern sense of mass compulsory schooling, made little sense.

This growth in the schooling of most of the population is of interest to sociologists who view education as one of the central social institutions of any modern society. Durkheim argued that education was important for the transmission of societal norms and values. He believed that if everyone in a society was submitted to the same educational processes, this would foster the development of value consensus and social solidarity, and so ensure a stable, well-ordered society. From Durkheim's point of view, schooling should include both formal and informal mechanisms for securing a stable society. The formal curriculum should include subjects such as history because this encourages students to see themselves as part of something larger than themselves and to develop a commitment to that larger social group. More informally, if students are encouraged to follow the school rules they learn to respect rules in general and to develop the habits of self-control and restraint – 'It is the first initiation into the austerity of duty' (Durkheim, 1925/1961: 149). Durkheim's view then, is that education is a valuable institution, working in the interests of society as a whole.

This general perspective was shared by the structural-functionalist Talcott Parsons writing some fifty years after Durkheim. Parsons was concerned to demonstrate two things.

> [Firstly] how the school class functions to internalize in its pupils both the commitments and capabilities for successful performance of their future adult roles, and second how it functions to allocate these human resources within the role structure of the adult society.
>
> (Parsons, 1959: 297)

Taking the first of these functions, Parsons argued that the school plays an important role in preparing students for the transition from the family (where children have an *ascribed* status established by their birth into a class, gendered and ethnic position, and where they are treated as individuals with *particular* tastes and abilities) to the world of work (which assumes that status is something to be *achieved* through hard work, qualifications, and so on). The school prepares children for these transitions by using universalistic standards (of school rules and assessment procedures) that are applied equally to all students regardless of their gender, ethnicity, or class location. In this way, Parsons argued, the school prepares children for their adult roles in the world of work. Furthermore the school plays a role in the actual allocation of individuals to their future roles by streaming and evaluating students so that they match their abilities and skills to the jobs for which they are best suited. Just as Durkheim saw value consensus as essential for the smooth operation of society, so too Parsons argued that schools worked towards this by instilling the values of achievement and of equality of opportunity. Schools foster the value of achievement by rewarding students who do well. The value of equality of opportunity is encouraged by giving all students the same experiences in the school. Both of these values are seen as being central in a **meritocracy** where status is something that is *achieved* rather than ascribed through birth. In meritocratic systems social rewards (of prestige and income) are distributed on the basis of merit and not by pre-determined social categories. Education is seen as major means by which individuals can overcome social inequality.

Contemporary sociologists have been critical of the notion that modern societies are meritocratic and that education is a means of social mobility. Marxist and feminist sociologists argue that the professed values of achievement and equality of opportunity hide the ways in which schools actually function to reproduce various forms of social inequality. A key concept shared by these theorists is the notion of the **hidden curriculum**, first developed by Ivan Illich in *Deschooling Society* (1971). Illich argued that schooling has developed in such a way that its main role is a 'custodial' one – keeping children 'off the streets' until they enter the labour market. Much of what is actually learnt in school has little to do with the official curriculum but is conveyed through the 'hidden curriculum'. This concept refers to the *form* that schooling takes, the ways lessons are organised, the routines of the school day, the forms of assessment, the mode of teacher-pupil interactions and so on. One of the main lessons that is taught through the discipline and regimentation associated with the hidden curriculum is 'passive consumption'. Students

---

Meritocracy refers to the belief that social rewards (of prestige and income) are distributed on the basis of merit and not by pre-determined social categories.

Hidden curriculum includes those aspects of learning in schools that are not part of the official curriculum, but that nonetheless result from the way that teaching and learning are organised in schools.

learn to uncritically accept the prevailing social order. For Illich this is a travesty of what education should really be about. He believed that education should be a liberating experience whereby individuals are enabled to explore their abilities and talents in a creative and open way.

Marxist theorists have also picked up on some of Illich's ideas, but they claim that he has not emphasised enough that when schools treat students unequally, they do so in the interests of industrial capitalism. An influential American study, *Schooling in Capitalist America* (Bowles and Gintis, 1976), argued that the main role of education is to reproduce labour power for employers. Schools do this through a series of mechanisms which demonstrate that there is a:

> close 'correspondence' between the social relationships which govern personal interaction in the work place and the social relationships of the education system.
>
> (Bowles and Gintis, 1976: 12)

This **correspondence principle** is manifested through the school's hidden curriculum. In particular, the hidden curriculum shapes students into future workers by encouraging them to be the kind of uncritical and passive individuals that employers prefer to employ. Through the organisation of the school, students are encouraged to accept hierarchies as necessary features of organisational life. Moreover, by teaching students to be motivated by external rewards (such as qualifications) rather than by an intrinsically satisfying experience of education they are taught to accept the basically unrewarding nature of most work in exchange for a wage. Finally, the fragmentation of school learning into different subjects corresponds to the fragmentation of work in which workers have little knowledge of the production process apart from the small area in which they work. The acceptance of this fragmentation ensures that workers remain divided and are less likely to work together against their employers.

Correspondence principle refers to the similarities that exist between the social relationships governing interaction in the workplace and the social relationships involved in schooling.

This particular Marxist perspective on schooling is now considered by many commentators to be somewhat crude. In general it is believed that Bowles and Gintis have overemphasised the correspondence between work and schooling. Their analysis also failed to explore how students *actually* responded to the hidden curriculum and other studies have illustrated the types of resistance that many students put up to the school system (e.g. Willis, 1977). Nevertheless, the notion that the school plays some role in the reproduction of class inequalities is one which deserves further attention and we will return to explore this more fully in the section 'Differences and divisions'.

While theorists such as Bowles and Gintis explore the role of the hidden curriculum in reproducing class inequalities, feminist sociologists have drawn attention to the way in which schools prepare girls for their roles as wives, mothers and particular kinds of workers. Although there is now a very strong discourse of equality of opportunity, the school through its structures and teaching practices continues to reproduce gender differences and inequalities. Sandra Acker (1994) has argued that there is a hidden curriculum of *gender differentiation* that operates despite the assumed gender neutrality of the official curriculum. This hidden curriculum manifests itself in several ways. Firstly, the existence of an uneven distribution of male and female teachers throughout the educational hierarchy (with women clustered at the lower levels of responsibility) reinforces the notion that men rather than women are more fit for high status and responsible positions. Secondly, numerous studies have demonstrated that teachers have different expectations of boys than they have of girls. For example, there is a tendency to underestimate girls' academic abilities while boys are seen as being more intelligent. In addition, teachers tend to reinforce gendered ideologies – seeing the destinies of boys and girls develop in stereotypical directions. Thirdly, the ways in which schools are organised continue to reinforce gender distinctions. For example, the organisation of primary schools mirrors the roles of the family with a female, maternal, caring teacher and a male, paternal, authoritative head teacher being the norm. Finally, although the official rhetoric of schools is that both boys and girls will be given equal opportunities to do the subjects they wish to do (girls are no longer prohibited from doing woodwork, and boys can go to cooking classes) there is still a very strong gendered division of subject choice. In particular, some feminist theorists have drawn attention the continuing low participation by girls in science, maths, computing and technical subjects. These subject choices have an impact on the kinds of jobs, or further education, that girls are prepared for. All of these aspects of the hidden curriculum add up to an educational space that reinforces gender ideologies. This is not to say that students and teachers do not resist or disrupt such norms, but that these norms continue to be powerful shapers of gendered identity and the future life chances of boys and girls.

While there are clearly very important differences between the functionalist, Marxist and feminist theories discussed here, all share a concern with identifying the functions that schools perform in society. To that extent they share an *analytical* approach that is functionalist. However, the functionalism of Durkheim and Parsons emphasises the way in which the school's preparation of children for their future roles is in the interests of both the individual and the larger social order. Marxist and feminist sociologists have been critical of this general perspective because it ignores the ways in which it is only *particular* groups of individuals that benefit from the education system.

The social and the personal: intelligence, school achievement and meritocracy

The discussion so far has been directed at a very broad level of analysis; however, much of the sociology of education is concerned with explaining a more immediate question, certainly one that concerns many parents: why do some children succeed and some fail at school? A common-sense explanation for differential school attainment points to the role of intelligence – some children are just brighter than others. The experience of achievement at school appears then, on the surface at least, to be the result of an individual's *personal* attributes. Moreover we assume that when *inherited* intelligence is combined with motivation and hard work this results in achievement and will be suitably rewarded. John Codd summarises this basic ideology of meritocracy in the following way 'Ability + Effort = Merit' which is translated in schools into 'IQ + Motivation = Achievement' (Codd, 1988: 260). Successful academic performance has further benefits when it is translated into social and economic success with well-paid and high-status jobs. This belief in the existence and legitimacy of meritocracy is commonplace in societies like our own. Certainly, this is the view of Paul Johnson writing in the *Sunday Star-Times*.

> The more intelligent are succeeding; the less intelligent are failing … the … poor have become poor because they are stupid and/or incompetent and therefore the likelihood is that their children will do even worse.
>
> (Johnson, 1996: C6)

We might characterise this as a 'common-sense' view. As such it is widely held and it assumes that the attributes of intelligence and hard work are *personal* qualities belonging to the individual. At the same time, it is also assumed that the potential to inherit a high level of intelligence is determined by whether one belongs to a particular class and/or particular ethnic groups. While Johnson talks of 'the poor', elsewhere low intelligence has been attributed to particular ethnic groups. This view shares with other common-sense beliefs an explanatory schema based on individualistic and naturalistic attributes. Sociologists caution against such approaches and argue instead that there are several interrelated social processes involved in the seemingly individual and natural quality of 'intelligence'. In this section we explore the development of the notion of intelligence and how it has been used to legitimate educational inequality.

The belief that intelligence is a mental ability that is *inherited* and can be accurately *measured* was developed by Francis Galton in the nineteenth century. Galton's ideas were part of a more general development at this time in a wide range of 'human sciences' concerned with measuring and categorising human characteristics. At much the same time, there came a concern, with the growth in public schooling, to identify those students who had special needs, and the first intelligence test was developed by Alfred Binet in 1905. While Binet himself did not assume that intelligence was a fixed quality, the more prevalent belief was that tests could provide an accurate measure of an 'intelligence quotient' that was both fixed and innate. IQ tests came to be used by schools to select students into 'suitable' academic and vocational streams. Students with low intelligence were thought to be more suitable for manual and technical subjects while high IQ scorers were streamed into academic and professional classes, preparing them for high-status, non-manual occupations. IQ tests became a central part of a meritocratic ideology. These tests legitimated the notion that poor school achievement was not the fault of the educational system but was connected to the personal failings of individuals who lack intelligence. Karier argued that the tests:

> created the illusion of objectivity which on the one side served the needs of the 'professional' educators to be 'scientific' and on the other side served the need of the system for a myth which could convince the lower classes that their station in life was part of the natural order of things.

> (Karier, 1976: 136)

This 'natural order' has also been reinforced through numerous studies that have demonstrated that there are significant differences in the IQ scores of working-class and middle-class children, and between black and white Americans. Similar differences have also been recorded between Maori and Pakeha children. However, the question remains as to whether these lower scores can be linked to inherited *genetic* differences. There are several pieces of evidence which lead us to reject the idea that the mental capacities measured by IQ tests are wholly genetic in origin. For example, if intelligence were solely an inherited characteristic, we would assume that identical twins, separated at birth, would have the same IQ scores. Studies have shown that this is not the case. There does, then, seem to be some environmental shaping of intelligence. This is also evidenced in the following example:

> If, for example, one treated the mean IQ scores of Dutch children in the 1970s [and] those of their parents' generation (there is a large difference in favour of the former), as the scores of contemporary black and white American children are treated by some workers in this field, then it would probably be concluded that these groups, from the same population and separated by one generation, were genetically different. Such results are sufficiently disturbing as to prompt the utmost caution in the interpretation of research studies in this field.

> (Nash, 1997: 60–61)

Other evidence which supports the notion that measured differences in IQ scores on the basis of ethnicity are not genetic is provided by the example of the Burakumin, a Japanese ethnic minority. In Japan, Burakumin children score around ten to fifteen fewer IQ points than other Japanese children (Giddens, 1997: 424–425). What differentiates these children is not their genetic makeup – since both groups are genetically the same. However, there has been systematic discrimination against the Burakumin since the eighteenth century when, 'as a result of local wars, [they] were dispossessed from their land and became outcasts and vagrants. [Interestingly] Burakumin children in America, where they are treated like other Japanese, do as well on IQ tests as other Japanese' (Giddens, 1997: 424–425). This provides an interesting example of the role that *social*, rather than genetic, inequalities play in the construction of intelligence. The measured IQ differences between black and white Americans, and Maori and Pakeha children may therefore not be 'racial' in origin but the outcome of social disadvantage.

We must also examine just what it is that IQ tests measure. It can be argued that they only measure certain kinds of linguistic, symbolic and logical skills that are more prevalent in particular class and ethnic environments. While intelligence is now generally defined as 'abstract reasoning ability' (Jensen, 1971: 344) this definition refers to only one very specific aspect of the 'mental abilities' of humans. These mental abilities actually include a whole range of other abilities (or 'intelligences'), for example of a practical, musical, spatial, and emotional kind. However, 'intelligence tests' only test for 'abstract reasoning ability' displayed through the following kinds of aptitudes:

> encoding complex logical-grammatical structures ('put a cross in the third circle from the left if the number above it is not odd'), deducing and mapping logical relations ('hand is to wrist as foot is to …?'), and manipulating non-verbal material with a similar underlying structure.
>
> (Nash, 1997: 59)

Therefore a score on an IQ test does not tell us about the whole range of other important mental abilities that individuals may possess. Low scores may also be related to cultural aspects of the individual's response to the test (Haralambos et al., 1996: 227). For example, when Stanley Porteus administered Western IQ tests to traditional Australian Aborigines in the 1930s he found that they answered the tests very slowly. In Aboriginal culture there is no value placed on hurrying, and problem-solving occurs through collective rather than individual responses. The intelligence tests used by Porteus were clearly more suited to a particular cultural environment that values speed, individual responses and particular kinds of abstract reasoning. In the context of desert and nomadic life these attributes were less well developed than other spatial and cognitive intellectual skills of more use in this particular environment. Such conclusions lead us to question the notion that intelligence can be measured in a culture-neutral way or that it is a simple genetic attribute of individuals. This argument does not imply that there are no inherited individual differences in ability, but that those inherited differences which do exist are not a 'natural' product of class or ethnicity. Sociologists argue that instead of focusing on the individual, and on his or her personal attributes, an explanation for differential school achievement must be found elsewhere.

Differences and divisions: cultural capital and the reproduction of class inequalities

The previous section explored how the notion of intelligence contributes to the ideology of meritocracy that is so strong in contemporary capitalist societies like our own. Associated with meritocracy is a belief that social mobility allows people to move out of their class of origin and to improve their position in life. Schools are assumed to play a major role in social mobility as they are said to provide everyone with an equal opportunity to work hard and gain qualifications that may lead to further education and then on to high-paying and rewarding jobs. From a sociological perspective, the ideology of meritocracy is undermined by the results of studies which explore the relationship between class and educational attainment. These studies demonstrate time and again that there is an on-going *reproduction* of class inequalities. In general, children from working-class families do less well at school than children from middle-class families. Both groups of children go on to have much the same kind of employment status and occupy much the same occupational position as did their parents. New Zealand studies have also come to the conclusion that:

> New Zealand is not the open socially mobile society the common myth of everyone getting a 'fair go' suggests. The reproduction of privilege and disadvantage from generation to generation is sufficient to create different class cultures which have a determining effect on school outcomes.
>
> (Lauder and Hughes, 1990: 55)

The recognition that such a pattern exists does not tell us about the mechanisms by which class inequality is reproduced. Some theorists have argued that class-based differences in school attainment can be linked to the culture of working-class students. These **cultural deprivation** or cultural deficit theories suggest that working-class culture is deficient in certain important respects. Typically, cultural deprivation theories argue that working-class children lack some important skills, attributes and values that are necessary for the attainment of school qualifications. In particular, they lack ambition and may be more concerned about the pursuit of immediate gratification rather than the kind of deferred gratification that is required with a commitment to education. In such an

Cultural deprivation theories explain working-class failure at school in relation to deficiencies in working-class culture.

explanation, working-class families of working-class children are blamed for not providing enough books, newspapers, travel, opportunities for conversation or even the right kinds of nursery rhymes or songs for their children. These family 'lacks' are said to add up to a poor start for working-class children at school. On the other hand, middle-class children are seen as possessing just the right kinds of attributes and values (of literacy, deferred gratification and so on) that will help them make the most of the educational opportunities with which they are provided. One of the policy outcomes of these kinds of theories is the notion that 'compensatory education' can make up for previous lacks. Disadvantaged children may be provided with a 'head start' through targeted pre-school programmes.

At first glance these theories may seem to have some explanatory power. They seek to make a causal connection between certain *social* characteristics of individuals (rather than the *personal* and 'natural' ones of intelligence) and particular educational outcomes. However, both cultural deprivation theories and compensatory education programmes are problematic to the extent that they assume that middle-class culture is superior to working-class culture, and that the source of working-class educational failure can be found within its culture. An alternative perspective is developed by the French sociologist Pierre Bourdieu who argues that it is not the culture of working-class children that is at fault but the way in which schools recognise only the culture of middle-class children.

> To penalise the underprivileged and favour the most privileged the school has only to neglect, in its teaching methods and its criteria when making judgements, to take into account the cultural inequalities between children of different social classes. In other words, by treating all pupils, however unequal they may be in reality, as equal in rights and duties, the educational system is led to give its de facto sanction to initial cultural inequalities.
>
> (Bourdieu, 1974: 113)

The main way in which schools help to reproduce class inequalities is by legitimating only the knowledge and cultural dispositions of the middle class. Bourdieu argues that the knowledge that is transmitted in middle-class homes becomes a form of **cultural capital** that gives students certain kinds of 'returns' in the form of educational success, qualifications and professional employment. Working-class children do not have access to this privileged cultural capital and so are disadvantaged in the school environment. Here Bourdieu turns the cultural deprivation theories on their head by placing blame on the culture and organisation of the *school* rather than a deficit in the culture of working-class children. Specifically, cultural capital refers to the privileged forms of language, values, style of presenting the self, tacit understanding and knowledge. This cultural capital is *embodied* within the **habitus** of individuals. That is, middle-class children and their parents act, think and speak in ways that fit in with

Cultural capital refers to the privileged forms of language, values, self-presentation and knowledge that is recognised by the school.

Habitus is the embodiment of culture within the individual's practices and sense of identity.

the ethos and culture of the school. Working-class children do not possess this cultural capital and their habitus (embodied working-class culture) is at odds with what is valued in school learning. Under these conditions it is not at all surprising that working-class students typically do less well than middle-class students in *this* school system.

While the discussion here has focused on the reproduction of *class* inequalities, the pattern of disadvantage is similar for disadvantaged ethnic groups. In New Zealand, educational attainment of Maori and Pacific Islanders* is below that of Pakeha students. This may be accounted for by the compounding factors of class inequality (as Maori and Pacific Islanders are found disproportionately in the working class) and ethnicity (where the ethnic cultures of these groups is marginalised within a Pakeha system). For Maori the growth in the provision of Kohanga Reo and Kura Kaupapa (where children are taught in the Maori language and with a school organisation based on Maori cultural values and practices) is one response to the educational disadvantage they face in the traditional school environment.

> * The term *Pacific Islanders* is used in the context of this book as a convenient, if problematic, way of referring to those who were born in, but have migrated from, the Pacific Islands to New Zealand, or who have been born in New Zealand of Pacific Island descent. There are, however, a number of problems associated with the usage of the term: for many New Zealanders, it has associations with some of the stereotypes that were deployed in the 1970s and 1980s and the racialisation of Pacific Islanders as 'problem migrants'. For Pacific Islanders themselves, the term collapses important cultural differences as well as reproducing a negative label.

In the following contribution, Alison Jones compares the educational experiences of two students – Sina, an New Zealand born Samoan girl, and Sue, a middle-class Pakeha girl. Jones' discussion fleshes out the concepts of cultural capital and habitus by giving detailed accounts of how two 'hardworking' girls came to attain different educational outcomes. This kind of participant-observation research allows sociologists to gather 'thick' qualitative data about values, dispositions and attitudes that are generally invisible in research that collects large-scale quantitative information linking categories such as class and educational attainment. Clearly both kinds of research are valuable – giving us different kinds of information that we can put together to help gain a fuller picture.

Telling stories about achievement: sociology in an Auckland school

Alison Jones

Why is it that schools still tend to 'give' more to some groups of students than others? Some secondary students, like Sina T, work hard at school but come away with few qualifications and a belief that they deserve little. Others, like Sue B, get more rewards from their time at school, and go on to 'cash in' those rewards to gain even more educational qualifications, and a decent job.

When I first met Sina, she was in the fourth form at an all-girls' secondary school in Auckland. She was sitting in a science class; her science book was neat and up to date, but she was looking gloomy, and looking forward to the end of the period. I was a researcher in her classroom, trying to work out what Sina learned in science (and her other subjects as well) and how she got through the 'boring' school day. Sina was serious about school. She usually kept up with her work, she tried to get it all correct, and she secretly took time off to catch up if she needed to. She could not understand why I should be interested in her and her friends, but she let me hang out with them.

Sina's parents had migrated to New Zealand before she was born in order to seek better opportunities for their children than those available in Samoa. The New Zealand Government and employers had encouraged migrants from the Islands in the 1960s and 1970s in order to fill the demand for relatively cheap labour in the increasing number of factories and service industries opening up in New Zealand. Sina wanted to get a better job than her cleaner mother, like 'a teacher or a policewoman'. I followed Sina around for a year and a half, until she left school. She did not do well with School Certificate, and went to work as a house-maid in a large new hotel in Auckland.

I also met Sue at the school. She was doing science as well. She was bored like Sina – and on this day irritated with her teacher who, she said, was 'incompetent' and 'didn't know a thing about how to teach'. Like Sina, Sue worked hard at school, and her book was tidy and up to date. She also took days 'off' to catch up on homework and 'to recover from being at school'. Her mother didn't mind, so it wasn't a secret that she 'wagged' now and then.

Sue's parents had also migrated to New Zealand to seek opportunities in work; her mother as a polytech teacher, and her father as an engineer. Both had come from Britain. Sina and Sue lived near each other, they knew each other by sight. I spent time with Sue and her friends around school. She eventually went to University to study for a BA.

The reason I was in these girls' classrooms was that, for my doctoral degree in sociology of education, I had decided to find out 'what was happening' in New Zealand classrooms at that time (mid-1980s). I was particularly interested in how it was that schools throughout the country managed regularly to give out far more rewards to some groups of young people than others, even though the students worked equally hard. And how come most people seemed to think this was fair?

When young people sit in a classroom and are taught by the same teacher, you would think that if they put in the same effort, they would all do pretty much the same. If they don't, you would usually put it down to difference in ability – some kinds are 'brighter' than others (whatever 'brightness' means – and no-one seems to agree on that. It is easy to get into a circular argument: you do better because you are brighter, you are called 'brighter' because you do better ...). 'Brains' or aptitude might explain *individual* differences, but what about differences between *groups* of students? Why is it, for instance, that girls tend to do better than boys, or – my focus here – Pakeha students tend to do better than Pacific Islands students?

At Sina and Sue's school, like all other streamed schools in New Zealand, why were the 'top' streams made up mostly of Pakeha girls, and the Pacific Islands students mostly bunched in the 'lower' form classes? This is a complex question, one with several possible answers – none of them easily arrived at, and all dependent on what kind of research methodology you might use, which issues you focus on, and which approach you take.

I chose to do ethnographic (or 'participant-observation') research. That is, I spent nearly two years in classrooms in a local all-girls secondary school in Auckland, documenting the experiences of two groups of 'hard-working' girls – a group of working-class Pacific Islands students, and some middle-class Pakeha girls. To narrow my focus, I decided to ignore the ones who thought school was a waste of time. I tried to 'be a student' (that is, a 'fly on the wall' – though I didn't wear the uniform, or do the work!) – sitting at desks, mucking around at lunch time, even wagging. The girls mostly tolerated me good-naturedly, after quizzing me about the research. I scribbled in code in my notebooks, trying to record their activities and our conversations in a systematic way. Sometimes I used a tape recorder.

One of the things I did was measure the amount of time the girls spent on project or problem-solving work. While the middle-class girls on average spent 70% of their time on this kind of work, the Pacific Islands girls did it for less than one quarter of the time. Most of the Pacific Islands girls' time in the classroom was spent listening to the teacher or copying – either from the teacher's notes or after waiting for the right answers from her. The Pakeha girls only spent a very small amount of their time listening passively to the teacher. This interested me a lot. Why the differences, and were they important?

When I talked to the girls, I found out that both groups had quite different ideas about what *counts* as 'hard work' at school. Both groups were, in fact, *working equally hard*, by their own definitions. The Pakeha middle-class girls were doing their own writing, and the working-class Pacific Islands girls were getting 'what they needed to know' from the teacher. Their hard work had different outcomes, it seemed. Only one group's definition of school work was rewarded. The examinations demanded that the students use their own words, and demonstrate their individual understandings, not that they repeat rote-learned phrases. Most of the Pacific Islands girls did not do well in the tests and examinations.

What was interesting to me was that the girls encouraged the teachers to participate with them in what they (the girls) believed to be 'school work'. When Sina and her friends were asked to do their own work they were often restless, and waited until the teacher had given them 'what they needed to know'. Sue and her peers complained bitterly when the teacher 'gave them the answers'; they were happy when they were given material to 'work out for themselves'. The students 'shaped up' their teachers' teaching practices towards what the students thought was appropriate to getting good marks. They engaged with their teachers in the *production* of classroom practice, as they sought the rewards ostensibly offered by the school to all who 'work hard'.

As part of their various Pacific and class cultures, the working-class girls I studied had learned to respect the teacher and other knowledgeable elders, to listen to their instructions and follow what they said. The middle-class Pakeha girls, on the other hand, as a result of their ethnic and class culture, believed that teachers were ordinary people and that their own and their parents' opinions and knowledge were equal to those of their teachers.

The school, then, without anyone intending it, rewarded one group's class and ethnic cultural assumptions, through making them valuable in the context of the school. It allowed the members of this group a good chance of further access to educational qualifications. In other words, the school played a key part in converting the middle-class students' cultural assumptions about school work and authority into *cultural capital*. 'Cultural capital' is a useful term because it indicates that aspects of some cultures – which we learn automatically from our families – can be 'capitalised' on (in this case, through access to more education).

At the end of exams, most of the girls thought their results were 'fair'. Nearly all of the Pacific Islands girls I talked to said they simply 'did not have brains' or 'didn't try hard enough' – that is, they blamed themselves for the results. Sina said 'God didn't intend everyone to do well'. Sue said she worked for her good results, and could have done better if she had wanted to. Hardly any of the students thought that the pattern of achievement suggested something other than individual ability as an explanation; no-one thought about 'cultural capital'.

People concerned that schools are not benefiting all students as well as they might have a range of possible solutions. Some think it is simply a matter of teaching Pacific Islands students and parents about how the system works. But Pacific Islands teachers and educationists say it is not so simple. Is this 'solution' simply another way of saying: be Pakeha and middle-class like us? That is neither possible nor desirable. Others think that Pacific Islands communities should 'have more say in schools'.

But simply following the 'Tomorrow's Schools' principle and letting communities 'get on with it' is not going to make much difference. We have seen this already – schools in poorer areas such as South Auckland are under severe stress. Most Pacific Islands people in New Zealand continue to be positioned as working-class, a social and economic position which limits access to resources of all sorts. The resources necessary to running successful schools are far more easily found in those communities which already have material and educational goods. Consider the 'saleable' educational skills available to Sue's and Sina's parents, and it is not hard to see how this works.

It is like a vicious cycle: when a group's cultural assumptions are not 'made valuable' in an education system, their desires, abilities, and opportunities to intervene in that system are limited. Lack of economic capital, too, inevitably has a significantly limiting effect.

Change is happening. Very slowly, but surely, Pacific Islands scholars in New Zealand are writing the story – and text-books, becoming teachers, training teachers, deciding on teaching practices, and addressing some of the ways in which their own cultural assumptions might become 'capital' within and against the education system.

Questions

On the basis of your reading of Alison Jones' research, attempt to answer the following questions:

1   Alison Jones suggests that the kind of answer one gets to the question about why Pacific Islands students are mostly bunched in the lower streams and do poorly at school has something to do with the kind of research methodology that is used. What kinds of information can be gathered through participant-observation research and what does this add to our understanding about differential school attainment?

2   Outline the main differences between the 'cultural capital' of the Pakeha girls and the cultural assumptions of the Pacific Islands girls.

3   Although both the Pacific Islands and Pakeha girls that Alison Jones discusses here 'worked hard' only one kind of 'working hard' was rewarded – why was that?

4   Outline the elements of the ideology of meritocracy that are present in the talk of the Pakeha and Pacific Islands girls. Discuss how this ideology helps the girls accept their educational outcomes. In what ways does a sociological explanation of cultural capital offer a critique of meritocracy?

The local and global: classrooms without walls and the global information society

As we have seen in this chapter, mass public schooling grew out of the processes of industrialisation and urbanisation. We are now entering another era of major change with the rapid development of new information technologies. These technologies are changing the way we communicate with each other and how we transmit knowledge. Some people have suggested that these developments in information technologies are of the same magnitude as the shift from feudal to industrial society. If this is the case then we are seeing the growth of a new form of post-industrial society – perhaps it might be called a 'global **information society**' (Martin, 1995). Here Martin brings together *globalisation* (a concept introduced in Chapter 1) and the information society. Although the two concepts are interconnected, we will take each aspect in turn in order to examine its potential impact on education.

'Information society' is a concept that was first developed in the late 1970s to refer to the changes that were occurring in work, education and the marketplace as a result of new information technologies. In particular, there are four on-going developments in technology that are having profound effects at many levels of society: the increasing improvements in the capabilities of *computers*, particularly personal computers; the integration of computer and telecommunications technologies made possible through the *digitisation* of data; developments in *satellite technology*, and the increased capacity of *fibre optics* to carry thousands of messages at once (Giddens, 1997). These new information technologies are changing the sphere of work – creating new jobs, getting rid of others, as well as changing the nature of the tasks involved in some occupations. While these changes do not affect everyone equally, they are extensive enough to challenge the notion that conventional forms of schooling are sufficient to prepare children for the world of work. As new technologies constantly change so too do the skills that are required to use technologies. This challenges the idea that the school is the end point of the educational process. Those workers who have the most flexible and updated skills are best prepared for the new work environments. Most 'post-industrial' societies are therefore experiencing an expansion in the post-compulsory education sphere with increasing numbers of people pursuing higher education in universities and polytechnics.

Developments in information technologies are also being used within the school environment. In particular, the growing use of personal computers connected to **the Internet** is challenging the once unquestioned centrality of the textbook. School books are by their nature solid, portable, relatively fixed repositories of knowledge. Although this knowledge is updated with new editions of the book, such updating happens relatively infrequently, perhaps every three to four years. Contrast this with the information that is available through the Internet. Not only is there a

Information society refers to a post-industrial form of society that is based on the production of knowledge through new information technologies.

The Internet is a global system of connections between computers.

Classrooms without walls refers to education carried out via electronic media.

huge amount of information available from the World Wide Web but this information is updated regularly – in some cases once a day. This instant and relatively easy access to information may fundamentally change the relationship of children to knowledge. 'Teacher-less classrooms' and '**classrooms without walls**' may replace more traditional forms of education as students substitute 'surfing the net' for interaction with their teachers.

Classroom without walls?

Commodification refers to the reduction of elements of social life to commodities that can be bought and sold for a profit.

While the developments outlined here are still some way from being a widespread feature of schooling they do raise questions about the meaning of education and the nature of 'information' that is available through the Internet. One outcome of the new information technologies is that they make possible the rapid and widespread transmission of information, potentially to all parts of the globe. New facts and pieces of information become available daily. It is possible to gather information on almost anything via the Internet. It could be argued, then, that knowledge has become a debased currency, reduced to pieces of discrete information – much of it subject to **commodification**. From an educational point of view this increase in the availability of information does not necessarily translate into an increase in *knowledge*. A rather crude way to distinguish between these two terms is to see information as data, while knowledge involves a cognitive process of *understanding* that information. Although surfing the net might produce a huge mass of information on, for example, alternative health remedies, the possession of this information is unhelpful until some process of sifting through the various pieces of information has been undertaken and judgements made about which remedies are most appropriate and why. For this reason it is difficult to imagine that new information technologies can fully replace the pedagogical processes through which students interact with teachers.

The new information technologies discussed here have made a *globalisation* of information possible. In particular satellite technology and the Internet have connected up the world in a way unthinkable even 40 years ago. The rapid change that is occurring in this area is almost unbelievable. While it took 40 years for radio in the United States to gain an audience of 50 million, the same number was using personal computers only 15 years after their introduction, and it took only four years after the Internet became available for 50 million Americans to be using it regularly (Giddens, 1999a). Communication can now occur instantaneously with the transmission of digitised data through trans-ocean cables and the more than 200 satellites circling the earth. Giddens argues that this new world of transformations that we live in:

> [affects] almost every aspect of what we do. For better or worse, we are being propelled into a global order … Globalisation has something to do with the thesis that we now all live in one world.
>
> (Giddens, 1999a)

The full reference to this quote:
(http://news.bbc.co.uk/hi/english/static/events/reith_99/week1/lecture1.htm)
is just one manifestation of the global information society.

Those of you familiar with the Internet will recognise that the reference given above is an address on the World Wide Web. A quick trip to this site will reveal that the quote comes from the first of Anthony Giddens's lectures for the 1999 Reith lecture series. This lecture series was initially established by the BBC in 1948 to mark the contribution made to public service broadcasting by Sir John Reith and to advance public understanding and debate about important contemporary issues. Giddens's lectures on aspects of globalisation were, fittingly, delivered in four different places on the globe (London, New Delhi, Hong Kong and Washington). These BBC lectures were delivered in the conventional manner (orally to a room full of people) and were also broadcast over the radio. However, it was also possible to listen to the fifth lecture, as it was being given, anywhere in the world, via the Reith lecture website using 'Real Audio'. For those who missed the lecture at the time it was actually presented, or who live in a different time zone, it was possible to see and hear the videoed presentation via a personal computer. And for those whose PCs lack the latest video and audio capacities, it was possible to download the text and read it in the old-fashioned way. Participation in the debates surrounding the lectures was encouraged through the use of e-mail communications which were compiled and made available via the website. At the time of writing, there were some 52 pages of text generated through e-mailed comments.

For sociologists on the other side the world this use of the Internet provided a fantastic opportunity to be part of a series of global debates about matters of sociological interest, as they happened. Previously we might have had to wait some weeks to read about Giddens's lectures in a journal or magazine, and participation in the debates would have been slow and relatively minimal. More generally, for students the world over, the Internet provides opportunities to hear about things that are happening in places distant from them much more quickly than was once the case. In addition, the availability of e-mail allows for a more active form of participation in these events than was previously possible. The Internet may give you as a student of sociology access to new forms of knowledge without the aid of a teacher or having to be in a lecture room at a particular time. However, while these innovations in globalised information technologies offer possibilities they are also limited in certain important respects. Let us take for example the website address given earlier. The assumption that you will be able to read the text is premised on a number of things. Firstly that you will have access to a PC that has Internet connections (this requires certain financial and material resources not available to everyone). Secondly that you will have the software that will enable you to access the World Wide Web. Thirdly, that the website will still exist at the time you read this textbook (months or years after it was written) – it may not.

Most of the popular discourse surrounding new information technologies is celebratory – seeing them as progressive forces that will improve the nature of work, education and even perhaps democratic processes. However, sociologists raise some important concerns that we might have about these technologies. Firstly, the changes that have been discussed here are not as extensive as often suggested and it is possible to see societies, and groups within societies that suffer from **information poverty**. For much of the world outside the affluent West (and for certain disadvantaged groups within it) new information technologies still play a minor part in everyday life. Secondly, the changes wrought by new information technologies may not be only beneficial. For example, the speeding up of social life helped by these technologies may contribute to new stress-related mental and physical health problems. Thirdly, we should be wary of attributing to technology the role of motor behind changes in work and education. This kind of explanation is a form of **technological determinism** and as such assumes that technology is an external and autonomous force which shapes social and economic relationships and organisations. On the contrary – most sociologists would argue that technology develops within already existing social relations of class, gender, ethnicity, global inequality and so on. These social divisions shape the ways in which technology is used and the impact it will have on people's lives. For example, the discussion to this point has assumed that technological developments are gender neutral. However, feminist theorists argue that gender relations shape the use, and value of, information technologies. For example Judy Wajcman (1994) has

> **Information poverty** may be suffered by those who have minimal access to new information technologies.

> **Technological determinism** is a form of explanation based on the notion that changes in technology are an autonomous force which shape social and economic relationships and organisations.

argued that girls have less access than boys to computing at home and in the classroom. This is both shaped by, and contributes to, a female gender identity in which technical competence or confidence is lacking. Furthermore, just at a time when information technology is becoming increasingly important in many jobs, the proportion of women taking computer courses in higher education is dropping.

Conclusion

Education is one of the most important social institutions. Schooling takes up a large proportion of the waking hours of school-aged children and thus we can expect it to be a powerful force in people's lives. Contrary to the popular idea that schools provide the meritocratic means for everyone, irrespective of their class, gender or ethnicity, to achieve their full potential, sociologists have argued that the schooling process actually contributes to the *reproduction* of social inequalities. While there are undoubtedly exceptions, most children end up in occupations at the same class and status level as their parents did. Recent changes in information technologies provide possibilities for changing some of the ways in which schooling happens, and also increase connections between people across the globe. However, these technological developments cannot be separated from the larger social and political context of which they are a part.

Study questions

6.1 Outline some of the features of the hidden curriculum that you recall from your school days. How does this curriculum help reproduce class, gender and/or ethnic inequalities?

6.2 How does the belief in an inherited intelligence contribute to the ideology of meritocracy?

6.3 Why are sociologists critical of the notion that intelligence is a personal and natural quality?

6.4 What impact is the 'global information society' having on educational processes? Do you think these changes will result in 'classrooms without walls'?

Further reading

Acker, S. (1994) *Gendered Education*. Open University Press, Buckingham.
Meighon, R. and Siraj-Blatchford, I. (1997) *A Sociology of Educating*, 3rd ed. Cassell, London.
Nash, R. (1997) *Inequality/Difference: A Sociology of Education*. ERDC Press, Massey University, Palmerston North.

7 Work and economic life

Chapter aims

- to provide an introduction to the debates on how work is defined by sociologists and others;
- to review the global and local changes in the way that economic production is organised and managed;
- to identify who participates in the labour market and paid work, and who is excluded.

Introduction: defining work

What sort of paid work an individual does is one of the most significant pieces of information for defining the status, **life chances**, and economic position of that individual. Moreover, unpaid work is viewed quite differently to paid work. Being a university student, a superannuitant, a welfare beneficiary or a housewife is not ranked highly in terms of social standing or economic productivity. This chapter looks at the social significance of work and the way in which the nature of work is changing – radically in many instances – as we emerge from the industrial age into the information age. There are still substantial inequalities in terms of who is able to obtain paid employment (especially full-time, satisfying jobs); and the continued marginalisation of ethnic and indigenous minorities, or females, is a feature of contemporary labour markets. But we start by defining *work*.

Work is fundamental to social and economic life. Work is what we do when we need to produce something, whether a car, a house, or a meal at home. Even the very wealthy have to work to survive even if that work is rather different to what others do. And work takes such a multiplicity of forms that it spans the full range of social activities, from work in the home, to various leisure activities, to paid employment. All but a very few of us work, whether that work is the smallest task or maintaining a

> **Life chances** is a Weberian-inspired term that refers to the different opportunities and experiences that occur over a lifetime for different social groups.

home over a lifetime. Those who are incapable of physical activity are possibly the only exceptions to this rule. At this point, work can be defined as virtually anything. A basic definition would describe work in the most general sense as the expenditure of human effort and energy in providing some good or in transforming part of the world, however small. To refine what we mean by 'work', and to contextualise it, sociologists are interested in the *social significance* of work, and in the way in which it is *defined and socially constructed* in a particular situation or society. The questions that arise are: what is work in a particular setting, who does it, how is it rewarded (if it is) and what significance is attached to the particular task or role?

This might sound like a reasonable approach, and one that is unlikely to present too many problems. However, it is not as simple as it appears. In many societies such as our own, work is often defined as *paid work* or employment. That is, work is something that you get paid for doing. By definition, this excludes those people who do not get paid wages, such as students, housewives or retired people. Moreover, that the boundary between work and leisure is unclear is demonstrated in Chapter 15. These are activities that can be either work or leisure, so that some people, for example, professional sports people, are paid to carry out activities (= work) that others do for fun (= leisure). However, if you work on a garden or a house as part of your leisure activities (and gardening is one of the most popular activities in New Zealand), and this activity adds value to your property, then you are being paid – at least indirectly. Or let us look at the case of someone who is responsible for the functioning of a home and for doing the myriad of things required to keep a home in good order, from cleaning or cooking through to nurturing children. Such a person might not be paid – but surely this is work that is vitally important? It is as important as paid work in maintaining the household / family and community, but it is seldom seen as equivalent in value to paid employment, although there are groups and political organisations that argue for 'basic income schemes for all' or 'wages for housework'. Even the question of who is 'unemployed' is a contentious matter, especially when keeping down the unemployment rate is central to political success. Sociologists need to explore the various perceptions of what constitutes work, and analyse the social and economic significance of various tasks or roles.

Sociologists can claim some success here. The founding fathers of the discipline – Marx, Weber, Durkheim – all contributed substantially to our knowledge of the nature of work in the context of an emerging capitalism. They captured the centrality of work, and especially paid work, to our social lives. Work defines who we are. As stated at the beginning of the chapter, it gives us status, provides life chances, determines the level of satisfaction and income of an individual and contributes to the collective social and economic activities of a community or society. Marx provided a powerful analysis of who benefits from various sorts of work, and built an argument on the role of work in creating a capitalist society

118 Exploring Society

What is work?

which benefited some, and exploited and disadvantaged others. Weber examined the organisation of work, and its bureaucratic and rational characteristics, while Durkheim was interested in the division of labour. Each saw work changing as capitalism evolved, and this contextualisation of work has provided an important theme that continues to be explored in sociology to the present. Indeed, the challenge is to provide a convincing analysis of the current social and economic changes and of how they intersect with changes in work and employment. To do so, we need to consider the economy.

The economy is how the production, distribution and consumption of goods in a society is organised. Broadly speaking, the economy is made up of three sectors: primary production, or the extraction of raw materials from the environment (e.g. farming, forestry); manufacturing, or the processing of materials into manufactured products (e.g. car assembly); and services, or providing a service rather than producing a good as such (e.g. education, health services, media). The significance of each of these sectors has changed as the nature of capitalism has changed. The industrial revolution confirmed the significance of manufacturing and saw the rise of mass production in urban-located factories. It had an impact upon work by separating home and the place of employment, and wages characterised the relationship between employer and employee. More recently, the nature of economic production and ownership have begun to change in revolutionary ways. Manufacturing in some countries is in decline, while the service sector, and part-time, casual work are growing in importance. There are various descriptive terms for this new type of economy: post-industrial, post-Fordist, the information/network society or postmodernity. As a result of these developments, the nature of work and employment are again changing in significant ways.

The social and the personal: the social and economic significance of paid work

In an episode of the television comedy Seinfeld, the character Kramer says: 'I didn't want to tell you that I was out of work. It is embarrassing.'

Paid work is a statement about our background and training, about our success in obtaining a certain status and income, and about whether we are engaged in something which is personally fulfilling. Kramer is expressing a commonly held sentiment, because when we first meet someone, one of the most obvious ways of evaluating that person is to ask 'What do you do?' and by this we actually mean, 'What paid work do you do?' Even if a person is unemployed, he or she will often reply by saying 'I am an unemployed sociologist/carpenter/dentist'. A reply which specifies a particular type of employment is a statement about social standing and what an individual or family can expect over a lifetime (what Weber called life chances). It helps locate where another person is situated in the complex social and economic systems of a modern society.

The industrial revolution set the scene for our contemporary understanding of work.

> By the twentieth century, the conventional view of work was very different from that of the pre-industrial period: work was now performed *outside the home, was waged, and performed predominantly by men.*
>
> (Bilton, 1996: 378)

Industrialisation confirmed the separation of home and place of employment and the significance of the wage in defining the relationship between employer and employee. Paid work was no longer done from home, or within a short distance of home. People left home to travel to work at 7.00 am and left work at 5.00 pm or later. The day was structured around the needs of the employer and the machinery of the factory. The shape of the city came to reflect the distance between a home, often in the suburbs, and the place of work in the shopping centre, the financial and headquarter areas of the downtown area or the industrial sectors where manufacturers were located. The contemporary city caters in very obvious ways to the commuting patterns of its 'workers'. In addition, most people are paid a salary or a wage for what they do. This is a crude but effective way of indicating the social and economic significance of a particular task. How much a person gets paid, and what supplements this direct wage or salary, is a measure of the economic bargaining power of a certain group of workers. It is always interesting to analyse why some get paid what they do.

In the past, under a system of mass production which relied upon sub-systems such as transportation for its success, those jobs which were important to the maintenance of the main system were occupied by workers who organised themselves into unions and were successful in gaining favourable work conditions and payments. In New Zealand, for example, the watersiders or the freezing workers used to enjoy relatively good work conditions as a result of their collective bargaining power in strategic industries. With the advent of **de-industrialisation**, de-unionisation and changes to the regulation of the labour market, these conditions, and even the certainty of employment, have all, by and large disappeared. This can be contrasted to the position of the medical profession. From GPs through to medical specialists, these workers continue to enjoy considerable social standing and economic returns. For all of us, our personal health or that of people close to us is a matter of considerable importance, and it is hard to avoid a degree of reliance on medical systems and people. Even so-called 'alternative' health professionals such as naturopaths or acupuncturists are unable to attract the confidence enjoyed by orthodox doctors or earn the same salaries. Doctors continue to occupy a strategic position in the modern economy, and their collective bargaining power and ability to organise politically

De-industrialisation describes the decline of certain types of manufacturing, especially of those industries and types of manufacturing which characterised Fordism.

is reflected in their conditions of work – especially how much they get paid, and how others see them.

The situation of doctors is a good example of how an individual's job determines social status and income. But what about the many people who do not take part in paid work? It is important to ask who is left out. Not being employed is just as socially significant as the type of paid work someone does. Those who are typically excluded from employment are the very young and very old, those who are involved in unpaid activity such as students or those helping in voluntary and community activities, and those on a benefit. There is also the informal economy, including the domestic economy, that is, those activities associated with work in the home. Bilton's comment (see p. 120) notes that work, by which he means paid work, was performed predominantly by men. Of course, some of the most important work in the community is done by women in the home. With the separation of home and place of employment, and the payment of a wage for work, the contribution of the work done in the home has been undervalued. It has become a form of non-work that women do to maintain the private sphere of the home, and it includes essential tasks such as cleaning, cooking, the nurturing of children and the care of older people. It is private, non-paid, typically done by females and is seldom considered to be economically significant. Feminist sociologists have repeatedly challenged these common-sense views of the social and economic significance of domestic work.

What is the value of work?

Gendered culture refers to the way in which social structures and behaviours are determined by gender issues.

The issue of unpaid work in the home has been critically analysed by James and Saville-Smith (1989) and they argue that New Zealand is a **gendered culture**. There are clear gender differences in who does what in the home, and research has indicated that women were (and are) primarily responsible for unpaid work. Even if they are in paid work, they are still required to do most of the work that is required to maintain a home. Unpaid work accounts for about 20% of a 24-hour day for women compared with 12% for men, and marriage substantially increases women's unpaid work (Du Plessis, 1994: 104). Even when women are involved in paid work, they organise it around their 'housework, childcare responsibilities and their husband's shift work' (Du Plessis, 1994: 105). One way of challenging the 'invisibility' of this work is to estimate the financial contribution of women's unpaid work, especially in the home, to the economy. In the early 1990s, the work done by the average housewife during a week was valued at £369 in Britain (Bilton et al., 1996: 211). In New Zealand, Marilyn Waring has factored the unpaid work done largely by women into the national economic statistics on production to make the point that this is a contribution to the well-being of society and the economy which is vitally important and typically ignored. It highlights the contrast between the paid work of men and the contribution of women to the domestic economy.

The local and the global: the evolution of economic ownership and production

Full-time jobs began to disappear as a result of changes in the workplace in the 1980s and 1990s, and the numbers of redundancies and long-term unemployed began to grow. These changes in the type of jobs that were available highlighted something that was becoming increasingly obvious: the nature of production and ownership was changing dramatically. At a local level, economies were described as having changed from Fordist to post-Fordist in terms of how production was organised, and concepts such as post-industrial and the network or information society were used to describe the characteristics of these evolving economies. Globally, new centres of production and power emerged, and new forms of ownership which spanned the globe were established.

In the early and middle part of the century, economies and jobs were built around mass production, mass consumption and the welfare state. Henry Ford's car assembly plants epitomised the dominant production systems in which many people worked, hence the term *Fordism*. But the period also saw a high degree of intervention by governments as they sought to encourage economic growth and provide universal forms of welfare. One important approach was Keynesianism (named after the English economist Keynes). Keynes argued for government intervention to smooth out the business cycle, to run budget deficits in order to boost demand and to ensure full employment. These policies were used to deal with the effects of the depression of the 1930s, and are generally seen as contributing to the long boom enjoyed by Western industrial economies in the post-war period (Anderson and Davey, 1996: 29–30). But by the mid-1980s, rising unemployment and rising inflation (stagnation), plus union militancy, the oil crises and the collapse of managed exchange rates sparked an important policy change in most economies. Keynesianism was out and the economic rationalists were in – and they influenced policy under politicians such as Thatcher, Reagan and Roger Douglas. The idea that you managed demand in the economy in order to protect employment went, as did the idea that the government should provide extensive and universal forms of state services or that government spending was important for social and economic purposes. The free market was now the mechanism for distributing jobs and services, not the government. The private good was privileged over the public good, and the individual consumer would determine what was needed in society.

These policy changes were accompanied by important changes in the nature of production. The Japanese had developed a just-in-time production system which was based around flexibility. You contracted or bought what you needed as you needed it. This week you might want 500 blue Toyota car doors, but next week you might need 1000. You contracted this work to suppliers, and reduced your dependence on large factories, large machines and large numbers of workers. Flexibility was the new buzzword. It was aided by the use of new technologies, and many jobs were either replaced by machines or were altered by the introduction of technology, especially computer-aided technology. The combination of the impact of technology and the need for flexibility saw a rapid growth of part-time and short-term employment. The cost of employment became a major consideration when companies had to decide where to produce their goods. Employers sought to reduce the costs of employing workers, and this included reducing the power of workers to obtain more favourable working conditions and the power of worker representatives such as unions. Internationally, firms moved to countries or regions which had a cost advantage, especially in terms of their wage bill. International organisations such as the International Monetary Fund put a lot of pressure on countries and firms to move away from the notion of life-long employment. Production and capital were now internationally mobile with location determined by the cost advantage of one area over another. This new flexibility has been labelled post-Fordism, or disorganised capitalism.

124 Exploring Society

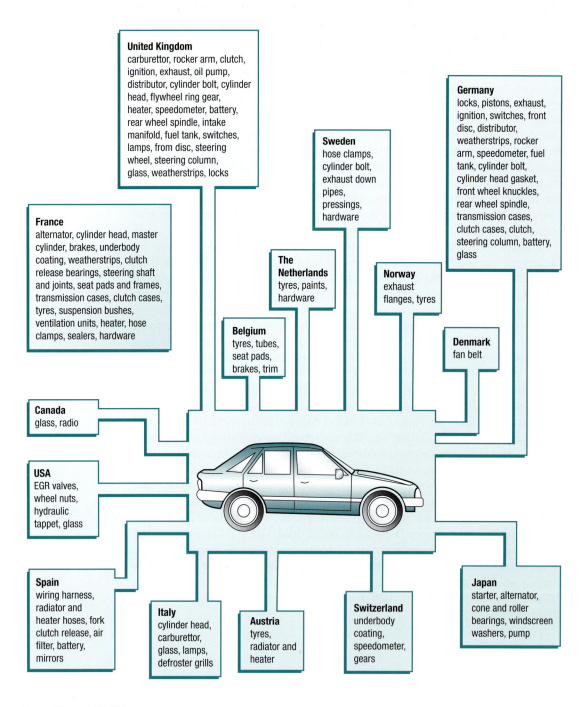

Source: Dicken, 1986: 304.

Figure 7.1 The globalisation of production

These developments confirmed the growing international nature of production and ownership. The degree of change in recent decades has been quite startling. In the last 25 years, the mobility of capital has grown 25-fold. Twenty-five years ago, $US14 billion was invested internationally compared with $US350 billion per year in the late 1990s. This capital chases profits on a short-term basis. By the late 1990s, 51 of the world's top economies were companies and 11 of the top 20 companies were Japanese. Increasingly, the significant decisions are made by international companies, not by the world's 186 states. The latter are at the mercy of global firms and currency markets. And the costs of production are often too high in the advanced economies so production continues to move to low-cost economies. There are about 250 million workers in the USA and the European Union, who each earn about $US85 per day. The significant economies in Asia – Hong Kong, Japan, Korea, Malaysia, Singapore and Taiwan – have about 90 million workers who produce the same goods to the same quality but at a lower price. Then there are the economies of South America, China, Indonesia and India which collectively have 1.2 billion workers, the majority of whom earn less than $US3 per day. With international links and competition, the low costs of production in the latter countries are attractive to global firms. The effect is that there is a major move in what is produced and where. In 1947 the USA was responsible for 60% of the world's steel production. By the 1990s, this figure had gone down to 15% while Japan's capacity in the same area had grown by 300% in the same period. However, what *has* grown is America's control of international brand names. In March 1998, an alliance between McDonald's, Disney Corporation and Coca-Cola was announced. This epitomises the nature of international linkages and production. Each of these companies has an important brand name associated with certain lifestyles and consumption, and sustained by huge marketing budgets. The product each produces is universal and can be purchased in some form practically anywhere. Each relies on casualised employment, and on making a standard product available globally, and each is capable of returning substantial profits to international investors. The combination of three already massive global organisations, with their internationally recognised brands and networks, signals a growing trend. The power of individual states, the attractiveness of a particular economy and the certainty of work or investment in a specific region are now at the mercy of international firms and investors. What work is available in New Zealand, and what rewards are associated with particular sorts of work, are all influenced by these global processes.

126 Exploring Society

	1970	1980	1985	1990	1991
Industry	34.0%	30.5%	27.7%	25.8%	24.9%
Services	66.0%	69.5%	72.3%	74.2%	75.1%
Goods handling	61.2%	57.3%	54.7%	52.6%	51.7%
Information handling	39.0%	42.7%	45.3%	47.4%	48.3%
Services: industry	1.9	2.3	2.6	2.9	3.0
Information: goods	0.6	0.7	0.8	0.9	0.9

Key:
Industry = mining, construction manufacturing
Services = remaining categories
Goods handling = mining, construction, manufacturing, transportation, wholesale/retail trade
Information handling = communications; finance, insurance and real estate (FIRE); services; government
Services: industry = ratio between information handling and goods handling employment

Source: Castells, 1996: 296.

Table 7.1 The decline of manufacturing and the growth of the service sector in the US economy, 1970–1991

These developments have also contributed to an interesting debate about the 'end of work'. Braverman (1974) provided a critique of the class base of work and organisations but he also focused attention on the de-skilling that was a growing feature of capitalism and the 'rearrangement of paid collective activities through a process of fragmenting skills' (Austrin, 1994: 239). The debate has moved on, and there is growing interest in the insecurity of work – for professional occupations as much as for the unskilled – and questions have been raised about the 'end of work as we know it'. On the one hand, the advent of the information or network society (Castells, 1996) has brought with it new relationships, new conceptions of identity, new forms of access to information and new experiences and types of employment, all based on the growing dependence on emerging technologies. Lifestyles and consumption patterns have changed, and affluence – and poverty – are expressed in different ways than previously. But all of this has taken place against the background of massive changes to employment as the nature of capitalist production has changed. Employment for most corners of the labour market has been casualised; new management ideologies of labour control, corporate identity and responsibilities have emerged; status and rewards are determined by explicitly defined merit and achievement contracts; there is less full-time and more part-time work with more workers being employed in a number of jobs at the same time; more overtime is being worked (in the case of manual and professional occupations) while at the same time there are significant rates of unemployment or **underemployment**. Insecurity of employment is an important feature of societies such as New Zealand, and it characterises the significant changes that have occurred in the nature of employment

Underemployment occurs when a person does paid work at a level below his/her capability and/or willingness to do more.

both locally and globally over recent decades. Certainly, the notion that you worked in one job for one company over a working life time has disappeared in many countries, and the old conditions and understandings of paid work have changed dramatically.

Looking for the action: rules of control and occupational style in casinos

Terry Austrin

The granting of exclusive public monopolies to run casinos to a mix of multi-national corporate leisure companies and local business consortiums has been a marked feature of service sector development in Australasia. Since 1973, the year the first legal casino opened in Hobart, Tasmania, 16 casinos have opened. The siting of many of these casinos in prestige central-city locations makes it very clear that gambling is favoured by governments pursuing development policies based around tourism.

As new sites of leisure, casinos are also new sites of work. What is the character of the work offered in these new sites? Are these jobs part of a de-skilled service sector typified by bureaucratically controlled work settings found in what Ritzer (1993) terms *rationalised*, *feminised*, *McDonaldised*, globalised industries? Or are they composed of a mix of unskilled and skilled labour markets loosely assembled through the ties between the workers themselves? I want to use the case of dealers and suggest that their jobs are neither one nor the other but both.

Let us look at the control argument first. Goodman, for example, presents casinos as gambling warehouses and, following Ritzer's (1993) example, he adopts the term *McGambling* to describe recent developments. In his version, the prestige of central-city siting is undone by the reality of mass gambling as a mindless form of action:

> … today's casinos are little more than theme-decorated warehouses filled with slot machines, designed for mass consumption – the new McGambling. They are largely populated by what the gambling industry calls 'grind players', a clientele who sit with plastic cups of coins, pulling levers and pushing buttons on clanging slot machines.
>
> (Goodman ,1995: 124)

In this account of North American casinos, then, dealers are no longer where the action is. Like the factory worker, the dealer has been subject to replacement through automation.

Goodman's account operates at one extreme of a continuum of writers who stress the similarity between factory work and the new prestige settings of central-city casinos. For other writers, the dealer remains the 'production worker' (Grey, 1986: 32), working the swing shifts in a twenty-four-hour-a-day industry. More significantly for Lafferty and McMillen (1989), dealers' actions promote an intensive surveillance apparatus to watch over them:

> ... the fear of crime and corruption has meant that casino workers are an extremely highly controlled workforce, whose every movement is strictly prescribed and supervised. Stringent controls, based on the principle of people watching people, have been introduced to counteract the worker's ability to exploit flexible and ambiguous situations.
>
> (Lafferty and McMillen, 1989: 45)

We have, then, the dealer presented as ritual prop, as production worker and as potential criminal whose every action has to be monitored.

These different accounts of control and action complement each other in their descriptions of the power of management and the insignificance of the worker in casino gaming. They emphasise that the rise of corporate gaming as a business has produced a form of managerial control which operates through intense surveillance, ritualised action, threats to job security and the potential of automation.

I want now to tell a very different story of work in casinos. This story looks at the action from the point of view of the dealers and the ties between them. In my own research with dealers in Australasia, aspects of all of the types of control discussed were referred to but what was emphasised most were claims concerning style. An aspect of these claims is elaborated on by Goffman:

> Casino personnel 'breaking in' on a job feel there is much profit if they make it but no practical way of ensuring that they will. During this difficult phase there will be many minor infractions of rules, which can serve as sufficient grounds for being fired: coming on shift a few minutes late; declining an undignified task; mishandling chips; being irreverent concerning a house loss; expressing impatience with one's rate of progress, and so forth. Once skill and reputation have been acquired, tenure is only somewhat more secure: runs of ill luck; ill-founded suspicion of theft; change in owner-sponsorship – all can provide grounds for sudden dismissal.
>
> (Goffman, 1967: 193)

Goffman's account is notable in so far as it draws attention to both rules of control and insecurity and the skills and reputations of dealers.

For Goffman, what was of interest was not the external surveillance but rather the controlled effort by the dealer to routinise composure under pressure. A dealer gives her own account of what this involves:

… dealing a card involves pulling out of a shoe with this finger while having the rest of your arm straight like this, don't have your elbow too high, don't turn your hand on the side, keep your fingers together, which I could never do, keep this thumb showing, take it down, flip it up, you put your thumb just like that and you have to practise where to put the card so that you are not holding the card and if you lifted the card off the pressure of the table it would drop, and at the same time wiggle your thumb around so that the card comes in a straight line with those fingers keeping your hand like this. This hand, the elbow stays over there comes in so that it is like this and you have to pick up the card so that it sits between there and there so that it cuts the diagonal bottom right-hand corner of the card so that you are holding it right in that niche there and you haven't got a very good grip on it and you have to sweep across the table, without moving your elbow, to the particular box, and as you get three-quarters of the way across the table you push your thumb slightly onto the table and once you're right at the thing you should have the card bent with your thumb on the table and you should slip your finger in and the card should fall exactly.

Each movement as the dealer described it, using her hands as she demonstrated it to me, was taught as a separate action in the training school and then has to be put into practice as a set of flowing motions.

Putting all this into practice requires a considerable degree of mind and body co-ordination. This degree of detail and standardisation of work is extraordinary. The descriptive language of the occupation speaks of both ritualised action and the awkwardness and fear regarding movement in the job. In this version, however, control operates from below, through the shame of being exposed for getting it wrong.

In casinos, new dealers are referred to as 'lumpies' and like apprentices in other industries are laughed at and ridiculed for their lack of speed, for their mistakes, for their inability to smooth their actions as display. The fears and the constraints associated with this form of control through shame do, however, have a pay-off for the new dealer. This takes the form of getting the action or performance right. A woman dealer explains that getting it right provides pleasure:

It was such an awesome task or it felt like it and sometimes, it was really dependent upon whether you were awake or you were having a bad night or having a good night, you know, just personally, for a woman whether you had your period or not made a hell of a difference, and nights when everything seemed to be going really well, it's just like yes, yes, you know you are really thrilled and really pleased and there is a lot of satisfaction in being able to do that but it was never there all the time it was, Oh my god what is it going to be like tonight – am I going to be able to do it?'

In the dealer's account the bodily control involved in the job encourages her to do her very best. For by doing her best she gains satisfaction. 'I would be buzzing' is how one dealer put it.

The significance of this is that the reputation of dealers is linked to their style on the tables. Dealers may be tightly monitored by the organisations that they work for but in so far as they develop occupational skills, they also develop their own styles of work, and their own reputations among their fellow dealers. In turn their reputations allow them to build both connections and careers for themselves by moving between casinos. When the Auckland casino opened in February 1996, a significant number of the dealers employed were from the Christchurch casino. Similarly, dealers from Christchurch can be found operating in Australia and Europe. The expansion of legal casino gaming, then, has involved the extension of a new legal labour market that informally links casinos. This new labour market operates both locally, within Australasia, and globally wherever the dealers' connections and reputations take them.

The minute detail of the bodily movements of casino dealers' actions may be under centralised surveillance within casinos but the decentralised personal moves of dealers among casinos are just as significant for understanding this occupation. Casinos in this last account are more than central-city sites 'where the action is' for clients; they are also sites within labour markets composed of networks and ties that dealers themselves assemble. For the dealers, a large piece of their action is located in these networks.

Questions

Having read Terry Austrin's discussion, try to answer the following questions:

1. Terry Austrin emphasises that it is possible to provide multiple interpretations of what happens in a particular workplace, in this case, casinos. Where does control lie in the example provided here: with the workers, or with the casino management, or with both?
2. In what way is the work described here an example of 'McDonaldisation', or 'McGambling'? Is the McDonald metaphor over-used or is it the best currently available for describing the nature of a great deal of contemporary paid employment?

Differences and divisions: work and inequality

Access to paid work, especially full-time, well-paid work, is fundamental to economic well-being. It is one of the most significant determinants in deciding who has access to credit and goods, including quality housing, health and education. It contributes to self-esteem and good health, and provides human and financial resources that then sustain future generations. Conversely, those who do not have access to paid employment, either because they cannot work, are reliant on a benefit or can only get part-time, poorly-paid employment face substantial social and economic difficulties.

The labour market divides out into those who are privileged – the top third – and those who are not – the bottom two-thirds. There are also those who are not part of the labour market. These differences have been long recognised. Marx discussed the issue in terms of positions in the system or means of production, and argued that the fundamental contrast was between the working class, who had little control over their working conditions, and were exploited, and the ruling class, who gained significant advantages as owners or managers of the means of production. Weber agreed that the position in the means of production – an individual's class – determined economic and social standing but was less convinced that class and class conflict was as all-important as Marx suggested. Weber noted that issues such as status were also important and together such factors determined life chances. From the emergence of capitalism, work was seen as pivotal in understanding inequality and political options, as the material on class elsewhere in this book makes clear.

Classical sociological approaches provide an important base in our understanding of the significance of work in our individual and collective lives. However, Marx did not anticipate the arrival of the welfare state in the middle part of the twentieth century, and its moderating influences on capitalism and the divisions that derive from the workplace. Nor did he – or could he – anticipate the changing nature of economic production and employment. He also tended to overlook some of the important distinctions that did exist, such as those associated with gender and ethnicity.

Sociologists have developed more sophisticated analyses of work and employment, and what this means in terms of major social and economic divisions. But in their defence, it must be said that the divisions that Marx and Weber identified still endure, and with the influence of economic rationalists on social and economic policy, those divisions are becoming more acute. Moreover, the segmentation of the labour market and the difficulties that some face in getting access to employment is still structured around some key factors.

The first of these key factors is still the gendered nature of labour, both in the domestic sphere and in terms of public, paid work. When sociologists talk of the **dual labour market**, they are highlighting the distinction between a relatively privileged primary sector of well-paid workers with good work conditions and career prospects, and a secondary sector whose work is less satisfying, well-paid, secure or acknowledged. Women have entered paid work in increasing numbers since World War II, but many have entered as part-time, casual, low-waged workers into the secondary sector. They often tend to do work which is an extension of

> Dual labour market refers to the division of employment into primary and secondary sectors, with quite different work conditions prevailing in each.

their domestic responsibilities such as child-minding or nurturing, cleaning or providing food. Even jobs such as teaching or nursing, which are relatively well-paid in terms of female-dominated employment, have faced pressures to downgrade their status or to put workers on contracts which casualise their work. There are also the responsibilities which are associated with the domestic sphere, and which either take precedence over employment or which need to be done in addition to the 'day job'. If a child is ill, the mother takes sick leave. If the ironing needs to be done, or the meals prepared, the female members of the household are typically responsible for these tasks, even if it means that they must do them after a full day's paid work. There is also the issue of whether a glass ceiling exists. Because of domestic responsibilities and the attitudes of fellow workers or employers, women face discriminatory barriers in spite of equal pay and other forms of anti-discriminatory legislation which have appeared in the last two decades. Even though we understand a lot more about the gendered nature of work, and have been exposed to the arguments of feminists, the position of women has not materially improved. If anything, women have entered those parts of the labour market which offer the poorest returns – inadequate pay, poor career prospects, little work satisfaction – and are still largely responsible for work in the home – hardly a major advance.

The second group that is likely to be disproportionately part of the secondary labour market, or to be excluded from the labour market altogether, are members of certain ethnic groups. In 'white' societies such as New Zealand, it tends to be the 'non-white' groups who face substantial difficulties. They might be indigenous groups who have experienced colonisation such as Maori, or low-skilled migrants such as Pacific Islanders* who came to New Zealand to fill certain positions in the labour market. Even though the latter are no longer migrants – they are New Zealanders who have now been resident for some generations – there is an intergenerational process which passes low education and low job skills, and poor employment histories down from generation to generation. This is, of course, a generalisation and not all conform to this pattern, but the current statistics of unemployment or underemployment, low educational performance and low income show that Maori and Pacific Islanders are disproportionately likely to be in the secondary labour market. They too face discrimination and their own glass ceiling, and the reforms of the 1980s and 1990s have not only reinforced their position in the labour market, they have clearly made it worse. With de-industrialisation, members of these groups have been made redundant and new generations entering the labour market have real difficulties even getting a foothold.

These experiences of the economic and labour market 'reforms' also apply to certain age groups and people in particular parts of a country. The 'baby boomers' have been privileged in their employment experiences

* See p. 106

especially as they had access to free education and health care as they grew up to find a buoyant labour market which paid well, offered careers and a choice of jobs. But even middle-class baby boomers have faced difficult times. In their forties and fifties, they faced redundancies as industry was restructured and downsized. Their children are confronted with greatly increased educational costs and a much more competitive job market. Since the 1980s, many have also faced major difficulties in getting employment. Those made redundant, especially if they are in their fifties, and those leaving school without qualifications or training have struggled to get work. This also applies to those outside the main centres of economic production. There is an important difference between the economy of a primate or global city, and that of declining regional areas. In both there are people who are struggling, but the numbers in a relative sense are much more significant in depressed regional areas.

The changing nature of economic production in both a global and local sense has had an impact on what sort of employment is available and who gets it. Long-term unemployment is now a feature of advanced capitalist societies, including unemployment amongst the middle class. The increase in low-waged and insecure employment '… means that many are both in work and in poverty' (McCormick and Oppenheim, 1996: 18). Paid work is now seen as a contributor to poverty in a more substantial way. McCormick and Oppenheim (1996) suggest that there are significant policy issues in this area, including questions such as: is it possible to generate employment which will provide decently paid jobs; is it possible to address major inequalities that are now associated with the nature of the contemporary labour market; is it possible to provide access for women, and others, to adequate earnings; and what can be done to address labour market failure in providing opportunities for young adults? All these policy questions recognise that the fundamental divisions which have long existed have become more deep-seated. The ability of some and not others to gain access to work has produced highly fragmented societies characterised by an obvious contrast between **work-rich** and **work-poor households**, with implications for income and education.

> **Work-rich** and **work-poor households** are terms used to refer to the histories of members of households in gaining, or failing to gain, paid employment.

In the 1980s, the increase in income inequality in the industrial world was greatest in New Zealand (followed by the UK), and this reflected the change from policies of full employment and welfare to higher joblessness and lower wages (see the Joseph Rowntree Foundation's *Inquiry into Income and Wealth*, 1995). In Britain, in 1979, there were 5 million people who received less than half the national average income; by 1989, this figure had grown to 12 million. Welfare has been replaced by 'workfare' and the assumption that even those on the dole should work. Employment circumstances often reflect the fact that there is a low level of trust between employers and employees, and that the employment situation is insecure. Countries like New Zealand have used the deregulation of the labour market to boost low-waged / part-time jobs, but this has happened at the expense of training, certainty and high-skill sectors which all rely on

The post-communist world has not delivered many winners

substantial investment in training and education, long-term financial investment and research. Not all economies or companies have adopted the New Zealand approach. There are some well-known companies such as Levi Strauss, Volvo, IBM or 3M which have sought to look after their various stakeholders, including employees, rather than focus on economic gains for the shareholders. Research indicates that the sales of such stakeholder companies grow as do the number of their employees, to a much greater extent than do those of shareholder-only companies. Japan is one country that has a major commitment to job security and a major investment in training, with the result that worker loyalty is very high, and it is much harder for competitors to poach skilled workers. This policy, which reflects a particular cultural attitude, is seen as a key competitive advantage for the Japanese economy. These approaches provide an interesting contrast with those of firms and countries that have opted for 'short-termism' – the chase for short-term economic gain.

Conclusion

What constitutes 'work' is an interesting and contested issue, in a public and political sense, as well as for the sociologist. The industrial revolution helped define work as employment, or paid work, which was done outside the home by men. Of course, this downgrades or ignores the very significant contribution made by non-paid workers in the home and community, and the contribution of women to the latter form of work. In the post-war period, women began to participate in increasing numbers in employment in the labour market. They were joined, in New Zealand, by Maori as they migrated to the cities and by immigrants from the Pacific Islands. Feminist sociologists examined the participation of women in paid work, the nature of this work and the barriers that continued to exist – and challenged the widely-held perception that unpaid work was economically and socially insignificant. But even as the level of participation grew and new understandings began to emerge about unpaid work, the nature of work itself changed.

These changes reflected local political changes, especially the rise of policies inspired by **economic rationalism**, and the impact of global changes. The meaning and characteristics of paid work were transformed. Work still continues to define who we are, but employment is now much more likely to be insecure, contractual, casualised, part-time, and subject to regular and often disruptive changes than was the case previously. We have referred to the 'McDonaldisation' of employment elsewhere in this book, and it is a useful metaphor for describing both the nature of the labour market and how people are going to be employed. One of the effects of the 'McDonaldisation' of the workplace has been to underline the disadvantage faced by women and members of indigenous/ethnic minorities in gaining access to appropriate forms of paid employment. In recognition of the changes in paid work, sociologists are developing new understandings of what constitutes work, the involvement of particular groups in particular types of work, and how work itself is changing.

A critical influence on these changes has been the evolution of ownership and production in a global sense and the significant impact that this evolution has had on economies like that of New Zealand. Post-Fordism encapsulates some of these changes as the need for flexibility in machinery and workers overtakes the Fordist ideal of mass production, mass employment and mass consumption. In reality, Fordist production still exists but it is accompanied by a reliance on new forms of technology, de-skilling and de-industrialisation; the existence of huge multi-national companies and the migration of production in search of lower labour – and other – costs. If McDonaldisation describes casualised, poorly-paid work, it also represents the 'global brand' and 'just-in-time', standardised production. As the nature of production continues to evolve, it will contribute to further changes in paid and unpaid work.

> **Economic rationalism** is a political approach which assumes that society is determined, or should be, by individuals acting in their own economic interests (see also pp. 93 and 199).

? Study questions

7.1 Provide a definition of work that includes both paid and unpaid activities.

7.2 Which groups are most likely to be excluded or under-represented in paid employment? Has their participation improved or declined in recent decades?

7.3 What characterises the nature of paid work in both Fordist and post-Fordist economies or workplaces?

7.4 What are the most significant global changes in economic ownership and production, and what is their impact on New Zealand?

Further reading

Austrin, T. (1994) Work. In Spoonley, P., Pearson, D. and Shirley, I. (eds) *New Zealand Society: A Sociological Introduction*. Dunmore Press, Palmerston North.

Castells, M. (1996) *The Rise of the Network Society*. Blackwell, Cambridge, Ma.

Dicken, P. (1986) *Global Shift*. Harper and Row, New York.

Grint, K. (1998) *Sociology of Work: An Introduction*, 2nd ed. Polity Press, Cambridge.

Oakley, A. (1974) *The Sociology of Housework*. Blackwell, Oxford.

Salaman, G. (1987) *Working*. Tavistock, London.

Sayer, A. and Walker, R. (1992) *The New Social Economy*. Blackwell, Oxford.

8 Stratification and class

Chapter aims

- to explore contemporary patterns of stratification, including wealth and poverty, at both the local and the global level;
- to review the sociological debates about class, and the nature and significance of class in contemporary society;
- to discuss the nature of poverty and economic marginalisation, and to examine which groups have been most affected by these in recent decades.

 Introduction

This chapter examines the way in which sociology has regarded class as one of the most significant elements of inequality in any society, but particularly in industrial-capitalist societies, and how sociology has contributed to theories about class. Class represents one of the most important dimensions of inequality, or has done. The chapter then goes on to question whether the changing nature of production and ownership at both local and global levels now makes this particular concept, class, redundant. The **stratification** which is associated with gender or ethnicity has intensified, as has inequality in general, and the issue is how best to describe and analyse these enhanced (they are hardly new) forms of stratification.

Stratification refers to the hierarchical divisions of a society according to socially determined criteria or characteristics.

Stratification, class and inequality

When people meet for the first time, they tend to use certain markers or characteristics to classify others. Inherent in these evaluations are assessments about status; sometimes such assessments are subtle and relatively minor, at other times, they have major implications for the options available to an individual. This ranking, which places an individual within a particular group, and then the group within a particular hierarchy, reflects the stratification which prevails in any specific community or society. Without exception, societies are stratified, whether it be by age, gender, economic background or ethnicity, family lineage or achievements. Sociologists take the presence of stratification as a given, but then go on to argue about the exact nature and causes of stratification, whether it is desirable or not, and what should be done about it.

There are some characteristics of stratification which are reasonably obvious. Despite beliefs to the contrary, nearly all stratification is socially determined. It is a product of the beliefs of a particular community and the way in which these beliefs are reflected in social relationships and structures. This gives rise to a second characteristic of stratification. The beliefs are translated into practice and major institutions in a society – families, the organisation of work, political groups of all sorts, education or health – are structured around assumptions about inequality. Stratification has important consequences for the opportunities available to all of us, and for what we might expect by way of resources and status. The third characteristic is the way in which members of a group face much the same expectations, opportunities and barriers. Stratification works by identifying group membership and then applying much the same beliefs and behaviours to most if not all members of the group. In societies such as New Zealand, gender or ethnicity are important markers of group membership, and therefore are the basis for stratification. But the stratification that does result is not benign: it empowers some and dispossesses others. It results in inequality.

From the very beginnings of sociology during the industrial revolution, inequality has been a central focus for the discipline. The term implies a certain disapproval. For most sociologists, the presence of inequality is a matter of concern because of the way in which it marginalises significant numbers of people. It results from beliefs and behaviours which discriminate unfairly. It means poverty, ill-health, poor education and housing. Inequality has been a major political as well as theoretical focus of sociology. In the 1999 Reith lectures the eminent sociologist Anthony Giddens spoke on globalisation, and he argued that:

> Along with ecological risk, to which it is related, expanding inequality is the most serious problem facing world society.

What has become apparent in the latter part of the twentieth century is the growing polarisation between ethnic groups, young and old, rich and poor, both within nations and between nations. Whatever gains in reducing inequality had been achieved during the middle part of the century, they were being reversed by the end of the century – or new forms of inequality were emerging. In political terms, some saw this as inevitable and desirable because it encouraged individual responsibility – as opposed to state welfarism – and economic competitiveness. While certain sociologists agreed with this view, most did not, and some exciting theoretical positions emerged as sociology sought to understand the dynamics and significance of this inequality.

8 Stratification and class

The enduring nature of stratification

A standard position, at least traditionally, has been to argue that class has been the major form of inequality. Karl Marx has been a central figure in the development of sociology, and he argued that capitalism produced a new form of class relations with the conflict between the working class and the ruling class a paramount feature. This has been a persuasive and central strand in sociological theorising right up to the present, although there are some powerful competing approaches as well as those which have radically altered the tenets of a classical Marxism. Therefore, class, as a particular form of stratification which results in inequality, is a major theme in sociology. The question is whether class should retain its significance given changes in the nature of capitalist production with major changes to the nature of work at a local level and new forms of ownership and production on the world stage. Sociology has also developed more sophisticated understandings of the nature of inequality, and has devoted more attention to the inequalities which result from gender and ethnicity as distinct from those which result from class stratification. Whatever the focus, stratification and inequality remain central to sociological theory and research.

Differences and divisions: the significance of class

The concept of class is one of the big ideas that sociology has contributed to debates about the nature of capitalist societies. It derives in the first instance from the work of Karl Marx, and an alternative reading is provided by Max Weber. Both theorists and their arguments about class have been covered in the Chapters 2 and 3, and we will simply remind you of the main elements of their respective positions before discussing how their arguments have been updated to address late twentieth-century concerns and issues. There is also the question of how much significance we should continue to ascribe to class as a central theoretical focus within sociology.

Marx was interested in the way in which different modes of production operated, or the way in which societies organised the production and reproduction of their material basis. Class inequalities and conflict were not the preserve of capitalism but were to be found in all human societies. However, the specific nature of the relations of production changed with the different modes of production, giving rise to different forms of expropriation or exploitation, and a particular set of contradictions between the social relations of production (class/ownership relations) and the productive forces (the application of science/technology). Under capitalism, workers sold their labour power on the market and worked under conditions which led to the alienation of labour as workers became divorced from the products of their own labour. This tendency was reinforced by the need to intensify the processes of production as the ruling class sought to sustain the process of accumulation. Capitalism then became characterised by the impoverishment of the working class, both in terms of the return they might expect for their labour and the satisfaction they might get from the work that they did. As they developed an understanding of their position – class consciousness – any political activity would inevitably bring them into conflict with those who exercised power in a capitalist system, those who owned and managed the means of production, the bourgeoisie, and those from the middle class who saw their interests as aligned with those of the bourgeoisie.

These arguments about the nature of capitalism and class had a powerful influence on sociological understanding of social stratification. This was particularly the case in Europe where the conditions, both structural and ideological, were amenable to Marxist analysis. Industrialisation and urbanisation produced clear class distinctions in terms of community and work. In Germany or Britain, the working class lived in distinct communities, worked at jobs that were as Marx described, and believed in the need for working-class organisations and political goals – or at least they did until late in the twentieth century when certain aspects of their lives, most notably work itself and the strength of working-

Class was originally seen as a product of classical industrial capitalism

class organisations such as trade unions and labour political parties, began to change. Not only did sociologists describe the reality of life for many, they contributed to the politics of working-class resistance. But the persuasiveness of Marxist class analysis was less obvious in the new world of settler societies such as the United States, Australia and New Zealand. Here, the ambition of those arriving was often to escape the confines of the class societies they had left, and their political beliefs emphasised the **'classlessness'** of their new home. There was some truth to the statement that the places they had moved to were 'frontier societies' which provided opportunities that were seldom available in the densely populated and well-established societies of Europe. In Europe, the ruling class of one era (feudalism) had merged with the ruling class of capitalism to confirm their hegemony. Societies such as New Zealand were also prepared to experiment with democratic changes such as the enfranchisement of women or the provision of universal welfare. But this spirit of experimentation does not adequately explain the differences, especially since European societies also adopted such measures, and at times went

Classlessness is the ideological position that either class does not exist or that it is not important in a given society.

much further in areas such as the welfare state. The more compelling argument derives from the lack of class-based traditions in the new settler societies and from the ideological belief that class was not relevant to these societies.

These views have been reflected in the approach of sociologists. Despite the presence of British-trained sociologists in New Zealand, there have been few who could be described as Marxists in a classical sense. One has been David Bedggood who has maintained a traditional Marxist analysis of class over some decades. His book, *Rich and Poor in New Zealand. A Critique of Class, Politics and Ideology*, which was published in 1980, provides a standard Marxist 'science of society'. He examines the emergence of a colonial class structure and what he refers to as 'the development of capitalist manufacturing ... established by means of the intense exploitation of domestic and wage workers' (Bedggood, 1980: 14). A number of elements are interesting as Bedggood adapts Marxism to explain the colonisation of New Zealand, the incorporation of Maori into the working class and the presence of a welfare state. He argues, however, that the welfare state was 'not a victory for the working-class' but rather a means by which the 'capitalist state was able to persuade the labour movement and the Labour Party to administer its own exploitation, redistributing taxation (or gross wages) to the capitalist class by cheapening the cost of labour and other "inputs"' (Bedggood, 1980: 15). This represents a form of Marxism that has been labelled 'vulgar', and it has not provided a particularly convincing explanation in the New Zealand context.

In contrast to this there is a neo-Marxist approach that is derived from the work of Erik Wright. Wright is still interested in issues of exploitation and domination, but has sought to provide a methodology which enables class to be identified in a contemporary setting, whether this is New Zealand or elsewhere. This methodology centres on asking four questions which then identify the four main classes – owners, self-employed, middle class, and workers – in a class-relational model. In contrast to Bedggood, New Zealand advocates of this approach such as Wilkes (1994) stress the political and economic significance of the middle class in the twentieth century; what he refers to as domestic labour; the fragmentation of classes (class fractions); and the significance of ideological relations. The four questions relate to whether a person owns his or her own business, whether he/she purchases the labour of others, whether he/she occupies a managerial/supervisory position and whether he/she is paid wages or a salary. Wilkes explicitly acknowledges the changing nature of production, from Fordism to post-Fordism, and the myth of classlessness, including the absence of class analysis from the intellectual agenda in the post-war period (Wilkes, 1994: 79). Even if this is a more persuasive account of class in a local context, it still has not produced a strong tradition of class analysis and understanding. There remains a reluctance – as much among sociologists as amongst a wider public – to see class as a central defining characteristic of New Zealand.

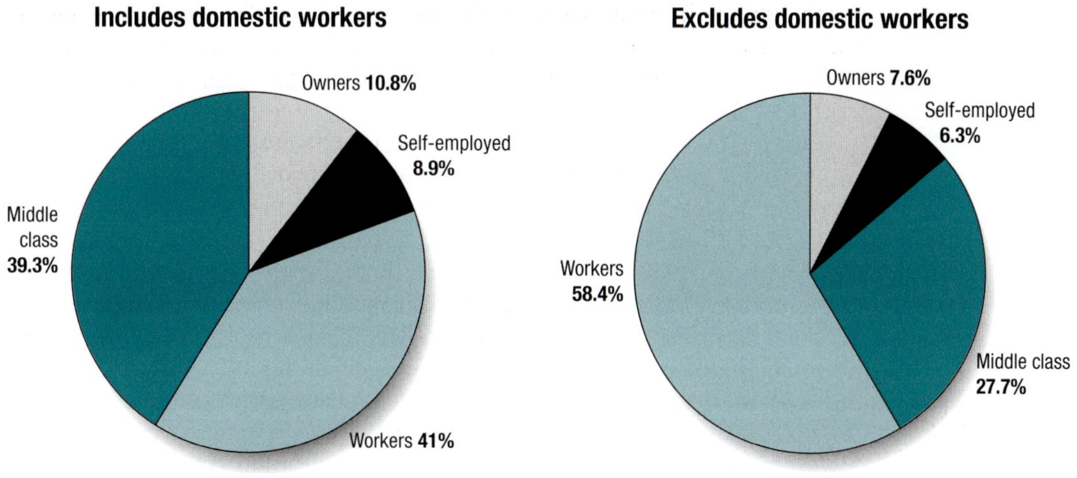

Includes domestic workers

Owners **10.8%**

Self-employed **8.9%**

Middle class **39.3%**

Workers **41%**

Excludes domestic workers

Owners **7.6%**

Self-employed **6.3%**

Workers **58.4%**

Middle class **27.7%**

Figure 8.1 New Zealand's class map, according to Chris Wilkes (mid-1990s)

The alternative in both a classical and contemporary sense is provided by a Weberian approach. Weber was not convinced by Marx's analysis of class and he provided a more diffuse definition of class, adding party and status as co-equal characteristics to be considered. Class was only one basis for inequality, and moreover, class was determined by the processes of the market as well as by position in the mode of production. Weber agreed that class was economically determined but status or party could be just as important and they reflected – or could do – non-economic factors. For instance, ethnicity is an example of a status that can determine life chances including economic rewards and position. Here, an ideological consideration can overrule the economic significance of class.

Neo-Weberians such as David Thorns, Peter Davis and David Pearson have contributed another approach to class or, more accurately, to inequality in New Zealand. Peter Davis (1982a; 1982b) talks of *life chances* and *lifestyles*, two concepts which indicate the interest in non-economic class characteristics, and he demonstrates that while health status is a function of class, there is also a factor that is related to a non-class matter, namely ethnicity. David Thorns, the author of the insert for this chapter, demonstrates the neo-Weberian interest in the middle class and the significance of consumption as opposed to the focus on production which characterises Marxism. In this particular case, Thorns looks at home ownership patterns as an important dimension of wealth distribution and a contributor to inequality.

Despite the fact that class is one of the enduring themes of sociology, it does not follow that this theme has necessarily been very important in the analysis of particular societies. New Zealand is a case in point. In the post-war period, there have been few examples of a convincing class analysis. One reason is the predominance of beliefs about the classlessness of New Zealand, but there are also other reasons. A powerful one has been the political and sociological significance of non-class forms of inequality, notably those based on gender and ethnicity. Post-war feminism, which has been a powerful player in New Zealand both sociologically and politically, has been disdainful of any class analysis which treats gender issues as reducible to a crude economic argument. The case is convincing when the class analysis in question assumes a particular model of household composition – including a male breadwinner; when there is not adequate acknowledgement of the gendered distribution of work and status; when there is an assumption of the same class position for both partners; or of the fact that class automatically takes precedence over gender. Gender and ethnic inequality, and explanations which are capable of dealing with non-class bases of inequality, have come to play a major role in sociological practice in the late twentieth century, displacing more conventional class analyses.

Class versus consumption

David Thorns

Theories of stratification have had as their objective the explanation of the causes of social inequality and the nature of systems of classes or other social groupings that have formed around particular levels of inequality. Such groupings may or may not be conscious of their position and therefore there has been a continuing debate regarding class consciousness and the extent to which class position forms the basis for social and political action.

The majority of the theories of stratification which have dominated sociology – Marxian, Weberian and Functionalist – have centred their concerns around economic inequality and seen the labour market as the chief source of wealth generation. This preoccupation with paid work has drawn considerable criticism in the last decade or so from feminist writers as it ignores the contribution women make to wealth generation through labour which does not receive payment.

As capitalist-industrial societies have developed over the course of the twentieth century, early predictions that the pattern of inequality would polarise around a dichotomous structure have proved to be unfounded and this has led to a theoretical concern for 'intermediate groups or middle-classes'. The structure of inequality has taken on a more fragmentary and fluid nature and there is a growing debate as to whether stratification in fact occurs at the point of production, i.e. in the labour market, or whether it is shaped more by consumption – spending patterns and lifestyle differences. This has led some writers to claim that the new 'fault lines' in contemporary society relate to consumption sector cleavages rather than production-based class differences (Saunders, 1990).

An area of research and debate that has contributed to this wider discussion regarding production versus consumption has been the one centred around the role that domestic property ownership has played. Home ownership provides the possibility of wealth creation for many people in societies where this form of tenure is available. The house one owns provides an alternative basis of wealth generation from employment in the labour market. Some writers have suggested that a 'family may gain more from the housing market in a few years than would be possible in savings from a lifetime of earnings' (Pahl, 1975: 291). Under some conditions, for example where there is price inflation at a rate greater than the Consumer Price Index, house owners can amass considerable real wealth which can then either be stored in the house as capital gain or used to enhance consumption expenditure through remortgaging and other similar equity release schemes. Such opportunities are clearly denied to the tenant of either public or private housing. Furthermore, house owners have an asset that their heirs are able to dispose of on their death. Consequently, the role that the inheritance of property-based wealth plays in the maintenance of or change to patterns of social inequality has also become an issue that has attracted the attention of researchers.

New Zealand is an interesting place to consider this particular debate as we have been a predominantly home-owning nation for most of the twentieth century. Currently, more than 70% of the population participates in this kind of tenure. The first question to explore is whether owner occupation has been a source of real income for New Zealand home owners. The answer is that it has – for some! The most dynamic period has been that of the last thirty years. Data produced by the Reserve Bank show that real returns from housing from 1961 through to the mid-1980s varied between 9.7% and 25% for people holding government mortgages and 1.7% and 21% for people holding private mortgages (Thorns, 1992). The higher rate for those with government mortgages arises from the presence of subsidised interest rates through the State Advances and later the Housing Corporation, indicating the strength of the state commitment to assisting people into home ownership.

The rate of return achieved by home owners compares very favourably with the returns that could have been obtained through alternative investment in the share market – varying from 0.9% to 1.8% – and from bank deposits – varying between 1.7% and 5.4%. However, these overall rates disguise the fact that the rate of return is very much linked to the point of measurement in the cycle of booms and slumps in the housing market that occurred in the 1970s and 1980s, and to the actual location of the property both regionally and locally. If the outcomes do vary quite substantially depending on place and time, is it possible to think of home owners as a single category (Dupuis and Thorns, 1997)?

New Zealand data have raised quite serious questions about the link between tenure and class situation which has been suggested – particularly in the British literature. The critique has been based on the uneven nature of the capital gains which have occurred and the extent to which this has reinforced other forms of privilege rather than creating greater levelling or equality. Research has shown that capital gains have been greatest in the wealthiest areas of the major cities, and that the major cities, especially Auckland, Wellington and Christchurch have been better places to buy property than regional centres such as Napier, Gisborne, Timaru and Invercargill. Furthermore, in the 1970s, 1980s and 1990s the gap between property values in Auckland and those in the rest of the country has increased. In early 1997, for example, the average Auckland house price was more than $300 000, compared to just more than $200 000 in Wellington, $160 000 in Christchurch and $84 000 in Invercargill. Given these differences, ownership per se is clearly not decreasing the extent of inequality but in fact contributes to its growth as the rate of wealth generation in Auckland is clearly much faster than in the South Island. The impact of this on geographic and occupational mobility are quite significant, making it much more expensive for South Islanders to move to Auckland than for the reverse to take place.

The possibility of gain thus exists through tenure for owner-occupiersand not for tenants. This creates a group that is excluded, whose ability to generate wealth is more restricted and whose capacity to assist a subsequent generation via bequeathing is more limited. The second major dimension of the debate has been the one surrounding the distribution of the wealth generated via inheritances. The British literature here has been the most enthusiastic about the possibilities of home ownership creating a more even distribution of wealth. However, empirical evidence is now accumulating to show that housing wealth tends to stay in the immediate family. For example, the study by Hamnett, Harmer and Williams in 1990 found that the majority of housing wealth was transferred to members of the immediate family, principally to the surviving spouse if any (48.3%) or to the children (22.9%). Further, it showed that inheritances were generally received in mid-life (most commonly by people over 50) when the recipients were already established in their housing and occupational careers (Hamnett, Harmer and Williams, 1990).

New Zealand data show a similar pattern, with property going to the surviving spouse (64%) or children (20%). These figures indicate a very low level of movement of accumulated wealth outside the immediate family circle, which suggests that such inheritance money is more likely to reinforce the current position of the family within the social structure than change it (Thorns, 1995; Dupuis, 1997). One factor which affects the amount accumulated but which has not been well-documented in the overseas literature is the necessity to use a greater proportion of accumulated assets to maintain oneself during a longer period of retirement. In the 1990s the changes made by the National Government to the asset testing regimes for elderly people in public hospitals has further increased the probability that a proportion of the accumulated wealth will be consumed during retirement and therefore that the amount to be handed on to the family after the death of the owner will be less.

A further local influence is the fact that many New Zealanders do a substantial amount of their own home maintenance; as they get older, their capacity to do this decreases and this can result in the value of their property falling rather than rising.

What this brief review of some of the elements and data generated in the debate about production versus consumption as bases for inequality has shown is that it is possible, through owner occupation of housing, to generate increased wealth for the owners. Home ownership does therefore separate people out on the basis of their tenure status and give them different sets of real interest. Owner-occupiers are, for example, much more interested than tenants in the booms and slumps of the housing market and in interest rates movements. There is therefore a prima facie case for the argument that tenure provides the basis for group formation and the generation of common political interest. However, this is a simplistic view because when the category of owner-occupiers is subjected to further analysis it is quite clear that it is a disparate category with considerable diversity of experience across all home owners. Sources of this diversity include the time at which the property was acquired or relinquished, the location of the property both within the specific urban locality as well as within the region, and the present and past labour market position of the household. Insufficient attention has also been paid to the ethnic and gender dimensions of differences in owner occupation and housing wealth accumulation. For example, in New Zealand the rate of home ownership for the population as a whole is 75% but for Maori the rate is 55%. Women have less wealth than men and a greater proportion of their wealth is held by the over-60s; this reflects the fact that women have greater longevity than men.

Questions

David Thorns offers a critique of some classical sociological approaches to stratification and class, and highlights the significance of contemporary patterns of consumption, specifically home ownership.

1   What characterises David Thorns's approach to stratification and class as neo-Weberian?

2   How does domestic property ownership contribute to class distinctions? Is it more important, or as important, as ownership of the means of production?

3   Who is most likely to be excluded from domestic property ownership or – at least – wealth-creating property ownership?

4   Do common housing circumstances produce collective political interests and organisations? Provide some examples.

The social and the personal: wealth and poverty

One of the enduring social policy concerns of the twentieth century has been the presence of poverty. Sociology has contributed to the debate about poverty and what should be done about it, most notably under the social contract which existed in most Western countries in the post-war era and which accepted the need for some form of the welfare state. The economic reforms that were ushered in by economic rationalist governments in the 1980s helped redefine the causes of poverty (individual inadequacy) but they have also contributed to growing levels of poverty. The question of who is most likely to be poor and who is most likely to be wealthy is now back on the research and policy agenda. These are bread-and-butter questions for sociologists, although there is a wide range of answers, especially when it comes to what is the most appropriate policy response.

The question – what is poverty? – now has a reasonably standard answer. Absolute poverty is defined as the absence of those things – food, shelter – which an individual needs to remain alive. Absolute poverty threatens an individual's chances of staying alive. Relative poverty is a measure which asks what is deemed to be an acceptable standard of living in a given society and then sets a benchmark below which it is considered that people do not have those services or resources that are essential in some sense. Running water or adequate heating, particularly for the elderly or young children, can be regarded as evidence of relative poverty. In New Zealand, the notion of relative poverty is the one that is mostly used. However, what constitutes 'poverty' is a highly charged question which almost inevitably is used by community agencies, social service providers and political parties to argue for or against particular measures to address the needs of the poor. Two questions arise. How best can poverty be identified and measured? Who are the poor?

There are some landmark studies of poverty. Townsend (1979) explored **relative deprivation**, a variation on relative poverty, and noted that up to half the population in the UK were likely to experience relative deprivation at some point in their lives. They did not have access to those things which were accepted as 'customary' or 'widely encouraged or approved' (Townsend, 1979: 31). What is defined as 'poverty' in such an approach has been criticised because of its seemingly arbitrary or generous nature, especially if televisions or phones are seen as 'customary', and the absence of either is seen as an indication of relative deprivation. As one way of countering these criticisms, sociologists have used the level of income as a benchmark, and anyone who falls below a particular level, and therefore can not afford basic requirements such as food, adequate housing, or medical care is defined as being below subsistence and therefore below the poverty line. This has been the approach adopted in New Zealand, and Easton (1995) has provided an interesting discussion

---

Relative deprivation is the idea developed by Peter Townsend that it is possible to establish what is considered essential or normal in terms of living standards, and who are therefore deprived because they do not have access to these accepted resources.

on how to draw the poverty line (the 1972 Royal Commission on Social Security suggested the income set for a couple on the 'pension' represented a minimum level) and on the numbers below it (485 000 to 593 000 in 1991/92). What is also apparent is the increasing number of people who are below or just on this poverty line. This is confirmed by sociological studies which have examined the distribution of wealth over recent decades. In the USA, 80% of working Americans' incomes fell by 18% in the period 1973 to 1995 which, translated into dollar amounts, means that $200 billion which used to go to the bottom three-fifths of Americans now goes to the top one-fifth (Gray, 1998b: 114). Similar trends are apparent in New Zealand. In the 16 years after the economic reforms which began in 1984, the top 5% of households increased their share of the national wealth; the next 15% held their own while the bottom 80% are worse off (Chatterjee in Campbell, 1998: 18). The distribution of wealth is becoming more unequal and the numbers of people in poverty are growing.

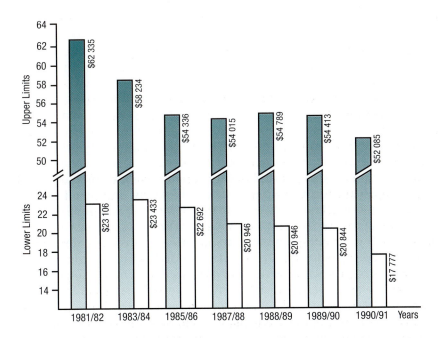

13% reduction in household incomes over a 10-year period
Graph shows the upper and lower limits of the mid-income range

Source: Social Welfare Department (1993) *Income Monitoring Report 1981/1991.*

Figure 8.2 Growing poorer – how middle-range incomes declined, 1981–1991

Who is most likely to be poor? The profile of the poor tends not to vary too much from country to country, at least in the Western world. In terms of households, disproportionate numbers of particular types are more likely to fall below the poverty line. These include single-parent families or those with large numbers of children (six or more), along with those households which are benefit dependent. Often size (single-parent or large families) and a reliance on a benefit income are a lethal combination leading to intergenerational poverty. The changes to economies and labour markets have produced work-poor households, or households which lack a history of involvement in adequately paid work. The poorly paid, of which there are growing numbers, constitute an important group, especially when their circumstances are made even more marginal by changes to welfare provisions, and specifically by a much tighter regulatory environment – i.e. 'tighter' in terms of who is able to receive a benefit. For similar reasons, the elderly also constitute a growing proportion of the poor. Early retirement, the lack of adequate personal resources and income combined with less generous state-provided retirement benefits, and the costs of being elderly (medical costs, reduced mobility, appropriate heating and housing) all have produced greater levels of poverty for the elderly. Poverty is also associated with ethnicity. Being a migrant, especially semi-skilled or unskilled, or a member of disadvantaged indigenous or ethnic minority, tends to be associated with higher levels of poverty. Gray (1998b: 117) talks of *Brazilianization*, a term that was coined by Michael Lind to discuss the way in which classes are separated by 'race', with the emphasis on racial disadvantage. This is very apparent in New Zealand, especially in terms of the situation of Maori and Pacific Islanders.

Whatever the measure – rates of ill-health, income levels, benefit dependence, educational performance, access to paid work – Maori and Pacific Islanders are significantly disadvantaged compared to national averages, and are routinely found in the worst-off categories. For example, Pakeha earn 7% more than the average New Zealand salary, while Pacific Islanders earn 50% and Maori 28% less (Chatterjee in Campbell, 1998: 18). Over 40% of Maori households are single-parent ones while nearly half of Maori households are benefit dependent. This is significantly different to the profile of other ethnic groups, with the exception of Pacific Islanders, and it indicates an ethnic underclass – that is, the coincidence of poverty and ethnicity. Pool (1991) demonstrates that this is not some passing moment, but that it has now become embedded in the contemporary experience for Maori with non-participation in the major wealth-creating institutions of New Zealand such as education and paid employment and with substantial intergenerational implications. Weberians talk of life chances, or the opportunity to gain access to those resources and institutions which can enhance status and quality of life. One example of such resources is appropriate education. But 40% of Maori leave school with no qualifications; they constitute 42% of those suspended or expelled from school, they are less than half as likely to obtain UE or bursary, and there has been no improvement in terms of Maori gaining sixth and seventh form qualifications since 1992 (Corbett et al., 1998: H3). Their life chances in terms of the benefits of a society that values educational credentials are poor. Maori represent one particular group that is likely to be poor, and that has noticeably lost ground since the 1980s.

Inevitably, the claim that there are more poor, that there is a definite poverty line and that certain groups are likely to be found near it or below it, is contested. It represents a failure of political management and social service delivery. It is seen as an indictment of a society, especially when it is compared to some international ranking such as a comparison with other OECD countries. It is one of the more political interventions that sociology can make, particularly when measures of poverty can be defended as methodologically robust and acceptable in a populist sense, even if they are not always politically acceptable. Poverty has profound implications for the quality of life experienced by particular groups, and sociology helps provide a human dimension to disadvantage. In this way, it fulfils its humanitarian tradition.

The local and the global: the changing dimensions of stratification and class

Changes in the world economy (especially in the nature of economic production and ownership), the focus of domestic policy in many countries on a reduced welfare state and the increased reliance on individual competitiveness in a market-driven economy, have had major implications for the nature of stratification and class.

For much of the mid-part of the twentieth century, and up until the 1980s, social policy and the economy complemented each other in many regards, with mass employment giving security to people (Glennerster, 1998: 11) and generating revenue for redistribution. In countries such as New Zealand, economic prosperity, the welfare state and full employment provided the basis for household and individual security, and a softening of class distinctions and significant inequality. But all of this changed substantially in the last two decades of the twentieth century, with the result that there is growing polarisation both within and between countries. The implications of this polarisation for class politics are not entirely clear, although the impact that it has had on some particular classes has already dramatically altered the standard of living and opportunities for many.

We have already referred to the exacerbation in unequal wealth distribution, in the 1980s and 1990s with those at the top gaining more of the national share and those at the bottom either remaining static or losing their percentage share. For many in the latter category, this was most obvious in the labour market as full employment gave way to casualised work and lower rates of pay. The impact of new technologies and an increasingly global labour market meant that tax resources were 'spent on rescuing the growing groups of poor people through cash benefits' (Glennerster, 1998: 11). Not only were greater levels of wealth transfer and welfare services required, but services such as health care and education were coming under attack for what was regarded as their poor quality of service. This presented an opportunity in many countries for a new regulatory and administrative approach to welfare, and the relative generosity of earlier decades was superseded by targeted and more strictly administered benefits and services. There was also a growing emphasis on individuals and households being responsible for carrying the cost of individual provision, especially in areas such as health care and education. The wealth transfers that had dampened inequality were being discarded, with the result that new levels of wealth disparity and poverty appeared. This was exacerbated by the lack of paid employment.

The de-industrialisation of significant regional and national economies and the McDonaldisation of employment – its casualised, low-paid, part-time nature – contributed to the creation of jobs that paid net wages that were often below the level of benefit incomes (Field, 1997: 30). As Field goes on to observe, in the 1970s, 14 000 Merseyside dockers handled 17 million tonnes of goods but by the 1990s, 400 dockers were responsible for 30 million tonnes. The traditional sources of income and employment were replaced, if they were replaced at all, by service industries. Jobs were simply no longer available for semi-skilled and unskilled workers, especially since, increasingly, those who were involved, were women entering the labour market. As Glennerster (1998) notes, paid employment is the 'essence of social security and dignity in our sort of society'. But employment in manufacturing and primary production disappeared and the new weightless economy appeared – weightless because it involves activities that are difficult to measure, with products that are often intangible. This economy includes growth in computing-related activities, telecommunications, biotechnology and entertainment (Coyle, 1997: 24). It has also forced more people to become active in the informal economy of undeclared earnings, unofficial employment and unofficial production. A whole new vocabulary, often politically inspired to justify what was happening, emerged. The emphasis on flexibility and individual competitiveness, along with attacks on the 'nanny state', that marked the era of Thatcher, Reagan and Roger Douglas has been replaced by action zones, clusters, stakeholding and the decent society. In reality, the words can not hide the fact that both economic and social inequality have grown substantially in this period of change.

New Zealand experienced one of the more radical experiments in economic reform. The neo-liberal experiment in New Zealand is the most ambitious attempt at constructing the free market as a social institution to be implemented anywhere this century ... Among the many novel effects of neo-liberal policy in New Zealand has been the creation of an underclass in a country that did not have one before.

(Gray, 1998b: 39)

Certainly, New Zealand has experienced the greatest increase in income inequality in the industrial world during this period (Joseph Rowntree Foundation, 1995). The marked wealth disparities of other countries are now a reality locally, and the nature of disadvantage, whether it is lack of adequate employment, housing, health or education, is now much more obvious. It has had an impact on the dimensions of class.

As elsewhere, the globalisation of production and de-industrialisation have contributed to the decline of what would have been considered working class jobs. It has given rise to one of the paradoxes of this period, jobless growth, with the effects obvious in the semi-skilled and unskilled sectors of the labour market. Along with the stripping out of jobs for the working class has been the collapse of working-class organisations such as trade unions, and a growing distance between working-class communities and their once traditional working-class political representatives, the Labour parties. Even the traditional bastions of working-class political dominance – at least in name – the economies of Eastern and Central Europe, have collapsed into what Gray (1998b: 135, 148) calls *anarchic capitalism*, with a halving of Russia's recorded economy in the decade after 1989. In these former Communist economies as well as those in the West which have undergone extensive restructuring since the 1980s, there are those who are excluded from employment and from adequate welfare support, and there is a much more obvious and extensive underclass. They are the new excluded – excluded from basic requirements such as minimal health and education services, as well as from adequate income and employment. They often deserve the evocative label of Marxism, the *lumpenproletariat*. Quite how they are likely to act politically or to be represented appropriately in liberal democratic societies is not clear. The arguments of classical Marxism do not seem to apply, and understandings which deal with global and local changes will be needed to analyse what is happening to the working class and a new underclass.

Lumpenproletariat is the somewhat derogatory term used by Marx to identify those below or outside the working class.

If there have been changes to the nature of the working class, there have also been changes that have had an impact upon the middle class. Gray (1998b) talks of the reversal of **embourgeoisement**.

Embourgeoisement refers to the process of becoming like or part of the middle class, typically in reference to the working class.

> The middle classes are rediscovering the conditions of assetless economic insecurity that afflicted the nineteenth-century proletariat … the incomes of middle-class Americans remain much higher that those of working people then or now. Even so, in their ever greater dependency on uncertain jobs, the American middle classes resemble the classic proletariat of nineteenth-century Europe.
>
> (Gray, 1998b: 111)

Affluence and employment has been eroded by insecurity and middle-class unemployment, even in the formerly safe areas of the highly qualified professionals. There is even some evidence in countries such as New Zealand of middle-class poverty. New Zealand research shows that the middle band of income earners slipped from a range of between $62 335 and $23 106 in the 1980s to one of between $52 085 and $17 777 in the 1990s (Chapple, 1994). These are adjusted figures so they represent a decline in the collective purchasing power and security of some in the middle classes in New Zealand. Moreover, people in the middle classes do not have the same level of subsidy or support from the state as they did in earlier decades, with more of a middle-class household's disposable income going on education and health spending.

The middle class has grown in size and diversity as the natural workers and employers of the service economy, but it has also experienced considerable disturbances to its security. Politically powerful, middle-class people have been unable to counter global influences or to protect their relatively affluent status or privilege.

Conclusion

Thorns's contribution to this chapter highlights the way in which the classical Marxist interest in stratification and class has had to be modified in the light of the developments of the twentieth century. The impact of welfare policies and the welfare state, the evolving nature of capitalist-industrial economies and production, especially in terms of the nature of paid work, the significance of women in wealth generation, the growth of the middle class and the increase in its political and economic power and the importance of consumption have all challenged the Marxist conception of a dichotomous class structure, and the realisation of unified class action. An adequate or convincing explanation of the contemporary nature of stratification needs to incorporate these elements, and Thorns provides one option, a neo-Weberian approach, which accords much more significance to the cleavages associated with consumption, rather than production-based class differences. Neo-Marxists have addressed similar issues but with a continued focus on the economic distinctions which derive from a location in the means of production.

In recent decades, interesting questions have arisen about the extent of changes to global and local societies as ownership and production have been transformed. A variety of descriptions has been used to illustrate the nature of these changes. What is clear is that the inequalities that marked the post-war decades – inequalities that were softened by the welfare state, active and affluent economies and full employment, at least in the West – are now being intensified. Inequality is growing in countries like New Zealand in the wake of an experiment with economic rationalism, and the degree and nature of polarisation has changed. Age, regional location, ethnicity, gender and participation in paid employment are all important characteristics in defining the new poverty and the growing degree of inequality. The very nature of production, ownership and control has changed, more so in some industries than others, along with the nature of labour markets and access to income, whether from the state in the form of benefits or from employment. Stratification has never been off the political or sociological agenda but the intensification of inequality has made it one of the major policy and humanitarian issues both within and between countries.

The remaining question is whether class is the most appropriate concept to use in analysing the stratification which now exists. Class has a long and honourable history in the discipline of sociology. The nature of class and its political significance has been intensely debated, but the presence of the concept has been one of the markers of the sociological tradition. However, class is associated with the emergence of a particular form of industrial capitalism, and with the nature of inequality based around ownership and labour in the means of production. Is such an approach and the concept of class still useful in describing the different world of the twenty-first century? Can the notion of class be rescued and modified to address the nature of social relations and economic production adequately? The answers to these questions rather depend on the sociological inclinations of those answering the questions and on whether they regard the changes of recent decades as so fundamental that existing concepts such as class are past their use-by date.

? Study questions

8.1 Why should sociologists focus on stratification? What is the most important form of stratification in contemporary New Zealand?

8.2 How has class been defined by Marxists and Weberians? What are the main differences between the two traditions?

8.3 How has stratification and class changed in the latter part of the twentieth century?

Further reading

Edgell S. (1993) *Class*. Routledge, London.

Morris, L. (1994) *Dangerous Classes: The Underclass and Social Citizenship*. Routledge, London.

Scott, J. (1996) *Stratification and Power: Structures of Class, Status and Command*. Polity Press, Oxford.

Wilkes, C. (1994) Class, in Spoonley, P., Pearson, D. and Shirley, I. (eds). *New Zealand Society: A Sociological Introduction*. Dunmore Press, Palmerston North.

Wright, E.O. (1985) *Classes*. Verso, London.

9 Politics, state and nation

Chapter aims

- to discuss the role of power, the state and national identity in social and personal life;
- to compare theories of neo-liberalism, Marxism, pluralism and feminism on the role of the state in constructing social divisions;
- to explore the future of the nation state in the context of processes of globalisation.

> **Power** can be defined as our capacity as human beings to act, to influence the actions of others and to shape the processes of interaction between people. Structural power refers to the powers of the state and dominant social groups.

> **The state** is the political apparatus that rules over a given territorial space through law, as well as having the monopoly over the legitimate use of force.

 ## Introduction

This chapter explores the interconnections between power, the state and the nation. The state's use of power is an important structural element of societies and here we examine how this power shapes our lives. Marxist, pluralist and feminist theories about the nature of state power will be reviewed. We also examine the nation – both its place within the global economy, and, at the everyday level, our identification with particular national identities.

 ## Power and the state

Power can be defined as our capacity as human beings to *act*, to influence the action of *others*, and to shape processes of *interaction* between people. In that sense, just about everyone has a certain degree of power, by virtue of being embodied agents and members of society. This 'micro' notion of power – the power relations that exist between various people, every day, everywhere, in all social relationships – provides limitless material for sociological exploration. Sociologists have also traditionally been concerned to develop a narrower sense of 'structural power'. Structural power in society is twofold. First of all there is the simple fact that (in Max Weber's terms) it is **the state** that has the 'monopoly of legitimate violence' in modern societies. Even in democratic states, governments ultimately rely on the presence of sheer force: if you drive on the wrong side of the road you will be fined – or jailed; if you take up violence against the state, this will be met by authoritative, organised and official violence.

The second form of structural power is that arising from the social positions of different groups in society. It is sometimes said, for example, that there is one law for the rich and another for the poor, that men have all the power and women do not, that immigrants are condemned to be 'second-class citizens', and so on. Power in the structural sense is therefore related to the way in which systematic *social inequalities* arise in a society, and it concerns the way in which the state facilitates or mediates social relationships under its supervision. Sociologists are always on the lookout for overlaps in the different forms of structural power, and the cumulative inequalities that they tend to produce, because such patterns of control tell us a great deal about the essential characteristics of particular societies, and can alert us to the ways in which those societies might fundamentally *change* over time.

The social and the personal: Big Brother, and national 'belonging'

In 1948 the English social-democratic writer George Orwell produced his famous novel *Nineteen Eighty-four*. It is a chilling fictional portrait of a totalitarian state, and although Orwell was clearly targeting the Communist and Fascist regimes of the 1930s and '40s, he also felt strongly that many of the features of state oppression that he identified could just as well apply to aspects of the liberal democratic states of the 'free world'. Amongst the memorable dimensions of the state depicted by Orwell were the following:

- a 'secret' and conspiratorial state apparatus of coercion, lying behind the benign, all-pervasive image of Big Brother (the idea in the book is that the people believe this figure, mistakenly, to be a real person, someone who is always looking after everyone's best interests);
- an all-powerful bureaucracy, producing its own language (Newspeak) which is able to justify almost anything that the state rulers are doing (e.g. the slogan 'War is Peace');
- a media propaganda machine (under the 'Ministry of Truth') which engages in systematic disinformation;
- an underclass of oppressed people ('the Proles') who have neither the means nor the motivation to engage in organised rebellion;
- an extensive process of 'thought control', directed at the middle strata and state functionaries rather than the Proles, involving rewriting history and the deliberate confusion of truth and falsehood (Doublethink);
- a sophisticated public philosophy of the good society, to which the top rulers constantly pay lip service, but which they neither believe in, nor ever try to put into practice.

Orwell's picture is obviously a bleak one! He is taking to fictional extremes the rather cynical view that the objective of power, especially state power, is more power; indeed, that it is *total* power. Orwell himself was not a complete cynic – he was really trying to alarm us into fundamental change, by asking, 'has it really come to *this*?' What are we to think about these issues today, when the official date given by Orwell to his speculative 'future' has already come and gone? On the one hand, the picture certainly has not in any complete sense 'come true'. Nevertheless, the challenge of a novel like this is to single out and exaggerate certain *trends*, and to remind us that even when we are sociologising, we too are ourselves individually *subject* to the power of state machines. Orwell's scenario gives us some compelling images of the state from the point of view of our individual *subjectivity* (i.e. our sense of self and identity), thus fitting in very well with our theme, 'the social and the personal'.

The state is one of the primary 'facts of life' in modern societies, impressing upon us that we are *social* creatures, and making it blindingly obvious that society is more than the sum of its component individuals. And in that sense, 'the social', as embodied in 'the state', has a very strong and potentially *oppressive* effect on ourselves as individual persons. After all, the state officially certifies our birth, and we are not officially dead until registered as such by the state. We cannot drive cars unless we follow the rules of the road as set by the state. Our redundancy payments vary according to variations in state policy. Our schooling system is predominantly state-run, and even if it were to be greatly privatised, this would still be a decision made by the Ministry of Education. There is the 'democratic state' of governments and elections which appears to follow the collective wishes of citizens, but there is also the 'secret state' of phone taps, lists of 'subversives' and other surveillance mechanisms, of 'emergency' measures, paramilitary policing and hidden bunkers in the event of nuclear catastrophe. The state regulates – or decides to de-regulate – our transport options, our dietary health, the air we breath, our 'cultural safety', and our superannuation entitlements. The state taxes us without our permission, and, if it wanted, it could still call upon us to make the ultimate sacrifice – to die for our country.

So far, we have been emphasising the oppressive powers of the state (= the social) over the individual (= the personal). But we also need to see the other side of this coin. Is it *bad* that we follow common rules of the road? Or that we have a standardised and fair education system? And would we expect governments to *broadcast* plans for military or civil emergency? Would we wish new schools, new roads, and health services to be paid out of a public purse filled only with the dollars of tax-paying *volunteers* perhaps? In fact, is not the very reason for having a state to give it *unusual* powers of compulsion? And if the state did not exist, would not powerful individuals and privileged groups simply take over the running of things in their own selfish interests?

These are intended as rhetorical questions – we only have to speak them out loud to know the answer most people would probably give.

When, therefore, we consider 'the social and the personal' as a sociological theme, it is important to see this relationship as a two-way thing: there are social *constraints* upon personal life, certainly, but this has also been seen as the necessary *condition* of civilised personal life. The state constrains and even oppresses the individual, but the state also enables individuals to do things that might otherwise be impossible.

Why do we accept the legitimacy of the nation state? This is partly a matter of sheer coercion – if we didn't pay taxes, we would go to prison. Partly, it is a matter of common humanity – if we didn't drive on the prescribed side of the road, innocent people would probably get killed. But we also tend to see the nation state as legitimate because we have been *socialised* into doing so. The reality of the state has become *our* reality, and we adjust our life strategies accordingly, imbibing at least some of the self-imagery of state and society. Thus, for example, many people regard the democratic state as a 'good thing' – or at least as not a bad thing – simply because it has become very familiar to us over time. It has become 'normal' to do things in the way that democratic states in a capitalist society need things to be done. This produces powerful psychological pressures to see **liberal democracy** as good and right, and thus many people come to see themselves as reasonably content citizens of liberal democratic states.

Moreover, we are bombarded every day with a barrage of social 'representations' which confirm our nation state as the 'normal' one, and our individual role within it as a 'natural' one. These representations include images and messages from the mass media, and some of them are actively propagated by the state itself. Above all, the discourse of *nationhood* is an extremely powerful one, and one that is being carried to us in myriad ways: the country-specific point of view of news programmes, government announcements and parliamentary debates, images of the 'essential' New Zealand in tourist brochures and TV ads, popular discussions of the deeds and merits of our country's sporting teams, bulletins about the national economy, geography and history lessons in schools, and so on.

The symbolic forms that nationalist representations take – flags, sports teams, portrayals of our physical landscape, anthems, a shared sense of history – are vital in constructing our subjective sense of identity within a national community. In that sense, the nation is 'flagged' on a humdrum daily basis (Billig, 1995). But of course it is also flagged to exaggeration on major ceremonial occasions, to the point where some sociologists say that we are witnessing a new kind of civil religion. The state itself, in other words, becomes the focus and agent of devotion and commemoration, creating a kind of secular mass faith.

The business of flagging your national belongingness is not, of course, exclusive to states or to those who possess political power. Flags can be potent symbols of *any* cause and identity (clubs, parties, universities, companies). Even in social movements which in some ways *oppose* the official state, flags are used too – as an emblem of aspiration rather than

> Liberal democracy is the system of democracy common to market economies and based on parliamentary governance.

Nationalism is a set of beliefs in which people with a common language, religion and/or ethnicity constitute themselves as having a distinctive political community.

achievement, as a promise given not to the nation that currently exists, but to the nation that one day might be. There is an important expression of this alternative sort of **nationalism**. An example is the Maori sovereignty movement in this country, which has its own unifying symbolism and its own 'national' flag.

Photo: *The New Zealand Herald*

Flagging New Zealand

As a way of visualising the general point here, look at the image above which circulated widely at the time of the victory of New Zealand's 'Black Magic' team in the America's Cup yacht race series of 1995. Think about what ideological baggage you as an individual might bring to your reading of these images.

Notice, for example, how the figure of Sir Peter Blake is pictured along with the New Zealand flag (the nation itself is being flagged), and how this man adopts his own typical style of presentation. He is personally excited underneath, of course, but outwardly it is a calm pride which is being conveyed. He is someone who earlier in his career, though successful, was slightly 'wilder' in his behaviour and approach. Now we see him, older, in a more managerial position, exuding authority and symbolising a great national achievement. The raised arms, the imposing countenance, fired but in control, manly but not masculinist, an individual for sure but a team builder too, architect of a big achievement for a small nation, a Pakeha achievement but somehow expressing New Zealand's Polynesian roots, its historic sea craft combined with expeditionary boldness, inflicter of defeat by the small over the large, the quietly confident over the loud and brash, the modest and hardworking over the rich and powerful, the margins over the centre, the red socks of the community over the big bucks of corporate finance. Who are you? You're a New Zealander.

Differences and divisions: theorising democracy

In many modern liberal societies, it is assumed that the state is a *democratic* state. **Democracy** means the rule of the *demos* (it's a Greek word originally), i.e. the mass of the people. Democracy thus is in contrast to terms such as *aristocracy* (rule of those privileged by birth) and implies a notion of popular self-government. Over the centuries, however, some very different interpretations of democracy have emerged, and democracy has been bound up with fundamental sorts of social division, depending on how two things have been interpreted. The first of these is: who is to count as being included in 'the people'? In Ancient Greece, for example, women and slaves were *not* seen as part of the demos, and so were politically and socially disenfranchised. Generally speaking, most democracies began with restrictions based on property ownership and it took two thousand years for (most) modern states to recognise women's equal right to vote. Similarly, some immigrant groups and ethnic minorities are today barred from political participation in some nation states.

> **Democracy** is a political system that allows people to participate in ruling.

A second potentially divisive issue is: 'how *directly involved* in the running of the democratic system should the demos/people be?' Some people, for example, think that if periodic elections are held, this is sufficient for a nation to be called democratic, whilst others believe that to be allowed to vote for a politician just once every few years is about as democratically minimalist as you can get. True, we have a vote, we can organise pressure groups, we can speak out, we have formal legal rights, and so on. But participatory democracy – rule *by* the people as well as *for* the people – is arguably still a very long way off. Democracy itself, then, is a term that is *struggled over*, both ideologically and politically.

> **Neo-liberalism** refers to the view that the state has become too large in recent years and that a shift back to free markets, economic efficiency, competition and choice is an appropriate response to the crisis of the welfare state.

How do social theorists line up on these issues? For theorists and politicians who espouse **neo-liberalism**, too much involvement by the people in their political system is thought to be a sign of 'unhealthy' democracy. Democracy is after all, a 'representative' system of power, in which the representatives, not the represented, take the big decisions. From a neo-liberal standpoint, by the 1970s there were simply too many interest groups from outside the official political sphere putting pressure on the democratic state, to the point where it could not respond effectively or efficiently. These societal groups (trade unions, beneficiaries, 'green' movements, peace movements, ethnic minorities, women, etc.) were all asking 'what about us?' and were not content to leave matters to the specialist politicians. The state could not cope with this volume of societal demand, and so there emerged a scenario – in the terms of neo-liberal theory – of government 'overload'. Overload in terms of the sheer amount of things the state was supposed to be doing for people, and overload in terms of its capacity to *finance* these multiple social initiatives. This overload thesis became very influential, providing much of the rationale for the widespread 'rolling back of the state' which began to occur from the mid-1970s onwards: the race was on to see how far the role of the state, and its budgets for social spending, could be pared back so that it would become a 'minimal' state, one concerned principally with defending the nation, guaranteeing basic law and order, and providing a minimal social security 'safety net'.

Pluralism emphasises the way in which several or many individual citizens organise themselves into social and political interest groups in their attempts to have their views represented at the level of the state.

The **pluralist** view of politics is that democratic politics is about the way in which individual citizens tend to form into social and political interest groups, and about the way in which the state responds to the claims of such groups. In the pluralist picture, social interests tend to come and go over time, and the democratic state, whilst it cannot really resolve or represent *all* group interests fully and fairly, nevertheless is in business to try to give a reasonable range of societal interests a legitimate hearing. And the state also *mediates* between various conflicts of interests – it acts as the 'go-between' for or 'broker' of conflicting interest-group demands. Pluralists, unlike neo-liberals, think that a high degree of interest-group pressure on government is a good thing, contributing to a robust and fair political climate of negotiation and bargaining. Such a political culture will probably produce some winners and some losers, but it is believed by pluralists to minimise the risk that political 'extremes' will emerge, because the inequalities of the political and social bargaining process do not usually 'stack up'. That is to say, those who lose today may win tomorrow; and the group that gains something in its economic demands may not be the same social group which gains in terms of, say, cultural resources. Pluralists hold that there are always many different interest groups in society, and that the strong and wealthy ones are sufficiently countered by others to minimise the emergence of any 'ruling' social group or class.

The Marxist response to the question of 'who rules?' is that pluralist accounts are too naïve – that they ignore the huge power resources at the disposal of big business in particular, and that they see the state rather naïvely as being fairly 'neutral' in its policies and responsiveness to social pressures. Marxism specifically highlights the socio-economic power of capitalists and those who administer all levels of the capitalist system, whether in industry or government. Even if individual state functionaries (i.e. those in government, parliament, the civil service, the police force, etc.) do not own blocks of company shares or come from a capitalist family background, the logic of the system itself nevertheless compels them to protect the interests of the capitalist class. For example, capitalism as a social system is based upon the unequal distribution of private property, and property ownership is sanctified in law. So judges and policemen and other law-enforcers, even if they feel themselves to be personally anti-capitalist or non-political, cannot really fail to reproduce those state forms (law, policing, etc.) which serve to uphold capitalist ownership and control of economic life.

There are other theorists who agree that there is a dominant ruling class within political and economic life (C. Wright Mills was one of them), but who are not committed to the Marxist idea that economic exploitation is crucial. Theorists like Mills prefer a slightly vaguer notion of the ruling class as the 'industrial-military complex' and its advocates in the governmental sphere. Such theorists are also less attracted than Marxists to the alternative of revolutionary socialism.

Orwell's 'Big Brother' was/is envisaged as a man, and feminist theorists of the state would argue that this is no accident, since historically the state has been dominated by men and operates, by and large, in the interests of men. The main principle of feminist theories of the state is that both historically and currently governments and agencies of social control are centrally concerned to uphold a *patriarchal* social order.

> The state is a site of patriarchal relations which is necessary to patriarchy as a whole. The state represents patriarchal as well as capitalist interests and furthers them in its actions. This conception of the state as patriarchal as well as capitalist runs counter to most other analyses of it; most accounts do not consider gender relations at all, focusing instead on class relations within capitalism and the relations between these and the state.
>
> (Walby, 1994: 24)

Feminist theories have perhaps been most persuasive in pointing to the patriarchal character of the modern **welfare state**. Gender is considered to be central to the existence and maintenance of modern male-dominated society, firstly because social provision has been premised on the notion of the typical traditional family, according to which the woman/wife/mother stays at home and the man/husband/father is the 'breadwinner'. The idea of the welfare state is that in circumstances of particular hardship, or in certain aspects of routine living, the state needs to 'top up' the resources of families so that they approximate to what would otherwise be a 'normal' average minimum family income, earned mostly for the whole family by the male breadwinner. In this scenario, the male is

The welfare state is premised on the notion that governments bear responsibility for the well-being of their citizens.

engaged in the public, paid world of economic production whilst the female is concerned with social reproduction in the private domestic setting. Even when they are employed in the world of work, and in the realm of the state itself, women tend to staff the 'caring' professions, which typically carry less status and remuneration than many men's employment roles. These processes and practices reinforce the typically greater rewards for, and visibility of, men in modern society, and so the welfare state, despite some 'good intentions' perhaps, could be said to operate in the interests of men rather than women.

The local and the global: the future of the nation state

Nationalism appears to be alive and well. Actually, many of the national movements today are in a way *sub-national* or *secessionist movements* (e.g. Scottish nationalism, First Nations nationhood, Maori sovereignty). Yet such movements exist at a time, apparently, of massive 'globalisation'. This contradictory social phenomenon is important, and it gives rise to the question of what the future of nations and nation states is likely to be. Sociology, we should remember, has tended to equate the modern nation state with 'society' itself. Today that equation cannot be justified.

The process of globalisation has several dimensions, one of which is economic. At its simplest this economic dimension means that, 'a recession in the United States, for instance, takes its toll in the factories of Europe, Japan, Latin America and Asia' (McGrew, 1992: 87). But this is not all. A great many nation states are party to international trade agreements, and to 'regional' economic and political alliances (such as GATT, the G7 group of dominant economies, the ASEAN countries, and so on). Moreover, enormous amounts of shares, bonds, and loans are transferred around the world's money markets every day, at the touch of a computer key. Turnover on this huge scale makes the control that each nation state has over the amounts of 'finance capital' within its national borders very slight indeed. Related to this is the fact that institutions such as the World Bank and the International Monetary Fund (IMF) are increasingly acting as major arbiters in the economic affairs and fiscal policies of domestic governments around the world.

Politically and militarily, similar developments are evident. There are supra-national agencies such as NATO, the UN, and the EU which generate their own huge governments and bureaucracies. The field of International Law is now extensive, as are various worldwide procedures and ideologies of human rights and social justice. All these semi-legal forms can often work *against* the laws of particular nations. Simply regulating communications processes between nations is a complex quasi-legal business – the world's airwaves, for example, now need to be carefully distributed and monitored transnationally by commonly accepted standards authorities.

On the ecological front, global warming and other planetary pressures on resources create an urgent situation in which it is almost impossible for individual nations to indulge in a policy of autarky or self-reliance. Such pressures are hugely intensified by the understandable desire of the nations of the Southern hemisphere to gain for themselves the industrial affluence which has become habitual in the privileged Northern hemisphere countries.

There has also been a proliferation of *cultural* institutions and associations, which makes it difficult to sustain the idea of a single national culture. Just one small-scale example of this process of 'cultural transfer' is the internationalisation of *sociology* itself as a professional circuit, illustrating how the knowledge industry now routinely engages in countless co-operative exchanges and practices across domestic borders. The globalisation of the media and of the entertainment industry generally provides many more examples of 'cultural transfer'. The possibility that we are, perhaps for the first time in history, moving towards 'one world' as a reality which exists over and above the innumerable 'local worlds' of individual peoples and nation states is a very real one.

The extent and depth of the globalisation process is therefore undeniable. However, we need to be quite careful about how far to take this development of 'one worldism'. Even if the obvious process of globalisation is undermining the traditional autonomy of nation states to be self-governing, it is not so obvious that 'the nation state is dead'. After all, since history is littered with instances of inter-national wars and relations of domination, it is debatable how many states, nations and peoples have *ever* enjoyed anything like self-determination. Moreover, we can question whether even the most 'universal' of supra-national institutions, the United Nations, has any real powers of intervention at its disposal which make it obligatory for individual nation states to comply with the UN's 'global' resolutions on, for example, world peace, or energy-saving, or education, or nutrition programmes. And when decisive, forceful action *is* taken by the UN, it is usually particular nation states (such as the USA) or particular alliances (such as NATO) that take the lead – often in their *own* interests rather than the world's or humanity's. Similarly, in economic terms, supra-national organisations such as the IMF or World Bank, whilst appearing to be empowering some weaker nations, often 'help them out' only by tying them into the model of the stronger capitalist nations. This sometimes *worsens* their relative position by saddling them with debt, and imposes an artificial solution which may not take account of their own specific situations and traditions. In terms of global culture, it can be argued that what we are now seeing is not so much a mutual sharing of wisdom, values and habits, but rather a remorseless 'McDonaldisation' of society – the final triumph of capitalist commercial culture. When we also bear in mind the continuing strength of national identities it would seem plausible to maintain that, for the foreseeable future at least, citizens are probably still going to prefer to see themselves as 'belonging' to particular nations or peoples or movements rather than to some global confederation.

166 Exploring Society

In the following contribution by Jane Kelsey, there is a strong message about what has been happening to New Zealand and to the New Zealand state in the past 15 years.

The New Zealand experiment

Jane Kelsey

We can easily identify elements of a crisis in the New Zealand state. In less than a decade New Zealand changed from a bastion of welfare interventionism to a liberal reformer's paradise. The rapid privatisation of power was carried out with unabashed ruthlessness. In contrast to the events in Chile, this was a bloodless revolution. First the Labour, and then the National government bolstered the power of capital through economic policies which promoted accumulation, free from government restraint and irrespective of the social or political consequences. They divested the state's power over many agencies, assets, and activities to the private sector by corporatisation, privatisation, and devolution. And they imported market measures, personnel and ideology into what was left of the state sector.

Real economic and political power was shifted outside the realms of the democratic state. The country came to be run by a handful of ideologues in Cabinet, in the bureaucracy, and in the private sector. These men were seemingly careless or contemptuous of the democratic process. Under their direction the corporatism of the welfare state, with its collaboration between employers, unions and government, gave way to a much more limited form of corporatism, or what might more properly be termed the privatisation of power. Control over economic intervention was delegated to the Reserve Bank, with its sole statutory objective being to secure price stabilisation, free from government interference. State commercial enterprises were placed in the hands of autonomous, ministerially appointed boards drawn from the private sector with an overriding statutory objective to run as successful businesses, or were sold to private enterprise. Public responsibilities, such as resource management, were delegated to regional and local government. Public utilities, such as electricity and water supply, public transport and waste disposal, were thrown open to market forces. Provision of basic social services was transferred to ministerially appointed commissioners, elected boards subject to ministerial disestablishment, or approved private-sector agencies.

In the process – and contrary to the rhetoric of freedom – state power became increasingly intrusive. The population was formally categorised according to income (or lack thereof). Identity cards were issued to prove the eligibility of the poor for state-subsidised services. A centralised state department was empowered to oversee information matching by a wide range of government agencies. Civil liberties began to be retrenched or came under threat. Racism and conservative morality were visited on schools, community organisations, and funding agencies, while the search got underway for the enemies within.

While both Roger Douglas and Ruth Richardson were hailed internationally for their unswerving dedication to the cause, at home they increasingly fielded brickbats rather than bouquets. Yet they seemed oblivious to the fissures being created within the political and social framework of New Zealand society. They showed no visible concern for the human cost of this huge and risky experiment. And they seemed untroubled by its effects on **hegemony** and legitimacy. Others within both their parties, and outside, seemed to be aware of the danger, but were unwilling or unable to reverse the slide.

> **Hegemony** is a concept developed by the neo-Marxist Antonio Gramsci to describe a form of power won through ideological and consensual means.

Despite Labour's promises of more 'responsible' and 'responsive' government, the Rogernomics juggernaut had rolled over parliamentary processes, and popular opinion. The experience of the Muldoon administration since 1975, through the Fourth Labour Government, to the National government in the 1990s, induced a deep-seated scepticism about electoral politics and parliamentary democracy. Manifestos proved meaningless, bringing an already fragile electoral process into greater disrepute. Traditional parties were rent by internal factions and defections, and were deserted by their traditional support base. Individuals dominated the direction and style of government decisions alongside a network of fellow travellers within and outside the state. The executive proved unaccountable to their own caucus, to parliament as a whole, and to the electorate. Laws were pushed through with minimal public input or regard for the niceties of parliamentary process and convention, or were formulated outside parliament by the executive by way of regulations or orders in council. Select committees became rudimentary. The official watchdogs were undermined. And media commentators who raised their heads were quickly subdued.

The deep-seated crisis which now afflicted the political system also threatened the judicial arm of the state. The courts were required to weigh their constitutional function in maintaining checks and balances on the rampant executive against the doctrine of parliamentary supremacy and a convention of judicial non-intervention in government. Fortunately for the courts such challenges were rare. Those which were made were usually unsuccessful. Despite an abundance of activist rhetoric, the courts adopted in general a hands-off approach to the exercise of government power. Deregulation of the labour market and devolution of government responsibilities also placed the common law of contracts back on centre stage. Here, too, the courts responded with orthodoxy when enforcing the rights of patently unequal contracting parties under the common law.

In the 1990s the Employment Court, the High Court, and the Court of Appeal were set to become the arenas in which struggles between labour and capital would be fought out, as the courts had been in the nineteenth century. Consistently anti-worker decisions would be seen as confirming the courts' structural alliance (as part of the state) with capital. Conversely, creative decisions which favoured workers would be condemned by private enterprise, be inconsistent with the doctrines of legal liberalism, and could provoke serious tensions between the political and judicial wings of the state.

The implementation and operation of the new order had placed the legitimacy of the state under threat. It also posed serious consequences for hegemony. The social impact of the liberal programme was devastating. National's 1991 budget formalised the stratification of New Zealand society which Labour had begun. The rich had to pay more for basic services. But they were also paying less tax and could afford to top up their state-provided entitlement or buy private insurance. Middle-income earners also faced increased costs for basic services. For them, this combined with lower pay, uncertain job security, higher indirect taxes, and increased insurance premiums, to produce a significantly reduced standard of living. But it was the purported beneficiaries of this new streamlined system of targeted state support – the poor, the sick, women and the unemployed – who bore the brunt of the restructuring. Faced with a daunting combination of unemployment, benefit cuts, enforced dependence and user part-charges, they were free to choose whether to use their scarce resources to buy housing, health, education, or other essentials like food, and free to choose which of these essentials to go without.

By 1992 an increasing number of New Zealanders were aware of where the country was being led. It was not the direction of their choice, nor was it to their liking. A survey taken in September 1992 showed that half of those polled believed New Zealand was heading down the wrong path. Only 38% thought the country was on the right track. Other polls conducted in 1992 showed: 72% of the population were opposed to user pays; 56% thought the state should buy back privatised state assets; 66% opposed privatisation in the electricity industry; and 51% disapproved of the Employment Contracts Act, although 71% of those polled said it had made no difference to them personally. Many New Zealanders remained wedded to a strongly interventionist state, universal provision of state-funded social welfare, and state ownership of strategic resources administered to meet both commercial objectives and social needs.

In a country where welfare ideology has been so dominant, such change could have been expected to provoke disobedience and disorder. By the late 1980s the consequences of the tensions between the liberal reforms and democratic government – the challenges to state legitimacy and the breakdown of popular hegemony – had begun to affect the strategy of the Labour government. These tensions continued under National. But while the mass of the Pakeha population felt uneasy with what was taking place, they remained isolated, insecure, defensive, unorganised, and politically inactive. Limited dissent was focused on specific issues and policies. Those who were even prepared to protest on the streets wanted adjustments to economic policy to produce jobs, a return to a decent standard of living, and basic social services at affordable prices – a return to the security of the past, not the radical redistribution of economic and political power. They retained an overriding loyalty to the social, political, economic, and institutional structure of the New Zealand state. But the state was not delivering what they wanted.

This raises the crucial question of state autonomy. The globalisation of the economy and power of transnational capital fundamentally altered the dynamics of power which existed in the middle of the century. When economic interests operated primarily within national boundaries, there were some limits on their power and government had more scope to intervene. Now they operate beyond and across those boundaries. The process involves a kind of pluralism in reverse: it is states, rather than interest associations, which compete with one another, on a global terrain they do not control and under rules they can only marginally change. It is hard to see how a revival of traditional corporatism or a modified version of interest-group pluralism, even with increased independent scrutiny or electoral reform, would fundamentally affect the way that power was exercised. Labour's promise of a negotiated economy, built on a revival of consensus politics and still committed to international free trade in a global marketplace, ignored this simple reality.

The New Zealand state has always been subject to political and economic power wielded off-shore. The international trend to globalisation of economic and political power has combined with the policies of recent governments to deepen New Zealand's vulnerability. Like most states New Zealand is now locked into a network of regional and international markets, alliances, and institutions. It can exercise only a limited degree of state autonomy. While the powers of government are restricted to national territories, the structure of business organisation and activity is multi-national. When governments lose their ability to determine their country's economic course, they also lose the power to control social and political consequences. They are dependent on the success of an economic structure which effectively holds them captive. Concessions can still be made to meet short-term crises or to pacify unrest. Governments can still regulate, but there are serious limitations. If the government goes too far, transnational capital can disinvest and move elsewhere.

To what extent the New Zealand state can exercise any political and economic autonomy, and what constraints and alliances are acceptable or desirable, are perhaps the most crucial questions for the future of the country and its peoples. Yet few politicians and commentators seem prepared to grapple with them. Liberalisation and globalisation have been treated as purely economic questions, ideologically and structurally removed from the political agenda. Liberal ideologues, free-trade

Exploring Society

supporters, and most economists simply assert that liberalisation and globalisation are in the 'national interest' and must be pursued. New Zealanders are treated as hypothetical consumers operating on the level playing field of the global marketplace. There has been no informed or independent debate over its implications for our everyday lives, or the options available.

Viewed against this theoretical backdrop we can see the causes of crisis facing the New Zealand state today as structural and endemic – not simply the product of overbearing and ruthless personalities or weak constitutional safeguards. Only by understanding the anatomy of the crisis can we hope to identify remedies and devise strategies to exploit the contradictions between liberalism and democracy within the economic, political, and judicial arenas. The state's desire to avoid coercion, and its need for legitimisation, can be played on to restrain the continued onslaught of the liberal agenda. But the ability of formal democracy to restrain the exercise of state power should not be overestimated. Nor should it be assumed that moves towards a more accountable and democratic state will increase the ability of New Zealanders to control the essential economic and political decisions which most affect our lives.

Questions

Having read Jane Kelsey's piece, try to answer the following questions.

1. What are the main social consequences she sees in the 'rolling back of the state', and how would this fit in with our *differences and divisions* theme?
2. With which overall theoretical perspective would you associate Jane Kelsey's position, and why?
3. In terms of the *global/local* issue, how does what Jane Kelsey says match up with the arguments for and against the idea that the nation state is dying?

Conclusion

Towards the end of her contribution, Kelsey writes of the need for a sociological understanding of the anatomy of the state in New Zealand, and it is worth underlining the significance of this point for the chapter as a whole, and indeed for all social understanding. When studying politics and the actions of government, we are sometimes tempted to take ruling politicians at their word, and to see the process of elections, policy enactment, cabinet reshuffles and so on in terms of the leaderly guidance of dominant personalities, or the securing of the 'national interest', or the way in which particular parties and politicians fulfil or fail to fulfil their manifestos and so forth. However, important as these details may be, it is the structural question of how shifts and directions in political life connect with longer, underlying developments in the society and economy as a whole that matters. And to get a sense of such 'structural' issues, we need to get underneath the surfaces and tissues of daily political life; we need to see what the anatomy of the state is, as a form of social regulation, in the context of the state of society itself.

For example, it would be easy to think, from a superficial or purely 'descriptive' point of view, that 'the state' ceased to play the interventionist role in the 1990s that it did in the period from the 1940s to the 1960s. In one sense this is true enough, since there have been huge efforts to turn back into private hands resources and functions that were once possessed exclusively by government. And yet, in another sense, state control and regulation of society is still growing all the time, and the state's demands for demonstrable 'accountability' from those who occupy authoritative positions throughout the ex-public services are stringent indeed. Moreover, the systematic effort of governments and states to shake society into line with the new 'less-state' regimes is very substantial. To understand the anatomy of the state, and not just to describe the actions of governments, thus demands in turn a structural and historical perspective, and it is the role of sociology in this as in other areas to try to develop that kind of 'anatomical thinking', and, one hopes, to bring to public attention any lessons that the deeper analysis can reveal.

? Study questions

9.1 In what respects or in what situations do you think the use of state power is legitimate?

9.2 What is meant by the phrase 'flagging the nation'? How does this notion illustrate the theme 'the social and the personal'?

9.3 Outline the main differences between neo-liberal, pluralist, Marxist and feminist theorists on the role of the state in modern societies.

Further reading

Billig, M. (1995) *Banal Nationalism*. Sage, London.

Carnoy, M. (1984) *The State and Political Theory*. Princeton University Press, Princeton, NJ.

Held, D. et al. (1999) *Global Transformations*. Polity Press, Cambridge.

Kelsey, J. (1995) *The New Zealand Experiment*. Auckland University Press/Bridget Williams Books, Auckland.

McGrew, A. (1992) A Global Society? In Hall, S. et al. (eds). *Modernity and its Futures*. Polity Press, Cambridge.

McLennan, G., Held, D. and Hall, S. (eds). (1984) *The Idea of the Modern State*. Open University Press, Milton Keynes.

Sites 30. (1995) Special issue on *National Identities/National Futures*. Department of Social Anthropology, Massey University, Palmerston North.

Walby, S. (1994) Towards a Theory of Patriarchy. In *The Polity Reader in Gender Studies*. Polity Press, Cambridge.

10 The city and city life

Chapter aims

- to explore the significance of cities for societies and economies;
- to highlight the evolution of the city and the characteristics of contemporary cities.

Introduction

This chapter begins by identifying the key features of the city, and what characterises life in an urban environment. Cities, especially cities that dominate regions and economic systems, continue to evolve into mega-cities, and there are new patterns of urban growth – and decline – as cities reflect new global systems of ownership and production. But urban growth often comes at a cost – notably poverty and crime. In the latter part of the chapter, there is a discussion of those who have gained through processes such as gentrification and those who are excluded or marginalised (immigrants, non-whites), as well as of the theories concerning these processes such as those offered by sociologists like David Harvey and Manuel Castells.

Cities

The city is very much a feature of contemporary life and yet, for most of human history, cities as we know them did not exist. Until the eighteenth century, cities were relatively few in number, but this changed dramatically in the wake of the industrial revolution. The city now dominates most aspects of modern societies and economies. Even in New Zealand, which in many ways remains influenced by rural images and history, cities are overwhelmingly important. In fact, New Zealand is one of the most urbanised countries in the world with the majority of its population living in large cities or towns. In New Zealand, as elsewhere, the city is the powerhouse of modern economies and societies.

What is a city? An important defining feature is its size. Basically, a city comprises a large number of people living in close proximity. However, that is only the beginning of what characterises a city. A city has its own **political economy** and this has developed into a variety of forms in the late twentieth century (the edge city, sunbelt cities). A large city tends to continue to increase in size (becoming a megalopolis) so that the largest cities in the world contain 20–30 million people. Most advanced societies have one or two cities which dominate national economic and political interests, and which attract enormous concentrations of economic and political power. These are **primate cities**. Cities contain complex social and economic relations with a division of labour which continues to evolve in its complexity, especially with the development of global networks which link the major cities of the world.

> **Political economy** is an approach, typically Marxist, that is concerned with the management of economic issues and institutions and the associated politics.

> **Primate cities** are those cities that completely dominate – politically, economically and socially – the country in which they are located.

Rank	Name	Country	Population (millions)
1	Tokyo	Japan	28.8
2	Mexico City	Mexico	17.8
3	São Paolo	Brazil	17.5
4	Bombay	India	17.4
5	New York	USA	16.5
6	Shanghai	China	14.0
7	Los Angeles	USA	13.0
8	Lagos	Nigeria	12.8
9	Calcutta	India	12.7
10	Buenos Aires	Argentina	12.3

Source: United Nations Population Division, 1999

Table 10.1 The world's largest urban agglomerations, 1999

There is also a particular way of living which is described by sociologists as urbanism. People interact, work and play in ways that reflect their urban location. The latte-drinking 'culture' of Ponsonby Road, the Saturday markets in Otara, the corporate world of Lambton Quay or the gridlock on a motorway, are aspects of living in a city which illustrates both the problems and the opportunities that city life offers – and that make it very different from life in rural areas and provincial towns. It is the variety of city life which is a key characteristic.

> On the surface ... [the city] seems a simple and physical entity but, like the human brain, it is actually so complex and flexible that virtually all theories about it are true – especially contradictory ones. It works both as a mediaeval village with the equivalent of 13th-century inhabitants pottering about, and a global network of 24-hour traders. Contradictory ways of life are necessary, as are so many other complementary economic activities ... the city is more like the uncontrollable process of the stock market than a fixed artefact.
>
> (Jencks ,1996: 26)

The forerunner of the city can be found in the settlements which were established with the domestication of animals and then turned into permanent communities. These continued to evolve and early cities which most typically correspond to their modern counterparts can be found in the Greek and Roman empires with Rome itself expanding by the first century BC to include almost one million people as the centre of a large military and economic empire. During the Middle Ages, cities in Europe began to grow as centres of commerce, but the most important factor in the establishment of cities was the industrial revolution. The demand for labour in the newly built factories in urban areas attracted migrants from the rural hinterland, and the evolution of capitalism encouraged the expansion of private ownership and the opportunity for workers to migrate in search of employment. As a result, the industrial-capitalist cities of Europe expanded rapidly in the 1800s, and by 1900, London had over six million inhabitants (compared with 900 000 a century earlier) while Berlin, Paris and Vienna all had between 1.5 and 3.3 million inhabitants. Industrialisation and urbanisation provided the impetus for the growth of cities.

The modern city continues to evolve, given the continuing urbanisation of populations, the economic power of the contemporary city and the networking which is a feature of global economic life, especially with lower costs and ease of travel and communications technology. Britain was the first country which can be labelled 'urban', with less than 20% of its population living in towns and cities in 1800, but 74% by 1900 (Giddens, 1993: 566). Two world wars disrupted the development of the city in Europe with a disastrous loss of life and buildings. The post-war period brought a new vitality to cities as a major period of capitalist expansion in both Europe and North America encouraged new and large migration flows from rural and provincial areas to major cities, but also from former colonies and the less developed regions of the world. The city was already culturally diverse and the post-war period has seen this diversity grow and become a feature of urbanism. Neighbourhoods are known for the ethnic groups which dominate in one area or another, and the growth of new businesses such as restaurants and markets, or the significance of ethnic enclaves such as Chinatown in San Francisco, reflect the pluralism of the inhabitants. Major cities such as Los Angeles, Toronto, London or Melbourne are epitomised by their cultural diversity.

Cities are also seen by the people who live in them, by governments and by outsiders as the source of various problems. The attempt at *planning* a city to overcome some of these problems has been made at various times this century, and there have been some notable examples of cities which have been established from the ground up to fulfil a particular purpose. These include the 'new towns' of Britain, as well as cities like Canberra and Brazilia. This development reflects the political views of the time, and the degree of intervention which was acceptable then, but is less so now. A key element driving such attempts was concern about the negative impact of the city on the life of its inhabitants, and the potential for environmental and social damage. These concerns have been justified with the appearance of the **megalopolis** or the mega-city. Cities of more than 10 million people constitute the latter while the term *megalopolis* refers to two or more centres that have merged with one another to form a continuous urban belt. For example, New York is the centre of a 650-kilometre urban belt which incorporates a number of major and minor cities and suburbs. In the 1950s there were only two megalopolises in the world, whereas the United Nations anticipates that there will be 26 in 2000, many in Asia and the developing world. Equally, there were 16 cities of more than 10 million people in 1996 (UN Population Division, 1999), and four of them will have grown to house more than 20 million people by 2010 (Castells, 1996: 401). Tokyo, Mexico City and São Paulo are the three most dominant of these. In the future, the continuous urban area of the Pearl River delta in China might include as many as 40 million people. Of course, mega-cities and megalopolises are often the same thing as the very large cities sprawl and incorporate surrounding suburbs and cities or towns.

> **Megalopolises** are very large, continuous urban centres with huge concentrations of people.

There are many other aspects to the modern city. Sociologists have been busy recording the changes that have occurred within the city, such as the growing pluralism and the implications of this in terms of the exclusion of some groups as cities become divided along ethnic and class lines. **Suburbanisation** has been a major feature of post-war city growth, with the growing decentralisation of particular forms of economic enterprise and the mobility provided by the car and the motorway. The growth of Auckland's North Shore highlights the 'edge city' growth of both employment and suburbs. In some cases, this has been hastened by those wanting to avoid the 'browning' of inner city areas, and the decay that coincided with the arrival of migrants. 'White flight' is apparent in many cities, including Auckland, but it has also been accompanied by a move back into the city centres. **Gentrification** is occurring in some areas, urban recycling in others (i.e. the conversion of industrial and other buildings to residences), while the celebration of alternative lifestyles (e.g. ethnic and gay neighbourhoods) is another aspect of modern city life. At a macro level, some cities have declined economically because the industries which sustained them have disappeared or moved elsewhere (**de-industrialisation**) while others (sunbelt cities) have expanded considerably. In the United States, cities such as Detroit, Chicago and

> **Suburbanisation** is the development of housing in areas outside and often some distance from the inner city.

> **Gentrification** is the process of renovating older houses and areas by, and for, the middle class.

> **De-industrialisation** is the late twentieth-century process of declining employment in heavy manufacturing industries.

Baltimore have seen a significant decrease in their populations as their economic base has declined, whereas Phoenix, Los Angeles and San Diego represent the sunbelt, or expanding, cities (Macionis, 1993: 605). Cities are far from being the same the world over. What they share is their size and their urban culture, as well as social and economic importance.

The local and the global: global influence and local problems

The evolution of the city in the twentieth century has made it an exciting subject for sociologists. One increasingly obvious development has been the way in which cities have become bigger, more powerful – both within particular societies and globally – and have come to represent some of the best and worst aspects of human existence. How big will they grow and what are the implications of such growth?

In the mid-1990s there were three world cities – London, New York and Tokyo. They reflect the shifting influence and the dominance of particular economies. As Short (1996: 68–70) explains, London gained its strength from its position at the centre of a colonial empire in the late nineteenth and earlier twentieth centuries. The rise of New York reflects the power of the US economy for much of the twentieth century and the concentration of financial institutions in the eastern United States. By the 1970s, Tokyo joined the other two as the centre of Japan, a major industrial and financial power of the late twentieth century. Each of these cities is home to large numbers of people (almost 28 million in the case of Tokyo) but they are also the location of corporate head offices, so they are the base for major concentrations of economic and political power. New York houses the headquarters of 59 of the world's largest transnational firms, London hosts 37 and Tokyo 34. But in terms of size and economic significance, these three cities are being joined by others. The urban agglomerations surrounding São Paulo, Mexico City, Shanghai, Bombay, Los Angeles, Seoul, Beijing, Rio De Janeiro, Calcutta and Osaka all have populations in excess of 10 million people. They are all spreading to include surrounding districts and towns.

The first of these urban agglomerations grew from the urban spread between Boston and Washington ('Bosh-Wash') and that between San Francisco and San Diego ('San-San'). The new mega-cities are in Asia and South America, and some of these are expected to include 40 million to 50 million people within the next few decades. Their population size and economic power is greater than those of most countries, and their growth is seemingly unstoppable. They are the centres for the new global networks, and yet are often disconnected economically and socially from the countries in which they are located (Castells, 1996: 404).

Cities are part of an increasingly globalised production and network system. Sassen (1991) and Castells (1996) are two sociologists who have analysed the way in which global cities operate. The growing cities of

Asia and South America have attracted industries because they are able to offer international opportunities, a sizeable market and low costs, notably in terms of labour. The cost and organisation of labour in the older industrial centres, the mass assembly plants of Fordism, have been replaced by the low-cost, disorganised labour to be found in cities in Asia and South America. A global shift has occurred with a new division of labour and new centres of production as the older industrial cities have experienced de-industrialisation and the cities of the third world have become the home to new globalised production systems (Short, 1996: 82). Short uses the example of Nike which is headquartered near Portland, Oregon, but which manufactured shoes in Japan in the 1960s, in South Korea in the 1970s, in Bangkok and Jakarta in the 1980s and in China in the 1990s. But the industrialisation of these cities in Asia and South America is only part of the story, as telecommunications networks further alter the way in which business is done. Castells (1996: 378) talks of the way in which the global economy is organised around 'command and control centres [which are] able to co-ordinate, innovate, and manage the intertwined activities of networks of firms'. These networks are built on advanced telecommunications systems, and confirm the dominance of some cities and not others.

If cities are the powerhouses of global change, they also produce some of the worst problems of contemporary social and economic life. They are exhilarating, interesting places to work and live; they can also be dangerous, depressing places. The sheer density of population and the reliance on individualised and inefficient forms of transport such as the private car mean that utilities such as water supply, transportation services and sewerage are stretched, that pollution is a major hazard and that there is chronic and debilitating congestion. The needs of such large concentrations of people are very demanding on the environment and as cities continue to grow in size, they present ever-growing problems, not simply in terms of the health of their citizens but also in terms of the impact they have on the surrounding countryside. However, there are examples of what can be done under such pressures. Ankara in Turkey began a reforestation programme in 1961 which has seen over 30 million trees planted – one million per year at the moment – to help the city breathe, while Berlin has an interesting programme of social housing and the provision of urban space, and Barcelona has provided 150 new public open spaces, has rebuilt slums and has made public transport work (Jencks, 1996: 28). These success stories exist alongside major environmental problems in many cities. Furthermore, cities also encompass enormous disparities of wealth. There are many examples of misery that reflect the hope people have of gaining access to the wealth of the city. Poverty is a characteristic of all cities, from downtown New York or London through to Bangkok or São Paulo. The city economy is significantly dependent on such impoverished communities for certain sorts of labour. Economically powerful cities might be, but equitable they are not.

The social and the personal: safety in the city

The growth of the city was an important focus for the growing discipline of sociology. Three of the founding fathers of sociology, Marx, Durkheim and Tönnies, were all writing and researching in the mid- and late nineteenth century when the modern city began to take form. However, all three were ambivalent about the city, reflecting the common-sense suspicion that the city held many problems. Marx was concerned about the poverty which was apparent in the new centres of capitalist expansion; Durkheim contrasted the mechanical solidarity of smaller rural communities with the organic solidarity of urban life and argued that the complex division of labour in urban communities replaces religion as the factor which binds people, and that anomie is the result. Ferdinand Tönnies (1855–1936), a German sociologist, developed two concepts to help compare rural and urban life, *Gemeinschaft* and *Gesellschaft*. The first is similar to Durkheim's notion of **mechanical solidarity**, and Tönnies uses it to describe the way in which people in traditional communities are bound by ties of kinship and tradition. *Gesellschaft* describes what he saw as the lack of community to be found in urban areas which reflects the self-interest of the individuals concerned. Urbanisation and the expansion of the cities reflected Tönnies's view that *Gemeinschaft* was on the decline and was being replaced by *Gesellschaft*.

This suspicion of the city and its failings in terms of personal and social life continues. It is often implied – or expressly stated – that rural areas and small towns have a sense of 'community' which is lost in a city environment, and that people help and care for one another in rural areas – a reflection of *Gemeinschaft*. The size, pace and complexity of the city fracture community solidarity, make interpersonal relations more impersonal and encourage a competitiveness and a materialism which demean social values. There will certainly be pockets within the city with quite different experiences of these problems – from fortress suburbia to scrap-heap economic activity on the margins. Moreover, it is felt that if there are going to be social problems of one sort or another – crime, poverty, congestion – they will happen in the city.

As with many common-sense ideas, there is some truth in this distrust of the city. Primate cities such as Auckland, London, Paris or Bangkok do contain within their boundaries major problems of one sort or another, and will always dominate negative statistics such as the rates of criminal offending simply because of their size. But is it true that people are more lonely and less involved in community and social networks in cities? Are you more likely to get burgled or beaten up in Auckland than you are in Gore or Tolaga Bay? The answer is a lot more involved than most people would assume. Even some of those sociologists who thought that the city represented the decline of the positive values and institutions of social life had to concede this. Louis Wirth (1897–1952), who coined the term

> **Mechanical solidarity** is the Durkheimian notion that traditional societies are bound by common beliefs and norms to produce high levels of social cohesion.

'urbanism' to describe city life, argued that life in the city was impersonal and lacked the moral code of rural life. But he also acknowledged that cities produced greater tolerance, more privacy and operated as 'melting pots' for diverse cultural groups. Smaller communities tend to be intolerant of those who are seen as departing from local norms. Questions of sexuality or culture can be negatively perceived and can be the source of comment or abuse in a non-city environment whereas these issues are more apparent – and often more accepted – in an urban environment. In a city where gays or lesbians, for example, may live in large numbers, there may be more support of one kind or another, and others may be more ready to accept their presence. The Hero Parade, for instance, would be unlikely to happen in many centres outside Auckland, San Francisco or Sydney. In San Francisco, gay communities have an important political influence and constitute an important market in the city. Much the same could be said about various migrant and cultural groups. In this way, the city does encompass very powerful examples of community, or social networks, and makes possible a sense of belonging and an acceptance that is unlikely to occur in smaller, less tolerant communities.

Photos: Jason Oxenham/Central Leader

Urban communities and cultures have traditionally been diverse

Of course, cities also include those negative things that come to dominate our nightly television news. Someone watching TV in Gisborne or Westport could easily be forgiven for thinking that their community is 'safe' compared to the mean streets of Auckland. A film like 'Once Were Warriors' reinforces such views, especially as the final scene encapsulates the idea of 'cities bad, rural communities good' – some of the central characters leave the city to escape the abuse and temptations of a depressed city neighbourhood. Again, we need to be cautious. If crime statistics are based on rates – the number of crimes committed in relation to population size – then a rather different picture emerges in New Zealand. Auckland is often 'outperformed' by much smaller centres. In other words, the rate for various forms of criminal activity is sometimes higher in small towns like Gisborne or Westport when it is calculated as the crimes committed *per number of people*. Auckland's appearance on television screens as the location of various social problems is a function of size; rates of crime may be higher elsewhere in New Zealand, especially in depressed areas which rely on informal and non-legal activities such as cannabis growing. We should not be too hasty in drawing conclusions about the nature of identity and the strength of the community in the city compared to that in smaller towns and rural areas. Different lifestyles are possible in different forms of community, and a simplistic conclusion that the city lacks 'community' or is less safe than other areas is far from sociologically accurate. It very much depends on the nature of the community being discussed, especially as the city encompasses a wide range of socio-economic, cultural and spatially-distinct communities.

That having been said, the city still offers constraint as well as opportunity. A major contribution to debates about the nature of the city and city life has been provided by feminists. An early and important contribution was made by Jane Jacobs (1961) whose book, *The Death and Life of Great American Cities*, was highly critical of the unsafe nature of public space. Later feminist researchers (Wekerle, 1980; Valentine, 1989) extended this to the fear women have of public space in the city because of the possibility of sexual harassment and violence. Feminists also added other concerns and observations to the sociological analysis of the city. Saegert, in *Masculine Cities and Feminine Suburbs* (1980), highlighted the association between women and domestic production and their location in the home and suburb. A New Zealander, Jacqueline Fahey, coined the term **'suburban neurosis'** to describe the problems faced by women who were largely confined to their homes in newly established suburbs in post-war New Zealand (although the term is often attributed to her husband, Fraser MacDonald). This has been an important reminder that a discussion of suburbanisation, for example, needs to consider the gendered nature of the work-home split and the link between 'domestic ties, locational restrictions, and the occupational segregation of women' (Short, 1996: 230). The design of urban space is seen as reinforcing this sexual division of labour and the decisions about the planning and construction of the city are dominated by men with the result that there

> Suburban neurosis is a phrase coined in New Zealand to describe the effect of isolation felt by women in the newly established suburban areas.

are important differences in the way that men and women 'experience the city' (Short, 1996: 230–231).

City life

Ann Dupuis

When I was growing up in the 1950s and 1960s, a common joke heard about New Zealand cities was that they were shut at weekends. While not entirely true (movie theatres and a sprinkling of restaurants and coffee bars were open on Saturday nights), it is more or less the case that cities closed when the shops closed at 9 pm on Friday nights and reopened at 9 am on Monday mornings. The same could not be said of New Zealand cities in the 1990s. Waterfront developments, casinos, multi-storey buildings, elegant shopping areas, wine bars and al fresco cafés have changed the face of New Zealand cities. Today's cities are places where locals and tourists alike come to play, be entertained, watch and be watched, and – above all – consume in the wide array of shops, markets, galleries, museums, restaurants, coffee bars and entertainment complexes that proliferate in our downtown areas (Thorns, 1997). From teddy bears' picnics to the Hero Parade, dragon-boat racing to opera and symphony under the stars, ethnic cultural displays to the Festival of Romance, New Zealand cities have changed dramatically from what they once were.

Another dramatic urban change has occurred in terms of where people live in the city. The 1950s and 1960s saw the development of suburbia across western countries (Thorns, 1973). In this regard, New Zealand was no different. The baby boom and the buoyant economy that followed the war years set the scene for the establishment of ever-mushrooming new suburbs across New Zealand cities. These post-war suburbs were made up of relatively indistinguishable, largely three-bedroomed bungalows, built for owner occupation and often purchased with state-subsidised mortgages. Suburban housing was depicted as the 'central motif in the post-war social pattern', expressing the dominant ideas of the time about family life, privacy and space (Dunstall, 1981: 404) and about suburbia as being integral to the New Zealand dream of home ownership (Ferguson, 1994). Austin Mitchell captured the social ethos of suburban New Zealand in these years with his now famous description of New Zealand as a 'half gallon, quarter acre, pavlova paradise' (Mitchell, 1972).

While the immediate post-war years were characterised by a population push outwards and the consequent development of new suburbs, more recently certain groups of people have moved back towards the city to live in either the inner city itself, or in what had previously been run-down, low-income, working-class neighbourhoods close to the inner city. This process is referred to as *gentrification*.

Initially, the term *gentrification* was used to describe the flow of middle-class residents into run-down, inner city areas for the purpose of restoring and renovating old, dilapidated, inner city houses with the intention of living in these houses themselves (Glass, 1964). Bourne (1993) refers to this definition of gentrification as a restricted definition. The gentrification of the Ponsonby area in Auckland is a New Zealand example that would fit this definition. The key feature of this definition is class – more specifically the encroachment into working-class neighbourhoods of middle-class people who, over time, not only change the class nature of the area, but also displace the previous working-class occupants as property prices and rents rise. The process frequently involves a tenure change from renting to owning and, as has often happened overseas, a change in the demographic and ethnic mix of inner city neighbourhoods (Hamnett and Randolph, 1986).

More recently, the concept of gentrification has been extended to include other forms of inner city change, such as the conversion into apartments of warehouses and other old commercial buildings in inner city and adjacent areas. Examples of these are the blocks of apartments just off Mount Eden Road in Auckland that were once warehouses, or the apartments in Christchurch that were formerly lecture rooms in the old University of Canterbury's downtown site. Included too in this definition are the new, purpose-built, high-rise, downtown apartment blocks. The units in these blocks range in size from studios, to three-bedroomed apartments, are often serviced, and supply residents with car parks. Echoing 'Melrose Place', many of the apartment buildings are also equipped with a gym, a pool, steam and sauna rooms for the residents' use.

A useful and very broad definition of gentrification into which all the above examples fit is that put forward by Zukin (1987: 13) who identifies gentrification as a process of spatial and social differentiation in which a segment of the middle class rejects the suburbs in favour of an urban lifestyle geared towards consumption. Such a definition can encompass not only class issues, but also those of gender, age and ethnicity and it makes very clear that gentrification is a much more complex process than merely the renovation of inner city and inner city fringe housing (Smith, 1987; Rose, 1988).

I have outlined the process of gentrification, but who are the 'gentrifiers' and how can the process be explained sociologically? Overseas research has shown that gentrifiers are, by and large, single people or childless couples with high incomes (Gale, 1979; Beauregard, 1986; Filion, 1991). Gentrified areas also tend to be chosen by artists, musicians, lesbians and gays, for whom urban living offers a tolerance of lifestyle diversity. There are a number of competing explanations as to why gentrification occurs (Hannigan, 1995: 176–178). Commuter costs and the increased costs of suburban real estate have been suggested as explanations. More important, however, are cultural explanations. These focus on the values, preferences and tastes of the middle-class gentrifiers themselves and their attempts to restore and recapture the perceived solidity of values of a past era (Williams, 1986: 68). From a perspective that shifts the emphasis to identity construction, Zukin (1991: 192) claims that moving back into the city is akin to demonstrating tolerance and an appreciation of ethnic diversity, as opposed to the white flight to the suburbs that had earlier taken place in many American cities.

Structural factors are the basis for alternative explanations for gentrification. These explanations tend to be Marxist in flavour, and view gentrification not as an isolated process, but in the context of the logic of capitalism as it is played out in the property sector (Smith and Williams, 1986). The key point of such explanations rests on the decline of profit levels in the suburban building industry as the post-war boom came to a close, resulting in capital flowing into the inner city as a site for increased opportunity for profits (Stilwell, 1993). The focus therefore is not on the movement of people but the movement of capital. Other explanations focus on the roles of politicians, bankers, the real estate industry and property speculators in the process.

In the 1970s and 1980s, studies of gentrification stressed the effect of the process on existing neighbourhoods, particularly on the hardships experienced by those who were 'pushed out' by rising rents and increasing property prices. Gentrification was seen as a significant problem for the low-cost rental market, as buildings that had previously been flats or bedsits housing a number of residents were turned into owner-occupied units, lived in typically by a young, professional, high-income couple. Gentrification was even identified as a factor in the increase of homelessness. This focus tends to disappear in the current climate of postmodernism, which views gentrification as a rejection of the homogeneity of suburban living, a celebration of diversity and the old over the new and, above all, the display of a certain type of distinctive taste with its focus on identity, style and consumption that is part of the postmodern city and the postmodern lifestyle (Mullins, 1991; Filion, 1991).

The study of gentrification has received much attention in overseas urban studies over the last two decades. Although not much New Zealand research has been done on gentrification, two differing local views on the topic are worth mentioning. One view put forward by Morrison (1995) downplays the importance of gentrification and suggests that while these inner city changes are interesting, they do not represent fundamental change in that city growth is still primarily growth on the outskirts of the city. Another view on gentrification is offered by Winstanley (1995) who, taking a feminist perspective, broadly points to the gendered nature of space, and the different understandings and experiences women and men have about space and its utilisation. In her analysis of women's experiences of gentrification in Wellington, Winstanley argues that gentrification theories that focus strongly on the economic and profit-making dimension, largely ignore women's experiences of gentrification. She claims that women's identities can be constituted through gentrification as women experience gentrification as a form of self-expression that offers them a freedom of lifestyle not available in suburbia.

New Zealand cities in the 1990s have changed enormously from the cities of my youth. No longer 'shut at weekends' like they once were, people now choose to live in apartments in the inner cities and in the elegantly renovated Victorian and Edwardian villas on the inner city fringes. These 'gentrifiers' are a highly visible and intriguing part of the changes cities have undergone. But the impact of gentrification spreads far beyond the inner cities themselves. If you're a suburbanite like me, think about this next time you're sitting in a trendy café or wine bar, sipping a cappuccino or swirling a Chardonnay. We're all part of it: the 'croissantisation' of society.

Questions

On the basis of your reading of Ann Dupuis' discussion, attempt to answer the following questions:

1. The process of regeneration in various areas of the city has significant implications for the existing residents and facilities in an area. Ann Dupuis refers to 'croissantisation', i.e. the appearance of French bakeries in an area undergoing gentrification. What other changes occur as a result of gentrification?
2. What is the significance of gentrification for the status and class distinctions of the city, and particularly for the areas involved?

Differences and divisions: inner city and outer suburbs

One of the most important aspects of post-war city development has been the expansion and growing political and economic significance of the suburbs. The process of suburbanisation, that is, the development of housing and service areas away from the city centre, has been encouraged by the availability of transport systems, notably motorways and the widespread ownership of cars. The suburban home has come to represent a desirable residence away from the built-up city and work, where it is possible to live in attractive surroundings with detached homes and gardens. Most suburbs reflect the changing nature of the housing market and the privatised preference for a particular type of housing and location although states have also been responsible for suburban housing developments. In New Zealand, suburbs such as Otara and Porirua were built as state housing areas for the expanding post-war of urban population.

Service areas such as shopping centres and industrial parks have followed as part of another stage of suburbanisation, especially as firms have sought 'greenfield' locations. Many of these suburbs, both as relatively wealthy housing areas which generate substantial tax revenues, and as the location of expanding service and industrial sectors of the economy, have had the effect of drawing investment away from the inner city areas which were marked by decay. These areas lost jobs, industries and the more affluent of their tenants. Revenue in terms of rates or other forms of taxes declined, and politicians were increasingly less willing to spend revenue on halting the decay. The inner cities became areas of destination for new and poor migrants and a place where the poor were trapped. In the 1970s and 1980s, these inner cities became the areas characterised by high crime rates, poor services, decayed housing, conflict and were the epitome of unattractive city life. In the UK, riots occurred in Brixton, Bristol and Toxteth in Liverpool. The Los Angeles riots, which were sparked by the beating of a black American, Rodney King, by white police officers, are a significant example of urban conflict. American inner city areas became dominated by blacks and Latinos who elected non-white mayors and councils who did not have sufficient tax revenue to do anything substantial for their constituencies.

This changed in the 1980s. Major new investment took place in many cities and downtown areas were revitalised and refurbished.

> Cities devised sophisticated public-private partnerships and transformed the design of downtown: assembling land, building parking garages; manipulating the tax code for office buildings and hotels; constructing cultural centres, convention centres, and festival market places; promoting downtown housing; improving the streetscape.
>
> (Barnett, 1995: 4)

Buildings were recycled – either they were modified to provide housing such as in the Docklands in London, or they were replaced by inner city housing developments – or the housing stock from earlier eras was seen as once again desirable. Houses were gentrified and upwardly mobile or middle-class residents lived alongside the urban poor, although the latter could not afford to buy in the neighbourhood any more. It was obvious that gentrification was under way when the French bakery (croissantisation) arrived in the neighbourhood.

Ann Dupuis has mentioned the rent-gap theory, and it is certainly one of the most influential explanations for the revitalisation of inner city areas and gentrification in particular. Certain demand-side factors have been highlighted as helping to explain the move back to the inner city by higher income groups, including the continued presence of high-income jobs in the inner city and the desire to be near the place of work in the face of increasingly congested transport systems, more single-person households or households without children and new expectations and

Urban forms continue to evolve: gentrification, suburbanisation, 'greenfield' locations and inner-city housing

patterns of consumption (Short, 1996: 182). But there is also a supply-side explanation offered by Neil Smith. Smith's basic argument is that there has been an effective disinvestment from many inner-city neighbourhoods. Capital has been invested in suburban locations. This produces a *rent gap*, the difference between the land value and the potential land value of an accessible inner-city location. The rent gap creates the conditions for new forms of investment. Gentrification is one outcome. But the investment in the inner city is quite selective, and gentrification occurs in some areas that are next to others which remain impoverished and poorly serviced. The inner cities of Glasgow and New York have seen the refurbishment of old buildings and an investment in new buildings, shopping areas and facilities, but these have often been confined to the downtown area and one or two highly localised inner city residential areas. Surrounding inner city areas remain decayed with poor services and housing stock. Gentrification, if anything, has highlighted the social inequalities of the inner city as decay exists alongside affluence, expensive lifestyles and housing alongside poverty, new consumption patterns alongside economic subsistence, security alongside crime. Gentrification has forced migrants and the poor to move to less expensive housing areas further out, which in turn means that those affected might be further from their work, and facing higher costs. Those who are left near the inner city form a pool of low-cost labour to clean and care for the new commercial and residential developments. Changing urban landscapes have reinforced difference and division.

Differences and divisions: theorising the city

The city, especially primate and global cities, contain the economic powerhouses of the contemporary world. Wealth continues to remain concentrated in these cities, and the wealthy reside here – or within commuting distance. Indeed, many villages or even towns and cities are dormitory in nature – people live there but commute to work elsewhere, in a bigger city. Cities also encompass exceedingly impoverished communities, and the stark contrast between the poverty and wealth of those who inhabit the city is a theme that has characterised sociology from its beginning. The city represents some of the most obvious and significant economic differences between people, which in turn reflect ethnic, gender, age, employment and education issues.

One aspect which has attracted urban sociologists since the turn of the century, when black immigration from the American South began to transform cities such as Chicago and New York, is the significance of ethnicity. Black communities were confined to crowded and impoverished neighbourhoods, or **ghettoes**. Italian or Irish immigrants lived in other concentrated communities. The Chicago School in the early decades of this century wrote about questions of integration and equilibrium in the city and these issues were raised again when the mass labour migrations of the post-war era took place, especially as this migration of Afro-Americans was associated with the decline of inner city areas.

Two sociologists, John Rex and Robert Moore, took up the same interest in Britain when they published an influential book in 1967, *Race, Community and Conflict*. They explored the process of succession in the inner city areas of Birmingham as Afro-Caribbean migrants replaced the white inhabitants of particular areas. These new migrants were excluded

Ghettoes are concentrated areas of poverty which contain excluded groups within a city.

from certain areas and types of housing by the operations of the housing market and specifically of gatekeepers such as real estate agents. Rex and Moore argued that these migrants occupied a housing class in a market, and their economic position reflected their ability to buy or rent certain types of accommodation. It is possible to see the same process in action in New Zealand cities with the arrival and concentration of Maori and Pacific Islands migrants in the 1960s and 1970s. Ponsonby and Newtown became inner city destinations along with state housing areas such as Otara or Porirua. Is this a result of choice or discrimination? Rex and Moore would argue that the latter is considerably more in evidence than the former.

A critical, neo-Weberian sociology of the city had an important influence on more recent understandings of urban processes, and the contribution of Pahl and others raised fundamental questions about the 'nature of the state, power, class and social action', in the context of the city. These contributions from neo-Weberians were soon joined by those from neo-Marxists, including David Harvey and Manuel Castells. They have focused attention on the structures of the city, both physical and institutional, and on how these reflect political and economic divisions. The city is an expression of the nature of contemporary capitalism and as such it is an important site of capitalist expansion – and contraction – and of the eternal class distinctions which characterise capitalist relations. Harvey (1973; 1978; 1982) has argued that the space of the city is constantly being restructured as economic decisions are made about the profitability of locating in one area or another (Giddens, 1993: 574). These decisions do not simply reflect local economic processes but are sensitive to international flows of capital and the position of specific cities in global networks. Apart from seeing the city as a manifestation of capitalism, Harvey is also interested in the way in which grassroots movements have contributed to the processes of urban change, and he has argued that such movements are a displaced form of class struggle: the community replaces the workplace as an important arena for the playing out of class interests (Smith and Tardanico, 1996: 94).

Another influential neo-Marxist is Castells, who has shared Harvey's interests in the process of urban development as an expression of global and local capitalist relations, and the way in which local forms of urban struggle and resistance are an expression of class politics. Castells sees urbanisation as the concentration of production in a locality and the incorporation of people and institutions into a set of cultural and economic practices, which are capitalist in nature. 'Spatial forms, then, are assumed to be material products of historically-specific patterns of social organisation' (Smith and Tardanico, 1996: 95). The city has allowed profit to be generated in new ways. Moreover, the city is an important site of consumption. For Castells, the city is an expression of the processes of capitalism, including the need to generate profit, the globalisation of production and contemporary forms of development and decline, but it is also the home of significant social movements, which have the capacity to alter the character of the city More recently, Castells (1996) has examined the role of cities in the economic, political and cultural networks that now determine and dominate global production. These networks will further confirm the significance of the city, and especially those cities which are at the centre of regional and global systems of power and production.

Postmodernists are also interested in the city as an expression of globalism, but approach the same issues somewhat differently. Postmodernism has many meanings (Hannigan, 1995), and postmodernist approaches have been used to explore contemporary architecture – a form of multinational globalised capitalism, style and beliefs. The emphasis is on the plurality of identity and social relations, and cities are typically seen as an expression of the transformations that mark postmodernity. Four aspects in particular are said to mark the postmodern city (Hannigan, 1995: 160–161). The first is its despatialised or uniform nature which means that contemporary shopping centres, hotels or urban landscapes could be anywhere. A chain hotel in Auckland is likely to be a replica of the same hotels in Ankara, Akron or Adelaide. The McDonalisation of production and consumption standardises many forms of city life. Brand names are global and what you purchase will be much the same, no matter where you purchase it, no matter what the city or country. McDonald's has provided a metaphor for this aspect of globalisation and how it impacts upon urban landscapes. Secondly, the postmodern city is 'obsessed with surveillance and security' (Hannigan, 1995: 160). Security is expressed in the privatised public spaces such as malls or play areas which are under intense security by security officers, who are often hidden from public view and monitor behaviour via sophisticated surveillance systems. Foucault has discussed the ability – and inclination – to monitor social behaviour, and a mall is constructed with security and control in mind. Note the cameras and security officers and the limited exits in your local mall. Thirdly, the postmodern city is often constructed to appear like something else; often themes such as a particular historical period, a media character or show, or another place dominate (Hannigan, 1995: 161). These constructions are designed as a representation of a theme and are deemed to be a way of encouraging people to travel to a themed shopping centre and to buy more. Finally, the city is said to be geographically and sociologically fragmented, and 'newly created postmodern landscapes do not arise in any organic fashion from the existing urban environment but are artificially inserted with little regard to the consequences either for the existing neighbourhoods or for the integrity of the city as a whole' (Hannigan, 1995: 161). Postmodernism has a lot to say about cities and urban spaces, and especially cities such as Los Angeles. Certainly, the social and spatial nature of the city has changed this century. Sociologists are particularly interested in processes of expansion and decline, and the impact that these processes have on where people live, work and shop.

Conclusion

We do not want to make the same mistake as the early sociologists and see the city as evidence of the breakdown of society. It certainly is the site of problems – decay, crime, environmental degradation, congestion, poverty – but equally, it represents economic growth, new lifestyle possibilities and new forms of community and work. The reality is that about half of New Zealand's population lives within an hour's drive of Auckland, and that this country is one of the most highly urbanised in the world. If we are to understand the daily life of New Zealanders, then our analysis needs to focus on the nature of city life. If we are to understand the modern economy or globalisation, then the city is a critical feature to be studied. The evolution of societies, economies and world networks hinges on what happens in cities. We need to get beyond the common-sense idea that the city represents an unfortunate decline of the integrated, bucolic life of the smaller community or rural area and to understand the dynamics and structure of the city – both good and bad.

Study questions

10.1 Which sociological concepts best describe the way of life in the city?

10.2 What have been the major influences on the development of the city in the latter half of the twentieth century?

10.3 Who is typically excluded or marginalised in contemporary cities? How is this manifested? What processes result in exclusion?

Further reading

Castells, M. (1996) *The Rise of the Network Society*. Blackwell, Cambridge, Ma.

King, A.D. (1991) *Global Cities*. Routledge, London.

Population Division of the Department of Economic and Social Affairs of the United Nations Secretariat. (1999) *The World at Six Billion*. (ESA/P/WP.154, 12 October 1999.) http://www.undp.org/popin/wdtrends/urb/urb/urbpcf.htm

Sassen, S. (1991) *The Global City: New York, London, Tokyo*. Princeton University Press, Princeton.

Savage M. and Warde, A. (1993) *Urban Sociology, Capitalism and Modernity*. Macmillan, London.

Thorns, D. (1994) Urban. In Spoonley, P., Pearson, D. and Shirley, I. (eds). *New Zealand Society: A Sociological Introduction*. Dunmore Press, Palmerston North.

United Nations Population Division – *see* Population Division …

11 Racism and ethnicity

Chapter aims

- to outline the practice of racism and to describe various forms of resistance to racism;
- to provide an analysis of identity, specifically ethnic identity, and its emergence in the late twentieth century as the basis of politics;
- to indicate some of the traditional and emerging sociological approaches to issues of racism and ethnicity.

Introduction

The sociology of racism and ethnicity has not always been a central, or indeed even a popular, topic in sociology. At sociology's birth in the nineteenth century, it was often thought that the reality of living in an industrialised, urbanised society would dominate social relationships and that the pre-existing concepts of who we are in terms of a specific locality or ethnic identity would disappear. Karl Marx, for example, felt that the identities and politics of the workplace would prevail over those of the community and ethnic group. Max Weber was not so sure. He argued that an important aspect of social status would be **ethnicity**. Ironically, for much of the latter part of the nineteenth century and for a good part of the early twentieth century, the world was divided up into nations which were all seen as the products of particular 'races'. What unsettled this view and invited sociologists to rewrite the analysis of identity was the Holocaust. It epitomised the excesses of racism and encouraged sociologists and others to reconsider how classifications like **'race'** were used and what alternatives existed. At the end of the twentieth century, the political reality of who we are in ethnic terms can hardly be ignored. In many societies – New Zealand included – it is one of the significant dimensions of identity and of difference, and a feature which is shared globally with many other countries. A sociology without an understanding of racism and ethnicity is now unthinkable. Accordingly, this chapter examines how questions of 'race', racism and ethnicity

> **Ethnicity** occurs when a group shares a particular history, a set of cultural practices and institutions, and is conscious of a shared identity as a result.

> **Race** is the grouping which results from the practice of classifying others by physical characteristics and the belief that this classification represents some form of innate difference in terms of ability or disposition.

manifest themselves in terms of our personal identities and as we interact with others, and in creating inequalities.

Who are we?

Many of us still feel uncomfortable with the importance granted to matters of racism and ethnicity. However, in terms of how we operate in our communities, in terms of national identity and issues, or in terms of social policy, contemporary debates are framed by concerns associated with ethnic identity. Sport and leisure, for example, involve distinct ethnic traditions and this often determines which group plays a particular sport. The practices of national teams such as the use of the haka at the start of an All Black game are examples of such traditions. Our education often requires a declaration of who we are in cultural terms and an exploration of what this means. In the wake of MMP, political differences have yet again come to reflect ethnic loyalties. All of these issues have as great an impact on the residents of rural or provincial New Zealand as they do on people in the larger cities or elsewhere in the world. In London or Liverpool, in Sydney or Melbourne, in New York, Toronto, Bangkok or Singapore, policy and political issues are often substantially influenced by cultural and ethnic considerations. Admittedly, the experiences are not always positive ones. The end of the century has seen the escalation of major ethnic conflict in the former Yugoslavia, in Rwanda and in Los Angeles. But, as sociologists, we want to understand the centrality and significance of these issues and perhaps, if we feel so inclined, do something about them.

At this point, it is worth drawing a distinction between ethnicity and racism. We need to accept that sociologists will use these and related terms in ways that are quite different from common usage. The common-sense definition of 'race' in contemporary New Zealand can often be a long way from what a sociologist might mean by the same term. When we talk about 'race' sociologically, we are essentially describing the common-sense classification of people into groups according to biological characteristics. The most visible biological characteristics are things such as skin colour or facial features. It is an easy and relatively quick way to categorise people into groups and a common way of defining and relating to others, even if there is no racist intent. However, behind this convention is a substantial history of exclusion and even persecution that was 'justified' by a scientific racism which argued that peoples' genetic background predetermined their behaviour and their potential. It is the continuation and the expression of these ideas that sociologists identify as *racism*. This label indicates the way in which these classifications lead to negative views (prejudice) and behaviours which exclude others (discrimination).

In distinct contrast to this is the notion of ethnicity. This developed as a result of the political developments of the latter half of the twentieth century and the growing interest in how cultural identity influences intergroup and inter-personal relations. Ethnicity is a product of how a particular group sees its history, its identity, how it defines membership, how it continues to uphold its practices and beliefs, and how it interacts with others. All of us belong to a variety of groups, including religious and sporting groups, groups belonging to specific localities and age cohorts. Ethnicity is one further dimension of such group identity. It captures the idea of belonging to a particular cultural group and the significance of this identity for an individual. Some people will marry out of or opt to move out of the group while others might well join it. The boundaries defining who is a member of a group are often relatively soft compared to the hard and exclusive boundaries imposed on 'races' in a country such as South Africa under the apartheid system. Ethnicity can be an opportunity to glorify your own group and discriminate against others, but equally, it often involves an acceptance of cultural diversity and a pride in an individual's cultural traditions and history. In fact, it is often so important that for many people it is *the* most significant form of identity.

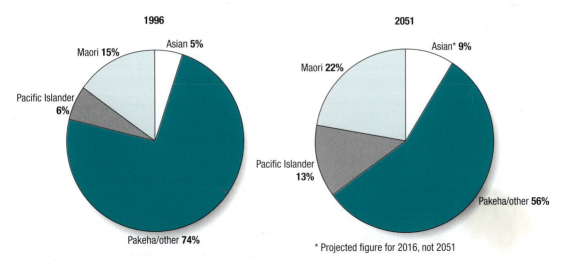

Source: Statistics New Zealand (1999) *Demographic trends, 1998.*

Figure 11.1 The growing significance of New Zealand's cultural diversity: ethnicity, 1996 and 2051

In the same way that feminism has challenged sociology to include gender considerations in our theorising and practice, the anti-racist and anti-colonial movements of the late twentieth century have invited sociology to give much greater consideration to ethnic identity and the products of a colonial past. Ethnicity is now a major consideration in areas such as access to health care, the way in which fishery resources are owned and managed, the inclusion of cultural practices and institutions into the mainstream of New Zealand society or the way in which New Zealand should be politically represented and governed. It is a world that Karl Marx might well have recognised, coming as he did from a

Post-colonialism describes an analytical approach and political position which is critical of the processes and impact of colonialism. It includes the attempt to establish new, non- or anti-colonial institutions and identities.

Rabbinical family and Jewish background, but he probably would not have been supportive of ethnic and nationalist movements. For many Marxists, racism and ethnicity serve as a smokescreen for more fundamental class-related questions. In contrast, Max Weber, who long ago recognised that the status of ethnic groups could be of significant advantage – and disadvantage – would have been much more comfortable with these arguments. The difference between Marx and Weber is certainly repeated amongst contemporary sociologists. Some, like many New Zealanders, might feel uncomfortable or indeed deplore the significance of ethnicity in New Zealand. Others, and we would like to think it is the majority, see ethnicity as one of the major dimensions of social life. Its significance also marks quite a substantial change which has occurred alongside the local economic revolution of the 1980s and 1990s. In a similar vein, we would want to talk about the 'cultural' revolution of the same period and the way in which ethnicity has now been inserted into many areas of life and, for many people, is a defining feature of social identity and interaction. This revolution also marks an interesting departure from the colonial links between New Zealand and Britain. **Post-colonialism** is one term which tries to capture the significance of these changes, not as somehow indicating the disappearance of colonialism, but as a way of critically understanding what colonialism has done for New Zealand and what we might do differently in the future.

Hostility towards Asian migrants has been a recurring theme in New Zealand history

A contemporary sociology must consider how best to understand the implications of such changes. Racism, or the way in which people are conceived of negatively and perhaps discriminated against, is an on-going issue which deserves attention in the same way that class differences do in an advanced capitalist society. How we conceive of ourselves in terms of an ethnic identity, or the way in which some people decline (often strongly) to be identified in ethnic terms, also requires attention, especially given the importance of ethnic claims for questions of public policy and justice. Whether this is best described as post-colonialism or something else will be explored later but there is little doubt that the New Zealand of the early and mid-twentieth century, with its links to Britain and its deference to all things British, has been replaced by a country in which there is a much greater interest both in local identities and concerns and in the geo-political realities of being part of the Asia-Pacific region.

The local and the global: the reality of 'race' and the resistance to racism

The construction and application of ideas about 'race' were essentially a product of European expansionism and the establishment of colonial empires. As a way of classifying and understanding others, 'race' was used by European nations as a means of justifying their dominance and exploitation of non-white peoples: later they were variously seen as pagan, uncivilised, backward, primitive, intellectually inferior and incapable of contributing to modernity. The expansion of these colonial empires, especially those that were capitalist in nature, involved complex arguments about the superiority and inferiority of certain 'races'. This is epitomised in the social and legal circumstances of the slave states of the southern United States where an absolute division between black and white was constructed, and was later justified by the science of 'race'. Scientists 'proved' that 'races' existed and that there were significant cultural, intellectual and physical differences between them. This tradition continues, particularly, but not exclusively, in the United States where a book that appeared recently, *The Bell Curve*, repeats such arguments about 'racial difference', as though the existence of 'races' is real and as though it is possible to quantify intellectual differences. Of course, 'races' are not 'real' in this sense. They are social constructions and are only made important by our social beliefs and values.

The colonialisation of New Zealand in the nineteenth century occurred during a period when slavery was coming under attack but when views about 'race' were still very powerful and widespread. New Zealand's colonial history is a mixture of patronising benevolence and beliefs about the superiority of the coloniser and the inferiority of Maori. Whatever criticism we might have of the missionaries, for example, many were motivated by a genuinely-felt, if patronising, concern for Maori. The Treaty of Waitangi was, among other things, a recognition of the rights of 'natives', voiced both here and in Britain. The story of nineteenth-century New Zealand includes explicit beliefs about the significance of 'race' and the right of the colonisers to impose their own institutions and beliefs, alongside some limited attempts to recognise and protect Maori – the latter attempts include the Treaty.

The history of 'race' is a dominant theme of the nineteenth century globally as it underpins national expansion and the internal and international policies of empires and colonies. It was re-emphasised by anti-democratic movements, especially **fascism,** at the beginning of the twentieth century. The attempt by the Nazi regime in Germany, with the help of other sympathetic governments and movements, to eliminate the 'landless' of Europe, the *untermenschen* (non-humans) represented by Jews and Romanys represents one of the worst (but by no means the only) excesses of racism in history. The latter half of the twentieth century has seen some interesting politics emerge. Anti-colonial, civil rights and ethnic groups have challenged the ideas about 'race' and the institutions and practises that have underpinned them. 'Racism' and 'institutional racism' have entered the sociological and popular vocabulary as a way of identifying, critiquing and dismissing the use of 'race' as a means of demeaning and disempowering others.

Fascism is the political philosophy of a totalitarian party or government which adopts an extreme form of exclusionary nationalism and may, as in the case of Nazism, pursue policies of genocide or ethnic cleansing.

The late twentieth century has witnessed an upsurge in ethnic conflict.
Kosovo, 1999

How did former colonised peoples escape from the disempowering ideologies and labels which had justified their subservience? A group of writers mostly from French colonies or former colonies, had a major influence. They included Aimé Césaire, and above all, Franz Fanon. They drew upon various sources for their theoretical inspiration, including

Freud, Marx and existentialism. Fanon provided a number of powerful arguments about the internalisation of racist beliefs by those identified as inferior, about the disempowering and exclusionary ideas and strategies of colonialism and racism, and about the need for decolonisation and the powerful forces that were going to be released as colonised peoples regained their confidence and cultural identity. He was a significant influence on those former colonies that were fighting for their independence, but he was equally influential on the growing civil rights movements of the USA and elsewhere. The sociological interest grew with the riots in various US cities in the 1960s and the growing influence of the black civil rights movement. Here were a set of arguments and strategies which denied the validity of 'race', or the policies and institutions which had sustained racial advantage and disadvantage, and they were to have a profound effect on many countries – including New Zealand.

Institutional racism was a concept that identified the way in which organisations, especially those that were responsible for health, education and justice, discriminated against particular groups, either intentionally or unintentionally. It was coined in 1967 in the midst of the civil rights movement in the USA, and first appeared in New Zealand in 1970 to be used by a younger group of Maori. They were the children of a generation of post-war migrants who had moved from their traditional iwi locations to the cities, who had limited contact with Maori culture and institutions, and who were inspired by the emerging arguments and strategies of anti-colonial and anti-racist movements. Throughout the 1970s and 1980s, they highlighted and attacked anything that was deemed racist, they challenged Maori leaders and institutions to provide leadership, and a defence of **tikanga Maori** and they sought to establish an acceptance of things Maori in the public domain. By the late 1980s, biculturalism had emerged as the basis for public policy and tino rangatiratanga as an ambition that embodied the notion of Maori control. These politics are epitomised in Donna Awatere's book, *Maori Sovereignty* (1984), and the influence of Franz Fanon can readily be seen in the arguments about colonialism and the need for decolonisation. The notion of who we are, individually and collectively, has not been the same since.

These emancipatory movements have been reinforced by one other development in the post-war period: the migration of large numbers of people in response to the demands of an expanding – and then restructured – capitalism. By the early 1970s, the significance of migration in altering the urban communities of advanced capitalism was apparent, and a group of neo-Marxist sociologists, including Stephen Castles and Bob Miles, developed an approach which focused on the political economy of labour migration. At the centre of this analysis was the role of **labour migration** in capitalist production, especially in the post-war environment when capitalism was expanding but there was a shortage of semi-skilled and unskilled labour. Large migration flows resulted, with former colonies providing labour to the metropolitan centres. Significantly, many of these

> **Tikanga Maori** refers to the whole which is Maori culture.

> **Labour migration** describes the flows of typically unskilled and semi-skilled workers in search of employment.

Racialisation is the process whereby a group is classified as a race and defined as a problem.

migrants were non-white. The labour needs of capitalism led to a new cultural diversity, and particular migrant groups were identified by the white host communities as responsible for social problems such as increased unemployment, the decline in particular urban areas, and the difficulty of obtaining resources in areas such as health and education. These groups were **racialised**, or seen as a 'racial problem'. The class communities which the migrants entered in the work place or community were increasingly divided over how these migrants were perceived and treated, and in many instances, a resurgence in explicitly racist political movements occurred in countries such as France, Britain and the USA. These non-white communities are no longer migrants but are products of the countries in which they have been born and brought up. Their struggles concern their location as non-white communities in white-dominated societies and what citizenship might mean for them in this context. In New Zealand, this has provided new identities, and what it means to be Tangata Whenua, Tangata Pasifika or Pakeha are significant social issues.

The social and the personal: ethnic identity and notions of citizenship

One of the most interesting – and challenging – developments of recent decades has been the growing significance of cultural identity. It is a universal phenomena, even for those who once did not have to consider such matters. Jeremy Paxman (*The English*, 1998) describes the English as once having been the top dogs in the world's top-dog empire who did not need to know who they were, but faced by devolution within Britain and membership of Europe, the question of Englishness now has an immediacy and importance that cannot be ignored. It provides an interesting counterpoint – and overlap – with marginal identities.

> ... the term 'black' was coined as a way of referencing the common experience of racism and marginalisation in Britain and came to provide the organisational category of a new politics of resistance amongst groups and communities with ... very different histories, traditions and ethnic identities.
>
> (Hall, 1995: 223)

Whether one belongs to a majority or minority group, the question of cultural identity is an important one in modern societies. Who we are as cultural beings and what this means in terms of social and economic opportunities, self-esteem and social interaction, are central social and political questions. Social identity comes – for many – to be expressed through membership of an ethnic group. We are continually asked the question 'to which ethnic group do you belong?' as we begin school, go to hospital or enter New Zealand. The nature of the question and the categories provided for the answer are all regularly contested. Social policies are routinely constructed around notions of ethnic need, and the targeting of services typically addresses ethnic issues. Sport, music and the media all reflect the way in which our respective ethnic identities are played out in public spaces – sometimes in a celebratory and positive way, at other times, in varying degrees of offensiveness or marked by silence. These developments are reflected in the move from a citizenship which was defined in welfare state societies largely by notions of universal need and national welfare to a situation where a much more limited conception of social and economic rights prevails.

There is an interesting tension in recent developments. As countries like New Zealand have restructured, the arguments of an **economic rationalism** have come to determine policies. Issues of economic efficiency and a limited role for the state dominate, together with the emphasis on being competitive in a global economy. Central to these political ideologies is an assumption that individuals will act rationally in a self-interested way when faced by choices in one market or another. The reality is that most of us live our lives as members of groups and communities where social considerations exist alongside strictly personal ones. A powerful example are ethnic groups where collective interests are internally negotiated – not always amicably – and come to influence how the members of that group live their lives. Ethnicity requires a degree of loyalty and collective agreement in order for it to work. Any benefits are collectively shared, whether in the personal sense (enhanced self-esteem) or through access to common resources such as capital to establish a business or buy a house. Being a member of an ethnic group can be frustrating and disempowering, but equally, it can be a significant and positive aspect of social identity. It influences what sports we play, how we celebrate significant events in our lives, what schools we attend and our educational performance, what jobs we get, and how we are perceived in public situations. The current significance of ethnicity for many people – certainly not all – is a major determinant in identity and social interaction. This reality contradicts the assumptions of an economic rationalism.

There is no better example in a New Zealand setting than the resurgence of Maori identity and culture in recent decades. Dismissed for much of this century as irrelevant to a modern society, tikanga Maori was relegated to an interesting but quaint element in education, and some token expressions such as the All Black haka. It was sustained within Maori communities and on marae, but the migration of more than half the Maori population in the post-war period from traditional iwi areas to the cities constituted yet another factor in undermining the reproduction of a language and culture. The realisation that this was the case and the strategies of an urban-raised generation produced a more assertive politics that combined traditional cultural concerns with the strategies of feminism and the civil rights movement. In the wake of these politics, the numbers claiming Maori identity – including both the urban Maori who do not

Economic rationalism is the monetarist-inspired politics of the 1980s and 1990s which assumes that individuals and markets act in economically rational ways (see also pp. 93 and 135).

claim an association with a particular iwi as well as those who do – has grown substantially and had reached almost 600 000 by the late 1990s. The Treaty of Waitangi is back as a constitutional document which identifies the rights of Maori as Tangata Whenua. It is much more difficult to ridicule or dismiss Maori culture in the public domain, and the language and culture are recognised in a range of policies and institutions.

One expression of ethnic revival in Aotearoa New Zealand

Ethnic revival encompasses the resurgence in ethnic identity of the last decades and the significance of this in political debates.

The resurgence of Maori culture and the claiming of Maori ethnicity is just one example of the **ethnic revival** that has occurred amongst indigenous peoples who had been colonised, as well as amongst minority ethnic groups who migrated at some point in the past. Settler societies such as New Zealand, Australia, Canada and the USA must now address the policy implications of a renewed importance given to ethnic identity, and increasingly, notions of citizenship encompass the differential rights attached to membership of an ethnic group. A sociology which does not address such issues fails to include one of the central developments of this century. However, it is not simply the ethnicity of minority and indigenous groups which is of interest. In countries like New Zealand, the bicultural policies and assertiveness of Maori have challenged what it is to be a member of the majority group. This question was given focus with the publication of Michael King's book, *Being Pakeha* (1985), and the label 'Pakeha' and what it means in terms of personal identity attracted a lively and, at times, angry debate in New Zealand in the late 1980s and 1990s. The simple process of naming yourself establishes certain claims, both about how social membership is defined, as well as what that membership means in terms of rights and resources.

Postcolonial Pakeha?

David Pearson

Naming oneself ought to be easy. But some questions about identity are tricky. I race through most of the census form with ease, knowing where I live, what job I do, and whether I own a washing machine. But then you get to those tick boxes that ask you to indicate what ethnic group you belong to. I used to tick 'European New Zealander' since that seems to describe me best. An English-born person, with British ancestries (Anglo and Celtic) who has lived in New Zealand for over twenty years. And the holder of New Zealand and European Union passports. Increasingly, however, the word 'Pakeha' is offered as a possibility for naming oneself, ethnically speaking. Is this a better alternative to 'European New Zealander'? Personally and sociologically, this is perplexing.

Over the past few years, we have witnessed the emergence of a fascinating situation whereby some members of the majority group in New Zealand name themselves using a word, Pakeha, that is taken from a minority group, Maori; whilst others, equally strongly, resist the label because of its source. Between these opposing positions one finds a broad range of people who are not sure, or who use the term Pakeha in some contexts but not in others. Meanwhile most Tangata Whenua seem comfortable using the term Maori, although here too there are questions to be asked about whether other names, of hapu or iwi for example, are more important in some or all contexts.

These processes of majority and minority group naming are thoroughly interwoven and can be traced through the colonial and post-colonial relations between two peoples. On the one hand, we can trace the gradual adoption of a 'national' categorisation, Maori, by socially and geographically distinct iwi and hapu, from the outset of colonisation. Paradoxically, the introduction of the category and the establishment of legislation and institutions designed to 'manage' the indigenous fostered new individual and political identities that were grafted onto senses of 'us' that pre-dated European contact. On the other hand, whilst the term *Pakeha* soon became a common Maori term for 'white strangers', and seems to have been used by some early settlers living alongside Maori, the use of Pakeha as a national identifier for European New Zealanders is a very recent phenomenon.

After the 1960s, aboriginal groups, like Maori, became increasingly assertive in their quest for self-determination and rights to land, fisheries and other resources – as 'First Nations' in the United Nations. In New Zealand, increasingly described in some circles as Aotearoa, the Treaty of Waitangi and the Waitangi Tribunal became, respectively, a potent symbol of a reconstructed history of partnership between indigenous people and settlers, and the vehicle for material and cultural redress of past wrongs within that history. Biculturalism, moreover, became a word that sought to encapsulate a shared Pacific existence and a framework for decolonisation processes that affected both Treaty partners. These names and frameworks can be seen as cynical attempts by the state to 'manage' ethnic politics, and as a liberative strategy for those seeking new avenues for reconciliation.

Names, particularly ethnic names, are indicators of political contestation. They reflect a dynamic process of boundary creation and reconstruction as relations between 'us' and 'them' shift in tune with changing meetings between social friends and strangers. The majority population in New Zealand is also experiencing a process of renaming. They too are contesting a change in their ethnic and national identities over the past few decades, partly because of the links with aboriginal peoples in their midst, but also because of the attenuation, possibly severance, of ties with the country, Britain, that previous generations once called 'Home'. New Zealanders of British ancestry, having established formal political independence and no longer reliant on the economic trading link with 'the mother country', are searching for a post-colonial social and cultural identity. At least this is how the argument runs for some who advocate the name Pakeha.

For cultural nationalists seeking a new identity for their country and themselves, naming oneself Pakeha is a political declaration. It positions them firmly in the Pacific and the identifier, being a Maori label, affirms an empathy with bicultural partners, with the Treaty representing a totem of national birth and renewal. But how forceful is this decolonisation movement, and how widespread is the support for Pakeha, as a name and as a political statement?

Research on these questions is in its infancy, but the study by Pearson and Sissons of Pakeha identity, for example, based as it was on a national survey, found that relatively few New Zealanders of European ancestry consistently name themselves Pakeha. In fact, 83% of those surveyed rejected the term outright or used it only occasionally. Why? Because they believed that the name had negative connotations in Maori and/or that it did not adequately link them to their European or British ancestry.

The people who were 'never Pakeha' were adamant that they had a strong sense of ethnicity. They implied that they did have a sense of 'us' that was distinctively their own and, interestingly, that their ethnic identity was not adequately covered by the term New Zealander. So this survey did not confirm the hypothesis that most New Zealanders in the majority group conflated their national and ethnic identity. Nor did it suggest that adding a British or European prefix to the term *New Zealander* was a satisfactory compromise for all.

What the survey appears to indicate is that many potential Pakeha do not want a borrowed name, particularly one that might denigrate them. But the British or European affiliation is not satisfactory either. Some people might be happy having a hyphenated label as it is often called in North America – they could call themselves British or European-New Zealanders. That's OK with me as a recent migrant. But what if you are a fourth or fifth generation 'European' New Zealander? These 'old timers' seem to need a sub-national, indigenous, non-Maori equivalent to iwi and hapu affiliation. If you come up with a likely name, rush out and patent it.

The research done by Pearson and Sissons also raised major doubts about assuming an automatic equation between accepting the label Pakeha and the assertion of a particular political standpoint. Their findings suggest that if you call yourself Pakeha, it does not necessarily mean you fully sympathise with biculturalism or Treaty issues, and support for Maori self-determination – tino rangatiratanga – is decidedly problematic. And, even more striking, refusing to name yourself Pakeha is not a sure-fire indicator of monoculturalism or worse. In the survey, both the users and non-users of Pakeha were internally divided on such issues as what we call our country and how widespread the experience, in daily life, of Maori culture and language should be?

If being Pakeha is an indicator of support for biculturalism, one would expect the highest levels of support for, for example, bilingualism among those who always called themselves Pakeha. This was indeed the case. Almost three-quarters of the 'always Pakeha' were happy with Aotearoa/ New Zealand as a national label, just over half believed we should have some understanding of Maori culture, and there was solid, if minority support (44%) for being able to pronounce Maori words correctly. Most 'never Pakeha' disagreed, but sizeable numbers (ranging from 24% to 45%) supported these ideas. Divisions between the 'always Pakeha' also soon became apparent when the limits of their sympathy for biculturalism were tested. A large majority (76%) weren't prepared to go as far as replacing New Zealand with Aotearoa and, on average, only about a quarter of them accepted the idea of seeing the Maori language on every street sign, on tins of baked beans, or on the coins in their pockets. So despite the fact that 'always Pakeha' were more committed to biculturalism than 'never Pakeha' on most indicators, their support was within strict limits.

Much the same pattern emerged when questions of rights and

self-determination were raised. Just over half (55%) of the 'always Pakeha' thought Maori should have more control over their own affairs at the iwi level – and the same proportion of the 'never Pakeha' agreed with them. But there was not strong support for special rights for Maori at the national level from any Pakeha. 'We are all New Zealanders' seemed to be the refrain. Overall, there appears to be a small subgroup of self-identifying Pakeha who share bicultural ideals and who are sympathetic towards the idea of greater Maori self-determination, and there is a somewhat smaller number of people who reject the Pakeha label but espouse similar sentiments. As for the rest, the cultural nationalist crusade has limited appeal.

Why should this be so? The majority's fear of having to give too much away to an increasingly assertive aboriginal minority, and their irritation with the perceived political correctness of a Pakeha intelligentsia, is only half the story. There is also hostility and unease about losing control to global political, economic and social forces. The shock of the new is embraced by some, rejected by others. Having access to new cuisines and the Internet is exciting, but the fear of losing your job if your company moves offshore is disconcerting. Where do you anchor yourself in a sea of new and old possible identities? While some Pakeha proselytise the Pacific way, others research their British genealogy. The word *postcolonised* is confusing. We are not witnessing a new linear stage of development, nationalistically or otherwise. We are seeing new processes of change grafted onto tradition, providing a heady transition to an uncertain future. What do we call this experience, and how do we name ourselves within it? What do you think?

Questions

Having read the contribution by David Pearson, what is your response to the following questions?

1   What is meant by the claim that '… ethnic names are indicators of political contestation'?

2   David Pearson highlights the confused use of ethnic labels such as Pakeha, and what this self-claiming means in terms of support for various political issues. Are ethnic labels used consistently? How significant are internal divisions within any ethnic group?

3   How new or different are these ethnic politics? David Pearson sees them as 'new processes of change grafted onto tradition' but is the nature of the change more significant than the tradition, or vice versa?

Differences and divisions: a racist society?

The charge that a society, an institution or an individual is racist is now a politically powerful one. In seeking to undermine the monoculturalism which dominated many Western societies for most of this century, anti-colonial and anti-racist movements invested the notion of racism with a critical accusation. To be racist was to have broken a social code. Of course, that social code of non-discrimination towards other 'races' had to be defined and legitimated – a difficult task when quite the opposite had prevailed historically. The task was helped along by post-Holocaust developments which established that the notion of 'race' was scientifically invalid; the politics of the newly independent countries and their activists; the civil rights movement in the USA; the promotion of universal human rights by international agencies such as the UN; and the ethnic revival. Sociologists contributed to these debates.

In the United Kingdom, some sociologists took an interest in the arrival of non-white migrants in major urban areas from the 1960s onwards. They included John Rex and Robert Moore who, influenced by Weber, used the notion of **housing classes** to examine the way in which these new Asian and Afro-Caribbean migrants were being excluded within an urban housing market. Arguments about class divisions were combined with an interest in racial disadvantage, and empirical research was used to demonstrate the extent of black exclusion from access to various sorts of housing in particular urban areas. It was part of a move to challenge commonly-held assumptions about the equity and acceptance of cultural difference within British society from the later 1960s onwards.

Other sociologists also contributed to these emerging debates, especially by documenting the exclusionary ideas and practices of a colonial past. Michael Banton, for example, wrote about the history of the idea of 'race'. The evolution of the idea, its support by the emerging biological sciences, the way in which the ideas about 'race' were used to justify slavery or genocide and the unscientific nature of the concept and its supporting arguments were all extensively critiqued by sociologists. This was broadened by the contributions of others from the late 1980s onwards. In particular, Edward Said argued that Europeans constructed a dualism between the West and the Orient in a way that strengthened 'Western cultures and imprisons those of the Orient' (Malik, 1996: 227). Orientalism helped define the 'Other', those who could justifiably be seen as different and/or inferior in some way, and thereby excluded. Said also analyses the various forms of resistance to these notions and extends the interest of Fanon in the process of decolonisation, the growing plurality of contemporary states and how this plurality is encompassed (or rejected) in civic life. However, the idea of 'race' and the construction of the Other has continued to evolve and British sociologists such as Barker (1981) and Americans such as Goldberg (1993) provide an analysis and critique of the ideologies which preserve racial exclusion.

> **Housing classes** is a neo-Weberian term that assumes that position in a housing market is broadly equivalent to class.

In the wake of monetarist-inspired New Right governments in Europe and North America, new forms of racism have emerged which owe little to the crude biological racism of the past, but rather are couched in the arguments of preserving cultural traditions and the importance of national unity and institutions. If you read the 'letters to the editor' columns of your local newspaper, you will see plenty of evidence of these evolving forms of racism. One recent and interesting development has been the attempt to invert the meaning of racism. Instead of being used to indicate the classification of others in racial terms and then discriminating against them, some members of majority groups use *racism* to describe anything which recognises minority ethnic or indigenous group identity and practices. They think the majority group are being excluded and want to use racism as the privileging of minority and indigenous groups. In this case, the definition of who is the 'victim' of racism is reversed. In fact, the empirical evidence demonstrates the nonsense of this position. Even though ethnic and indigenous groups have been more widely recognised in policy terms, the sociological research demonstrates that they continue to face disadvantage in a way that is not true for majority groups such as Pakeha. Whether in the area of access to health care, or education, justice, employment or housing, Maori and Pacific Islanders* typically experience much higher negative rates than is true for Pakeha. A crude but reasonably consistent measure is to say that the rate for Maori/Pacific Islanders will be twice to four times worse than Pakeha rates. This is also apparent in areas such as unemployment, illness, imprisonment or sub-standard housing. The question is whether this state of affairs is primarily the product of racism.

The answer is a lot more complex than one might expect. In the case of the health statistics, some of the difference can be accounted for by class. Death or illness resulting from accidents or certain diseases is a direct product of the class position of individuals and families. If working-class Maori and Pakeha are compared, then the differences are reduced. However, proportionately more Maori are working class for historical reasons which is one reason why Maori appear in negative statistics. Demographically, Maori have a much younger age profile and constitute a greater proportion of the 'at risk' age groups. If teenage males are responsible for burglary and car accidents, and Maori make up a much greater proportion in this group (compared to the proportion of the total population in this age group), then more Maori will end up in court or hospital. Maori also migrated to urban areas in the 1950s and 1960s when urban manufacturing industries were expanding. They are now to be found in the declining and de-industrialising sectors of these urban economies, with the result that they have faced significant levels of redundancy and unemployment since the late 1980s. These factors – class, age, location in labour markets and in certain communities – all contribute to the negative statistics and social problems. But the cumulative effect,

* See p. 106.

especially when combined with the marginalisation of indigenous cultures and institutions, and a history of colonisation, is to produce disadvantage which can justifiably be labelled as racist. Some of these issues are being addressed, by both the state (in a limited way), and by Maori (in a more significant way), but the extent of the problems faced is such that these inequalities are not going to be easily addressed or eliminated.

Theorising racism and ethnicity

A number of approaches to the theorisation of racism and/or ethnicity have already been canvassed in this chapter. For example, the political economy of labour migration has helped revolutionise the way in which sociologists, and others, have viewed contemporary racial and ethnic relations. Theorists such as Miles and Castles have encouraged social scientists to look critically at the use of 'race', to take care with the concept racism, and to recognise the significance of contemporary forms of resistance and cultural identity. In addition, they have combined an analysis of racism with the demands of capitalism, and focused attention on the migration and settlement of culturally different groups in the main centres of capitalist production. In this way, relatively isolated countries such as New Zealand have been as much affected by the global movement of people as any other. In the post-war period, such migration began with that of Maori from the rural hinterland. This was followed in the 1960s by the arrival of various groups from the Pacific Islands, which supplemented the on-going immigration of British and Dutch migrants. Polynesian migrants were welcomed in the expanding industrial sector because of the demand for semi-skilled and unskilled labour. However, by the 1970s, with an economic downturn which was signalled by the oil crises in 1973, some of these groups were racialised. Local problems such as growing unemployment, what was perceived as a decline in law and order, and the deterioration of certain city areas, were interpreted by many as associated with the arrival of 'Pacific Islanders'. The overstayers campaign, which took place during the mid-1970s through to the late 1980s, explicitly linked Pacific Islands groups with illegal overstaying, despite the fact that many overstayers were North Americans and Europeans. The police, immigration officials, politicians and the media all contributed to the common-sense racism which justified the targeting of Pacific Islanders as 'problem' groups. Miles refers to this as racialisation, the process of defining some groups as 'races' and then seeing their presence as problematic in some way. This helps understand the processes and politics of a period of mass labour migration that took place in many countries between the 1950s and 1970s.

Capitalism had changed significantly by the late 1980s, with the nature of production being subject to new global pressures, the withdrawal of state support and the deregulation of the labour market. The demand for semi-skilled and unskilled labour evaporated as de-industrialisation occurred, and the geo-political interests of New Zealand swung from

208 Exploring Society

Hegemony is a concept developed by the Marxist Antonio Gramsci to describe a form of power won through ideological dominance.

Post-colonialism involves a critical understanding of the experiences and effects of colonialism, as well as resistance in various forms. It does *not* mean 'after colonialism'.

Europe to the Asia region. The migration flows changed again, and an increased flow of migrants from Taiwan, Hong Kong and South Korea entered New Zealand between 1990 and 1995, before the flow decreased substantially. These migrants, often wealthy and skilled, were also racialised and seen as a threat to the cultural 'homogeneity' of New Zealanders. When political candidates, especially from parties such as New Zealand First, used the word 'immigrant' during the 1996 election campaign, and talked of the problems they had created, audiences understood that it was Asian immigrants to whom reference was being made. Once again, immigrants were racialised, and political struggles around 'race' became significant.

Stuart Hall, a Gramscian-inspired, British-based black sociologist is one who has contributed to an understanding of these contemporary struggles. Hall, as a neo-Marxist, continues to focus on the capitalist and class nature of Western societies, but he then goes on to examine the forms of resistance adopted by Afro-Caribbean and Asian communities to racist ideas and practices. The use of music to critique racism is one interesting example. Secondly, Hall has been concerned with the way in which conservative leaders such as Thatcher were able to convince others that their views and policies best represented the interests of all Britons whereas the effect was to marginalise many, including non-whites. He offers an approach which explains the power of New Right politics and the way in which racist arguments have been recast. They are still racist in the way in which non-whites are portrayed but they avoid the biological racism of earlier eras. Thirdly, Hall focuses on the role of the state and of institutions such as the media in sustaining racism. As a Gramscian, he is interested in the establishment and maintenance of **hegemony**, and Hall examines the role of state agencies such as the police, or the contribution of the media, in creating and circulating certain ideas about non-whites (and whites for that matter) and thereby mediating relations between the core institutions of society and non-white communities. Hall retains a Marxist interest in the economic relations of capitalism, but he argues that racial divisions are characteristic of the economic and ideological relations of capitalist societies in the late twentieth century. Not only are there new forms of racism, there are also new forms of ethnicity based upon the resistance of non-white communities to the disempowering effects of racism.

Stuart Hall has been influential in an approach which has collectively been labelled 'post-colonial'. The term is confusing because it implies that colonialism has been replaced whereas it is accepted by those interested in **post-colonialism** that new forms of colonialism are occurring, often as an outcome of new types of economic or cultural sovereignty. Post-colonialism refers to the 'process of resistance and reconstruction' (Ashcroft et al., 1995: 2) that results from the interaction between the 'imperial culture and the complex of indigenous cultural practices' (Ashcroft et al., 1995: 1). In the case of a revisionist history, the aim is to give voice to those groups who have been silenced, who have not been able to have their story told, as well as to adopt a much more critical understanding of the actions of the colonists. The experiences of the colonised are discussed, and the ideologies that have sustained colonial oppression, especially those that are racist, are challenged. It is this challenge to the racism of colonialism which has been an important characteristic of post-colonialism. It obviously encompasses the resistance of Maori but it also includes the activities of supportive Pakeha. Indeed, the label itself indicates a willingness to resist the ideologies and practices of a colonial past, although the term is problematic in that not all who use the label are sympathetic to the politics of resistance or to Maori ambitions for tino rangatiratanga. As members and beneficiaries of a settler colonial culture, majority group members (Pakeha) are '… poised … between the centre from which they seek to differentiate themselves and the indigenous people who serve to remind them of their own problematic occupation of the country' (Ashcroft et al., 1995: 152). These forms of resistance and the critique of society and institutions as racist have not gone unanswered. Some have sought to portray dominant 'white' groups as the new disadvantaged and therefore the targets of minority 'racism'. Others want to focus on nationality.

> Blackness and Englishness are constructed as incompatible, mutually exclusive identities. To speak of the British or English is to speak of white people.
>
> (Gilroy, 1990: 268)

Yet others have stressed the imperatives of the market and an economic rationalism which dismiss ethnicity as irrelevant.

Conclusion

Ethnic identity and racial exclusion are a central focus for contemporary sociology, especially the ethnic identity politics which has emerged as a major expression of resistance and community mobilisation in the late twentieth century. Looking back over the century, racism has been an enduring thread, from the genocide of European fascism to apartheid in South Africa to the beliefs and practices of racism in many countries. Equally important have been the various forms of resistance such as the black civil rights movement in the USA and Maori expressions of tino rangatiratanga. It is our task as sociologists to provide a convincing analysis of such developments, and to write racism and ethnicity into the very core of sociological understanding and practice.

210 Exploring Society

? Study questions

11.1 In relation to the twentieth century, what have been the major expressions (or examples) of racism?

11.2 In thinking about your own identity, how would you describe your ethnicity (or ethnicities)? How would you define ethnicity sociologically?

11.3 What are the key features of a post-colonial approach to issues of racism and ethnicity?

Further reading

Ashcroft, B., Griffiths, G. and Tiffen, H. (eds). (1995) *The Post-Colonial Studies Reader*. Routledge, London.

Durie, M. (1998) *Te Mana, Te Kawanatanga. The Politics of Maori Self-Determination*. Oxford University Press, Auckland.

Fleras, A. and Spoonley, P. (1999) *Recalling Aotearoa: Indigenous Politics and Ethnic Relations in New Zealand*. Oxford University Press, Auckland.

Miles, R. (1989) *Racism*. Routledge, London.

Solomos, J. and Back, L. (1996) *Racism and Society*. Macmillan, Houndsmill, Basingstoke.

Wilson, M. and Yeatman, A. (eds). (1995) *Justice and Identity. Antipodean Practices*. Bridget Williams Books, Wellington.

12 Health, illness and medical power

Chapter aims

- to outline differing definitions of health and to examine the dominance of the biomedical model;
- to outline the ways in which health, disease and illness are socially produced and distributed;
- to examine how the personal experience of illness is connected to broader social ideologies and identities;
- to examine the role of medicalisation in modern social life.

Introduction

This chapter explores three important elements in the sociological study of health. Firstly, sociologists are interested in the question of *who gets sick and why*. The answer to this question is by no means a straightforward one about disease, accident or lifestyle choice. Rather it involves exploring the role of social structures and historical processes such as colonisation and capitalism in shaping patterns of morbidity and mortality. A second question asks: *how is the experience of illness socially constructed*? Here the focus is on the ways in which personal experiences of illness are shaped through the ideological beliefs and identities of both doctors and patients. Sociologists are cautious about granting medicine a wholly altruistic role in the interactions between lay people and medical professionals. Rather, we approach medicine as an institution of considerable power in shaping our experience of illness, cure and care. Thirdly, sociologists are interested in how formal health care has come to be provided for most people in modern societies by the *medical profession*. Medicine's capture of health care has now developed to the extent that the medical way of seeing things has come to infiltrate more and more aspects of 'ordinary life'. Thus 'medicalisation' of once non-medical facts of life, such as childbirth and menopause, is now an everyday element of life in modern societies.

What is health, who 'has' it and can medicine help?

Health and illness are issues that concern us all at some time in our lives. That we will die is one of the few universal human experiences that can be counted on. Typically, however, our health is something that we take for granted until it is threatened through illness and disease. This might be in the form of a fairly mild cold, or more profoundly through diseases like cancer. And there are a range of other illnesses and diseases in between that inconvenience, pain and trouble us to varying degrees. Some of these are acute and pass quickly (e.g. broken bones); others are more chronic and we have to live our whole lives in their shadow (e.g. arthritis or diabetes). These personal concerns about ill-health take a more global form in the World Health Organisation's strategy of 'Health for all by the year 2000' (World Health Organisation, 1985). While this goal seems eminently desirable, it is also somewhat ambitious and it raises a number of pressing questions. What, for example, are we to understand by the notion of 'health'? At first glance, *health* appears to be a relatively self-explanatory goal, but on closer examination health and illness are concepts embedded within particular cultures and social relations. There are many different views on what healthy and unhealthy states of being are. How people decide on what they mean by *health* depends very much on their social location.

> Health may be perceived very differently in a community in which many children die within the first year of life and in which adult life expectancy is low, than in a situation in which everyone is well-fed and where adults live into their 60s and 70s. Similarly there are those for whom the term *health* currently conjures up visions of jacuzzis, saunas, health farms, and designer tracksuits – imagery that may be similarly unthinkable in fifty years' time. *Health is therefore a relative quality – relative that is to the surroundings and circumstances in which people find themselves.*
>
> (Aggleton, 1990: 4 – emphasis added)

What is the nature of this relative quality, health, in Aotearoa/New Zealand? At the level of cultural and ethnic difference it is clear that there are a variety of beliefs about what counts as health. For example, Maori culture tends to have a *holistic* understanding of health that has been symbolised by the image of the strong house – whare tapa wha. In this model health is compared to:

> the four walls of a house, all four being necessary to ensure strength and symmetry, though each representing a different dimension: te taha wairua (the spiritual side), te taha hinengaro (thoughts and feelings), te taha tinana (the physical side), te tahu whanau (family).
>
> (Durie, 1994: 70)

This way of talking about Maori health is only one model. Alternatively, it could also be symbolised as an octopus with intertwining tentacles (Pere, 1984). What both models share, however, is the *holistic* approach to health in which it is difficult to separate out the body from the wider interpersonal and familial context in which it is situated. While this particular version of the holistic model of health may be specific to Maori, many non-Maori also work with a holistic concept of health in which they believe that they are healthy even when they have diseases that from a medical point of view would suggest 'ill-health'. For example, in a study of the health beliefs of elderly people living in Aberdeen in Scotland, Rory Williams (1983) discovered that some people felt that they were healthy even though they suffered from diseases. What seemed to be important to these people was that they retained a sense of their 'wholeness', their integrity, their inner strength and an ability to cope. Such lay health beliefs are therefore important in shaping how individuals understand health and illness.

While these cultural health beliefs are very important in shaping the experience of illness, they exist in a context where the privileged model for *explaining* disease comes from a **biomedical model**, the dominant Western medical paradigm. This view is focused very much on the presence of disease and pathology. It is based on five key assumptions (Nettleton, 1995: 3).

> The biomedical model is the dominant Western medical paradigm. Biomedicine focuses on the diagnosis and explanation for individual illness in relation to a malfunction of biological processes.

1   *A mind-body dualism* in which the body and mind are treated as if they are separate entities.

2   *A mechanical metaphor* where the body was treated as if it was like a machine. Doctors are therefore like engineers, using technical knowledge to repair the machine-like body. Moreover, this body is treated as if it were a series of separate anatomical parts and physiological systems.

3   Because the body is treated like a machine, *a technological imperative* operates. It is sometimes assumed that technological interventions are the most important factors in making people healthy.

4   *Biological reductionism* means that disease is explained in terms of the biological structures and processes of the body to the neglect of wider social and psychological factors.

5   *A doctrine of specific aetiology* works on the basis that every disease and illness is caused by a specific agent that can be clearly identified (e.g. a parasite, or bacterium or virus).

One effect of the biomedical model is that individuals are treated as if they were simply the asocial, neutral, biological and passive hosts for disease mechanisms. In sum, 'the body is isolated from the person, the social and material causes of disease are neglected, and the subjective interpretations and meanings of health and illness are deemed irrelevant' (Nettleton, 1995: 3). In contrast to this, sociologists emphasise the social influences and context of health and illness, and in this chapter we will examine the social relations involved in the production of disease, the experience of illness and the role of medical power in shaping the health care we receive.

Perhaps the dominant theme in the sociology of health is the critique of medical power. Biomedicine is popularly held to provide the best model for explaining, and curing, illness and disease. There is a commonly held belief that medicine, with its emphasis on science and technology, has been a great progressive force, responsible for the amelioration of disease and illness and the decline in certain diseases that once were major causes of death. However, sociologists take a wider view and there is a now well-documented case to show that the decrease in deaths from infectious diseases (such as cholera, typhoid, tuberculosis and plagues) that has occurred in industrialised nations from the end of the nineteenth century is not due to the role of medicine but rather to increased standards of sanitation, improved housing and better nutrition (McKeown, 1976; Powles, 1973). These social factors were in fact much more influential in decreasing mortality than medical interventions such as immunisation. Figure 12.1 illustrates that many infectious diseases were declining as a cause of death decades before the introduction of immunisation or medical cures. There is also evidence to suggest that medicine's emphasis on surgical and chemical interventions may often have disastrous results in the form of iatrogenic illness. For example, overuse of antibiotics has contributed to the development of drug-resistant 'superbugs' that are far more dangerous than the original bacteria targeted by the antibiotics.

In addition to these criticisms of the biomedical approach, sociologists have highlighted how biomedicine's explanation of why people get sick focuses on the individual and is not able to explain the *pattern* of disease and illness that occurs across the world and within particular societies. It takes a sociological perspective to explain these patterns and the mechanisms by which they continue to exist and it is these questions that are the focus in the following section.

Differences and divisions in health status: who gets sick and why?

Being healthy is a status which is not enjoyed by all alike. Even a superficial investigation shows that there are profound inequalities across the world, in death rates (i.e. patterns of mortality) and prevalence of disease (i.e. morbidity). For example, the average age of death ranges from the high seventies in Western developed societies to around fifty in some poorer countries. The infant mortality rate (IMR) also provides an important measure of the overall national health status. These rates vary from a low of 4.8 per 1000 live births in Japan through to over 100 in 1000 live births in 28 African countries (Nettleton, 1995: 191). In addition, the rate of maternal mortality is much higher in poor countries, where the risk of dying during or just after childbirth is up to 200 times greater than in a rich country.

How do we explain these differences? It would be tempting to attribute poor health in 'developing' countries to a lack of food caused by having too many children, or to the prevalence of nasty 'tropical' diseases.

12 Health, illness and medical power **215**

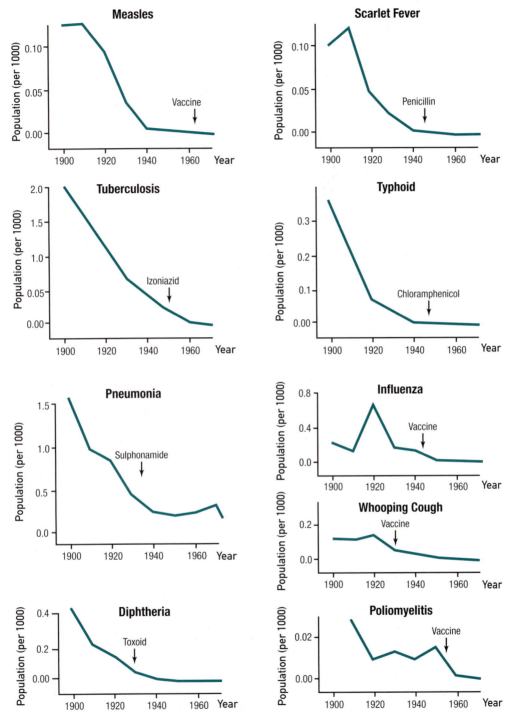

Source: McKinley, John B. and McKinley, Sonya (1977) The questionable effect of medical measures on the decline of mortality in the United States in the twentieth century. *Milbank Memorial Fund Quarterly*. 55: 422–423.

Figure 12.1 Decline in infectious diseases in relation to medical interventions in the United States, 1900–1973. These graphs depict the fall in the standardised death rate (per 1000 population).

However, both of these explanations greatly over-simplify what is really going on. Firstly, having a large family, instead of simply being a drain on resources, may be a rational strategy for poor families. In the context of a high IMR, children are important because of the work they perform for the family and for taking care of parents as they age. Moreover, it has been noted that as the standard of living increases and infant and child mortality falls, fertility patterns are accordingly adjusted downwards. Secondly, the major cause of ill-health and death in poor countries is not endemic tropical disease, but rather malnutrition and infectious disease. Doyal and Pennell suggests that 'these are not "natural", but arise in large part from the particular social and economic relationships characteristic of imperialism' (Doyal and Pennell, 1979: 27). Here the authors are drawing on a Marxist tradition in which poor health is explained not by looking at these poor societies in isolation but rather by examining the world system in which there are social relationships of exploitation between the 'first' and 'third' worlds.

Colonialism is the historical process by which Western societies have occupied and exploited other territories and societies.

The current world system has its historical origins in **colonialism**. This pattern of exploitation began in the sixteenth century and reached its apogee in the nineteenth century by which time several European countries had gained power over colonies in Africa, Asia, South America and the South Pacific. While this process was often portrayed by the colonisers as one of bringing 'civilisation' and generally improving the lifestyles of less developed people, colonisation has in fact had a deleterious effect on many aspects of life, including health. Early contact between the colonisers and indigenous peoples introduced previously unknown infectious diseases such as measles, smallpox, influenza and venereal diseases. It is difficult to be precise about the impact of these diseases but they clearly contributed to remarkable decreases in the local population. It has been estimated that the Maori population numbered between 200 000 and 500 000 at the time of first European contact but this had declined to a low of 42 000 by 1896 (Durie, 1994: 31). While the introduction of such infectious diseases was unintentional, other deliberate economic and social changes wrought by colonisers led to the destruction of traditional modes of life and productive forms of agriculture in favour of the development of an economic system that has benefited the colonial centre. As Doyal and Pennell suggest:

> there is always a close relationship between economic and physical health, so that the ability of a population to maintain a given standard of health is always directly related to its capacity to maintain and control the material means of production. Colonial expansion in bringing about the destruction of the vital social and ecological relationships which enabled people to feed themselves, also destroyed the health of local populations on an unprecedented scale.
>
> (Doyal and Pennell, 1979: 107)

Most previously colonised societies have now gone through a process of decolonisation and have become independent states. However, they have entered a global economy that works largely in the interests of the first world. Poor countries have been encouraged to 'modernise' or become 'developed', usually along Western lines of industrialisation, urbanisation and increasing production (Petersen, 1994: 49). While the provision of aid and development projects has lead to an overall decrease in mortality rates, improvement has not been distributed evenly within populations. For example, aid projects have often focused on men's rather than women's work and so women's health and position in these societies has become even more precarious. Aid has also sometimes come in the form of food imports that have actually had little positive, and often very negative, health consequences. The most striking example of this is the way in which baby milk formula, freely distributed as aid to third world countries 'has done more to aid the assiduous efforts of multinational companies to promote bottle feeding, than to alleviate malnutrition' (Doyal and Pennell, 1979: 128). The move away from breastfeeding has had dire consequences for infant health with the rise in diarrhoeal disease often leading to brain disease or death (Jellife and Jellife, 1977: 250).

In addition to major inequalities in mortality rates between first and third world countries, there are also differences in the kinds of diseases that are suffered. In the Western industrialised world, infectious diseases are less important than the so-called 'diseases of affluence'. These diseases are the result of an 'epidemiological transition' in which there has been a shift in the major cause of death away from infectious and towards degenerative diseases such as cancer, heart disease, strokes and lung disease. These diseases now account for around 70% of deaths in such countries (Giddens, 1993: 606) and have been associated with the move from agricultural communities and production toward industrial cities and production (Powles, 1973). Powles speculates that this shift can be related to the fact that humans are not biologically adapted to the changes in lifestyle and diet that have occurred in the last 200 years. Because our bodies have not had the time to evolve to a lowering of physical exercise and to changes in eating habits (away from what used to be a high-fibre, low-fat diet) we now suffer from previously uncommon diseases. This view seems to be supported by the fact that as developing countries have become increasingly urbanised, industrialised and developed along Western lines, sections of the population are increasingly developing these diseases of 'affluence'.

While these degenerative diseases are the major causes of death in Western societies, they do not affect all groups in the same way. In particular, there are major differences between men and women, social classes and different ethnic groups. For example, the following patterns have been identified in Aotearoa/New Zealand:

- Lower social class is linked with higher death rates overall, and with higher rates of most of the diseases which are common causes of death.
- Social class differences in mortality rates/patterns are widening.
- Women experience more ill-health than men, when ill-health is measured by incidence of disease, use of health services or self-report.

- Life expectancy for Maori is considerably lower than for non-Maori.
- Maori women have substantially worse health statistics than non-Maori women; for example, the rate of lung cancer amongst Maori women is four times that amongst non-Maori women.

These very broad statements suggest that there are significant patterned differences between people in terms of experiences of disease. For the sociologist, these differences highlight the significance of the *structuring* effect of class, gender and ethnicity on patterns of disease and illness. There are, however, a number of different ways in which these structural differences can be explained. One increasingly popular explanation for these differences in health status focuses on how the 'lifestyles' associated with class and ethnicity contribute to the development of cancers and heart and lung diseases. In particular, high rates of smoking, poor diet and inadequate exercise are targeted as behaviours that put people at risk of degenerative disease. Such a perspective is *behavioural* and *individualist* in that it explains ill-health in terms of the actions of individuals, and it encourages interventions based on individual behaviour change as a way of preventing disease. What this approach fails to recognise is the way in which individual behaviour is deeply rooted in sets of social relations that are – for the most part – outside the control of the individual.

The failure of this behavioural approach is illustrated in a study of the Multiple Risk Factor Intervention Trial Group (1982) which attempted to change the diet, smoking habits and exercise patterns of white men identified as having the highest risk of coronary heart disease. Although these men used every effort over six years, they succeeded in making only minimal changes.

> This means that as an approach to prevention, the behavioural route is unlikely to realise anything like the reduction in heart disease which behavioural risk factors appear to contribute. Clearly, behaviour is related to the social context in which people live and is difficult to change in isolation. Indeed, if behaviour was not partly determined by the social environment, there would presumably not be a social class gradient in smoking, in dietary composition or in the amount of leisure-time exercise which people take. In other words, *to change behaviour it may be necessary to change more than behaviour.*
>
> (Wilkinson, 1996: 64 – emphasis added)

In this discussion, Wilkinson highlights the structural nature of the social production of disease. Such an approach encourages the development of materialist theories of health. These theories focus on how class, ethnic and gender relations may place individuals directly at risk from environmental factors (such as pollution, dangerous working conditions, poor housing and education, male violence and so on) as well as constructing situations in which stress or working conditions encourage particular diseases. For example, it has been argued that 'high strain jobs' are associated with high blood pressure and high rates of smoking. These jobs, where demands are high but the degree of control is low, are also typically low-status ones. They are associated with a capitalist system of production that makes more and more demands for higher productivity, while at the same time giving workers less control over their work (Burdess, 1996: 177).

One outcome of these higher demands for productivity can be seen in the increasing numbers of workers, from supermarket checkout operators to university academics, reporting what is called variously Repetitive Strain Injury (RSI), Occupational Overuse Syndrome (OOS), or muscular-skeletal discomfort. While it is not uncommon for individuals to blame RSI on their own lack of attention to posture or some other *personal* failing, it is possible to explain these injuries by examining the *social* organisation of work. In particular, the way in which the labour process is organised is a key determinant in the development of RSI (Willis, 1994). In jobs where there is little job rotation and few rest breaks, there is a high risk of developing RSI. Moreover, there are other structuring factors of the work environment such as 'deadlines, peak demands, machine pacing, bonus systems, incentive payments, electronic monitoring and work rates' (Willis, 1994: 141) all of which are demands of the job that lie outside the control of the individual worker. These factors can be seen as components of a capitalist labour process which has developed two governing features (Willis, 1994: 142). Firstly, there has been a search for greater *efficiency*. This has entailed trying to eliminate 'inefficiencies', by dividing work into discrete tasks. There has also been a gradual mechanisation of work tasks, in which the worker increasingly becomes defined as an extension of the machine. Work therefore requires a greater *consistency* of physical movements but less physical labour. Secondly, there has been a quest for more effective *control over workers* through technical developments which attempt to measure the productivity of individual workers and time the absences of operators.

What the discussion in this section suggests is that differences between individuals in their experience of health and illness can only be explained by looking at the 'big picture'. This picture has several different levels and dimensions. At the level of national differences in mortality and morbidity rates, colonialism and an inequitable world system played an important part in producing the different patterns of disease between countries. *Within* these societies, as well as in countries like New Zealand, there are also differing experiences of health according to gender, class and ethnicity. While lifestyle differences are often blamed for the worse health statistics of those from the working class and ethnic minorities, it has been suggested that factors such as diet, exercise and smoking are related to more complex social constraints that encourage and support such behaviours. It is also possible to explain the prevalence of some diseases by examining the way in which work is organised, and it is to this issue that we turn in the following contribution by Kevin Dew.

Poisoning workers?

The poisoning of New Zealand

Kevin Dew

New Zealanders have traditionally prided themselves on their close relationship to the land, finding in their landscape a source for their national identity. The imagery has changed over time from the pioneering spirit of taming a wild country, to a mystical contemplation of nature, and more recently, to a pride in our 'clean green' image as a source of tourist dollars and a marketing strategy for our primary products.

But lurking behind this clean green image is another story, a story of a land poisoned by the effects of chemical contamination. Such a vision is a threat to our nationhood, and when this story is told it provokes a dramatic response, often a response which leads to policy innovations to clean up this contamination, and to provide regulations to prevent such contamination recurring.

And yet there is something that is missed in this response. When the land is contaminated, the people are contaminated too. All too often this is overlooked, ignored, or placed in the 'too-hard basket'.

A case in point is the story of the sawmill workers, victims of New Zealand's timber industry. Many workers were contaminated and poisoned when they worked on a particular chain in the sawmill – the Green Chain – where timber was graded and sorted after having been dipped in chemicals to prevent discoloration. In New Zealand, up until 1988, the chemical used was Pentachlorophenol (PCP). Commercial grades of this chemical contained contaminants, including dioxin, one of the most potent poisons ever made and a poison never found naturally in the environment. New Zealand was a very heavy user of PCP, with 200 tonnes a year being used over a 40-year period. The dioxin content of this PCP is still a major source of dioxin contamination in New Zealand.

In 1992 a report was released showing that PCP from sawmills had contaminated the sites where it was used, where it was dumped, and also in some cases the surrounding environment. Most notable here was the Waipa Mill site, where PCP had seeped into the local stream and flowed into Lake Rotorua. Studies showed that the trout in the lake had been contaminated. These studies, commissioned by government departments, had gone to the trouble of examining the fish in the lake, but did not look at those who worked in the mill.

When these studies were given media attention, workers who had been sick for no apparent reason, and who had never related their illness to their work, suddenly realised that there could be a link. They started coming forward, and asking questions, and found that many of them were suffering from the same conditions. They suffered from fever, fatigue, weight loss, nausea and neuropsychological dysfunctions. Such chronic illnesses strained relationships. Sons and daughters of deceased workers wondered if their fathers' cancers had been caused by work conditions, and they came to realise that many of their fathers' colleagues had also died from cancer. Groups formed to lobby for inquiries into the extraordinary high levels of sickness and early death that had afflicted the workers employed on the Green Chain.

But whilst the government established protocols to clean up the contaminated sites, and deregistered PCP in 1991 so that it could not be used again, no government agency looked at the workers, or at their mysterious health problems.

What could account for such a strange situation where concern is raised about the state of our fish, and the state of our land, but no-one looks at the state of our people? At one level this is an issue of the use of government resources. The Ministry for the Environment played the major part in identifying the toxic sites, but its resources were limited, and its brief never extended to a consideration of 'toxic people'. No other government department took up the cause.

The Occupational Safety and Health Service of the Department of Labour (OSH) and the Department of Health failed to pursue the issue for a number of reasons. At first it was assumed that the workers would not have been contaminated because they wore protective clothing. But this assumption, typical of many similar cases where workers have been poisoned, ignored actual work practices. For the workers, protective clothing hindered the work process. Protective goggles steamed up, making it impossible to see, so they were discarded. Aprons got in the way when timber had to be moved, so they were not worn. And these breaches of safety codes were not policed. The workers' clothes would be soaked in PCP, and the spray from the high pressures systems used would be in the air around them. Workers had little idea of the risks they were facing.

Even if these poor work practices were taken into consideration, there was a greater obstacle to the workers gaining a sympathetic hearing. This was the requirement to provide scientific proof: that is, of establishing causal links between exposure to the toxins and the physical condition of the workers. If a worker died of cancer, was that because dioxin (a carcinogenic agent which is a contaminant of PCP) caused the death, or was it a natural occurrence – a result of lifestyle choices or of a genetic predisposition?

To try to answer this question epidemiologists would need to carry out studies of a large population of workers and compare this with the study of a 'normal' group. Blood samples of workers would have to be taken to see if they have dioxin in their system, and to compare the health of those contaminated with those that are not. But there are major problems with this approach. First of all, such a study would require a lot of money and take a long time – and no authority has the will to carry out such a study. Secondly, because many of the workers have already died, the most seriously contaminated may have already been eliminated from the study. In addition, to measure the dioxin levels of a person, one litre of blood needs to be taken. Some workers are too sick to have this much blood taken from them.

The obstacles to gaining proof have been too great. In 1996 the Occupational Safety and Health Service did finally release a study of 137 workers which indicated that there was an association between exposure to PCP and various symptoms. But the study was regarded as too small to indicate associations with more serious, or fatal illnesses, and the wood industry dismissed the study as not being rigorous enough to justify claims for worker compensation. The Ministry for the Environment is hoping to carry out a study to measure the 'normal level' of contamination in New Zealanders – but sawmill workers are expressly excluded from such a study as their suspected high levels of contamination may distort the data.

Establishing scientific proof is not the only way to convince politicians of the need for action. If there were enough public pressure, politicians might feel obliged to look at the issue more closely. So far there has been no such public pressure. In 1993 articles appeared in overseas publications like *New Scientist*, and *The Times* of London, claiming that New Zealand was a poisoned paradise, with over 10 000 contaminated sites. In response to this there was great media attention and immediate government reaction. Those responsible for the articles were regarded as being unpatriotic and a threat to our clean green image and therefore to our tourism and agricultural export industries. The government was at pains to show that it was indeed doing something about the contamination of the land, and cleaning up the sites. No such media attention has been paid to the workers.

Why does the media show so little interest in such an outrageous situation? We might suggest that the sawmill workers are not the sort of people that get the appropriate response from the media. For a start they are working class, secondly they are mostly Maori. In New Zealand there is often a very negative image of the working-class man – he may be a malingerer. If he claims he is sick it is probably because he wants to get something for nothing. These sick and dying men are not from the more articulate and self-promoting middle classes. They do not have the same traditions of lobbying and public protest that the urbanised middle classes have. They are geographically more isolated, and have not been able to successfully form alliances with other groups to push their case.

In New Zealand we have a number of articulate pressure groups who promote the defence of the land – the foremost of these, particularly in the case of PCP contamination, is Greenpeace. But we have no such pressure groups who mobilise around the defence of the sick worker – and this situation has been exacerbated by a decline in union membership and subsequently union power.

Finally, it can be suggested that as a nation we feel much more for the land than we do for the people. Our clean green image is not only a source of pride, but a marketing strategy, an economic boon. But we have no such places for images of strong, healthy and happy workers. Rather, such images smack of Stalinism, of the Stakhanovite worker. So if our clean green image is tarnished, we quickly mobilise to its defence, but we feel no need to take such action when our workers are sick and dying. Action may be warranted to protect our fish, but not to look after our workers.

Questions

Kevin Dew discusses the way in which a particular industry in New Zealand has contributed to the development of illness in a group of workers. He uses a similar materialist approach to that explored above by Doyal and Pennell, Wilkinson and Willis. In your reading of this piece you might like to reflect on the following questions

1   Who do you think is responsible for the workers' failure to wear protective clothing?

2   What role has the state played in the social production of dioxin-related illness in sawmill workers?

3   Do you think that Kevin Dew is correct in suggesting that sick workers, particularly working-class workers, are a difficult group for which to secure public support? Why might this be so?

Social and personal dimensions of illness: interaction, identity and ideology

Whereas the previous section discussed the *social production* of health and illness, this focus tells us very little about the personal experience of illness, about what might be called the *social meanings* of illness. Submerged within the statistical evidence of different rates of mortality and morbidity there are individuals who suffer, who seek medical care, and who try to make some sense of what is happening to them. While this often feels uniquely personal, as has been suggested throughout this text, individual experience is always embedded within particular social contexts and has its origins outside the individual. One way of exploring the interconnection between the social and the personal dimensions of illness can be illustrated by examining doctor-patient interactions. These interactions are important components in the social construction of illness and are also linked to questions of self-identity and ideology.

An early sociological study of doctor-patient interactions, developed by Talcott Parsons (1951), aimed to demonstrate that the personal experience of illness was more than simply a biological malfunction; rather it could be viewed as a *social role* that was in some way *functional* for society. As a functionalist, Parsons was interested in the overall structuring and maintenance of social order. From this perspective, health could be defined as a normal state that is necessary for individuals to fulfil their social roles. Disease and illness are seen as deviant states because they mean that individuals are unable to fulfil the expectations of their social roles. Therefore illness has to be socially managed to provide the least disruption to the social order. Parsons argued that it was through the four aspects of the **sick role** that individuals lessen the negative impact of their illness on the social system. Firstly, by taking up the sick role the individual is able to legitimate his or her withdrawal from work and family obligations. Secondly, the sick role exempts individuals from responsibility for their medical condition. The third aspect involves the individual taking on the social obligation to get better. Finally, those taking up the sick role are expected to seek out medical care from a suitably qualified person. Such a perspective assumes that being sick is legitimate only when individuals accept their responsibility to seek medical intervention and eventually return to their normal social roles.

While this perspective has the advantage of showing the ways in which illness is as much a social as a medical condition, Parsons' focus on doctor-patient interactions ignores the other social roles and relationships that shape the individual experience of illness. In addition, there is little attention in Parsons's model to active processes of *negotiation* between individuals, medical workers and others in making sense of illness. Both of these criticisms have been taken up by sociologists working from an interactionist perspective who emphasise the meaning-making processes involved in the experience of being ill. Rather than focusing on the level

> **The sick role** was the concept developed by Talcott Parsons to describe the social expectations that sick people were expected to enact.

of the social system, the interactionist perspective examines how interpretations of the situation are made by individuals in relationships with significant others. For example, our interactions with family, friends and work colleagues may be very important in helping us to decide how sick we 'really' are. Aggleton illustrates the process in the following way:

> Imagine that you wake up one morning feeling slightly under the weather. [...] you might decide to share the information with other people. Depending on their reactions, you may not decide you are seriously ill. Imagine how you would feel if, on hearing the news, your best friends said, 'Now you've mentioned it, you've looked really ill for weeks'. Think about how you would feel if they said, 'Oh, forget about it, it's probably nothing, just too many late nights, that's all'. Both of these reactions could easily be triggered off by exactly the same evidence, your comment about not feeling too well, but each could have very different consequences for how you subsequently feel about yourself.
>
> (Aggleton, 1990: 68–69)

This interpretive process of defining illness may also be shaped through labels that identify particular diseases as signs of madness, moral degeneracy, irresponsibility and so on. Particular individuals who suffer from diseases that appear to be highly infectious, that reach epidemic status and that seem to be associated with disreputable personal characteristics, are often subject to a stigmatising labelling process. This involves making negative value judgements about such individuals and believing that they are personally culpable for their own illness. In the past, leprosy provoked this response from the healthy population who stigmatised sufferers and forced them to live in colonies outside of the rest of society. The belief that lepers were sinners being punished by God illustrates the way that illness is often linked with personal identity, that is, with beliefs about the particular distinctive characteristics of individuals. Today, the best example of illness as **stigma** is found in relation to the experience of people with AIDS. These individuals are often blamed for their illness and they are marked with the stigma of a sexually transmitted disease. This stigma leads people with AIDS to be accorded less respect and sympathy because they are believed to have brought the disease upon themselves through their own actions. In particular, gay men are targeted as 'guilty' victims because their sexual practice and identity are already marked out as 'deviant' and morally reprehensible. Being gay and having male-to-male sex are identified as 'lifestyle choices' that could be rejected, thereby protecting the individual from HIV. This view fails to take account of the fact that while in the Western world HIV infection may be much more common among gay men, in African and South-East Asian nations it is a disease resulting from so-called 'normal' heterosexual practice. This suggests that the stigmatising of gay men with HIV may have less to do with some 'natural'

Stigma refers to attributes that are believed to be demeaning for individuals.

or moral order than with ideological processes that have marginalised gay sexuality and identity.

While this process has often worked against gay men, it would be misleading to suggest that gay men have therefore been completely powerless and passive in the face of AIDS stigma. On the contrary, in the face of such stigma and because there is a strong link for many gay men between sexual practice and their sense of self, a strong gay culture has developed. The existence of a gay culture and community has facilitated a vocal and collective response to the medical and AIDS research profession on matters of treatment, prevention and care. Gay men have rejected the label of 'AIDS victim' and have sought to become active partners in decisions about AIDS research, prevention education and treatment.

The example of AIDS clearly demonstrates connections between ideology, identity, sexuality and the experience of health and illness. These connections can also be seen in the 'unfortunate experiment' that occurred at New Zealand's National Women's Hospital in the late sixties (Coney, 1988). This experiment involved withholding treatment from some women who had *carcinoma in situ* (CIS) of the cervix in order to monitor the 'natural history' of the disease. Contrary to the dominant view of the time, namely that CIS often leads to invasive cancer of the cervix, Dr Herbert Green believed that a more cautious approach was called for because cervical cone biopsies, the main procedure for treating CIS, might reduce women's fertility. Because Dr Green believed that fertility was a key component of women's identity and their place in society he avoided the use of cone biopsies. The result of the experiment was the development of invasive cervical cancer and subsequent death for many women. This example contradicts Parsons's view of doctors as largely beneficent and altruistic and starkly illustrates how interactions between doctors and patients are often structured through ideological notions about gender and sexuality.

Health care: the globalisation of medical power and local resistances

In the face of disease and illness, societies have developed complex social arrangements for the diagnosis and treatment of disease and for the care of patients. In modern Western societies it is largely taken for granted that biomedicine, with its associated medical profession, hospitals and pharmaceutical industry, is the appropriate place to seek advice, care and treatment for illness. However, medicine, as we now understand it, is a relatively recent form of knowledge – only appearing over the last 300 years. Just as sociology, as a form of knowledge, can be associated with the rise of modernity, so too medicine has been located in this global process. In particular, the development of medicine has involved the following processes of modernisation (Haralambos et al., 1996: 158):

- *rationalisation* in which objectivity, experimentation and reason were privileged as components of medical knowledge;
- *secularisation* which encouraged replacing religious ideas about sickness with medical knowledge; and
- *differentiation* which encouraged the separation of medicine from religion and its transformation into a profession with privileged knowledge and power in the realm of health care.

The globalising nature of modernisation, coupled with the development of capitalist forms of social organisation has seen the gradual replacement of traditional and community-based healers with the institutionalisation of the medical profession as the privileged model for health care. While other local forms of health care still exist and while there is still resistance to the medical model, medical power is pervasive everywhere and has a number of important social consequences for the kind of health care that we can expect at the end of the twentieth century.

The early sociological work of Talcott Parsons tended to be supportive of the medical profession, seeing it as a positive means by which society could be stabilised. However, other sociologists have drawn attention to oppressive features of the all-pervasive nature of medicine. For example, Ivan Illich (1975) argued that the dominance of the medical profession has led to a **medicalisation** of society in which more and more everyday aspects of life have come to be defined as medical problems requiring the input of medical specialists. A good example of this is childbirth. Once thought of as a natural process, and solely the province of women as mothers and midwives, it has come to be seen as a medical problem that requires monitoring, treatment and intervention by doctors. In New Zealand, this process began in the 1920s and 1930s with attempts by the medical profession to displace midwives and to move birth away from the home and into the hospital (Fougere, 1994: 151). Contrary to popular belief, medicalising childbirth did not lead to a decrease in maternal mortality. In fact, doctor-assisted births in hospitals were for a time associated with a higher rate of death. However, doctors eventually succeeded in gaining control of the process of childbirth through a complex process involving state intervention and occupational licensing whereby only doctors, and not midwives, were able to administer effective anaesthetics. (See Fougere, (1994), for a more detailed discussion of how the medical profession gained control over childbirth in New Zealand.)

> **Medicalisation** refers to the processes by which non-medical problems come to be defined and treated as if they were medical issues.

More recently, the medicalisation of women's bodies is apparent in the increasing popularity among the medical profession of the use of hormone replacement treatment (HRT) for menopausal and post-menopausal women. Sandra Coney (1992) documents the pervasiveness of this idea at the international and national levels, and within the lay media. For example, at its 1991 Congress, the International Federation of Gynaecology and Obstetrics voted unanimously for the routine use of HRT and argued that:

> Doctors should offer hormone replacement therapy (HRT) to all menopausal women to use indefinitely, *irrespective of whether they have menopausal symptoms.*
>
> (Barnes, 1991, quoted in Coney, 1992: 180 – emphasis added)

Coney demonstrates that this view is also shared by some New Zealand doctors:

> Currently in New Zealand fewer than 10 per cent of post-menopausal women use HRT. If anything, the menopause for New Zealand women is *under medicalised* and many women are unaware of the benefits that HRT may give them.
>
> (Farquhar, 1991, quoted in Coney, 1992: 180 – emphasis added)

Both of these quotes illustrate the view that menopause is a disease state, regardless of whether women suffer any ill-effects of a lowering in oestrogen levels. In particular, becoming menopausal is seen as an endocrine deficiency that should be monitored and treated with drugs and it has increasingly come to be seen as a disease, rather than a natural aspect of ageing. While it is undoubtedly true that some women suffer significant health problems with the onset of menopause, for many women these are passing in nature and do not require medical treatment. This process of medicalisation has also been combined with an ideological view which treats women's ageing as unattractive. The lay media has often played on this theme by encouraging the view that HRT has youth-preserving features. For example, a writer in *New Zealand Women's Day* made the claim that many women 'feel younger and more beautiful... When cells have the oestrogen they need, the facial skin and breasts have a healthy, fleshy appearance' (Donaldson, 1991, cited in Coney, 1992: 185). These claims are commonly made despite the lack of evidence that oestrogen has any positive effects for skin appearance.

Medical gaze is a means for the observation and surveillance of patients by the medical profession. This gaze joins together power/knowledge so that what might seem like objective medical knowledge becomes a means for the regulation of individuals.

Disciplinary power involves the medical profession in making decisions about how individuals should behave and so is a form of self-regulation.

The example of HRT clearly demonstrates how medical discourse now permeates many areas of life that were previously thought of as non-medical. Michel Foucault has theorised this general process by arguing that since the end of the eighteenth century medicine has incorporated a **medical gaze**. This gaze is not an innocent means for observing symptoms and treatment but is a form of power/knowledge that is used to regulate the behaviour of individuals. Foucault argues that power and knowledge are deeply interconnected so that 'there is no power relation without the correlative constitution of a field of knowledge, nor any knowledge that does not presuppose and constitute at the same time power relations' (Foucault, 1977: 27). This view highlights the way in which forms of knowledge, including the so-called objective, rational and scientific views of medicine, are means by which people have their lives regulated. For Foucault, regulation often occurs through processes whereby people govern themselves rather than being oppressed by structural forces from outside. This self-regulation, a form of **disciplinary power**, occurs as individuals accept ideas of medicine or science as saying something 'truthful' about their own selves. This process is clearly at work when women accept the idea that ageing is unattractive and demeaning and that HRT can restore youthfulness. Medical and lay knowledge about menopause, ageing, female beauty and so on interact to constitute women as a certain kind of subject; they are then *subjected to* the suggestions for self-improvement offered by medicine. Where menopausal women use HRT it may tie them into a regular regime of drug use that is inappropriate or perhaps even harmful (given that oestrogen use has been linked with endometrial cancer). The development of medicine and the medical profession are therefore not to be viewed as unproblematically progressive, but rather as inevitably involved with strategies for social control.

The medical gaze at work

Foucault's perspective clearly differs from that of structuralist theorists in that it does not identify particular class, ethnic or gender groups as orchestrating these strategies of power/knowledge. Foucault prefers to view these strategies as involving shifting sets of relations that may vary in their effects. While this perspective may be useful in identifying the complex way in which medical knowledge has been created and linked to pervasive power relations, it does not explain the power and influence of those aspects of medical dominance that can be linked to capitalism. Sociological studies of the pharmaceutical industry have demonstrated the way in which the production and promotion of drugs may have more to do with profit than with health (Davies, 1992; Chetley and Mintzes, 1992). For example, certain drug regimes may be favoured not because they offer useful treatments but because it will be more profitable for companies if they can patent and market these drugs. For example, control over the development and supply of AL721, a possible new anti-viral drug that might be useful in the treatment of HIV infection, was stymied by a pharmaceutical company seeking to maximise its profits. While this substance is now available as a food supplement (because it is derived from egg lipids), initially the patent holder for AL721 withheld its development and marketing in a bid to have it classified as a new drug. As a drug, AL721 could have enabled the patent holder to make a larger profit than is possible from a food supplement.

While it is clear that the way in which health care is provided at the local level has been shaped by global processes of medicalisation and the dominance of the medical profession, it would be a mistake to assume that there is neither resistance to medical power nor the provision of alternative health care. On the contrary, since the 1970s various groups have organised themselves in opposition to medicine. For example, feminists have attempted to resist the patriarchal nature of medical knowledge and practice through the establishment of women's health collectives that offer everything from general health advice to cervical smears. Similarly, there has been a growth in whanau- and iwi-based health providers for Maori. Gay men have also formed political and health organisations for the prevention of HIV infection, and the treatment and care of people with AIDS. It must be said, however, that while these local forms of resistance to medical power have had many beneficial effects, they are still situated in a context where medicine continues to be the privileged form of knowledge about health and disease.

Conclusion

Where does this discussion leave us? You might well want to protest that medical interventions for the treatment of cancer, heart disease and all the other major diseases that plague us are vital. Certainly, much of what medicine has achieved is indeed life-saving and life-enhancing. However, it would be naive to ignore the very real, and often major, costs associated with medical dominance. A sociologist might well be grateful for life-saving surgery but can at the same time be aware of the way in which her treatment is informed by ideological processes and power relations that are disempowering. The sociology of health therefore cautions us to be critical of the connections between medicine and power. Such a perspective can only enhance our understanding of how health and illness are produced and might well contribute to a more just provision of health care.

? Study questions

12.1 Outline the biomedical approach to disease. Why are sociologists critical of this way of understanding disease?

12.2 What role do colonisation, the global economy and capitalist labour processes play in the production and distribution of disease and illness?

12.3 Discuss how the inter-connections between ideology, identity and sexuality help shape individual experiences of AIDS and cervical cancer.

12.4 What do sociologists mean by 'medicalisation' and why are they critical of this feature of modern societies?

Further reading

Davis, P. and Dew, K. (eds). (1999) *Health and Society in Aotearoa New Zealand*. Oxford University Press, Auckland.

Doyal, L. and Pennell, I. (1979) *The Political Economy of Health*. Pluto Press, London.

Germov, J. (ed.). (1998) *Second Opinion: An Introduction to Health Sociology*. Oxford University Press, Melbourne.

Lupton, D. (1994) *Medicine as Culture: Illness, Disease and the Body in Western Societies*. Sage, London.

Nettleton, S. (1995) *The Sociology of Health and Illness*. Polity Press, Cambridge.

13 Deviance and crime

Chapter aims

- to define deviance and who is most likely to be deviant, or defined as deviant, in a particular social setting;
- to explore the process and effects of identifying certain behaviours in legal codes as crimes, and how the judicial system then deals with crime;
- to discuss the growth, and decline, of certain crimes, and the involvement of particular groups in deviance and crime, both as instigators and as victims.

Introduction

Deviance from accepted norms is inevitable, and in many ways, to be welcomed. It helps confirm what is acceptable – and unacceptable – behaviour and, in the process, reinforces social solidarity. This chapter looks at the processes which define deviance and who is most likely to be defined as deviant. We take a particular interest in crime. Certain behaviours are deemed so unacceptable that they are described in legal codes and a process involving the police, security organisations, the judicial system and corrective or custodial institutions then seeks to identify and punish offenders. With growing economic insecurity, levels of crime have also grown thus requiring greater resources. The involvement of Maori and Pacific Islanders* in crime, the courts and the prison system is a significant social policy concern. Sociology contributes

* See p. 106

13 Deviance and crime — 233

to debates about why this should be and what alternatives exist. It has also helped sensitise society and key institutions to crimes which target women and children and this has led to more appropriate policies dealing with, for example, sexual offending. Deviance and crime provide a useful insight into political processes that shape communities and countries.

Defining deviance

Deviance is the act of violating or contravening an accepted norm of a community or a society. As Durkheim observed, defining what constitutes deviance is an important mechanism in confirming what is acceptable and unacceptable behaviour in a community. It reinforces solidarity as well as setting limits to, or guidelines on, our interactions with others. It helps define society. Because of its significance in helping shape society, deviance helps focus attention on some of the fundamental issues around how notions of 'society' are constructed and reinforced. How do societies create a moral code which defines acceptable and unacceptable behaviour? Is deviance always present and inevitable? How do societies sanction some behaviour and what do they do about unacceptable behaviour (see Macionis, 1993)? Sociology provides useful insights into all these questions, as well as into the efficacy – or otherwise – of the institutions, policies and processes which are designed to 'deal with' those defined as deviant.

The most obvious of the latter are the **laws** which codify social norms. Laws generally embody the norms of a particular society. Note the qualification 'generally'. Sociologists focus as much attention on who does the defining and who gets defined as criminal or deviant as on the fact of deviance itself. Paradoxically, deviance – with the exceptions of major contraventions such as murder or theft – is often not self-evidently deviant; rather, what is defined as deviant tends to reflect the dominance of particular groups and their ideas of what is, or is not, acceptable. There is considerable variation between societies, or groups within a society, as to what is deviant. This even applies to laws. The line between avoiding tax legitimately and evading it illegally is a fine one, and while tax evasion may be unlawful, others may not regard it *as* deviant as other forms of behaviour. Laws reflect norms, but there are a lot of laws in a society such as New Zealand, and not all are equally important. We therefore want to ask whose norms are embodied in laws and whose interests are being met.

Law is a description for behaviour which is codified in a legal statement, produced by a political institution such as a parliament and which is administered by government agencies such as the police.

Who creates laws, and for what purpose?

We also want to ask questions about the levels of and trends in crime. In New Zealand, Britain, Australia, the USA or Canada, criminal offending has increased in recent decades: more crimes are being committed. In Britain, in 1971, there were 1.666 million instances of recorded crimes. By 1993, this figure had increased to 5.526 million (Bilton et al., 1996: 449). This raises inevitable questions about why this is occurring and about what can be done. The answers are rather complicated, and are the subject of considerable political debate. We know that the rates of offending have gone up but, in part, this can be accounted for by more comprehensive surveillance systems, by more awareness in the case of some offences (such as sexual abuse), and by economic imperatives – the requirements of insurance claims, for instance. Even so, many criminal acts go unreported. It is estimated that one in two burglaries, four in five woundings, and nine out of every ten acts of vandalism or theft go unreported in the UK (Bilton et al., 1996: 449). Even though crimes are the most clearly defined forms of deviance, crime rates only tell part of the story. There is a hidden or 'dark' side of crime which is often unacknowledged when we discuss issues of deviance and crime.

Then there is the whole complex structure designed to monitor and do something about deviance and crime. The police, and at times the armed forces, are an important part of this process, and they are increasingly supplemented by private security organisations and the surveillance involved in the protection of homes, businesses and public spaces. Most people would be amazed – and perhaps horrified – by the extent to which their activity is now monitored by unseen people or machines. It is estimated that 81% of British streets are under video surveillance (Fiske, 1998: 71) and taking a book out of the library, making charitable donations, or attending courses at university can all provide information that can 'be turned into knowledge by which the powerful may "know" what we think' (Fiske, 1998: 76). Then there are the institutions that are part of the justice system which deal with those who contravene laws. There is a complex, highly rationalised and centrally administered system of social control which defines and sorts deviance and then hands over responsibility for dealing with an offender to various 'helping occupations' and remedial and custodial institutions (Scull, 1992: 33). Prisons are an important part of the system, and they are being used more and more to 'deal with' crime. In most countries like New Zealand, the numbers of people in prison has increased quite substantially in the last two decades. In California, more money is spent by the state on prisons than on higher education; 2% of the US population is under the control of the penal law system and there are 69 prisoners per 100 000 of the population (Bauman, 1998: 106, 115). Social control is big business for governments and private providers. Apart from describing these processes, and what happens in the justice system, sociologists ask the same question as anyone else: how successful is the system in preventing crime and dealing with deviance? We are all concerned with *Sicherheit* (safety, security, certainty), no matter what our class or political persuasion, and this threat to safety drives the politics and concerns of many societies such as New Zealand (Bauman, 1998: 117, 118–122). Deviance and what we do about it is one of the enduring themes of social groupings because it is so central to questions of social order and identity.

The issue of how effective prisons are in dealing with criminal behaviour is an enduring one

The local and the global: economic decline and growing crime

Bauman's comment that *Sicherheit* is a central concern of modern societies has gained significance because of the economic uncertainty that now characterises the industrialised world. There is a central paradox here. The influence of economic rationalists in the 1980s resulted in a concerted move by politicians like Thatcher, Reagan, and Douglas or Richardson in New Zealand to reduce the provisions and role of the state. In its more extreme forms, this policy meant that the state was to be minimalist – its role in providing welfare, health care and education was to be reduced significantly. Protection was to be accorded to individual citizens and property in order to enhance the productive capacity of an economy. Labour markets were to be freed up and the cost of labour reduced. As Bauman (1998) observes, economies needed to be attractive to global investors who were interested in local flexibility and costs. But in the process, crime increased and governments spent more on crime prevention, the processing of criminals and their punishment. Stuart Hall labelled Thatcher a '**moral authoritarian**'. Law and order was one of her frequent catch-cries, and state intervention was justified in preserving law and order in the interests of safe communities and orderly business.

Moral authoritarian describes someone who adopts a particular moral code or position and then insists, often from a position of political advantage, that this code be adhered to by everyone. The code is possibly enforced by government agencies.

While the state has reduced its activities in most areas, it has increased its costs and involvement in trying to contain the growth of what are socially defined as illegal activities.

There are two aspects to this growth. The first is the expansion of global criminal activities. An obvious example is drugs-related activities, with parts of Asia and Latin America responsible for production and the affluent cities of North America and Europe important consumers. Some drugs have long been part of international trade, but they have not always been illegal. In the eighteenth and nineteenth centuries, morphine or opium were commonly used, and only became controlled substances at the beginning of twentieth century. In New Zealand, those most likely to be charged and sentenced for drug offences, at least up until the mid-1960s, were local Chinese. Drugs became much more widely used as part of the hippie movement from the late 1960s, and something of a moral panic took place. There was growing political and popular concern at drug use or, at least, the use of certain drugs. It was partly a reflection of growing usage. Many hallucinogenic drugs are now part of an international trade that provides an important income flow for countries. Within New Zealand, marijuana is an important if illegal aspect of the economy of declining rural areas such as Northland or the East Coast. Of course, not all drugs are international commodities, and some of the most destructive in terms of costs to a community, such as alcohol and tobacco, are perfectly legal (see Newbold (1992), for an indication of the effects and costs in New Zealand of various sorts of drugs), although, there are increasing measures to reduce the use or abuse of these drugs.

Globally, other illegal activities have also increased, especially terrorism and prostitution. The Locherbie disaster is only one example of the internationalisation of terrorism, and since the 1970s, the costs of terrorism – increased security, lost tourist income, the loss of life and property – have become much more significant. Prostitution is another international commodity which may involve illegal activities. Attempts to reduce the sex tourist trade which has contributed to child abuse in Asia have been only partially successful, while the arrival in New Zealand of Asian sex workers who operate outside the labour laws in local brothels and massage parlours provides another dimension of globalisation. Although these are aspects of international illegal activities, they are a relatively minor influence on the explosion of crime within societies such as New Zealand. Much more significant is the relationship between the economic reforms of the 1980s and 1990s, and the increase in offending within societies.

As economic changes have impacted on communities, producing greater levels of unemployment, underemployment and economic stress, rates of offending have increased. It is not a simple relationship. Sometimes the offences are new ones. There has been a noticeable increase in laws concerning driving. There are now 21 categories of driving offence in Britain, and 1000 people are jailed each year for failing to pay fines for these offences. Electronic crime, involving hacking, access to or theft of

238 Exploring Society

Sexual offending refers to any sexual activity that is identified as being a criminal act. Sexual deviance includes sexual behaviour that may or may not be defined as criminal.

Blue-collar crime includes those types of offending, such as burglary, or car conversion, that are most likely to be committed by members of the working class.

White-collar crime includes crimes such as fraud that are committed, in a work-related context, by professionally qualified people.

information, illegal financial transfers, or pornography, are all growing rapidly, and require new responses. In other cases, there is a greater awareness of offending. **Sexual offending** and child abuse are now more likely to be described as such and reported to officials than in previous decades. These considerations aside, the reported figures indicate that there is more crime, both blue-collar and white-collar, that mirrors the growing economic stress of communities. Violence has increased, along with theft of various sorts. Burglary, a **blue-collar crime** generally committed by working-class males, has increased – but so has fraud, typically a **white-collar crime**. Economic rationalist policies appear to have contributed to a substantial increase in criminal activities, and as the state has reduced the level of intervention in the market and the provision of universal welfare, it has had to step up its social control activities. In the USA, for instance, the prison population doubled between 1985 and 1995, and it now costs $20 billion per year to house this population (Macionis and Plummer, 1997: 227). Governments in New Zealand and elsewhere have minimised their responsibility for welfare and their level of intervention in economic activities, but they have had to spend more as the costs of social control have increased, often dramatically.

So far, we have suggested that the effects of recent economic policy changes have played an important causal role in increasing the crime rate. But economic rationalist arguments have been used to provide sociological explanations of crime. The argument is that people make an assessment of the risks and benefits of offending, and act accordingly. Much more powerful in sociological circles is an approach that appeared in opposition to neo-liberal arguments – Left Realism. Marxist approaches to crime had previously stressed the capitalist nature of society and stated that offending reflected the effect of inequality – both in who committed crimes and who defined and controlled the process of legislating for crime, and the processing of criminal activities. According to Marxist criminologists in the 1970s such as William Chambliss and Richard Quinney, capitalism is a crime-creating system (Bilton et al., 1996: 457). But often, in this broad approach, there was little acknowledgement of who was the victim of crime, of the processes which led to certain crimes, and there was a silence on domestic and sexual violence. Marxist arguments need to be refined, and Left Realism offered a more convincing approach. Led by criminologists such as Jock Young, this approach argued that the increase in crime was significant, and that it had an impact particularly on the working class, women and ethnic minorities. Crime was often intra-class with both offenders and victims from the same class. Furthermore, the increase in rates of crime were real, and could not be explained away as simply a construction of a system, capitalist or otherwise. Left Realists argued that to explain and understand offending, the square of crime, involving the state, society or the public at large, and the informal control that is exercised, the offender and the victim, all need to be considered (Bilton et al., 1996: 464). For instance,

> ... although police and judicial practices and prejudice may exaggerate the involvement of black youth in crime, they [Left Realists] insist that the higher levels of officially recorded black crime are a reality which is not merely the product of racist law enforcement, prosecution and sentencing.
>
> (Bilton et al., 1996: 465)

Left Realists went on to argue that the nature and levels of offending are a product of the structural inequalities of capitalist societies, and of how individuals and groups perceive themselves relative to others and the level of marginalisation which they experience. In response, Left Realist solutions to criminal offending focus on three levels. At the macro level, issues of social justice – including access to employment, housing and community facilities and material rewards – need to be addressed. At another level, there needs to be greater trust in the police and justice system, more co-operation and new options for dealing with offenders. It is agreed that prisons do little to address criminal offending and that non-custodial options should be explored. Finally, at the street and community level, the opportunities for crime should be reduced (see Bilton et al., 1996: 466). Communitarian approaches which use 're-integrative shaming' whereby the victims and their families confront the offenders and their families are used to re-establish community and informal social controls in order to inhibit crime (Milne, 1996). The way in which courts have traditionally operated is seen as being too removed from the crime and the solutions offered too uncertain and too punitive to be effective. Left Realists have contributed to debates about the nature of crime, the rates of crime and what should be done, although the growing level of crime and the tendency to punish (including high and growing levels of imprisonment), are still the current reality in most western, industrial societies. Sociological explanations and political responses often diverge significantly in terms both of explaining crime and its recent increase, and of suggesting what should be done by way of a series of policy responses.

Differences and divisions: defining the deviant other

It is useful to ask why some crimes are given more – or less – prominence than others, and why, as the Left Realists argue, people from some groups are more likely to be involved in crime. These are well-established questions for sociologists or criminologists, although they are asked and answered in ways that are rather different from popular 'theories' of crime and who offends.

Blue-collar crimes such as burglaries or theft (see Newbold, 1992) are often portrayed as the most significant form of criminal activity, while it is only recently that white-collar crimes have been given any attention or resources. The term was coined in 1939 by a sociologist, Edwin Sutherland, to describe '… crimes committed by persons of high social positions in the course of the occupations' (Macionis, 1993: 221). As Newbold (1992: 27–28) notes, white-collar crime has been consistently overlooked by sociologists, and by politicians and the public. It is carried out by people, often professionals, who have some social standing in the community, who are in positions of trust and who are well-educated, articulate people. Their offending often involves complex legal and accounting transactions which are not easily identified or understood by the public. Even the police are not particularly interested because the privacy and complexity involved make these crimes difficult to investigate and also make it difficult to obtain successful prosecutions (Clarke, 1992: 43). However, the level of white-collar crime is substantial. Soon after the Serious Fraud Office was established in New Zealand, it was investigating white-collar crimes which involved four times the value that was involved in conventional property offences reported to the police each year (Newbold, 1992: 36). Newbold goes on to calculate that for every dollar stolen through conventional crime, $40 are stolen via white-collar crime. Few comprehend the level of white-collar crime, or consider it as great a threat to themselves or the community as blue-collar crimes such as property theft. And in New Zealand and elsewhere, the level of white-collar crime has increased dramatically since the 1980s, even allowing for the effect on statistics of a greater awareness and more police resources. This is a classic case of labelling.

Durkheim made an interesting observation in 1893 to the effect that:

> … what confers a criminal character upon an act is not the nature of the act itself but the definition given to it by society. We do not reprove certain behaviour because it is criminal; it is criminal because we reprove it.
>
> (Durkheim, quote in Newbold, 1992: 9)

This is a radical observation which challenges popular views about the nature of crime and who commits it. It was taken up in the 1960s by labelling theorists such as Howard Becker and Edwin Lemert. They reflected the challenges to authority that were part of the political landscape of the 1960s and helped shift the focus from the question of why an individual committed a crime to questions of who was doing the defining: which behaviour is defined as criminal and why? (Bilton et al., 1996: 456). It was part of an approach called **symbolic interactionism** which focused on the social definitions used by social actors as the basis for social interaction. The point here is that symbolic interactionism in general, and labelling theory in particular, argued that crime was a social construction, and that people learned to be criminals; they were often criminals as a result of stigmatisation, or were confirmed in their 'criminality' by the process of stigmatisation. Returning to the issue of white-collar crime, labelling theory offers an explanation of why such

Symbolic interactionism is a sociological approach which is interested in the role of symbols and language in social interaction.

crime is defined and labelled quite differently to blue-collar crime: white-collar crime involves powerful people who work in powerful, 'respected' occupations and institutions – the very people who are influential in defining which activities are crimes and which people are criminals.

The same questions can be used to interrogate the issue of why some ethnic minorities are so over-represented in crime statistics. In New Zealand, Maori and Pacific Islanders are more likely to be charged, successfully prosecuted and sent to prison than Pakeha. Are they more criminally inclined or are there other reasons for this? Left Realists point to the structural inequalities of capitalist societies and the economic and social marginalisation experienced by some groups while labelling theorists focus on the process of defining who is a criminal. Both help explain the position of Maori. Their disproportionate numbers in working-class occupations and communities, and a history of colonisation, explain why they appear in blue-collar crimes involving theft and burglary, and domestic violence. A powerful Maori criminology (see Pratt, 1994: 229) articulated by Moana Jackson since the late 1980s, has linked the levels of crime amongst Maori to their low socio-economic status and the destruction of Maori culture. This has led to calls for Maori to develop their own criminal justice system to deal with addiction, sexual and violent offending, principally because the existing justice system is seen as irrelevant to Maori. One important issue is the degree to which non-Maori, or institutions which are bound by the culture and conventions of the dominant group, can ever be appropriate given a lack of understanding and the presence of stereotypes and hostility.

Here there is some evidence to support the labelling approach. It dates from the 1970s when Oliver Sutherland and Marti Grönfors sat in a Nelson court and recorded the treatment and sentencing of Maori and Pakeha who came before the court. Even when the incident was the same and the background and previous offending of those charged were similar, Maori were more likely to be given harsher, and often custodial, sentences. Subsequently, the actions of the police Task Force on the streets of Auckland in the mid-1970s indicated that police dealt with Maori and Pacific Islanders quite differently to Pakeha; they paid more attention to their activities, were more likely to confront them, take them into custody and charge them. Once Maori and Pacific Islanders appeared in court, they received tougher sentences. This raises some important questions about the impartiality of justice systems, and returns us to the questions raised by labelling theorists. Is there prejudice, especially amongst those responsible for dealing with crime? Certainly, some high-profile US cases indicate that there are substantial racial divides in the way that American blacks are perceived and in the treatment they receive.

The freeway chase involving O.J. Simpson was the second-most watched television event in American history (the most watched was the first day of the Gulf War (Fiske, 1998: 67)). From then on, the Simpson case because a test for American justice, with significant political implications to the extent that it polarised the public along racial lines.

A key part of the defence was that Simpson was dealt with unfairly by prejudiced police. He faced two juries, one which was largely white which found him guilty, and one which was dominated by blacks which found him not guilty. In the first trial, the lone black juror said that 'Simpson got a raw deal'. Public opinion echoed this divide with three-quarters of the white community thinking Simpson guilty while only a quarter of blacks agreed. How do two juries, both claiming to be 'colour blind', reach two different verdicts? Fiske (1998: 67) suggests that blacks represent the most obvious criminal threat in the USA and surveillance is typically designed to monitor the activities of American blacks:

> … O.J. Simpson, Rodney King, Clarence Thomas, Willie Horton, Mike Tyson, Marion Barry are all different people, but they all figure in the racial anxieties of the 1990s because they are all hypermediate Black men whose racial identity was sexualised, whose masculinity was racialised, who were all, whether found guilty or not, criminalised.
>
> (Fiske, 1998: 67)

The O.J. Simpson freeway chase was a 'high-tech replay of the old nigger hunts of the South' (Fiske, 1998: 68). Similarly, the beating of a black man, Rodney King, by Los Angeles police officers 'scandalized the normally unseen operations of white power by making them visible and thus contestable' (Fiske, 1998: 76), and resulted in the Los Angeles riots which underlined the racial divides of the USA. Foucault's arguments about the nature of surveillance in a modern society endorse those of the labelling theorists in suggesting that questions need to be asked about whether there are expectations about who is most likely to commit crimes, who represents the greatest threat to the public order, and how equitably the police and justice system operate. These questions focus attention on who does the defining and who is most likely to be defined and treated differently in matters of crime and deviance. The evidence in both New Zealand and the USA, as well as elsewhere, indicates that certain ethnic minorities, or racialised 'others', are most likely to be labelled as deviant, or potential deviants, and that these definitions impact on their treatment by the police and the judicial process. Obversely, there is the question of how white-collar crimes and criminals are treated.

Low life in high places: the fight against white-collar crime

Greg Newbold

In his presidential speech to the American Sociological Association in 1939, the sociologist Edwin H. Sutherland addressed the topic of 'White-collar Criminality'. The focus of the talk was the huge amounts of crime which are hidden within America's corporate sector. Thus did the term, 'white-collar' crime, come into being. That very same year, using a similar theme, singer and songwriter Woody Guthrie wrote 'The Ballad of Pretty Boy Floyd'. In it were the lines:

Now as through this world I ramble,
I've seen lots of funny men,
Some will rob you with a six-gun,
And some with a fountain pen.

But as through this life you travel,
And through this life you roam,
You will never see an outlaw,
Drive a family from its home.

In 1939, the suggestion that businessmen could be worse criminals than robbers was a novel one. By the same token, Sutherland's paper, published in the *American Sociological Review* in 1940, stunned a generation of criminologists who for years had talked about crime in the streets, without even thinking about crime in the suites. But despite the great impact which Sutherland's paper had, it was fully two decades before the crimes of big business became important in the realm of mainstream criminology. Recognition in New Zealand was even slower. When in 1968 the first major study on crime in New Zealand was published by the Department of Justice, the corporate offender was almost forgotten. Indeed, the New Zealand government generally has ignored this type of crime until very recent times.

To some extent, the obscurity of white-collar crime is understandable. Business rip-offs are seldom detected and evidence of them is hard to get. Up to the beginning of the 1970s, in fact, there had been only two major fraud trials in the entire history of this country. The first involved the Investment Equity Trust Group in 1934; the second was the Intercity Distributors case of 1958. In both cases, special legislation was required to enable prosecution to proceed.

For years, impotent law, weak forensic power and poor resources hobbled agencies appointed to investigate corporate fraud. Repeated complaints by those agencies generally fell on deaf governmental ears until the advent of crisis. It took the four-million dollar collapse of JBL in 1972 and a five-year Committee of Inquiry into the Companies Act before a special unit was created within the Department of Justice to police such crime. It took a surge of bankruptcies in the late 1970s and the collapse of Hoffman Holdings in 1984 before a dedicated business crime agency, known as the Corporate Fraud Unit, was set up in 1985. But, under-staffed and under-funded, within three years this unit was crushed by work pressure and hugely inadequate means.

It was not until the late 1980s that the true extent of white-collar crime started to become publicly visible in New Zealand. The monumental losses sustained by high-profile companies like Judge Corp, Renouf Corp, Goldcorp, Rada Corporation, Landbase and Registered Securities after the 1987 sharemarket crash, heightened awareness of the dangers of corporate rip-off. In 1984, two senior public accountants had already announced that in two-thirds of the receiverships they had undertaken, serious fraud had been encountered. By 1989, 30 commercial enterprises were under investigation or awaiting investigation for crimes totalling between $50 million and $70 million. An assessment conducted in the 1990s placed the value of possible frauds committed between 1985 and 1988 at around $2.3 billion.

It was in this atmosphere that the Serious Fraud Office was established in March 1990, with the purpose of attacking head-on the problem of white-collar crime. Its work has given us our first insight into the true extent of white-collar crime in this country.

From the beginning, the impact of the Serious Fraud Office was dramatic. Within its first two months of operation, the office received 59 complaints about matters involving more than $100 million. By November 1990, the amounts involved had reached $200 million and in December the massive Equiticorp inquiry, alleging almost a billion dollars in fraud, began.

In 1996, Charles Sturt estimated that 80 000 New Zealanders had been directly victimised by the work of serious fraudsters with 800 000 – the children, wives, creditors and employees of the victims – suffering indirectly. By mid-1997, the Serious Fraud Office had taken 83 prosecutions, involving a combined total of $800 million. At that time, 21 cases were awaiting to be determined. Of the remainder, 62 cases had resulted in convictions and only five had been lost. Prison terms – of up to seven years – had been imposed on the majority of the convicted.

In February 1993, following the jailing of Equiticorp boss Allan Hawkins for six years, the Minister of Justice suggested that because they are not really 'dangerous', white-collar criminals might better be put to work in the community than serve time in prison. This is an old theme, and it reflects an older fallacy.

The fallacy is that people who steal with the stroke of a pen are a lesser menace than those who use violence or threaten it. Such a claim is easily answered. Violent criminals get heavy sentences because of the trauma they cause, and few people would argue with that. But the majority of people who are robbed or attacked suffer no lasting injury. Cuts and bruises heal, broken teeth can be fixed. People who suffer violent attacks may be traumatised for a while, but in the great majority of cases they get over their experiences and go on to lead normal lives.

Not so the victims of white-collar crime.

A person who loses $50 000 will forever be $50 000 worse off. People who lose their life savings, their assets, their livelihoods, their homes, may never recover. They may stay poor for the rest of their lives. Children may falter in their education and life chances, marriages may come under strain and collapse. The emotional stress endured by the victims of white-collar crime can be extreme, and has driven several to suicide. For these unfortunates, there is no recovery.

But not only do individuals suffer from the depredations of corporate crooks, the country as a whole degenerates as well. Since 1984, New Zealand has moved increasingly toward a market economy. The success of this strategy depends on investors providing money, so that entrepreneurs can set up business, so that workers can get jobs. In order to work, the market requires that people play by the rules. But the white-collar criminal does not play by the rules, and in doing so he derails the whole process. He steals from his investors, he cheats his competitors, he exploits the consumers, he defrauds the tax department. As a result, legitimate competitors collapse, potential investors lose confidence and squirrel their savings, consumers pay higher prices for goods and services, interest and tax rates stay high and the economy stagnates. A market system can never work efficiently while fraudsters are sabotaging its mechanism. Unlike the short-term damage caused by blue-collar crimes such as burglary and robbery, therefore, the consequences of white-collar offending are chronic and profound.

The solution to the scourge of white-collar crime is vigorous prosecution by agencies such as the Serious Fraud Office, combined with heavy deterrent penalties. In contrast to the impetuous opportunism of the average blue-collar criminal, the corporate offender meticulously plans his activities, carefully assesses the chances of success and failure, and weighs possible profits against potential losses. The crooked businessman is a calculating criminal who responds to measured risk. Consider the case of Allan Hawkins, former director of Equiticorp. He received a sentence of six years for stealing $87.7 million. Of this, he served less than two-and-a-half years, or one year for every $35 million. To any businessman, that has to be a pretty good deal. It is small wonder that white-collar crime continues to thrive.

Overseas authorities agree that for every dollar stolen by conventional crime, about fifty are lost to corporate offenders. In 1997, Charles Sturt estimated the total amount of suspected fraud that had come to the notice of the Serious Fraud Office to be about three billion dollars – many times more than the $30 million reported stolen each year by conventional means. By these measures, commercial fraud must be one of the most serious crime issues facing New Zealand today. It undermines the economy, it wrecks thousands of lives, it is committed by greedy, calculating con men who seem to care not a damn for the misery they create. From a practical point of view, deterrent penalties are necessary to give meaning to the force of law.

Exemplary sentences are also justified, no less than they are for crimes of serious violence. Because the armed robber or the gangster looks mean and nasty, few people have compunction about sending him to jail for long periods of time. But the well-attired and genteel businessman somehow seems a lesser evil. As we have seen, however, the activities of the elite criminal are no less sinister than those of his working-class counterpart. True, the armed robber might terrify his victims as he relieves them of their wallets. But the charm of the corporate outlaw is cold comfort to honest, trusting investors who have been driven from their homes.

White-collar crimes such as fraud have increased substantially since the 1980s. Nick Leeson under arrest.

Questions

Greg Newbold highlights the role of sociology in first naming and then focusing attention on white-collar crime. The following questions help demonstrate the importance of white-collar crime, and the reluctance to do much about it.

1   Why is it difficult for the general public to fully comprehend the nature or scale of white-collar crime?

2   Greg Newbold indicates that the late 1980s saw a significant increase in white-collar crime. What general political and economic developments contributed to this growth?

3   Why does the general public, or the police and justice systems, see white-collar crime as 'less dangerous' than other crimes? Greg Newbold feels differently. Do you agree with his arguments about the impact and seriousness of white-collar crime?

The social and the personal: personal safety and gender

To continue the theme of the social construction of crime, we might ask, as Carol Smart (1976) has done, whether crime and control are gendered. In general, women are considerably less likely to commit crimes, to be charged or to be imprisoned. But they are certainly the victims of crime, and the fear of crime is an important issue for women, especially as they get older. An obvious area of crime which involves women as victims is domestic and sexual violence, including rape and sexual abuse. The rate for these has increased as the level of reporting and awareness has increased since the 1970s. Given the subjugation of women, and the unwillingness of the legislators, the police and the courts to recognise the rights of women for much of this century, those offences most likely to involve men as the perpetrators and women as the victims have typically received little attention in the past. But the women's liberation movement of the 1960s through to the 1980s politicised the position and treatment of women, with significant results. The reporting of sexual offending increased rapidly as organisations and individuals acted as advocates for those abused; as police and courts were confronted and challenged to take sexual abuse seriously, and as new policies were introduced to recognise the needs of those facing abuse. Women's refuges were an obvious example of this recognition. However, the gendered nature of crime and control has not always worked against women's interests. While homosexual acts between men were a criminal offence until the passing of the 1985 Homosexual Law Reform Act, homosexual act between consenting adult women have never been a crime in New Zealand, primarily because Victorian society did not believe that women 'indulged' in such behaviour (see Newbold, 1992: 72). Such examples do tend to be an exception.

Sexual orientation is variously defined as deviant or acceptable according to cultural and social values

As happens in many areas of sociological – and popular – understanding, the gendered nature of deviance and crime has been ignored. In particular, the focus has been on male involvement to the exclusion of females – and children – as either offenders or as victims. The politicisation of feminism since the 1960s, and the growing influence of feminism within sociology, has encouraged a feminist criminology best represented by Carol Smart (1976) and Frances Heidensohn (1985). A tradition which had been built around the study of male criminality was rejected as an inadequate basis for the understanding of female deviancy and criminal activities. Ann Campbell (1981; 1986) provided interesting insights on female involvement in deviant and criminal sub-cultures, including the role of girls in New York gangs. What she clearly demonstrated was the central role they played in gang activities, and that they were involved in much higher levels of violence than was commonly thought. Newbold (1992) offers similar comments on the situation in New Zealand, and goes on to observe that the differential expectations of male and female criminality are reflected in the assumptions and procedures of the criminal justice system.

> Much of New Zealand's criminal law and procedure [was] created at a time when a proper sense of adult responsibility in women was denied, and when men's dominance over them was unquestioned … Where deviance is concerned, this has led to a severe under-representation of women's criminality in published statistics.
>
> (Newbold, 1992: 54)

The other aspect was women – and children – as victims. The levels of victimisation experienced by women and children, particularly in terms of sexual offending and domestic violence, were not widely appreciated or acknowledged until the influence of feminist sociology in particular and feminism in general challenged existing perceptions. For example, rape has attracted considerably more attention since the 1960s than it did previously, even though it is clear that most rapes are still not reported (possibly only one in five rapes is reported; see Newbold, 1992: 97) and even though there are still ambiguities in terms of definition and the processing of complaints of rape between married couples. Nevertheless, the reporting of rape and the conviction of rapists has increased significantly in recent decades. While it is a direct product of the influence of feminism, it parallels the broader issue of personal safety, or *Sicherheit* (Bauman, 1998: 118–122). Bauman goes on to argue that one of the prevailing issues of contemporary society is the concern with personal safety, which he attributes to the anxieties which derive from the media preoccupation with violence. It helps emphasise the 'stranger danger' anxieties of vulnerable individuals and communities, especially children, women and older people.

> Stranger in the street, prowler around the home … Burglar alarms, the watched and patrolled neighbourhood, the guarded condominium gates – they all serve the same purpose: keeping strangers away.
>
> (Bauman, 1998: 122)

Industries that provide security – in the form of household burglar alarms, surveillance, and security checks – have all grown, and provide a new dimension to both personal and public life. They constitute part of the redefinition of what is a threat (from dangerous dogs to sexual harassment) and what can be done to protect individuals. Unfortunately, while there are new options and a new awareness by agencies such as the police and courts, those that are vulnerable and who have been victims, are still at risk.

Although awareness may have increased, this does not mean that women – or indeed children – are any safer. Fifty per cent of all murders involve family members. As violence has increased generally over recent decades in line with economic stress and the levels of unemployment or underemployment, so has violence involving women and family members. New Zealand has had some high-profile cases such as that of Delia Witika, in which those who are dependent are shown to be vulnerable in ways that gain considerable public sympathy. It raises an interesting question of how old someone needs to be before he/she is regarded as being criminally responsible. In medieval times, seven was considered to be the age of reason, and it was held that prior to this age, children were incapable of sinning. In 1933, in Britain, the age was increased from seven to eight, and then, in 1963, to ten. Under this age, a child is regarded as incapable of committing serious wrong. Yet in 1995, two 10-year-olds murdered 2-year-old James Bulger in Liverpool. And those under 20 years of age account for 40% of all offenders in the UK while the peak age for offending (in the case of males) is 18.

Conclusion

Definitions of what constitutes deviance and crime evolved significantly during the twentieth century. At first, explanations of who committed crimes was often based around a crude biologism ('criminals are born criminal'), deviance was often defined in fundamentally different ways (religious non-conformity or sexual preferences attracted considerable hostility) and punishment was often primitive, either in terms of what was administered (e.g. flogging) or the conditions of prisons. In the second half of the century, many of the existing definitions of deviance and criminality, and what was the most appropriate response, were challenged and, at times, dramatically changed. Some activities, such as male homosexuality, were decriminalised whereas drug misuse, sexual offending and illegal immigration attracted new laws and punishments. We might better understand, now, what produces deviant and criminal behaviour, but we also imprisoned considerably more people (including

250 Exploring Society

women) as the twentieth century progressed, while those who are mentally ill have been moved from institutions out into the community. White-collar fraud is now recognised as a much more significant form of criminal activity although blue-collar crimes such as burglary or assault attract most attention and resources. And at the very time when individual and group rights have been more comprehensively enshrined in law, we are subject to much greater surveillance and monitoring.

The sociology of crime and deviance is one of the most significant traditions in sociology, particularly as sociology is able to contribute an understanding to an area of immediate and major personal and policy significance. And yet, while there have been notable advances in sociological understanding (feminist criminology, Left Realism), many of the well-established sociological questions – and responses – still prevail. Sociologists continue to assume that no behaviour is automatically deviant or criminal, but instead to focus attention on why the behaviour is labelled inappropriate or an offence, and by whom. The process of defining deviance and crime highlights the social construction of norms and of acceptable and unacceptable behaviour. It also highlights the social construction of what sanctions or punishments are considered appropriate for such forms of behaviour. The sociology of crime and deviance is as much about conformity and establishing social regulation, as it is about inappropriate behaviour. It is central to the process of community and society building, and sociologists want to focus on political power and control, on the process of defining some forms of behaviour as acceptable, and others as not, and on why some groups are routinely cast as deviant or criminal.

? Study questions

13.1 Provide examples of activities that typify (a) white-collar crime and (b) blue-collar crime. What sorts of crime are of particular concern to the public?

13.2 How do social divisions such as class, ethnicity, age and gender reflect on deviant and criminal statistics, and how are such divisions reflected in the punishments handed down by the judicial system?

13.3 What are the central arguments of Left Realism and feminist criminology?

Further reading

Baumann, Z. (1998) *Globalization: The Human Consequences*. Polity Press, Cambridge.

Cohen, S. (1985) *Visions of Social Control*. Polity Press, Cambridge.

Downes D. and Rock, P. (1988) *Understanding Deviance*, 2nd ed. Clarendon Press, Oxford.

Newbold, G. (1992) *Crime and Deviance*. Oxford University Press, Auckland.

Smart, C. (1976) *Women, Crime and Criminology*. Routledge, London.

Walkgate, S. (1995) *Gender and Crime*. Prentice Hall, New York.

14 Social movements

Chapter aims

- to outline some key features of, and theories about, contemporary social movements;
- to explore the connection between globalisation and local protest in transnational social movements;
- to examine the interrelationship between social movements and collective identities;
- to discuss elements of ideological conflict within social movements.

Introduction

Social movements have come to be familiar features of the political landscape. On almost any day if you open a newspaper or watch the television news you are likely to read about a street march, protest, sit-in, or demonstration of some kind happening somewhere in the world. Such methods of protest are associated with social movements as diverse as environmentalism, feminism, the peace movement, animal rights activism, Islamic fundamentalism, the New Christian Conservatism, indigenous peoples and pro-democracy movements, gay rights activism, and so on. Given their diverse ideological positions, value commitments and forms of political organisation and activity it would seem that there is little that links these movements. However, sociologists have sought to identify the common features that such social movements seem to share. This chapter examines the key defining features of social movements and outlines five broad sociological perspectives on this phenomena. Drawing on the text themes, the chapter explores (a) how the process of globalisation has contributed to the development of social movements – particularly new forms of 'transnational social movements'; (b) the role of identity in mobilising individuals to act; and (c) ideological divisions that can exist *within*, and can weaken, social movements.

Social movements can be broadly defined as groupings of organisations and individuals who through collective action challenge particular aspects of the social order. For the most part this form of political action occurs outside established institutions.

Protest, collective action and social movements

One common feature of all the social movements named above is that they represent forms of collective action. Collective action includes 'crowd behaviour' of all sorts (e.g. riots, panics, mob activity and hostile outbursts) as well as other kinds of mass behaviour (e.g. fads, fashions and crazes). These forms of collective behaviour are characterised by 'socially shared but relatively spontaneous and non-institutionalised responses by a large number of people to uncertain and problematic situations. (Thompson and Hickey, 1994: 522). While social movements are in some respects expressions of collective action they can be distinguished from these other forms of collective behaviour by virtue of their more *organised* and *goal-directed* efforts to produce change (Thompson and Hickey, 1994: 522). These features highlight the fact that social movements are *political* in character. They protest against certain features of social life and at the same time they are 'collective enterprises to establish a *new order of life*' (Blumer, 1995: 60 – emphasis added). This definition emphasises social movements as forms of 'moral protest'.

While both organised and spontaneous forms of protest have probably always been a feature of social life, the nature, meaning and significance of protest movements have varied throughout history. James Jasper (1997: 6–9) argues that it is possible to distinguish between three historically different forms of protest. Pre-industrial protests can be seen as responses to *immediate threats* associated with such things as grain scarcity, high bread prices and the enclosures of grazing land. In pre-industrial societies actions were directed at the local level and were relatively short-lived. Protests were directly targeted at those who were perceived to have erred, and they sought to directly redress the perceived wrongs. The changes associated with the industrial and French revolutions brought new forms of 'citizenship movements'. 'These efforts were organised by and on behalf of *categories of people* excluded in some way from full human rights, political participation, or basic economic protections' (Jasper, 1997: 7 – emphasis added). These movements were therefore demands for the full inclusion in society of particular collectivities (e.g. industrial workers, women, and ethnic minorities). The trade union, feminist and civil rights movements are the best examples of such industrial or citizenship movements. In comparison with pre-industrial movements, citizenship movements are more national in scope, better organised and they direct much of their activity against the state. These citizenship movements continue to be important elements of the political landscape, yet it has been argued by a number of different theorists that the post-industrial age we now live in has given rise to *new* forms of social movements that are significantly different from citizenship movements. These movements for social change are simply called new social movements (NSM) by many theorists (e.g. Offe, 1985; Melucci, 1985). However, Jasper more precisely calls these NSM 'post-citizenship' movements because they do not have such clearly defined collectivities on behalf of whom they are working.

Moreover, for the most part such movements are made up of people whose motivation for activity is not that they are excluded from political or economic power. Rather, post-citizenship movements are made up of people

> who pursue protections or benefits *for others ... Ambivalence toward modern science and technology,* occasionally even outright hostility, are common themes in the recent wave ... These protestors are especially interested in *changing their society's cultural sensibilities.*
>
> (Jasper, 1997: 7 – emphasis added)

These new post-citizenship movements also differ from citizenship movements in that their target is as likely to be the media or science and technology as the state. Table 14.1 identifies some of the ways in which NSM (or post-citizenship movements) are differentiated from 'old' (or citizenship movements) in terms of the issues, actors, values and modes of action of each movement.

	'old paradigm'	**'new paradigm'**
Actors	socio-economic groups acting *as* groups (in the group interest) and involved in distributive conflict	socio-economic groups acting not as such, but on behalf of ascriptive collectivities
Issues	economic growth and distribution; military and social security, social control	preservation of peace, environment, human rights, and unalienated forms of work
Values	freedom and security of private consumption and material progress	personal autonomy and identity, as opposed to centralised control, etc.
Modes	(internal): formal organisation, large-scale representative association (external): pluralist or corporatist interest intermediation; political party competition, majority rule	informality, spontaneity, low degree of horizontal and vertical differentiation protest politics based on demands formulated in predominantly negative terms

Source: Offe, Claus. (1985) New social movements. *Social Research* 52(4):832.

Table 14.1 The main characteristics of 'old' and 'new' social movements

While Jasper distinguishes between citizenship and post-citizenship movements, this distinction may not be as clear-cut as it might first seem. For example, feminism is in many respects a citizenship movement particularly where protest is directed towards extending human rights sometimes denied to women. However, feminism also shares elements of post-citizenship politics in that many feminists are opposed to the dominant cultural constructions of femininity reproduced for example through the media, science and medicine. Much feminist protest may therefore be less a case of eliminating discrimination and seeking redress for legal disadvantages than of protesting against certain cultural practices. While these distinctions between citizenship and post-citizenship movements may be helpful in some circumstances, in this chapter we will focus less on the differences between these movements than on what they have in common. One such common feature of both citizenship and post-citizenship movements is that they can clearly be distinguished from the activities of the state and from other political actors such as single-issue interest groups and political parties who have become an integral part of the *formal* political process. This suggests, then, that at a very general level we can define a social movement as 'a collective attempt to further a common interest or secure a common goal, through collective action *outside the sphere of established institutions*' (Giddens, 1997: 511 – emphasis added). Giddens refines this definition further by adding that social movements exist in 'relations of conflict with organizations whose objectives and outlook they frequently oppose' (Giddens, 1997: 585). This definition highlights the *oppositional* nature of social movements (although to what or to whom particular social movements are opposed may vary greatly). For Sidney Tarrow, this opposition can more precisely be thought of as a form of 'contentious collective action'. This action is the basis of social movements because it is 'the main and often the only recourse that ordinary people possess against better equipped opponents or powerful states' (Tarrow, 1998: 5). Contentious collective action differs from the more routine and formalised means of political representation and lobbying because it brings ordinary people into *confrontation* with their opponents, elites and the powerful.

Tarrow argues that social movements should be defined as '*collective challenges, based on common purposes and social solidarities, in sustained interaction with elites, opponents and authorities*' (Tarrow, 1998: 4 – original emphasis). Here we can identify four empirical properties of social movements. Firstly, social movements mount a collective challenge to particular elites, authorities, groups or cultural norms. This challenge is typically *contentious* in that it takes the form of disruptive social action of various kinds. Often this disruption is public (for example through demonstrations) but it can also include the co-ordination of individual acts of resistance and the affirmation of new values. It is the 'contentious' nature of the challenge posed by social movements that distinguishes them from interest groups who engage in more traditional forms of political organisation. However, having said that, social movement organisations may also on occasion use more traditional means of lobbying, public relations and legal challenges (conversely, interest groups occasionally use contentious politics). Nevertheless, what characterises social movements in particular is their use of *contentious collective challenges* because they do not have the same access to financial resources or the state that is available to interest groups and political parties. 'Movements use collective challenge to become the focal points of supporters, gain the attention of opponents and third parties, and create constituencies to represent' (Tarrow, 1998: 5). Secondly, social movements are places where the expression of a *common purpose* can be articulated. People become involved in particular social movements because they share in the interests and values that are the basis of these movements. Thirdly, these interests are only mobilised to the extent that they are experienced by individuals as deep-seated feelings of solidarity or identity. This issue of shared *collective identity and social solidarity* is what distinguishes the relatively isolated incidents of riots and mob activity from the activity of social movements. Riots and mobs may well involve a temporary expression of solidarity but unless this solidarity can be sustained beyond the initial incidents the people involved in the riot will not coalesce into a social movement. Finally, contentious politics (which are relatively common across history, e.g. in food riots, tax rebellions and religious wars) are transformed into social movements through *sustaining* collective action against antagonists through time and in a number of different settings. Tarrow sees this aspect as vital to the success of social movements. While common purposes, collective identities, and identifiable challenges help in the construction of social movements, he argues that:

> unless they can sustain their challenge, they will either evaporate into [a] kind of individualistic resentment ..., harden into intellectual or religious sects, or retreat into isolation. Sustaining collective action in interaction with powerful opponents marks the social movement off from earlier forms of contention that preceded it in history and still accompany it today.
>
> (Tarrow, 1998: 6–7)

 ## Theorising social movements

One of the central attributes of theory is that it provides a particular way of looking at an issue. Different theories may focus on different aspects of the same phenomenon. In this section we briefly examine five different theoretical perspectives on social movements. Each perspective seeks to explain a different element of the phenomenon of social movements. Neil Smelser's structural-functionalist approach is most concerned with seeing social movements as part of the broader category of *semi-rational* collective behaviour. Partly in response to this analysis, resource mobilisation theorists have focused on the *rational* and *deliberate* use of resources by social movements in their attempts to secure social change. European theorists have explored the question of *why* new social movements have arisen post-World War II in relation to the concept of post-industrial society. Others have argued that a concept such as post-industrial society is too all-encompassing and that it would be better to

256 Exploring Society

The cultural construction of protest emphasises the ways in which forms of protest are constructed through cultural interpretation and the interactions amongst protesters and between protesters and their opponents.

Resource mobilisation theories focus on *how* social movements are organised around the deployment of resources.

examine particular political processes that contribute to the development of protest. Finally, we explore theories that take the question of the **cultural construction of protest** as their main focus.

Early sociological studies tended to focus on social movements as forms of crowd or collective behaviour. For example, in *Theory of Collective Behaviour* (1962) the American structural-functional theorist, Neil Smelser argued that social movements are forms of collective behaviour that are characterised by their 'semi-rational' nature. For Smelser, collective behaviour 'involves a belief in the existence of extraordinary forces – threats, conspiracies etc. – which are at work in the universe … The beliefs on which collective behaviour is based (we shall call them generalised beliefs) are thus akin to *magical beliefs*' (Smelser, 1962: 8 – emphasis added). This way of talking about social movements reinforces their similarities with panics and riots, and emphasises their 'intellectually deficient' beliefs and less than fully rational nature. It also lumps together relatively *simple* forms of action such as panics with the *complex* processes involved in social movements. Other theorists responded to Smelser's characterisation of social movements as semi-rational and symptomatic of 'pathological' conditions by stressing the rational and relatively 'normal' nature of social movements. Rather than seeing these forms of collective action as unusual and irrational, some theorists have argued that social movements are normal and almost ubiquitous forms of social behaviour.

Because grievances always exist in societies, **resource mobilisation theorists** (RMTs) have focused on how social movements mobilise a range of both *material* resources (such as money, goods and services) and *non-material* resources (such as mass publicity, popular support, friendship and moral commitments) to influence policies. For RMTs these methods are clearly both rational (i.e. calculative, deliberative and institutionalised) and normal (in the sense that they are part of, rather than completely outside, the political process). RMTs focus their attention on the importance of social movement organisations and the role of movement leaders and activists within these organisations in setting goals and strategies for action. Central to this process are the resources of consensus and the dedication of movement participants. RMTs argue that successful social movements are able to attract individuals to their cause if they have clear objectives and strong organisational structures. These theorists assume that support can be gained from prospective supporters if they believe they have something to gain and little to lose. Individuals are therefore viewed as acting largely out of self-interest. This American tradition of RM theory has the advantage over the earlier collective behaviour approaches in that it recognises the rational and complex nature of social movements. However, the focus on *how* movements operate has sidelined the question of *why* social movements arise in the first place. RMTs are also unable to explain those situations in which strong organisations and resources are available, but where there is a lack of mass support – for example the situation for European peace movements in the 1960s and 1970s (Kitschelt, 1991: 335).

The question of *why* social movements arise when they do has been taken up by European theorists concerned with identifying the general *structural* conditions that give rise to social movements. These **post-industrial theorists** have tended to focus on the 'new social movements' (NSM) associated with post-industrial society. Here the emphasis is on explaining those movements that have emerged during the last four decades – in particular, second-wave feminism, and the student, peace, and environmental movements have been the focus of attention. One point of difference between the RMTs and post-industrial theorists is to be found on the question of 'grievances'. Whereas RMTs believe that grievances always exist in society and therefore cannot be seen as determinants in the development of social movements, theorists such as Alain Touraine (1971; 1981) argue that there is something about the new form of post-industrial society, as it has developed since the 1960s, that gives rise to new grievances and hence to new social movements. Touraine argues that in post-industrial societies production is primarily organised around knowledge-based industry rather than around the manufacturing base of industrial societies. This shift has led to a movement away from workplace-based conflict towards conflict organised by social groupings who are opposed to the technocracy, bureaucracy and instrumental rationality associated with post-industrial society. These elements of post-industrial society are rejected because they are viewed as leading towards the destruction of humans' harmony with nature. Progress as a goal in itself is viewed with suspicion and the elevation of technology, bureaucracy and markets as ends in themselves is seen as reducing the value of human beings and nature. Many post-industrial theorists focus particularly on the *ideology and values* of the various social movements. This emphasis clearly differs from that of RMTs with their analysis of the organisational and resource level, and it allows us to explore divisions that exist between groups in societies as well as divisions *within* social movements.

> **Post-industrial theorists** of social movements explain *why* new forms of social movements have arisen over the last 50 years in relation to the development of new grievances surfacing in post-industrial society.

Another contemporary theoretical perspective examines the broad political processes that exist within societies. In particular, such theorists focus on the **political opportunity structures** that contribute to the development and success of protest. Political opportunity structures can be defined as the 'consistent – but not necessarily formal, permanent or national – dimensions of the political struggle that encourage people to engage in contentious politics.' (Tarrow, 1998: 19). This approach differs from post-industrial theories in suggesting that the existence of grievances is not in itself enough to explain the development of particular examples of contentious collective action. Rather, contentious politics arises when political opportunities become available and, at the same time, individuals perceive that there are high costs associated with *inaction*. Tarrow identifies four 'dimensions of opportunities'. He believes that these are part of the broad political process and that they facilitate the development of social movements. Firstly, where there is an *expansion in access* to formal political processes (such as elections) people have more incentive to organise

> **Political opportunity structures** refer to those consistent dimensions of political structures and processes that encourage people to engage in contentious politics.

themselves against their opponents. Secondly, *unstable and shifting political alignments* provide new opportunities for social movements. Tarrow gives the example of the political realignments that occurred within the American Democratic party in the 1950s over the question of black civil rights. Initially the Kennedy administration had only a very thin electoral majority; however, this majority was increased when the administration took the initiative for black civil rights. This movement at the Federal level led to an increase in the political opportunities available to the civil rights movement. Thirdly, where there are *elites that are divided among themselves* resource-poor groups may be provided with a further incentive to engage in collective action. Finally, where social movements have *influential allies* who can 'act as friends in court, as guarantors against repression, or as acceptable negotiators on their behalf' (Tarrow, 1998: 79) they may be encouraged to take collective action. 'The concept of political opportunity structure emphasises resources *external* to the group. Unlike money or power, they can be taken advantage of by even weak or disorganized challengers' (Tarrow, 1998: 20).

The *structuralist* emphasis of both the post-industrial theorists and the political process approach focuses on a level of analysis that is some distance from the humans who are the actors in social movements. For many sociologists, the missing dimension in such analyses is the role that *culture* plays. Doug McAdam argues that 'expanding political opportunities do not in any simple sense produce a social movement ... [Instead] they only offer insurgents a certain "structural potential" for collective political action. Mediating between opportunities and action are people and the subjective meanings they attach to their situation' (McAdam, 1982: 28). These subjective meanings are not simply the idiosyncratic views of individuals but are created through culture. Theorists who have picked up on the cultural construction of protest emphasise the fact that humans are symbol-making creatures. As James Jasper argues

> Protest ... is *constructed*. No individual or group has goals or interests that are objectively given without any *cultural interpretation*. In interaction with others we perceive what our interests (economic, moral, emotional and other interests) are, and build political goals in accordance with them. We also decide what tactics are appropriate, even what organisational forms fit our moral visions.
>
> (Jasper, 1997: 10 – emphasis added)

Culture therefore plays a key role in many different aspects of social movements. An example of the role that broader cultural meanings play in the construction of social movements is given in William Gamson's book *Talking Politics* (1992). Gamson identifies four pervasive themes and counter-themes in North American culture that provide a cultural resource for the language of protest. These themes and counter-themes help organise how protests are talked about and organised.

Issue	Theme		Counter-theme
Technology	'Progress through technology'	vs	'Harmony with nature'
Power	Interest-group liberalism	vs	Popular democracy
Interpersonal	Self-reliance dependence	vs	Mutuality
Nationalism	America first	vs	Global responsibility

Table 14.2 Four themes and counter-themes shaping the language of protest

While these pairs are rather broad, they do provide a general framework of cultural interpretation that is understood by most North Americans and that social movement organisers can appeal to in their attempts to garner support for their cause.

The local and the global: globalisation and transnational social movements

The central slogan of the environmental movement, 'Think globally, act locally', recognises the interconnected nature of environmental concerns in places as distant from each other as Germany and New Zealand, and at the same time advocates that protest should happen in the places we live. There is a double edge to this recognition. On the one hand it is a response to the negative aspects of globalisation – the growing rationalisation and standardisation of human life spheres and the world wide consequences of industrial development with its degradation of the environment. On the other hand, many social movements, not just the Green movement, make use of aspects of globalisation to their own advantage – e.g. the use of worldwide media to publicise their activities. This is not a straightforwardly positive process given that there may be costs associated with linking organisations and rhetoric across nations, however, the logic of globalising power relations leads to a logic of globally co-ordinated resistance. In this section we outline some of the issues raised by Sidney Tarrow in his discussion of transnational social movements.

There are two main aspects to globalisation that are relevant here. Firstly, the growth of a global economy, in which transportation, finance, distribution, marketing, labour and raw materials are integrated on a global scale, changes both the nature of power and the best means for resisting such power. Secondly, the development of new information technologies such as satellite TV, the Internet, fax machines and so on, have enabled the rapid communication of troubles and protests around the world. 'The expansion of worldwide markets and global communications brings citizens of the north and west and those of the east and south closer together, making the former more cosmopolitan and the latter more aware of their inequality' (Tarrow, 1998: 179). The increasing connection between people from around the world through travel, migration and information technologies has also enabled social movements in different parts of the world to speak the same language and hence draw on a wider pool of support than might otherwise be the case. For example, a protest against the new repression of women in Afghanistan since the fundamentalist Islamic Taliban took power in 1996 has sought support from women around the world through an e-mail petition. The language of protest in this example (e.g. 'waging war on women') draws on feminist rhetoric that is found around the world. At the same time, the e-mail communication seeks to take advantage of the possibilities opened up by the Internet – spreading information about a repressive regime quickly and safely. This, and other technologies, also link up indigenous peoples who live in isolated areas and are geographically distant from each other but who share similar problems, for example 'groups as diverse as Andean Indians and northern European Lapps are now in contact across national borders' (Tarrow, 1998: 180). It is possible to see in these examples forms of transnational political opportunity structures. Some theorists have gone so far as to argue that the structures that now help mount collective action are actually *replacing* previously common national structures (e.g. Pagnucco and Atwood, 1994). Others have chosen to see these changes as merely different kinds of *resources* (such as overseas travel and communication through e-mail across national borders) that have become available through globalisation.

> **Transnational social movements** are social movements that are organised in a sustained way across national borders.

These changes in the global economy and communication technologies have contributed to a new form of **transnational social movement** that Tarrow defines as 'sustained contentious interactions with opponents – national or non-national – by connected networks of challengers organized across national boundaries' (Tarrow, 1998: 184). This definition is similar to Tarrow's general definition of social movements but emphasises the fact that challengers are both rooted in their domestic setting (the local) as well as being connected to one another at a global level in on-going ways through informal or organisational ties. To be a truly transnational movement, challenges must be 'contentious in deed as well as in word' (Tarrow, 1998: 184). The most obvious example of a transnational organisation is Greenpeace with its millions of supporters and members around the world connected through a transnational structure, a common world view held by its members and the on-going confrontational action against governments and multi-national corporations. Much of Greenpeace's protests happen outside national boundaries, for example those in opposition to French nuclear testing in the Pacific. Other movements that lack a single organisational focus, but are truly transnational in scope, include Islamic fundamentalism (including the Afghanistan Taliban and Iranian nationalism) and the European and American peace movements of the 1980s. As well as these highly organised transnational social movements and organisations there are other more diffuse and loosely connected 'transnational advocacy networks' that exist across national borders (Keck and Sikkink, 1998: 2). These networks include people working on issues internationally who share common values and forms of discourse, and use interconnected information sources and services. These networks of people may be drawn from governmental as well as non-governmental organisations and are particularly common in human rights, women's rights and environmental politics.

An example of a transnational social movement in action

We began this section with the environmental slogan 'Think globally, act locally'. This strategy of 'global thinking' is also found in the *rhetoric* used by many social movement organisations as they seek to widen their support base and recruit outsiders to their cause. Jasper (1997) argues that social movements will use 'globalising rhetoric' when they want to avoid the charge of self-interest and NIMBYism ('NIMBY' stands for 'Not In My Back Yard'). For environmental groups who commonly target *local* expressions of environmental destruction the use of only locally-based rhetoric (e.g. 'This factory is bad for *our* community') is avoided because it may not mobilise enough support to mount an adequate challenge. Global rhetoric of the 'Not in Anybody's Back Yard' (i.e. NIABY) kind is thought to be more successful. In addition to globalising rhetoric, many social movement organisations make use of coalitional politics in an attempt to gain strength in numbers. While this may have certain advantages, these are also risks associated with such moves.

> By entering into a coalition with others, a group may gain numbers, prestige, institutional authority or other advantage. But group members may find that these advantages are purchased at the cost of diffusion of their issue and involvement in other issues in which they have little interest. Their own troubles may be considered only a part of the larger problem by their allies, and thus be given a low priority.
>
> (Spector and Kitsuse, 1987: 145)

The social and the personal: framing collective identities

So far we have been discussing social movements at a macro level – as forms of *collective* action. Yet clearly these movements are made up of thousands of *individual* women and men who play various roles as leaders, activists, members and supporters. One issue that is raised when we turn our attention to social movement participants is the question of how individuals become motivated to take part in movement activities and culture. Moreover, the success of collective action may very well be dependent on participants sharing the understanding and identities generated by social movements. Individual participation in social movements is not simply a matter of a natural or pre-existing coincidence between individual and movement beliefs. Rather it becomes a matter of sociological enquiry to explain why and how individuals join, remain active and sometimes leave social movements. These questions take us onto the territory of identity – both personal and collective. While post-industrial theorists have focused on how the collective identities of social movements have been historically determined by the *structural* forces of post-industrial society, this perspective does not explain how particular identities are 'interactionally accomplished' (Hunt, Benford and Snow, 1994: 189). Symbolic interactionists have drawn our attention to this level of analysis when they argue that social movements do 'framing work' that actively connects individuals to social movements. At a very general level, **framing** refers to 'the conscious efforts by groups or recruiters to craft their rhetoric and issues in such a way that they appeal to potential recruits' (Jasper, 1997: 77). This process contributes to the construction of both the personal identities of individuals as well as the collective identities associated with social movements.

Framing refers to the efforts by social movement organisations to craft their rhetoric and issues in such a way that they appeal to potential recruits.

We can think of collective identities as the perceptions that exist within a culture about a group's *distinctiveness* and the boundaries that surround their interests. The collective identity associated with an environmentalist is quite different from that associated with an anti-abortionist or Islamic fundamentalist. The identities associated with movements (or indeed any other collectivity) only exist insofar as people agree upon them, argue over them, enact them and internalise them (Jasper, 1997: 86). While collective identities require the interactions of humans to create and sustain them, these identities are larger than any particular individual. An individual may incorporate the collective identity of, say, 'feminist' or 'animal rights activist' within her personal identity but in the process the collective identity may take on different meanings as it becomes part of an individual biography and sense of a personal self.

But how does an individual come to take on board any collective identity? Turning an uncommitted, but sympathetic, observer into an active participant in a social movement is most likely to occur when the frames that are used by social movements fit in with individuals' already existing beliefs, their life experiences and the narratives that they use to describe their lives and the world around them. As suggested above, symbolic interactionists argue that one important element in this process is the 'framing work' that social movements do to help secure new recruits to their cause. This framing work is intended to shape grievances and concerns into broader claims that will have some resonance with individuals. The framing of issues also helps to define 'us' and 'them', 'good' and 'bad', 'the problem' and 'the solution'.

> At the organizational level of analysis SMO actors provide 'appropriate' vocabularies and stories for participants and sympathizers to *(re)construct their personal identities in ways that link or further commit them to the movement or SMO* ... Collective action frames focus attention on a particular situation considered problematic, make attributions regarding who or what is to blame, and articulate an alterative set of arrangements including what the movement actors need to do in order to affect [sic] the desired change.
>
> (Hunt, Benford and Snow, 1994: 190 – emphasis added)

One of the most important frames used by SMOs in their attempts to recruit new members is an 'injustice frame' which provides a precursor to collective action by focusing on 'the righteous anger that puts fire in the belly and iron in the soul' (Gamson, 1992: 32)

Any social movement constructs for itself a particular collective identity that involves protagonists, antagonists and an audience (Hunt, Benford and Snow, 1994). Each of these three groupings, or identity fields, has a particular relationship to the social movement. The protagonist identity field includes attributions about people or groups who are supporters of the movement. This might include stories about movement heroes and heroines, activists and 'star supporters' (e.g. politicians or movie stars). Boundary frames are also used to make distinctions between members *within* a social movement, e.g. between those who take more 'extreme', 'radical' or 'risky' actions and who castigate other activists who take 'easier' and 'safer' options. These distinctions between more and less militant wings of a social movement help to establish its collective identity and may be important in the personal identities of particular movement participants. Social movement actors also make claims about their antagonists' identities. Typically, negative characteristics are imputed to antagonists – they are 'unscrupulous', 'immoral' and perhaps even 'evil'. This framing process also has the effect of making implicit claims about the protagonists who have positive and moral characteristics in comparison with their opponents. Finally, attributions are made about the individuals and collectivities who are believed to be neutral or uncommitted and who may report on movement activities.

> Audience framing is particularly important because SMO actors use these frames to determine what kinds of other frames will resonate, what kinds of 'evidence' need to be marshaled to support movement claims, and how audiences' cultural symbols and narratives can be used in advancing movement claims.
>
> (Hunt, Benford and Snow, 1994: 200)

To conclude then, the feelings, beliefs, fears and hopes of individual movement participants are culturally constructed through framing work undertaken by social movement organisations. An initial interest or inclination felt by a person may, in the right circumstances, be shaped into more active commitments to, and support of, an SMO.

Differences and divisions: ideological conflict within social movements

In the chapter thus far we have been discussing the phenomenon of social movements in a fairly dispassionate way – identifying their key social characteristics, discussing how they are the product of particular social, historical and global processes, and examining the role of personal and collective identities. In many respects this analytical angle seems to sit outside the 'moral' and impassioned nature of the social movement phenomenon itself. For if there is one thing that all social movements share, it is their passion for change, their vehement opposition to elements of the social world, and their vision of a different future. Many progressive social movements are concerned with healing divisions that exist in the social world. However, social movements are not themselves immune from conflict. They are often riven by dissent. This section examines in particular the ideological divisions that have troubled the environmental movement.

As we have seen, one of the defining features of social movements is their ideological opposition to aspects of contemporary social life. It is sometimes said that social movements even contribute to social divisions in their attempts to secure their desired goals. Through protest they highlight their difference from a world they object to. In the process of constructing ideological and value positions, social movements are themselves often subject to *internal* conflict and division as different social movement organisations and individuals debate ideological positions, matters of internal organisation and structure, and political strategies to use against their opponents. Sometimes these differences within social movements can be explained in terms of 'generational cleavages'. For example, Nancy Whittier uses this notion to explain differences within the women's movement in Columbus, Ohio from the late 1960s to the early 1980s. She argued that 'micro-cohorts' entered the movement at particular moments in its history, when it was engaged in particular activities, and each had a specific political culture and feminist collective identity. 'Each [micro-cohort] defined the type of people, issues, language, tactics or organizational structures that "qualified" as feminist differently' (Whittier, 1995: 56). At stake for different cohorts of women was the issue of what was to count as a 'real' or 'authentic' feminist position.

This sort of division is one that also applies more generally in many other movements. It is one of the issues that has troubled the Green movement around the world. In the former West Germany, where the Green movement has a long and well-established position, the debates between the 'Fundis' (fundamentalists) and 'Realos' (realists) has touched on this issue particularly in relation to the question of what an authentic 'green' position is. Does 'being green' mean rejecting everything about modern capitalist, industrialised and technologised society (the view of the Fundis) or does it mean a focus on 'conserving' the environment we have now but within the context of modern capitalist states (the view of the Realos)? For fundamentalist greens the ecological balance of the world is severely out of sync and only a whole-scale reassessment of the social order can ensure the continued harmonious co-existence of humans and nature. The realists, however, take the view that such a principled position will be ineffective in shifting policies and practices towards ecologically desired goals. In the following contribution, Carl Davidson picks up these points and makes an impassioned plea for a particular understanding of the ideological conflicts within New Zealand of the 1990s and the environmental movement more generally.

Where have all the Greens gone?

Carl Davidson

In 1972, at Victoria University in Wellington, the world's first nationwide 'Green' party was formed. The 'Values Party of New Zealand' contested that year's general election and, despite being less than 6 months old and standing candidates in fewer than half of the available seats, it won 2% of the vote. The *Sunday Herald* described the party's manifesto as 'the most original political policy for at least a generation' (in Brunt, 1973: 90). A decade before Green parties became the darlings of European politics, one had arrived in style in New Zealand.

That this was something other than a trendy fad was established at the 1975 election. There the party increased its share of the vote to 5.2%. Overseas commentators and theorists were soon taking notice. Hazel Henderson, a well-known ecological activist and writer, argued that the success of Values showed how New Zealand led the world in 'the politics of reconceptualisation' (1978: 368). Jonathan Porritt would go on to describe the Green vision of 'reconceptualisation' as 'the most important political and cultural force since socialism' (Porritt and Winter, 1988: 3). Others would simply call the arrival of Green politics a 'revolution' (Parkin, 1988: 17).

Fast forward to 1990: In that year's election things looked even brighter for the Greens. They won 6.9% of all votes, more than any of the other minor parties and, for a brief while, this result established the Green Party (as the Values Party had by then been renamed) as New Zealand's third most important political party. This was despite the fact that the Greens stood candidates in only 76 of the then available 99 seats. If they had stood in all seats, it is likely the Green vote would have been up around 10% of the total (Chapple, 1997). For the second time, the Greens had bettered the 5% threshold that would have seen them win parliamentary representation in the present MMP system.

This brief overview of Green politics in New Zealand has all the elements of a great story; talking about how the Greens 'arrived in style' and then went on to become the 'third most important political party' in the country is one that strikes a cord with many New Zealanders. It connects with a collective image of ourselves as 'clean and green'. But the story of Green politics goes even further. It provides another example of New Zealand leading the world – just as we did when we became the first country to give women the vote, or when we took our nuclear-free stand. The appeal of this kind of story tells us a lot about the way we like to see ourselves – New Zealand as clean and green *and* first.

Unfortunately, this view is almost entirely an illusion. Any close examination of Green politics in New Zealand soon reveals an entirely different story. To begin with, while the numbers suggest that New Zealand would have had members of the Green Party in its parliament if only it had introduced proportional representation earlier, this denies the very context that brought the Greens most of their support. The Greens did so well in both the 1975 and 1990 elections *precisely* because of New Zealand's first-past-the-post, 'winner-take-all' two-party electoral system. The level of support experienced by the Greens was much more a product of discontented voters registering a protest against National or Labour than it was an expression of solidarity with their 'green' convictions. In 1975 Values did well because of disaffected National supporters who couldn't bring themselves to vote for the Labour opposition. In 1990, the Green Party's vote came largely from traditional Labour supporters angry at the direction of the Labour Government but not mad enough to choose National. Even the founder of the Values Party, Tony Brunt, understood clearly that Values flourished because it was a seed planted 'in a soil made fertile by manure' (Brunt, 1973: 79).

That the highs of the 1975 and 1990 elections were inflated figures which give a false impression of the support for the Green movement in New Zealand can be seen in the poor performance of the Greens in our first MMP election. In 1996, as part of the much broader and seemingly appealing Alliance, the Green Party shared in just 10.1% of the vote. The Progressive Greens, a break-away and stand-alone Green party, netted just 0.26%. As Chapple put it, in 1996 it looked as though the green vote in New Zealand 'simply may have vanished' (1997: 7).

And it is not as if the Green message had become superfluous by 1996. Indeed, if anything, things had got far worse. Writing in 1995, Jeremy Seabrook talked about how, now more than ever, capitalism was 'scything brutally' across the world, 'bringing irreversible ruin to the earth's resources [and] creating unimaginable social injustice' (Seabrook, 1995: 22). Nobel Laureate Konrad Lorenz spoke of how 'every human being remain[ed] in peril of a slow death through poisoning and desiccating the environment [because of our] blind and unbelievably stupid conduct' (1987: 3). In this kind of context, it is easy to see how the Green message should make *more* sense than ever before.

The Greens didn't attract support partly because they had largely been eclipsed by a programme of macro-economic reform which would dominate New Zealand politics for more than a decade. This restructuring, driven by the neoclassical economic philosophy of 'the New Right', has been described by Jane Kelsey (1995) as 'the New Zealand Experiment'. It was an 'experiment' that makes Hazel Henderson's claim about the politics of reconceptualisation in New Zealand look sadly out of place. Or, more accurately, 'the New Zealand Experiment' means we lead the world in another kind of 'politics of reconceptualisation' altogether – one that is anathema to the Green agenda.

Still, the question this leaves spectacularly unanswered is why the Greens never responded with an alluring and practical alternative to the New Right's obsession with 'free' markets. In many respects, the Greens were uniquely placed to provide such an alternative because environmental issues encompass so much more than economic considerations. The questions the Greens raise demand solutions which require something more than the workings of blind market forces. At a time when their message would seem to make more sense than ever, when it could perhaps uniquely have provided an alternative to the rapid descent into rampant consumerism, where were the Greens?

While it is true that joining the wider Alliance became part of the problem for the New Zealand Greens (because, as Chapple pointed out, many Greens 'didn't want their green ideals composted with someone else's social and economic policies' (1997: 7)), the real problem goes much deeper. To understand why the colour ran out of the Greens at the very moment when you might have expected them to flourish like never before takes us to the heart of the green agenda. There we find the issue which split the Greens in New Zealand as it had done everywhere else in the world – the issue of what it means to be 'truly' Green. On one side of this debate are what the (West) German Green Party, *Die Grunen*, calls the 'Realistic Reformers' or 'Realos' for short. They are opposed by the 'Fundamentalist' Greens, or 'Fundis' (Papadakis, 1984; Parkin, 1984). Elsewhere this split has been called a division between the 'light' Greens and the 'dark' Greens (Porritt, 1989; Capra and Spretnak, 1986). It is perhaps easiest to understand this 'split' by seeing it in terms of those who pushed conservation issues on one side and those who had a much more radical idea of what it meant to be Green on the other. And the split was no less destructive in New Zealand (Rainbow, 1993, 1989; Davidson, 1992).

While the conservationist agenda seems to share many of the goals of the Greens, in reality it was never interested in rejecting the structure of the modern capitalist state. Instead, the conservationists simply wished the modern capitalist state would clean up after itself a little better. In stark contrast to this, the 'dark' Greens were clear that there was no way to be truly 'green' within the existing state boundaries. For them, being 'green' is not about curbside recycling or landscaping landfills. Instead, it is about reconceptualising the way humans relate to the natural world. Fritjof Capra summed up the difference in purpose when he wrote that the conservation movement 'is concerned with more efficient control and management of the natural environment for the benefit of man (sic) [whereas the 'dark' Green] movement recognizes that ecological balance will require profound changes in our perception of the role of human beings in the planetary ecosystem' (1982: 411–412). Rudolf Bahro, the famous German Green, captured the mood of many of his contemporaries when he described the conservation movement's 'shallow' approach as akin to 'cleaning the dragon's teeth and scraping away its excrement' (in Porritt and Winner, 1988: 213). Bahro's 'dragon' metaphor is instructive because it demonstrates the extent of opposition to the present economic and state system; dragons are for slaying, not for forming coalitions with.

For this type of Green, all of the modern world's ecological, political, social and economic problems are seen as the inevitable manifestations of a deeper, metaphysical problem. Essentially their view is that the core values of the modern world mean we are incapable of living in harmony with the natural world or with ourselves. This desire to make peace with the world can be seen in the manifesto of Green parties everywhere. For instance, it is no coincidence that New Zealand's first green party was called 'Values'. Its founder, Tony Brunt, was clear that it was responding to 'a new depression ... a downturn not in the national economy but its national spirit' (Brunt, 1973: 79). Stephen Rainbow tells us how a former General Secretary of the Party wrote that Values 'wasn't even particularly an environmental movement ... just an expression of anti-materialism' (1989: 184).

Green movements throughout the world commonly draw on the traditions of indigenous people to represent the kind of alternative world view they are seeking. It is one which attributes equal value to all elements of nature and reconceptualises humanity as just another component of a complex web. The Green agenda is captured beautifully with a phrase from the Hopi, a tribe of Native American Indians, who label the dominant industrial-materialist-scientific world view as an example of *'aan Koyaanisqatsi'*. This means 'life out of balance' or 'way of life that calls for another way of living'. It is a seemingly simple idea but one which demonstrates how radical the Green challenge really is. What is being demanded is nothing less than 'another way of living' based on a reassessment of what human society is and how it needs to work.

I believe this is the key to the failure of the Green movement. This sort of agenda, that one journalist called more akin to a 'secular religion than ... [a] political ideology' (*The Press*, 1990, 16 June), has no room for compromise. And this explains why no 'practical and alluring' alternative could come from the Greens: the praxis they offered held little allure for the mainstream of society, while the things they said which were alluring were simply not practical.

As a result, it is hard to see the Green movement as anything other than a failure. Anthony Giddens tells us that social movements provide glimpses of possible futures and are in some part vehicles for their realisation. But in New Zealand, as elsewhere, the no-compromise nature of Green vision means that it will remain little more than a fading glimpse. As a 'vehicle' for realising a possible future, it has been overtaken by the race for the gas-guzzling, smoke-belching, tyre-burning, single-seat supercars of the free market.

Questions

1   How does Carl Davidson explain the relative electoral success of the Values and Green Parties prior to the introduction of MMP?
2   Why does he think that this success declined with the introduction of MMP?
3   Do you agree with Carl Davidson's assessment that the 'no-compromise nature of Green vision' has led to its failure as a social movement?

Conclusion

Social movements take many different organisational forms and include a variety of ideological positions. In many respects then there is little that connects them. However, sociologists have sought to identify some common features shared by groups as opposed to each other as Christian Conservatism and Islamic Fundamentalism, anti-abortionists and the feminist movement. These similarities have to do with the political sphere in which social movements act – i.e. to some extent outside the established political institutions. However, sociologists also debate which aspect of social movements is most important in their organisation and success – is it their ability to mobilise resources or their willingness to take advantage of political opportunity structures? Should we look to the level of historical and structural change or the cultural construction of protest? These are on-going debates and we do not need to resolve them here. That sociologists care about such matters reflects as much a commitment to active politics as to issues of theoretical coherence and validity.

? Study questions

14.1 Using the example of a social movement that you know a little about, outline it in terms of Tarrow's definition of social movements and the four empirical properties he argues they possess.

14.2 What role has globalisation played in the development of transnational social movements?

14.3 How does framing contribute to the construction of collective identities?

Further reading

Denton, M. (1998) Theoretical Perspectives on Social Movements. *New Zealand Sociology*, 13(2): 208–238.

Jasper, J. (1997) *The Art of Moral Protest: Culture, Biography and Creativity in Social Movements.* University of Chicago Press, Chicago.

Larana, E., Johnston, H. and Gusfield, J. (eds). (1994) *New Social Movements: From Ideology to Identity.* Temple University Press, Philadelphia.

Lyman, S. (ed.). (1995) *Social Movements: Critiques, Concepts and Case-Studies.* Macmillan, London.

Tarrow, S. (1998) *Power in Movement: Social Movements and Contentious Politics,* 2nd ed. Cambridge University Press, Cambridge.

15 Sport and leisure

Chapter aims

- to explore the significance of the difference between 'leisure' and 'work';
- to examine how social rituals associated with sports contribute to the social construction of masculinity and national identity;
- to discuss the ways in which local expressions of sport and leisure are connected to global processes;
- to discuss how social divisions of class, ethnicity, age, gender and ability are reproduced through sports and leisure activities;
- to compare the figurational and postmodern approaches to theorising sports and leisure.

 Introduction

This chapter explores the meaning and place of leisure in modern social life. Our leisure pursuits range from highly organised sports media events beamed around the world, through to the more everyday acts of watching television. Sociologists draw attention to the ways in which these activities are *shaped by broader social structures, institutions and power relations*, and how at the same time, sports and leisure pursuits *shape our own social identities*. Here we examine some of the ways in which rituals associated with sports and leisure are connected to constructions of masculinity and nation. In addition we explore how the consumption of leisure has become globalised. We then turn to examine the ways in which social divisions of class, ethnicity, age, ability, and gender are involved in producing the leisure experiences of individuals. Finally, 'figurational' and 'postmodern' ways of theorising sports and leisure are compared.

Leisure as 'not work'

The sociology of sport and leisure is an increasingly popular area of study and research. There is, in fact, at least one plausible sociological explanation for this steady growth of interest, and it goes something like this. Leisure and sport are usually understood as the things in life that are *not work*. Leisure is what starts when we clock off at the factory or supermarket, or finally put the kids to bed, or turn the office lights out. And in recent decades, at least in the established industrialised nations, and at least until the 1990s, the world of work appears to have been 'shrinking'. One British study, for example, estimates that from 1961 to 1984, men had gained approximately 10% more leisure time, and women had gained somewhere between 12% and 20% more. Another long-term trend is for more people to have more *disposable income* to spend on leisure activities. So, as more people get more time and resources to put into leisure, it makes good sense for sociologists to try to get a handle on this vast and important area of social and personal life. When you think of all the energy and variety of activities that make up 'sport and leisure' – netball, holidays, making love, rugby, eating out, keeping fit, reading books, gardening, visiting Disneyland, climbing a rock face, listening to music, playing music, getting drunk, chatting, biking, DIYing (to name just a few) – then you immediately realise that there is a real treasure trove of sociological interest to be found under that label. Whether we are focusing on the mass rituals of sporting audiences or the obsessions of the individual sportsperson who wants desperately to 'succeed'; the music-making habits of young people or the music listening habits of older people; the world-wide cloning of commercial theme parks and shopping malls or the quest to go 'to the edge' in order to experience authentic fulfilment; visiting friends or being on the marae, there is a huge amount of social interaction to observe, understand and explain in this topic.

There is more to investigating sport and leisure than meets the eye. Even that initial distinction between work and leisure, for example, is quite problematical. Some areas of work, such as the manufacturing industry and agriculture, may well be diminishing as sources of mass employment, but many people spend at least part of their increased leisure time working and earning in the 'informal' economy. For example, there has been a great increase in the amount of time and money spent on home maintenance and self-servicing: in 1990/91 alone New Zealanders spent $17 million dollars a week on property maintenance goods.

Moreover, whilst there has been a decline of full-time jobs in many traditional work roles, there has been considerable growth in part-time and casual work in the last decade (much of it being taken up by female and ethnic minority workers). Is this to be counted as an increase in leisure opportunity, or the opposite? Furthermore, the 'non-work' activities of some people in an ever-more commercialised society means 'more work' for others, because the fast-food shops and wine bars have to be staffed, the trendy sportswear made, the obsolete home computers upgraded, the flight tickets or big match tickets sold, and 'feel good' images promoted in every available public space, if what we recognise as modern leisure is to happen the way it does. Perhaps the biggest irony of modern leisure is that in order to be attractive, it has to signal *escape* – from work, from hassles, from routines, from other people; and yet there is a certain social *tyranny* about leisure, which is every bit as routinising, hassling, and socially constructed as anything in the sphere of 'work'. The classical sociologist Max Weber would have been interested in the creation of all this 'routinised' work around leisure – the creation of tourist boards and local officials, and the endless images and documentation signalling our leisure choices, and the calculated, rationalised way we organise our spare time and allow others to organise it for us. Weber would have seen modern leisure developments as further evidence for his thesis that society was becoming relentlessly bureaucratised and corporatised, with the element of spontaneity and charisma in social life diminishing all the time.

Karl Marx would have added that the key thing about the leisure industry is that it is an industrial *capitalist* sector of production and services. We should not be surprised, therefore, to find that leisure is a social sphere colonised by profit goals and 'false' imagery. Marxists are likely to be negative about much that goes on in the leisure world for that reason, but other sociologists are more positive. They think that the worlds of work and leisure are indeed collapsing into each other, and that if this is not happening now then it *will* be in the future, and that this is basically a good thing. Think about the very current notion of 'lifestyle'. In one sense, this is just a marketing idea, encouraging you to see yourself positively as a certain type of person, and in control of your life. You then, literally, 'buy into' the image that suits you, accumulating the appropriate goods and services that help express the niche you're in. But arguably the 'lifestyle' ploy also signifies an important shift in (post)modern life, prefiguring how the worlds of work, domestic life and leisure are beginning to intersect and overlap in a major way. Greater numbers of people work flexible hours, greater numbers work from home, more people organise their work around child care options, more workplaces are 'family-friendly', more people are striving to be multi-skilled and able to add to the value of their homes without bringing in separate experts (the home may well double up as an office too), and more organisations appear to value autonomous, multi-skilled and balanced individuals: such initiatives recognise that mechanised, industrialised and routinised work practices are not only bad for *people*, they are also, in today's conditions, bad for *business* too. In this scenario, a more fluid 'lifestyle' orientation, where there is greater harmony between work, leisure and family commitments is seen, affirmatively, as the future trend. 'We should be so lucky!' might be the response of critical sociologists who feel that such 'lifestyle' hype remains very much the prerogative of white, affluent, able-bodied men.

There are several different models and styles of sport and leisure. In sport, the 'power and performance' model can be contrasted with the 'pleasure and participation' model. The first of these can be seen as an *extension* of the competitive, individualistic, closely monitored, and ever-aspiring world of work or 'business' – some people are always busy working at leisure as well as working at work. The 'pleasure and participation' model reminds us that for many of us, sport is – or should be – for relaxation, sociability and recovering a holistic perspective on life; it expresses the need to *get away from* pressured activity and competitive values. Both these very different images of leisure time, it should be noted, are activity and out-of-home oriented, although actually the 'big five' leisure pursuits in terms of spending and doing are based around watching TV, consuming alcohol and tobacco, betting, and sex. This 'leisure core', as it is sometimes called, takes up the bulk of what happens outside the 76% of New Zealanders' total time that is occupied by work, sleep, personal care and domestic labour; and within that 'spare' 24%, watching TV is the single most popular activity, taking up 8% of total time (Gidlow, 1993: 161).

A striking example of the great social and economic power of such 'ordinary' leisure pursuits is the fact that, in Japan, people's obsession with the simple bagatelle arcade machine game 'Pachinka' generates more than twice the amount of revenue that the Japanese motor industry does. In New Zealand, a new type of paid work has emerged in order to service the sharp growth in popular gambling (think of Lotto, Keno, Telebingo, casino openings, and the removal of previous restrictions on what type of event we can bet on); but there is also the 'work' created for families and counselling agencies as we attempt to cope with the social 'down side' of this soaring leisure pursuit. The need for such help work is indicated, for example, by the rapidly growing use of the Hotline of the Compulsive Gambling Society of New Zealand.

The social and the personal: rituals, masculinity and nationality

The case of gambling shows how easily, even in the sphere of our leisure activities, a 'personal' problem can become a 'public issue'. But because of their association with 'free time', we often think of our leisure preferences as very much our own, and outside of the realm of the social and public – they express our personal tastes and individual aspirations. This 'private' sense of leisure is captured in the notion that we have 'hobbies', although that term and its homely connotations probably seem a bit old-fashioned these days – as if trainspotting or collecting stamps could possibly compete with Nike fashion or a passion for rap music. The 'social' element, however, is in fact just as inescapable in sports and leisure, as in any other aspect of life – how could it be otherwise? Social *values* and *ideologies* are promoted in and through sport and leisure, around such notions as excellence, leadership, discipline, character, fair play, teamwork and so on. Sport and leisure are closely linked into other '*subsystems*' of society like the economy, politics, culture and education, and they provide many and great occasions for *social ritual* and *solidarity*. Sport and leisure pursuits, moreover, vary considerably according to *class* and *ethnic* interests (rap originated as the sub-culture of young 'disadvantaged' black kids in the USA).

Two examples can be given of the way in which sport serves to reproduce social relations in a ritual way. The first concerns the norm of masculinity and its crucial importance for the sporting image and success of many young men, even today. Physical contact team sports, especially, create the kind of on- and off-field culture in which toughness, tough talking, and heterosexual male locker-room culture strongly condition the participants' sense of their aesthetic and qualitative sporting achievement. Here is how one American football player describes his own beginnings and progress in the sport:

> The initiation rites were inauspicious. My flesh was pricked with thorns until blood flowed, and hot peppers were rubbed into my eyes. I was forced to wear a jockstrap around my nose, and I didn't know what was funny. Then came what was to be an endless series of ways of proving myself. Callisthenics until my arms ached. Hitting hard and fast and knocking the other guy down. Getting hit in the groin and not crying. Striving to be a leader ... The object was to beat out the other guy. I already had it in my head that the way to succeed was to be an animal. Coaches took notice of animals. Animals made the first team. Being an animal meant being ruthlessly aggressive and competitive. If you saw an arm in front of you, you trampled it ... The idea was to slap backs, but not to get too close emotionally. As for friendships with women, they were virtually impossible. All that boys and girls were supposed to do were neck and pet, and the cheerleaders were the most sought-after girls. On the sidelines and in the stands the boys, and probably the men, watched the girls' breasts bounce and waited for cartwheels.
>
> (Messner and Sabo, 1994: 11–12)

Clearly, this kind of report refers to a particularly aggressive context, and it is written in a heightened emotional style because the writer has, since that time, come to loath the 'competition, misogyny and homophobia in the sports world' (Messner and Sabo, 199: 3). Even so, such images and rituals of masculinity are pervasive and powerful, recruiting huge numbers of boys into them, becoming perhaps the most important and committed aspects of their young lives.

Another 'classic' integrative function of sport and sporting contests is that they serve to 'bind' the *nation* together, over and above social and political differences that may exist. In Chapter 9, reference was made to how the America's Cup campaign in 1995 led to a strong sense of common

cause amongst all New Zealanders, and the public celebration of the subsequent triumph was a truly mass affair. It felt *good* to be a New Zealander, and to feel proud knowing what *sort* of people good New Zealanders are. Sporting rituals thus contribute to and galvanise our sense of national identity and belonging, bringing to great public apotheosis the countless small-scale rituals and customs taking place in parks and within families every weekend. Rugby, of course, has a special place in this process for New Zealand cultural and national identity.

> What is achieved through rugby is the symbolic uniting of men over and against all of the differences of background, occupation, education, income, experience and belief that otherwise divides them. This vision of male comradeship is not imposed from above, but built painstakingly from the level of the local club through provincial and national levels. At the peak of this structure, giving final definition to its meaning and purpose, are the games between the All Blacks and other national teams.
>
> (Fougere, 1989: 116)

The local and the global: leisure globalisation

New provincial rugby associations have formed in New Zealand, and the national team has gone explicitly professional as it has become involved in world cups, tri-series, hemispheric contests, and so on. Sport and leisure have 'gone global' in a dramatic way in recent times, with multi-national corporations and sponsorship deals crossing state boundaries. The 'mediafication' of big sport and leisure events is ensuring their reception on the scale of the world market. Tourism and travel provide one of the most obvious and pervasive examples of leisure globalisation. The whole essence of the tourist experience is that we are meant to sample the 'exotic', the different and the local in other cultures. Tourism and travel are also meant to convey the idea of a 'unique' experience – a treasure of special vistas, activities and modest learning curves all of our very own. And yet, travel is actually a truly *mass* phenomenon today. Even advertising campaigns for places (like New Zealand) which emphasise how unspoilt, congestion-free and 'out of time' the destination is, ironically signal the possibility that soon those unique features will disappear, as more and more people arrive to spoil, congest and contaminate that unique atmosphere – aided, as Weber might have noted, by an army of Kiwihosts and Tourist Board officials. As one commentator puts it:

> The agents and structures of the tourist industry seemed to reduce the experience of travel from home and abroad to a state of equivalence. The tourist leaves the airport terminal in one capital city and arrives in its replica three thousand miles away. He or she is searched and questioned by one set of customs officials upon departure, and is searched and questioned again by their doubles on arrival. The tourist takes a cab from the hotel to the airport terminal in one continent, and takes a cab from the airport to the hotel in another continent. The depthlessness and transparency of travel experience matches the depthlessness and transparency of the surrounding culture ... De-differentiation has weakened the contrast between home and abroad. One has only has to walk along the shopping and amusement areas of any metropolis to find evidence of this: Korean and Indian restaurants in London; Chinese film theatres and Indian fashion shops in Los Angeles; African music and Latin-American galleries in Paris. In some complexes, de-differentiation is formally incorporated as a design feature. For example, Chaney (1990) refers to the Metroland Centre in Gateshead which is advertised as the biggest shopping centre in Europe. Various sections of the centre have been built to incorporate simulations of 'foreign' locales and different times. Examples include the 'Antiques village', the 'Forum'

and the 'Mediterranean village'. Time and space compression techniques which earlier, in the discussion of Busch Gardens and the 'World Showcase' pavilion at Disneyland I mentioned as attractions in amusement parks, are here presented as part of the normal facts of daily life.

(Rojek, 1993: 199–200)

> **De-differentiation** refers to the tendency in contemporary culture to blur the boundaries between such things as the local and the global, representations and reality, the past and the present, politics and culture.

What Rojek means by **de-differentiation** here is the tendency in contemporary culture to blur the kind of boundaries in social life that in earlier modernity were clearly separated out. For example, the difference between the local and the global, or between the past and present, or between 'representations' of events and cultures, and their 'reality'. In New Zealand too, the past-present distinction is fast being made an item of leisure consumption, with all sorts of gold-rush towns, Victorian rural villages, and Maori heritage sites being presented for 'authentic' display, even if these are just single items on a long agenda of visits and samples for tourists to get through (Bell, 1996). The condensation of the past into the present, and the 'instant' evocation of exotic cultures within a 'home' culture, all as it happens quite carefully standardised across the globe and filtered through the electronic mass media, is what some sociologists refer to as the intense 'time-space compression' of late- or post-modern times. The globalisation of leisure is a crucial part of that phenomenon.

Differences and divisions

We have suggested how sport and leisure on a mass scale can help *integrate* society, through shared pleasures and rituals, through a common national identification, and through the acceptance/transmission of dominant societal values. But few modern societies are seamlessly integrated: there is always room for ideological contestation. For example, the masculinity of male sporting culture, which is often contrasted in its 'manliness' with the homophobic stereotype of 'effeminate' and HIV-vulnerable gays, is challenged in the notable worldwide trend of gay men's bodybuilding. The point of this movement demonstrates that bodily power and manly imagery have intrinsically nothing to do with sexual preference. Another example would be the way in which the protests over the 1981 Springbok rugby tour tore open the previously integrating consensus around rugby, with divisions emerging within and across all social groups and families, within the sporting public, and between the sporting public and the state.

Sport and leisure, then, provide ample material for analysing the ways in which society is integrated *and* the ways in which it is divided – in terms of class, ethnicity, gender, age ability/disability, and so on. The sporting profile of *differently abled people*, for example, has been improved quite markedly in recent years, with the emergence of annual events such as the Paralympic Games, and the statutory provision of adequate access to sporting and leisure facilities for those with disabilities. However, whilst this increased visibility of a previously disadvantaged minority group is obviously to be welcomed, it also serves ironically to *underline* rather than eliminate the relatively greater advantage and visibility of the able-bodied.

With regard to *age and generation*, there are distinctive leisure divisions to be studied. One structural disadvantage felt by many older people is simply an economic one: many senior citizens are poor, and their participation in majority leisure pursuits is often a matter of resources than of any 'disability' that comes with getting older. Everywhere, 'Grey' movements are on the increase in our 'ageing society' as senior citizens come to terms with governments across the democratic capitalist world· who have been cutting away at the welfare state, state pensions, and other subsidies for people who have contributed a great deal throughout their lives to their nations' well-being. Clearly, the quality of older people's leisure time is fundamentally dependent upon such material provision, whatever the nature of the leisure or sport engaged in. Driving for pleasure, for example, is apparently a popular preference amongst older New Zealanders, particularly older women: but their ability to pursue this preference is strongly conditioned by their ability to own and run a car. More by way of 'difference' than 'division', older people have distinctive preferences for leisure pursuits, and these will obviously contrast with the preference of other social groups, such as urban youth for instance. Gardening, listening to music, walking for exercise, reading, TV, indoor crafts: these are prominent activities for older people.

Ethnicity poses a great challenge to the sociologist of leisure and sport. One aspect of that challenge is simply to understand that cultural differences will produce very different leisure patterns and priorities. For example, the role of family eating and family gambling games such as mah-jong and fan tan in the activities of Chinese New Zealanders have no real equivalent in the mainstream culture. And it takes a little research to find out that team sports as a rule do not feature as leisure activities for Chinese New Zealand youngsters, but in cases where they do take up sports, basketball and soccer are more popular amongst them than rugby. Another prominent question in ethnicity research is to try to explain why it is that in two different countries where there is a general situation of ethnic social disadvantage for certain groups (say African Americans in the USA and Maori in New Zealand) these groups become either 'over-represented' in the number of sporting stars in one place (America) but remains 'under-represented' across the full range of sports in the other (New Zealand).

The participation of Polynesians in some sports (rugby, netball, softball) but not in others (cricket, equestrian pursuits) also reflects cultural and class processes. As Maori and Pacific Islanders* have migrated to the urban areas of New Zealand, they have brought their strong commitment to

* See p. 106

certain team sports, and introduced new sports such as kilikiti, the Pacific version of cricket. This alteration of the sporting profile of Aotearoa is reinforced socially by the large numbers of spectators and participants attending Maori or Pacific festivals and competitions, and the widespread use of the haka at major sporting occasions.

A further challenge arises when we try to fit Maori activities into taken-for-granted categories like leisure and sport. Perhaps for urban Maori, whose cultures tend to be less traditional than those of rural Maori, there are ways in which leisure can be understood in much the same way as we understand Pakeha leisure. But Maori communities which retain traditional practices and ideas might well object to the very distinction between 'work' and 'leisure/sport', because this distinction is a product of the industrial world view. In other words, it is arguably a culturally specific way of understanding activities, and one that often 'forgets' that it *is* culturally relative. The extensive ceremonial features of iwi interaction, inextricably involving both work *and* socialising or 'entertainment', co-ordinated physical performance and celebration but *also* relaxation, exchanges of food and gifts, and the crucial role of the marae – which is itself unclassifiable into any particular pigeon-hole of work, domestic, or pastime activity – all these things make key aspects of Maori practice difficult to encompass within the Western, industrial and individualist notions of time divisions based on a work/leisure split.

Social class has long been a focus for sociologists of leisure. They ask: 'what are the differences in cultural taste/behaviour between different class groups, and how do these relate to material and cultural inequalities between classes?' In many ways, the class struggle in leisure is about which groups succeed in defining and exhibiting 'the good life', and this will tend to be closely related to the economic and social resources a class has more generally in society. In the terminology of the French sociologist Pierre Bourdieu:

> The production of cultural symbols, be they high culture, popular culture, or consumer goods, is the subject of an endless process of struggle on the part of classes, class fractions and groups to rename and legitimate the particular set of tastes which reflect their interests. Those classes which possess a high volume of economic capital (the bourgeoisie) and cultural capital (the intellectuals) are clearly in a stronger position to define what is legitimate, valid and 'pure' taste.
>
> (Featherstone, 1987: 122)

Thus, to indulge in sociological caricature for a moment, the working-class British male spends his leisure time smoking, drinking beer in pubs, doing exercise for virile strength, eating carbohydrate-rich food in decent portions, watching soccer, going to discos, and pursuing 'realistic hedonism' when on mass package holidays. In contrast, the middle-class person prefers exercise for health and enhancement of self-image, seeks serious aesthetic appreciation, drinks good wine and selects from refined menus, reads tastefully for education purposes, avoids vulgar crowds on vacation, and worries about over-indulgence. One notch further up the pecking order, the upper classes engage in sports and leisure performances (sailing, hunting, Ascot, Henley Regatta, stately home balls) which require early training and very considerable luxury resources. One goal of this is to appear to be natural and comfortable (as the middle class is not) in ostentatious but high-quality display, sending out the message that such sheer *class* is not to be acquired, only inherited; and another goal of glamorous but 'natural' social interaction amongst the elite is simply to ensure that the elite itself, and its 'superior' style, is reproduced to the exclusion of pushy incomers.

The *gender* dimension of sport and leisure is also a crucial one for any sociological assessment. We have already noted the role of images of masculinity, and it is a fair bet that if, as an *average*, 76% of people's total time is devoted to non-leisure activity, then the non-leisure time of women, taken separately, is going to represent an even higher proportion. The reason for this, of course, is that it is still women who do the bulk of time-consuming domestic labour and child-care, as feminist sociologists have consistently argued.

> Women generally have less time available for leisure than men and make choices about how to spend their time from a more limited range of possibilities. Women's housework and childcare responsibilities do not fit neatly into a conventional working day, and many women are almost constantly 'on call', which makes it difficult to plan leisure in advance with any degree of certainty. Making arrangements to spend leisure time outside the home is particularly problematic, resulting in most so-called free time being spent in the home. Women are generally financially poorer than men, with most married women still being financially dependent on their husbands. Women's leisure is given low priority in household budgets, with men's right to personal spending money more widely accepted. Finally, many groups of women are expected to choose their leisure time activities mainly from within the limited range of home and family-oriented activities which are socially defined as acceptable, womanly pursuits.
>
> (Green, Hebron and Woodward, 1990: 25)

Cartoon: Jock Macneish

Clare Simpson extends the theme of gender relations in sport in the following discussion, arguing that for the past century, sportswomen have had little but 'mis-attention'.

Women, sport and the media

Clare Simpson

When women began bicycle racing in Europe in the late nineteenth century, thousands of spectators jostled for the best vantage point. Reporters sensationalised their stories by focusing on scanty clothing and the shape of the women's legs, or by dwelling at length on what the disapproving public had to say. Similar press responses to New Zealand women's cycle racing also in the late nineteenth century, exemplify how media have, in subsequent years, persistently mis-represented the achievements of sportswomen, and have focused instead on trivial or irrelevant issues such as personal appearances or domestic arrangements.

Studies of sports media coverage in New Zealand show differential treatment for women and men, regardless of the national significance of the sports in terms of participation figures or the singular achievements of certain individuals. Research on newspaper, magazine and television coverage of women's sport shows that, despite women's increased participation in sports, these media have failed to reflect sporting reality in their reporting.

In print media such as newspapers and magazines, women's sports are accorded less space, fewer pictures, and are positioned in less prominent places on sports pages. Analyses have shown that between 1980 and 1992, for example, New Zealand newspaper coverage of women's sport has increased from 7% to 11.3%, an insignificant improvement given the increased funding, policy, and marketing aimed at women's participation in sport which have occurred during that period. Magazine coverage of sportswomen is likewise inadequate, with women's sports persistently under-reported, despite large numbers of participants and the internationally outstanding accomplishments of some women.

The portrayal of sportswomen on television is also mis-representative of sporting reality. A 1984 study of sports coverage on prime-time television news, for example, showed that male sports dominated disproportionately: women's sports made up just 13% of sports news items compared to 69% of items covering men's sports, and 18% mixed sports. Similarly, the duration of items was much longer for men's sports; the largest proportion of items dealing with women's sports (21%) lasting only 15 seconds or less (O'Leary and Roberts, 1985). More recent studies show that there has been no significant improvement since 1984, with women's sports receiving only 20% of television sports coverage. Like the newspaper studies, these television studies conclude that coverage has failed to keep pace with reality by persistently under-reporting women's sports.

Male sport also predominates in other kinds of sports programmes. A content analysis of a sports quiz show, 'A Question of Sport', for example, found that questions focused on men's sports disproportionately more than women's, that women were less likely to appear as contestants on the show, and the sports represented by those contestants were restricted to just seven codes: athletics, netball, cricket, bowls, hockey, triathlon, and squash. Given that many other sports are more popular with women than the last four listed, there seems no logical explanation for this choice. The inclusion of triathlon, bowls, and squash can be attributed to the popular successes of Erin Baker, Joyce Osborne, and Susan Devoy, current at the time of the programme's creation. It is unlikely they would have been included otherwise.

The way women's sport is reported reflects what the media believe is important to consumers. One of the arguments for the deficient portrayal of women's sport is that their performances are considered less exciting to watch. The fact that women may not move as fast as men, or play contact sports, suggests that their sporting skills are not in themselves valued when compared to the entertainment value that men's sport has for mass audiences. Sports which attract large numbers of female participants have been persistently overlooked. Netball, for example, drew minimal televised coverage until very recently. That its coverage has increased in the last five years suggests either that the public has changed its mind and now finds netball exciting to watch, or that some other factors have played a part in persuading television managers to increase coverage of this sport. The advent of indoor netball has found appeal for large numbers of men, and has generated amongst men a greater understanding of and interest in netball generally. The corresponding capture of effective sponsorship for netball and recent changes in its executive administration, together with increased audience ratings may have combined to influence more extensive coverage of netball. Most significantly, it has only been since men have expressed interest in the game that ratings and coverage have expanded.

Whilst women's sporting performances may not be considered very newsworthy, their conduct and physical appearances are. Sports media research has shown that all media routinely comment on the feminine images of sportswomen, and universally agree that the portrayal of sportswomen is consistent with stereotypical images of femininity; i.e., it is the femininity of athletes rather than their athleticism which becomes the central focus. Compare how the press has reported netballer Julie Townsend and swimmer Toni Jeffs, for example. Townsend has always been portrayed as 'pretty' and 'pleasant', whereas Jeffs has a reputation for being 'difficult' and 'rebellious', and her tattoo additionally promotes a dubious feminine image.

The way media report about sportswomen also suggests that sport is of secondary importance in their lives, and not taken too seriously by them. Press reports usually focus on the home and family of sportswomen, implying that these are their primary concerns. Furthermore, those sportswomen whose lives do not revolve around a heterosexual partner, or who participate in more masculine sports, usually receive sensationalised coverage. Compare how the press has reported marathon runner Allison Roe and tennis player Martina Navratilova, for example. The private lives of both women have frequently been the focus of reports. Roe has often been portrayed as the typical feminine stereotype: graceful, feminine, and devoted to caring for her husband. Since Navratilova does not fit this image, her muscular body and lesbian sexuality have been targeted as the most salacious, and therefore newsworthy, aspects of her non-sporting life.

A fundamental explanation for the inadequate media coverage of women's sport might be that, subconsciously, most people believe that sport is essentially a masculine concern. This notion is reflected in both the nature and extent of media coverage, devoting more space and time to men's sporting activities, and depicting masculinity as active, strong, and competitive. Femininity, on the other hand, conjures up qualities such as passivity, gentleness, and co-operation, attributes which have no place in sporting discourse.

Media ratings selectively increase the exposure of what audiences already see. This is problematic for top-level sportswomen in particular, since securing and maintaining a high media profile significantly contribute to the continuation of sponsorship deals which, in turn, ensure continued participation in their chosen sports.

Since ratings can be interpreted to suggest that the public prefers to see images of attractive women, sportswomen are compelled to emphasise their femininity in order to capture and hold media attention, colluding with viewer and media preferences to appear stereotypically feminine. Recognising that the media did not consider her feminine enough, tri-athlete Erin Baker, for example, soon realised that she should outwardly adorn herself to reinforce her femininity. She began to wear lipstick and jewellery, a strategy which has helped her maintain a more positive profile in the media. Her elite status had not been sufficient in itself to secure consistent coverage. Her outspoken views about racial discrimination, whilst finding favour with like-minded individuals, did not make for good sports news either, but her marriage and subsequent motherhood gained widespread and positive press attention.

Despite increased female sports participation over the last one hundred years, sports coverage by media has persistently failed to reflect changes in women's sporting participation and to uphold sport as a primary consideration in the lives of sportswomen. In an accommodative response, sportswomen over the century have been obliged to collude with audience and journalist preferences for feminine images, to gain, maintain and generate more positive media profiles. Unlike their nineteenth-century counterparts who had to fight for acceptance and prove they could play sport, today's sportswomen must not only display their sporting prowess, but must also become highly politicised in order to pursue their sporting ambitions.

Questions

Having read Clare Simpson's contribution, try to answer the following questions.

1. How can the media coverage of women's sports and sportswomen be *increasing* and yet also *mis-representative*?

2. Clare Simpson mentions that one 'fundamental explanation' of the priority given to coverage of male sports might be that 'subconsciously', people see sport as essentially a masculine concern. How could this basically *psychological* explanation be countered by a more *sociological* perspective?

3. Whilst Clare Simpson notes the increases in the profile of women's sport over the last decade or so, the strong impression given by her piece is that sport is still very much a *patriarchal* domain. What would have to change in social relations and attitudes for there to be a fundamental improvement in the status of women's leisure and sport?

Theorising leisure

Already in this chapter, many possible ways of theorising leisure have emerged, though so far we have not explicitly drawn attention to this. For example, it is a theoretical framing exercise just to consider leisure and work as distinct from one another, or to see leisure as either 'integrative' or 'contested'. Furthermore, in terms of social divisions, the Marxist theoretical emphasis would be on the primacy of social class in explaining the social division of leisure, whereas a feminist outlook prioritises male privilege. You should note that theoretical disputes in the sociology of leisure, as in other areas, are not always antagonistic. It may be possible, for example, to come to a combined view of the role of class and gender in understanding sport, and it is an important venture to see if Maori and 'western' perspectives on the very definition of the field of study can be productively brought together in some way, or whether this is a case of strict 'cultural relativism'.

One prominent perspective in sport and leisure theory which attempts to 'synthesise' a number of different angles on the role of sport in society is the so-called **figurational approach** associated with the sociologist Norbert Elias and his followers. This school emphasises the way in which, over many centuries of Western historical development, there has been a 'civilising process' going on in which many emotionally charged and 'vulgar' social activities have become increasingly regularised according to ever more refined conventions. (Once it was OK to blow your nose without a handkerchief at the dinner table, now it is not.) This civilising process is not necessarily regarded as a 'good thing', nor does it mean that 'uncivilised' behaviour is bad, or that it has been eliminated from social interaction. What it does suggest is that the threshold of personal crudity, public celebration and group violence in everyday life has been significantly lowered over time, and controlled ever more carefully by the state. Nevertheless, human beings still display a deep 'quest for excitement' and this social phenomenon increasingly gets transferred to, and ritualised within, the domain of organised competitive sport, which itself has become more 'civilised' over time (think of the decline in popularity of blood sports, once very popular and acceptable). The precise form taken by this ritualised quest for excitement depends greatly upon the 'figurations' of class, ethnicity and gender, which 'filter' and interrupt in various ways the underlying trend towards self-restraint and disciplined customs (Dunning and Rojek, 1992).

> Figurational analysis was developed by Norbert Elias to explain the 'civilising process' by which many emotionally charged and 'vulgar' social activities have become regularised according to ever-more refined conventions.

Another controversial recent theoretical contribution has been that associated with *postmodernism*. Unlike figurational sociology and other even more 'structural' perspectives like Marxism and feminism, postmodernists do not see the point in distinguishing between underlying 'real' social processes and their supposedly 'superficial' representation in the countless powerful images that literally *saturate* contemporary society. Postmodernists do not accept any simple division in social life between work and leisure, or between the 'material' aspect of living and the way we perceive ourselves through images of society and self. Instead, postmodernism suggests that the whole world has become mediafied to the extent that we can never really tell what is 'image' and what is 'reality' any more. Take Disneyland: a very postmodern leisure experience. The various component 'worlds' of Disneyland – Frontierland, Fantasyland, Toontown, Futureland, and so on – are elaborate technological constructions which absorb us into their reality, and Disneyland as a whole achieves this 'simulation' effect too. Having been absorbed into it, it takes us some time to re-adjust to the real world which exists outside the gates of this 'hyper-real' experience. And we think: 'amazing', then try to get on with our 'ordinary' lives. But, say postmodernists, what 'really' exists outside those gates is not something essentially different from what is inside the gates – it's more and more of the same! In America at least – postmodernists tend to focus on the USA – the whole world of modern society is actually a vast, invented and technologised construction of consumer signs and satisfactions, of hotels, mass car parks, shopping centres, fast foodstores, image industries, media information and media role models. In fact, in a sense Disneyland is *more* 'authentic' than the so-called real world, because at least it is aware of its inventedness, and celebrates it, whereas we somehow 'forget', or cannot bring ourselves to realise, that non-Disney experience is every bit as constructed and sign-saturated. We are living, say postmodernist thinkers such as Jean Baudrillard, in a seamless world of 'simulations' and **hyper-reality**, and we are all involved in the very serious business of incessant play, consumption and fantasy.

Hyper-reality refers to the way in which there is now no longer a clear distinction to be made between *communication* about reality and *reality itself*.

Disneyland: authentic, a sham or hyper-reality?

Conclusion

The postmodernist perspective on leisure today is a fascinating one, though it actually poses considerable problems for traditional sociology. This is because sociology usually aspires to distinguish clearly between reality and its representations, truth and illusion; yet postmodernism asserts boldly that there is no 'real' reality to be found lurking 'underneath' the messy world of hyper-reality and simulation. Postmodernists are thus content to describe our leisure images and pursuits rather than explain or moralise about them. The feeling is that what we make of the different sign systems and lifestyle images will depend on our own preferred images, fantasies and cultural preferences. We pursue the challenge of postmodernist sociology in the final chapter of this book.

Study questions

15.1 Drawing on the examples of masculinity and national identity, discuss how sport reproduces social relations in a ritual way.

15.2 What role does 'de-differentiation' play in the globalisation of leisure?

15.3 How do the social divisions of class, ethnicity, age and ability shape individuals' access to, and quality of, leisure pursuits?

15.4 Compare and contrast the 'figurational' and 'postmodern' theoretical approaches to leisure. Which perspective do you favour and why?

Further reading

Cashmore, E. (1996) *Making Sense of Sport*, 2nd ed. Routledge, London.

Critcher, C. et al. (eds). (1995) *Sociology of Leisure: A Reader*. Chapman Hall, London.

Featherstone, M. (1987) Leisure, Symbolic Power and the Life Course. In Horne, J. et al. (eds) *Sport, Leisure and Social Relations*. Routledge, London.

Fougere, G. (1989) Sport, Culture and Identity: the Case of Rugby Football. In Novitz, D. and Wilmott, B. (eds) *Culture and Identity in New Zealand*. GP Books, Wellington.

Green, E., Hebron, S. and Woodward, D. (1990) *Women's Leisure, What Leisure?* Macmillan, Basingstoke.

Messner, M.A. and Sabo, D.F. (1994) *Sex, Violence and Power in Sports: Rethinking Masculinity*. The Crossing Press, Freedom, Ca.

Perkins, H.C. and Cushman, G. (eds). (1993) *Leisure, Recreation and Tourism*. Longman Paul, Auckland.

Rojek, C. (1993) *Ways of Escape: Modern Transformations in Leisure and Travel*. Macmillan, Basingstoke.

16 The story of sociology III: from the past to the post

Chapter aims

- to outline some of the key features of postmodernity and to assess the adequacy of postmodern theory;
- to discuss elements of Eurocentrism within sociology and assess the on-going relevance of the classics;
- to outline the critique made by postcolonial theorists of modern sociology;
- to discuss three images of the sociologist.

 Introduction

In this chapter, we consider two of the most prominent concepts that are current in sociology right now – **postmodernity** and **postcoloniality** – and reflect on what it means to be a sociologist as we enter the twenty-first century. In doing this, we are trying to bring the 'story of sociology' of Chapters 2 and 3 up to date, but we are also keen to emphasise that the politics and culture of where we are situated – Aotearoa/New Zealand – crucially affect our sense of the relevance of sociology today.

Postmodernity

The thesis that we now live in a postmodern society is intuitively appealing. It suggests, for example, a 'post-industrial' society, one in which far fewer people work as typical 'proletarians' in big factories producing mass goods uniformly for a mass market. Indeed, classical 'productive' labour (factory production, mining, steelworks, shipbuilding, engineering, agricultural industries, etc.) would seem to have given way to innumerable sorts of rather different 'service' jobs and information-driven occupations. Lots of ordinary people

Postmodernity refers to the modes of social life that have developed in late twentieth-century societies. Postmodern society is said to be characterised by post-industrialism, 'virtual reality', media saturation and a general sense of disconnectedness.

Postcoloniality describes an analytical approach and political position which is critical of the processes and impact of colonialism. It includes the attempt to establish new, non- or anti-colonial institutions and identities.

own shares, have a stake in firms and trusts. Work is becoming more flexible in terms of both time and task. Leisure and consumption are more important to people these days, and management strategies seem to be subtle and ever-changing attempts to tailor and design products to the needs and tastes of specific lifestyles, social niches and company/brand ethics. The post-industrial economy has thus become more fluid, more design- and consumer-led, and indeed the market and its participants have gone 'virtual': with the enormous advances in home-based information technology and the 'Net'. Consequently, it is maintained, the old division between 'material' life on the one hand, and 'consciousness' on the other, is an anachronism. We are all the creatures, and also the authors, of the diverse, ever-changing, virtual network that is postmodern society.

It is part of the strong postmodern thesis to argue that along with these changes in material life, production and consumption in particular, profound changes in *social identity* have occurred. Instead of the solid and reliable identifications stemming from social class position, we are now cross-cut, as individuals, by a great number and variety of identities – age, gender, dis/ability, ethnicity, sexuality, lifestyle, subculture, leisure practices, political and social movements of the day, and so on. Each of these social influences, moreover, can be seen as forming a mosaic of social and personal discourses, sets of ideas, images, rituals or practices, which appeal to us in various ways and 'speak to' how we choose to live our lives. Some writers have even suggested that in the postmodern world, life is so saturated by media images and representations of all sorts, that the very distinction between real social relations and our images of them is no longer credible. We live in a network of **hyper-reality**: where signs and images collide, liaise and feed upon one another, whether in the realm of work or consumption or politics or information.

> Hyper-reality refers to the way in which there is now no longer a clear distinction to be made between *communication* about reality and *reality itself.*

From this sketch, it is important to note, firstly, that in postmodernity no one social identification or discourse can be seen as dominant over, or more 'real' than, others, and secondly, that these formations of social identity are *chosen* by, as much as *imposed* upon, us. A third conception is also crucial: that the resulting brew of postmodern identity formation produces a society not oriented to social *sameness*, as in the past, but to social and cultural *differences*. The overall sense of postmodernity is of an ever-changing, fragmented, and almost unreal society, in which multiple discourses and meanings compete and overlap. A society, indeed, where there is no such thing as 'society' at all – if this terms signals a coherent totality that is structured in any definitive way.

What about postmodern politics? The idea here is that, in modern times, politics basically followed the rather simple social structure that once existed. As we had mass production and mass consumption, so we had mass politics: big and few parties appealing to the homogeneous voter, working out from its natural base in particular and predictable class alliances. So, the working class tended to vote for Labour parties, the privileged and aspiring classes for the conservative/National Party.

But clearly, with the fragmentation and multiplication of social identities and the 'death of class', this form of politics becomes increasingly dated. One could perhaps see the onset of proportional representation as one consequence of the proliferation of social interests, these being better served by a politics of many minorities rather than of solid unchanging majorities. Moreover, the old party politics operated within the taken-for-granted dominance of the centralised *nation state*, whereas, increasingly, individual nation-states may be giving way as sovereign powers simultaneously to global and regional forms of government, and to local expressions of political autonomy.

The idea of postmodern *culture* is also a very potent one. If social groups are diverse and multiple, then clearly so are the cultures and values they create and sustain. If social relations are inextricably media-ted by their various representations, then ideologies and realities, aspirations and experiences cease to be 'ontologically' distinguishable from one another – we live in a rather 'flat' world of competing images. As for the ultimate meaning of the traditions people inherit, the social routines and pleasures they practise, their customs, music, food, relationships and hierarchies – none of these things can any longer be assumed to share a common basis in 'universal humanity'. Attempts to undersell cultural differences could even be criticised as a form of assimilationism or even cultural imperialism. At the same time, in postmodernity, one can expect increasing cross-cultural exchanges and the emergence of innumerable *hybrid* forms of culture and identity, fragmenting further still the social map of groups and beliefs. If you think of the increasing ways in which young people from different ethnic or cultural groups relate, socialise and inter-marry, or of the significant and growing numbers of individuals and groups who move to other places and countries to work and live, then you can readily envisage examples of what this idea of **cultural hybridity** refers to.

Such propositions have huge consequences for how we theorise about society, because an avowedly postmodern brand of social theory would also have to respect and foster diverse multiplicity. In a sense, the job of postmodern sociology is to heighten, not to appease, our consciousness that things are off the rails. According to postmodernists, 'modernist' social theories, just like modernist politics and society, essentially treat people as *the same* the world over, because they posit a single 'thing' called 'society', whose general principles of operation and progressive development we can scientifically understand. With the results of these theories, we can then proceed to control the social world, and change it for the better – make it even more 'progressive'.

But, say the postmodernists, the theories we invent and use are not neutral and objective and universal just because we sociologists like to think they are. Theories, just like our tastes in sport, art, religion and food, are *culturally variable*; and so if culture is multiple and diverse, the theories we develop to imagine how society works will be culturally variable also.

> **Cultural hybridity** refers to the exchange of cultural forms and beliefs, and to the intermixing of cultural groups, so that new forms of identity emerge which draw on two or more origins.

How are we to evaluate these provocative claims about postmodernity? The point so far has been mainly to show how a powerful new picture has developed in social theory, and how it squares quite well with many things that seem to be going on around us. As sociologists, however, it is important to approach all ideas in a *critical* manner, even if we are sympathetic to them. And there is very little in the strong postmodern picture that could not be strongly challenged by a resolute modernist sociologist.

One counter-argument would be that the postmodern scenario relies on a highly caricatured version of the relatively recent past, giving the impression that no-one valued leisure or consumption; that everyone was easily pigeon-holed into a social class and always acted accordingly, en masse; that there was social and cultural homogeneity. Unfortunately for the postmodern position, all these things can be shown to be misleading. As for contemporary society, it is just as plausible to point to *continuities* with the modernist past as it is to highlight postmodern discontinuities. For example, there is little conclusive evidence that a post-industrial, far less a 'virtual', economy exists in New Zealand, or that work is hugely less important for people nowadays than it was in the past, or that lifestyles are extraordinarily diverse, or that what flexible labour exists has been *chosen* by workers for its attractive qualities, or that cultural understandings are totally different across different traditions and groups.

Take as a brief encapsulation of the anti-postmodernist case what is probably the icon of the new 'virtual' and egalitarian post-material civilisation we are supposed to have entered: the PC (personal computer). The much-heralded revolution symbolised by the growing millions of PCs is nothing of the sort, we might want to suggest. For one thing, the hardware machines and their associated software are not at all 'immaterial', being physical products which are assembled by a mass of workers from scarce resources. PCs, like any other capitalist commodity, are hyped and produced for huge profits by companies who engage in the time-honoured cycle of competition and merger. They are bought by masses of people who may not really need them or be able to afford them and who run a high risk of getting physically damaged through over-use or mis-use. Already there are clear social divisions of competence and advantage in the use of computer technology amongst social groups and societies, and these tend to reinforce familiar inequalities of class, ethnicity and gender in our society. PCs have not, as speculated, led to the decline of paper goods and uses, and consequently pose a serious additional environmental hazard in terms of their disposal and replacement through rapid built-in obsolescence. PCs and the communications revolution they represent, in other words, might best be understood as the latest expression of perfectly familiar modern, capitalist cultural and industrial products.

In short, whilst the postmodernity thesis is very stimulating as a research project, and points to lots of things around us that do seem to be changing in new ways, the jury is still very much out. It is now accepted by many sociologists that the advent of the postmodern should not after all be understood to suggest that the modern era has been completely superseded, but rather that there is a complex process of continuity and change going on.

Eurocentrism and the relevance of the classics

Previous generations of sociologists have been dominated by the idea that sociology should aspire to be the scientific study of social relations. More recently, it has been recognised that this conception of sociology, and the reverence it shows for science more generally, is the product of specifically *Western* culture. When we do see theory and science in that way, it becomes impossible to understand the role of social theory as providing 'objective' knowledge, applicable universally across all times, places and cultures. Rather, social theories are stories or narratives of self-understanding. Such narratives are powerful and persuasive, no doubt, but *your* narrative of understanding, coming from your standpoint and background, may not be *mine*, coming from where I do. Mainstream sociology, it follows, would have to be seen as a modernist enterprise because it tries to give a universalist and scientific picture of what society is, and of how it develops. A postmodern sociology, by contrast, would require us to accept that there is always going to be a variety of sociological visions, that none of these will be objective, and that no amount of invoking 'social reality' will decide us in favour of one rather than another, because our very notion of social reality is itself culturally constructed.

One of the exciting themes in the postmodernist position is that it is time for sociologists of the here and now to stop revering those old 'Dead White European Middle-Class Males', i.e. the sociological 'classics'. Not only did they write of a society that was very different from our own today, but – as mentioned a moment ago – their conception of sociology as a science in the service of Progress is very much dated now as an 'Enlightenment' vision. And this vision, it is argued, is inappropriate for our own fragmented society and contested knowledges.

But that picture of thinkers such as Marx, Durkheim and Weber, whilst certainly exciting and challenging, is in other ways rather superficial. It would be absurd for us to expect these writers to have predicted everything about the world as we experience it today, and yet we do still draw extensively on their ideas to understand what is going on.

Take the central ideas of Karl Marx. Many people would say that developments in the modern world have made Marx's contributions outdated, and his 'predictions' preposterous. For example, Marx maintained that capitalism would be overthrown in a social revolution triggered by growing and unsustainable contradictions between social needs and private ownership, between the potential of science and technology and its human consequences. And yet none of this has come to pass. Indeed, with the ignominious demise of Marxist-inspired socialist states, capitalism has come to be the only game in town. Marx also predicted the growing polarisation of the two main classes in capitalist society, the bourgeoisie and the proletariat, but once again this has not come to pass, with Marx missing altogether the phenomenon of 'affluent' working-class segments and a huge, growing 'service' or middle class of employees who simply do not fit the bill of classical manual workers.

Such protests against Marx's relevance are important, but they cannot be taken too far. For one thing, the very term *capitalism* and its meaning has entered the vocabulary of all social scientists and many others largely through Marx's usage. It seems not only impossible to understand the world in which we live without the concept of capitalism, but, as Marx predicted, capitalism has become ever-more global and pervasive in character – more and more goods and services are becoming 'commodities' in Marx's sense (i.e. produced for profits in a competitive market), and more and more places around the world are being turned into full-scale capitalist societies, or would like to become such. Large enterprises continue to merge, compete and expand, in line with what Marx called the tendency of capital to become 'centralised' and 'concentrated'. In that context, it is difficult for individual nation-states, and almost impossible for any governments hostile to the dominant capitalist mode of production, to resist the dictates of the international production and finance markets, which remain fundamentally driven by profits or 'returns' rather than any sense of what is for the public good. It further seems impossible to make much headway in the struggle to improve much of the earth's environment, protect its limited resources, and sustain the health of all its peoples, because (Marxists would say) the industrial capitalist economies which have been responsible for environmental deterioration simply do not operate according to those kinds of human priority. Perhaps this type of problem is what Marx meant by the contradictions and instabilities of capitalism, contradictions that certainly still produce crises and crashes and revolutions around the world. Certainly, many people in all walks of life today seem to feel that the global capitalist economy is, literally, getting *out of control*.

As for contemporary New Zealand, there has been in the last 15 years or so, a definite 'rolling back of the state' (and of social democratic politics more generally) in order to accommodate the intensification of commercialisation and international 'competitiveness'. The economy, as a result, has almost become defined in terms of the idea of winning overseas markets for New Zealand goods, offering an 'attractive environment' for overseas firms to invest in, and generally getting public spending reduced so that it does not act as a 'drag' on resources that could be profitably employed elsewhere. Now, it is very difficult indeed to see this recent social 'experiment' as anything other than a decisive swing in favour of capitalism and against general public interests, including the interests of most workers. Marxists would go on to argue that the whole logic in terms of which the welfare state in New Zealand and elsewhere has hit a cycle of crisis and decline is revealed by Marx's identification of a central mechanism of capitalism, namely the tendency of the rate of profit to fall. According to this theory, in order to sustain the production of surplus value – the source of capitalist 'profits' – capitalist industry is compelled constantly to substitute 'dead' labour (machines, technology) for 'live' labour. But as a result, the rate of surplus value (not necessarily the total amount, however) declines; more and more people are either made unemployed, or casualised, or transferred to the (generally cheaper) 'service' sectors of the economy; this in turn leaves an ever-more-burdensome role for the welfare state to cope with, a burden which in conditions of severe capitalist competition around the world, it cannot 'efficiently' bear. The overall result is the need to cut back on the welfare state, and generally to try to make more 'efficient' and 'commercial' the activities of all manner of public goods and services, from rubbish disposal to health care and university teaching.

Well, the debate on Marx goes on. Would Marx have seen the 'revolutionary' process that is supposed to replace capitalism as a gradually unfolding one or as a sudden 'activist' event? Does the collapse of 'communist' states around the world from the late 1980s contradict or confirm Marx's analysis about the development and success of capitalism and the timing of its decline? Is capitalism efficient and beneficial or irrational and destructive? This debate continues to be a live and important one, not a relic from the past.

Emile Durkheim also contributes invaluable tools for understanding our times, and indeed, if it is felt that Marx's materialist perspective has failed to capture the *non-material* nature of contemporary life, then the legacy of Durkheim might be seen as the necessary antidote. Durkheim, you will recall, understood his key concept of the division of labour as a way of understanding the changing forms of *social solidarity* in modern life. In some ways, Durkheim was positive about the break away from the undifferentiated 'mechanical' solidarity of traditional societies and the break into the specialised, differentiated, interconnected society heralded by an advanced division of labour and 'organic' solidarity. The latter, Durkheim felt, was a precondition for the true achievement of both social integration and genuine individuality. But Durkheim held that the instrumentalism and utilitarianism of modern life (the 'looking-after-number-one' ethic, if you like) constituted a 'false' form of individuality, breeding widespread *anomie*, and posing severe obstacles to the achievement of a more rational and responsible society. One key index of the state of health of the social body, he thought, was the rate of suicide in cases that could be classified as 'anomic', i.e. resulting from a certain modern 'normlessness' or disorderliness in moral regulation.

Interestingly enough, there could be no better focus for the relevance of Durkheimian sociology today than the relatively high level of suicide amongst young people in New Zealand. How prevalent is this problem? What is the ratio of boys to girls, or Maori to Pakeha, and is this ratio changing? There are already some answers to these questions, but much remains to be found out, and there is a fair chance that such research could favour Durkheim-like interpretations. The youth suicide rate, for example, might be explained partly in terms of the relatively recent 'opening up' of a previously small and close New Zealand culture and identity to the powerful, international and seemingly uncontrollable forces of the free labour market. For Maori youth, the continuing erosion of the bonds of tribal society in conditions of increasingly impersonal and disadvantaged modern, urban life may be a factor. The increasing pressure and stress of an 'achieving' culture, one which means that the difference between surviving and failing is an ever-earlier entry into the desperate scramble for credentials, status and a proper 'plan' for one's whole life ahead may also play an important role. In a country which has held on longer than most to the ideal of a carefree, and classless early phase of life (spent largely outdoors), these pressures of individualism and status present a particularly sharp contrast with the norms of the past – and perhaps, literally, a depressing one.

In such an atmosphere of 'unhealthy' individualism, it might seem difficult for forms of solidarity and collective morals to prevail. According to Durkheim, individualism, however unhealthy, is itself a form of collective consciousness and morality, and it is regulated, as in all societies, by definite processes of ritualisation/socialisation. The task of the sociologist, now, as then, is to document and understand these social processes – for example, the way in which new varieties of individualism are reproduced through competitive professional sport, or reward structures within hierarchical organisations. Durkheim also expected, however, that even in an anomic, individualist society, solidaristic and altruistic forms of ritual would act as powerful bonding mechanisms. This was partly because Durkheim felt that in all societies, people are in a broad sense essentially 'religious'. They collectively invest in constructions of what they feel is 'sacred' or 'profane' in their culture, and organise their collective life around the significance of these symbolic meanings. One striking example of this kind of phenomenon might be the death and funeral of Diana, Princess of Wales, in 1997. In a climate of widespread consumerism, with increasing scepticism about the motives and abilities of monarchs and politicians of all sorts, and in a modern capitalist world where there is a sharp gap once again between the 'haves' and the 'have nots', from a Durkheimian point of view, Diana's death could be seen as a dramatic rediscovery of the sense of the 'sacred', an unorchestrated celebration of the collective moral consciousness. It was not simply that people were expressing agreement with some of the things Diana did, or expressing adoration of her personality; they were expressing a longing for some kind of more wholesome and effective social bond, a sense of true belongingness, in an anomic age. In a world of drugs and crime, stress and aggression, body and lifestyle obsessions, Durkheim would sense the deep need for a re-establishment of the collective moral conscience of society.

We are not inviting you necessarily to agree with that Durkheimian point of view. For one thing, more finding out is necessary: how many people in Britain, for example, really shared the media's and mourners' view of the significance of the Princess and her death? Was it experienced more in the way of an 'away match' atmosphere than a deep personal grieving for noble ideals? And how lasting have the various religious and altruistic sentiments been since that time – have they affected people's views and behaviour in any serious way? Such research might well lead us to be critical of the 'new Durkheimianism', but its relevance and interest are surely not in doubt.

As for Max Weber, he was always the most 'postmodern' of sociological classics. Weber did not really share the aspiration of Marx and Durkheim to give a complete 'scientific' picture of social reality, and he was more sceptical about whether modern society was 'progressive'. Weber was therefore something of a sceptic, and certainly a pluralist, and this fits in very well with the climate of our own times in sociology. Pluralism here means that, for example, there are always a large number of *different* ways of looking at things, not just one way, and that there are always a *range* of factors, not just one, to consider in explaining any social phenomenon. Thus Weber accepted to an extent, with Marx, that social class was an important social factor – but in his opinion so were issues of status, political identifications, and the varied practices of social closure that characterised all in-group/out-group dynamics, whatever the type of group in question.

In terms of Weber's sense of the relentless march of instrumental rationality in modern capitalism, as mentioned in Chapter 1, interesting work has been done which understands that quintessential symbol of our age, the McDonald's restaurant, in Weberian terms. Everything that goes on in a McDonald's – the drive-past window service, the continuous flow delivery of food, the limited and standardised range of products, the extra customer rewards if the service is poor, the constant monitoring of the work and attitudes of the low-paid service staff – is geared to precise calculability and utter effectiveness. Room for error, creative variation, and genuine worker personality is totally minimised, as the production and consumption of the product is governed by extremely tightly specified rules and norms.

Weber's related notion that the modern world is an increasingly 'bureaucratised' one might now seem to be a little out of date if we think of how the public sector bureaucracies have to a large degree been dismantled. But we should remember here that the old notion of 'public service' was an *ethical* one which exercised a hold on many workers and managers in public service departments. In that sense, the move to privatisation and commercialisation represents a further stage in the *disenchantment of the world* in Weberian terms, because issues of calculation and efficiency are even more privileged and the sense of non-instrumental goals in social life are further diminished. If you look closely at any large organisation today, whether public or private, there has been an *increase*, not a decrease, in precise rule-following, supervision and monitoring/ surveillance. Every part of an organisation, and every individual within it, have to have a 'mission statement', aims and objectives, performance indicators, systematic feedback on performance, appraisal and review mechanisms, and a whole stratum of people who are given glorified titles to undertake humdrum supervisory roles, just to sustain the sense of work discipline for a common end. And all too often (as in a modern university, for example) that common end is specified in terms of the delivery of a 'product' rather than an intrinsic public good. Students – like hospital patients or rail and air passengers – have become 'customers' and 'consumers'.

With that kind of defence of the relevance of the classics in mind, it seems important to warn against 'mindlessly' assuming that because an author lived some time ago, and in another cultural context, *therefore* he or she has no value whatever for us today. We need to remember, with C. Wright Mills, that *historical perspective* is fundamental to the sociological imagination, and indeed one of the very worrying things about the culture of immediate experience that is prevalent today is that our very sense of history is being either lost or continually 'media-fied'. It would be a great pity if sociology itself contributed to that loss of historical bearings.

Having said that, there can be no doubt that the 'founding fathers' of sociological theory were to a large extent dictated to by the norms of their culture – how could it be otherwise? In particular, the gender-blindness and ethnocentrism of their work stands out. Mary Wollstonecraft – long before Marx wrote – pointed to the fundamental inequalities between men and women in the modern world, going so far as to advocate that just as women required greater access to, and recognition within, public life and thought, so men for their part needed to become active participants in personal and domestic life. That message, brilliantly articulated in the 1790s, fell on more or less deaf (male) ears for a century. The basic concepts and images of Marx, Durkheim and Weber continued to reflect predominantly male social roles and masculinist forms of political action. The division of labour, exploitation, rationality and charisma: these notions and many more were formulated as though the social division between men and women was entirely a secondary matter. And again, when, one hundred years after Wollstonecraft, Charlotte Perkins Gilman from a feminist perspective further transformed the accepted understanding of the relation between domestic labour and work in the wider economy, this too seemed to have little impact on the work of 'malestream' sociologists, from that of the Chicago School to that of Talcott Parsons to neo-Marxism. Only with the next revival of feminist social thought in the 1970s did some of the basic messages of these earlier feminist thinkers really hit home.

As for the ethnocentrism – **Eurocentrism** – of the classic male thinkers, this is not exactly a matter of overt bias as such. Marx, certainly, wrote furious critiques of the brutality of several aspects of Western imperialism. At the same time, the classical sociologists, like the Scots thinkers before them, were obsessed by the question of why it was that North-West Europe took the 'lead' in the development of capitalist modernity. They were obsessed by the difference between modern and traditional society.

> Eurocentrism is the tendency to see everything from the perspective of European values and beliefs, and to judge things accordingly.

They drew clear contrasts between the 'progressive' West and the 'stagnant' and 'corrupt' East in their own day, and felt that, for good or ill, modern Western society would irreversibly transform the world in its own image. They wanted to understand that transformation in terms of an 'objective' and 'progressive' analysis – terms which themselves are centrally part of the Western scientific tradition. Again, it is important to say here that they did not think that European modernity was necessarily in reality an ideal or good society, but they did all see it as a *necessary condition* for the emergence of a more 'progressive' world. To that extent, the classical sociologists helped to intellectually and politically *marginalise* those cultures that were on the receiving end of Western 'progress' and domination.

A final important point about the Eurocentrism of sociology past and present is this: sociology tends to encourage us to see social change as the result of forces and developments *internal* to particular societies, and tends to conceive of such societies as equivalent to particular *nation-states* (American society, New Zealand society, and so on). These emphases push us always to identify changes in society as structural and deep-rooted. But such an intellectual style, it has been argued, must inevitably play down the fact of political domination of some societies over others, and ignores the fact that many 'modern' social changes, since the 'discovery' and 'exploration' of the 'New World' have been the product of external *conquest*. To dignify such events, as sociological theory occasionally tends to, with the pseudo-scientific vocabulary of evolutionary structural development, could be seen as complicit with the policies and advantages of the (predominantly European) conquerors.

Prescient and valuable as the theories of the classical male sociologists may have been, then, it is relevant and plausible to wonder whether their at least partial gender blindness, and their at least partial Eurocentrism disqualify them for active service today. And this is not to mention the obvious 'fact' that the world continues to change in unpredictable and novel ways, another reason why it is imperative that sociology today should develop resources which go beyond the classical ideas and findings. Continuing in this interesting, but also controversial, vein, some would argue that, especially in a place like Aotearoa/New Zealand, sociology must become *postcolonial* in ethos and focus.

Postcoloniality

The concept of postcoloniality overlaps with that of postmodernity, but 'postcolonial' intellectuals tend to be almost as critical of postmodernism as the latter are of modernist sociologists. Why? One reason is that postcolonial writers are inclined to think that 'strong' postmodernists are as much the product of the *metropolitan culture* of European and North American nations as are their modernist predecessors. The strong postmodernist picture is one in which reality and representations merge into one hyper-real neon blur; where there is an infinite number of identities, images, and scenarios for politics and culture, none having any intellectual priority; and where society and thought itself are seen as disconnected rather than forming a coherent totality. That being the case, intellectuals and academics, to put it bluntly, are off the hook – they can 'play' with ideas rather than advance them, and identify with particular cultures without feeling themselves to be an essential part of them.

Ironically, then, postmodernism can be accused of simply *reversing* all the terms of the modernism it overthrows, and of producing an equally 'universalist' image of society. Instead of a general principle of societal coherence, there is a general principle of societal incoherence; instead of social thought being thought capable of scientific objectivity, all we have to go on is our own particular discourse or 'narrative'. The idea of postcolonialism, by contrast, is one of an *engaged* and *located* theory and practice, not a disengaged and free-floating one. Postcolonial thinkers are less likely to argue that the contemporary world has broken completely with the old modern regime. The 'post' in postcolonial therefore does not simply mean 'after', as if colonialism and oppression are things that have magically left the social fabric of nations such as Aotearoa/ New Zealand. Rather, the process of political and cultural decolonisation is a complex and on-going struggle, one pitched against oppression where it exists, but not one which seeks to defend in any way unjust or irrational traditional practices and world views simply because they exist.

Having said that, postcolonialism *does* overlap with both strong and moderate postmodernism in regarding the influence of Eurocentric modernist culture – not to speak of its history of genocide and economic exploitation in 'the colonies' of the European states – as largely baneful, and the process of decolonisation as seriously incomplete. For example, indigenous or 'first nations' peoples, such as Maori, are still battling to have their significant differences from metropolitan and settler cultures recognised as valid; to have their distinctive forms of economy, society and knowledge seen as legitimate and strong. Most people tend to assume that the direction that the world is headed in will produce an 'advanced' condition which will leave little room for the protection of traditional social forms. The relentless pressures of the world capitalist system, the relentless pressures of economic growth, national unity, the growth of science, and individualist achievement – these are still the norms of social organisation.

Postcolonial thought wants us to challenge those norms – or at least see that they are, precisely, 'norms' that stem from Western history rather than 'eternal truths' that we should take for granted. In the course of that challenge, say postcolonialists, we might well want to argue that the social, economic, and political forms given by the West to the rest of the world through a long process of conquest and cultural domination, need not apply to our own specific here and now. Why, for example, 'copy' exactly the parliamentary and voting systems of Western democracies? Might it not be that democracies can be established in many different ways, and that democratic consultation can take different forms? (Think, for example, of the very thorough and respectful process of consultation and consensus-building that often takes place within Maori political culture.) In the light of the catastrophic downside of technological growth, the hazards and technologism of western medicine, the global deprivation and inequality caused by much free-market economics, and the separation from emotional and personal life that is often implied in the disinterested rationalism of the Western analytical mind, might it not be that a better way of meeting our spiritual and material needs can be achieved through a strenuous *re-negotiation* between traditional and modern ways? If that is to be a viable option for us, we have to take the first step in making it possible: recognising the validity, suppleness and extraordinary survival value of many aspects of 'traditional' culture and 'local' life-strategies. Notably in the areas of ethnicity and cultural politics, discussed in Chapters 11 and 14 of this book, Aotearoa/New Zealand is well placed to understand these complex negotiations, and its sociology consequently has a more prominent and genuinely postcolonial thread running through it than have many other national sociologies.

Three images of the sociologist

The discussion of postcoloniality was intended to provoke further discussion, not only about the debates surrounding the concept, but about what exactly students of sociology are to understand, nowadays, by the role of the sociologist and the skills that she or he possesses. What is the sociologist's purpose? There are several main options.

The scientist

One option involves resisting the temptation to go completely postmodern and postcolonial, but instead defending aspects of the Western intellectual heritage stemming from the Enlightenment, and continuing to think that the sociologist's main goal is to be a *scientist*. This means that sociologists should strive to be disinterested, in the sense of not letting immediate political sympathies get in the way of describing and explaining how things are. To that extent, even though complete objectivity may be an illusion, the scientific sociologist has objectivity as an ideal. He or she may feel that the results of sociological enquiry are directly relevant to public understanding and policy. He or she might want sociological explanation to lead to the right kinds of moral and political evaluation, but this process is far from automatic, because sociological explanations must be judged on their intrinsic scientific merits, not on their social consequences.

This picture of sociological endeavour is a little old-fashioned today, and indeed since Durkheim first tried to establish it as the mainstream, it has probably become a minority taste amongst academics. However, its continuing applicability should not be underestimated. We are always trying to put the different pieces of the sociological jigsaw together; for example, to construct one coherent story – even if, as in postmodernism, the story is: no story. And even the most committed sociologist is likely to argue that her view is the right one because 'that's how things are', not because 'that's how things ought to be' or because 'that's what I've just dreamed up'. For example, a committed sociological theory such as feminism is strongly governed by anti-patriarchal values, but its claims are still 'objective' and even 'factual' in character: that patriarchy exists and that it systematically favours the interest of men, for example. All sociologists are also likely to accept the idea that their favourite theories can, in principle, be overturned if shown to be sufficiently inconsistent with known evidence, or if major theoretical inconsistencies or omissions can be identified. This is not a simple matter – people are rarely knocked off their hobby horse on the basis of isolated counter-evidence or logic-chopping. But still, whilst sociologists would probably acknowledge that their work and ideas are ideologically motivated in some way, they would not wish their resulting theories and research findings to be regarded as 'mere ideology'. They will hope to have been too systematic, probing and respectful of possible alternatives for that accusation to stand. This indicates the continuing power of the 'sociology as science' model at a time when the whole human value of the scientific world view is being questioned once again.

The revolutionary

Particularly in the 1960s and 1970s – the time when sociology blossomed as a university subject – a much more 'revolutionary' view of the purpose of sociology was adopted by many people. This was the time of student revolt, of working-class militancy, of exposure of government corruption, of the Vietnam war, of feminism and gay and green activism, of anti-racism and civil rights movements, and generally of an ethos of 'liberation', especially amongst liberal middle-class, youth and anti-colonialist cultures. It was felt that in a world so obviously full of inequality and exploitation, the 'scientific' image of the sociologist was a dismal abdication of moral consciousness – a cop-out. Indeed, the very idea that social science could be 'above' the clash of political movements, or that it could be 'value-free' in its consequences, was denounced as being part of the dominant ideology of the Western, capitalist, patriarchal system. That ideology was militantly challenged by revolutionary sociologists, who were quite happy to see their 'scientific' endeavours as part and parcel of *this* world, not some bucolic ideal of middle-class isolates from reality. Instead of asking for objective studies of the social world – a sheer impossibility – revolutionaries wanted to know: 'Whose side are you on?' If sociology really matters, they argued, sociologists have to get off the fence and throw in their efforts with emancipatory movements.

This kind of model for sociology was very influential. First of all, Marxist sociological thought was revived under its influence, then feminist sociology; indeed, the postcolonial movement in critical social thought described above is the most current version of the emancipatory project. It remains a powerful source of motivation. After all, we do not take up a subject such as sociology thinking that we will be treating our subject matter in the same way as an astronomer regards cosmic bodies, or in the way a chemist looks at molecules. Sociologists are always *an active part* of the world they study, and a concern with simply making the world a better, more equal, peaceful and humanly fulfilled place is often what draws students to the subject. The world today certainly contains many social problems, puzzlements and multiple forms of oppression to keep us busy and motivated. If the sociologist cannot contribute, through knowledge, research and argument, to the wider goal of human emancipation for all, then it is hard to know why he or she has *not* gone into astronomy or chemistry.

A final point here would be that simply in terms of the vitality of the discipline, it is usually the new emancipatory perspectives, rather than the sober presentation of scientific findings, which stimulate true interest, debate and enquiry in sociology. The most obvious example of this in recent times is feminist sociology. Sociology was probably the most hospitable of the academic disciplines towards feminist thought after the latter revived, militantly, in the later 1960s, but even so, the predominantly male culture of sociology departments (exemplified by leading male 'names' in the discipline) took quite some time to change, and feminists encountered – still do encounter – resistance to their 'emancipatory' work. Though by no means completely 'feminised', sociology today probably no longer 'ghetto-ises' feminist work, it being widely accepted that gender is not just one corner of the subject matter, but that all corners of the subject matter have a crucial gender dimension. Without the strong emancipatory impulse behind feminism, it would not have made that kind of impact on the very nature and practice of sociology.

The professional

In the world of the 1990s, the image of the sociologist as a *professional*, rather than as a scientist or a revolutionary has strongly come to the fore. In a situation in which students and their families pay hefty fees for their education, and where there is a very competitive market for jobs and careers, both the ideal of a pure analyst and that of a world-transforming activist, could be regarded as a little luxurious or even escapist. The reality is that the skills and knowledge acquired through sociology must be pertinent to the kinds of employment available to graduates. And even when a sociology-relevant occupation has been attained, most sociologists are engaged in mediating, or at best *reforming*, society rather than changing it altogether or looking down on it from a lofty height.

This change in the image of what it is to be a sociologist goes along with the shift in emphasis in New Zealand and elsewhere over the last decades from the notion of *education*, something that is intrinsically valuable in its own right, to that of *training*. 'Training' signals a process that from the outset sees the acquisition of knowledge as geared to the particular needs of the prevailing forms of economic life, and likely employment prospects within that economy. Indeed, the acquisition of knowledge is, in reality, the acquisition of *credentials*, the kind of credentials that will – it is hoped – take their holders into one of a variety of middle-strata occupations. In the case of the sociologist, this type of professional role will most likely be in the following sorts of area:

- research for public or private agencies, where information is needed about the social constituencies with which the organisation has to deal;
- human resources, where organisations require the people-skills and communicational abilities of sociologists to identify and reconcile different perspectives on issues;
- policy analysis, where the conceptual and analytical skills of sociologists, and their awareness of the problems and potentials of informational data combine to deliver strategic 'big pictures' and identify strategic problems.

Some 'revolutionaries' and 'scientists' would maintain that, in those sorts of role, the sociologist becomes merely a functionary of the system, offering no real independent or emancipatory perspective on the world around us. Her/his job becomes one of simply oiling the wheels of the existing order. The 'professional's' response to this is that, actually, this is what most sociologists always have done, because sociology is inevitably *part of* modern society, and sociologists must, obviously, get jobs like anyone else if they are to thrive and survive. And anyway, the professional would go on to argue, sociologists *can* improve and change society and its institutions, and modestly 'enlighten' others around them. But the emphasis here is on the modesty of the ambitions to change things. Sociologists must be like anyone else, realistic, and must, like everyone else, simply contribute what they can, where they can. Any greater ambition involves either romanticism or delusions of grandeur.

Conclusion

We do not propose to sum up or close the debate on the issues raised in this chapter. Whether and to what extent the issues of postmodernity, postcoloniality and feminism are transforming the traditional sociological perspective; whether a sociological perspective is truly relevant to our experience and understanding of contemporary life, and what sort of role and self-image is the best for sociologists to adopt – these issues are ones involving a great deal of on-going discussion, research and personal evaluation. Accordingly, as is the case with many of the other vital sociological matters raised in this book, we think it is appropriate for us to hand the issues on to you, the students and teachers, for it is you who will take forward the challenge of developing the general relevance of sociology in the specific context of Aotearoa/New Zealand.

? Study questions

16.1 According to postmodern theorists, what are the key features of postmodernity? To what extent do you think these aspects of 'postmodern' life have displaced modernity?

16.2 Do the critiques of postmodernists mean that the sociological classics are no longer relevant?

16.3 What is the problem with Eurocentrism within sociological theory?

16.4 What is postcolonialism and what is its relevance for sociological theory?

16.5 Which of the three images of the sociologist do you find most appealing and why? Can you propose any other plausible self-images for us to adopt?

Further reading

Du Plessis, R. and Alice, L. (eds). (1998) *Feminist Thought in Aotearoa New Zealand: Connections and Differences*. Oxford University Press, Auckland.

Easton, B. (1997) *The Commercialisation of New Zealand*. Auckland University Press, Auckland.

Kelsey, J. (1995) *The New Zealand Experiment*. Auckland University Press/Bridget Williams Books, Auckland.

Marshall, G. (1986) *In Praise of Sociology*, Unwin Hyman, London.

Mongia, P. (ed.). (1996) *Contemporary Postcolonial Theory: A Reader*. Arnold, London.

Ritzer, G. (1993) *The McDonaldization of Society*. Pine Forge Press, Thousand Oaks, Ca.

Rosenau, P.M. (1992) *Post-modernism and the Social Sciences*. Routledge, London.

Smart, B. (1993) *Postmodernity*. Routledge, London.

Spoonley, P. et al. (eds). (1996) *Nga Patai: Ethnic Relations and Racism in Aotearoa New Zealand*. Dunmore Press, Palmerston North.

Walker, R.J.I. (1990) *Ka Whawhai Tonu Matou: Struggle Without End*. Penguin, Auckland.

References

Abbott, P. and Wallace, C. (1990) *An Introduction to Sociology: Feminist Perspectives.* Routledge, London.

Acker, S. (1994) *Gendered Education.* Open University Press, Buckingham.

Aggleton, P. (1990) *Health.* Routledge, London.

Anderson, P. and Davey, K. (1996) A Farewell to Keynes. *New Statesman and Society*, 23 February: 29–31.

Ashcroft, B., Griffiths, G. and Tiffen, H. (eds). (1995) *The Post-Colonial Studies Reader.* Routledge, London.

Australian Bureau of Statistics. (1994) *How Australians Use Their Time.* Cat. no. 4153.0. ABS, Canberra.

Austrin, T. (1994) Work. In Spoonley, P., Pearson, D. and Shirley, I. (eds) *New Zealand Society: A Sociological Introduction*, 2nd ed., pp. 237–252. Dunmore Press, Palmerston North.

Awatere, D. (1984) *Maori Sovereignty.* Broadsheet Publications, Auckland.

Backett, K. (1982) *Mothers and Fathers: A Study of the Development and Negotiation of Parental Behaviour.* Macmillan, London.

Bahro, R. (1986) *Building the Green Movement.* New Society Publishers, Philadelphia.

Barker, M. (1981) *The New Racism.* Junction Books, London.

Barnes, L. (1991) HRT Suggested for all Women. *New Zealand Doctor, 7*: 1. October.

Barnett, J. (1995) *The Fractured Metropolis: Improving the New City, Restoring the Old, Reshaping the Region.* Harper Collins, New York.

Bauman, Z. (1990) *Thinking Sociologically: An Introduction for Everyone.* Blackwell, Oxford.

Bauman, Z. (1998) *Globalization: The Human Consequences.* Polity Press, Cambridge.

Beauregard, R. (1986) The Chaos and Complexity of Gentrification. In Smith, N. and Williams, P. (eds) *Gentrification of the City*, pp. 35–55. Unwin Hyman, Boston.

Bedggood, D. (1980) *Rich and Poor in New Zealand: A Critique of Class, Politics and Ideology.* George Allen and Unwin, Auckland.

Bell, C. (1996) *Inventing New Zealand: Everyday Myths of Pakeha Identity.* Penguin, Auckland.

Billig, M. (1995) *Banal Nationalism*. Sage, London.

Bilton, T., Bonnett, K., Jones, P., Skinner, D., Stanworth, M. and Webster, A. (1996) *Introductory Sociology*. Macmillan, Basingstoke.

Bittman, M. and Pixley, J. (1997) *The Double Life of the Family: Myth, Hope and Experience*. Allen and Unwin, St Leonards.

Blumer, H. (1995) Social Movements. In Lyman, S. (ed.) *Social Movements: Critiques, Concepts and Case-Studies*, pp. 60–83. Macmillan, London.

Bourdieu, P. (1974) The school as a conservative force: Scholastic and Cultural Inequalities in Contemporary Research. In Eggleston, J. (ed.) *The Sociology of Education*, pp. 32–46. Methuen, London.

Bourne, L. (1993) The Demise of Gentrification? A Commentary and Prospective View. *Urban Geography, 14*(1): 95–107.

Bowles, S. and Gintis, H. (1976) *Schooling in Capitalist America*. Routledge, London.

Brannen, J. and Moss, P. (1987) Dual Earner Households: Women's Financial Contributions After Birth of the First Child. In Brannen, J. and Wilson, G. (eds) *Give and Take in Families*. Allen and Unwin, London.

Braverman, H. (1974) *Labour and Monopoly Capital: the Degradation of Work in the Twentieth Century*. Monthly Review Press, London.

Brunt, T. (1973) In Search of Values. In Edwards, B (ed.) *Right Out*. A.H. Reed, Wellington.

Burdess, N. (1996) Class and Health. In Gribich, C. (ed.) *Health in Australia: Sociological Concepts and Issues*, pp. 163–187. Prentice Hall, Sydney.

Callinicos, A. (1999) *Social Theory: An Historical Introduction*. Polity Press, Cambridge.

Campbell, A. (1981) *Girl Delinquents*. Blackwell, Oxford.

Campbell, A. (1986) *The Girls in the Gang*. Blackwell, Oxford.

Campbell, G. (1998) For Richer or Poorer. *Listener,* 8 August: 18–21.

Capra, F. (1982) *The Turning Point*. Fontana, Glasgow.

Capra, F. and Spretnak, C. (1986) *Green Politics: The Global Promise*. Bear and Co., Santa Fe, New Mexico.

Castells, M. (1996) *The Rise of the Network Society*. Blackwell, Cambridge, Ma.

Chapple, G. (1994) Losing the Middle Ground. *Sunday Star-Times,* 13 March.

Chapple , G. (1997) Vanishing Greens. *Listener,* 1 February: 7.

Chettley, A. and Mintzes, B. (eds). (1992) *Promoting Health or Pushing Drugs?: A Critical Examination of Marketing Pharmaceuticals*. Health Action International, Amsterdam.

Cheyne, C., O'Brien, M. and Belgave, M. (1997) *Social Policy in Aotearoa/ New Zealand*. Oxford University Press, Auckland.

Chodorow, N. (1978) *The Reproduction of Mothering: Psychoanalysis and the Sociology of Gender.* University of California Press, Berkeley.

Clarke, M. (1992) The Nature of Business Crime. In Giddens, A. (ed.) *Human Societies: An Introductory Reader in Sociology*, pp. 41–46. Polity Press. Cambridge.

Codd, J. (1988) The Case Against TOSCA: Psychometric, Ethical or Political? In Olssen, M. (ed.) *Mental Testing in New Zealand: Critical and Oppositional Perspectives*, pp. 252–270. University of Otago Press, Dunedin.

Coney, S. (1988) *The Unfortunate Experiment: The Full Story Behind the Inquiry into Cervical Cancer Treatment.* Penguin Books, Auckland.

Coney, S. (1992) The Exploitation of Fear: Hormone Replacement Therapy and the Menopausal Women. In Davis, P. (ed.) *For Health or Profit? Medicine, the Pharmaceutical Industry, and the State in New Zealand*, pp. 179–207. Oxford University Press, Auckland.

Connell, R.W. (1987) *Gender and Power.* Allen and Unwin, Sydney.

Corbett, J., du Chateau, C., Burge, K., Boland, M.J. and Knight, R. (1998) Which Failed – System or Kids? *New Zealand Herald*, 29–30 August: H1–H2.

Coyle, D. (1997) We Need New Ways to Measure the 'Weightless' Economy. *The Independent*, 6 February: 24.

Daniel, C. (1998) The Concise NewLabourspeak. *New Statesman*, 1 May: 28–34.

Davidson, C. (1992) Green Politics – A Fresh Green Breast of the New World? *Department of Sociology Working Paper No. 11*. University of Canterbury Press. June.

Davis, P. (1982a) Stratification and Class. In Spoonley, P., Pearson, D. and Shirley, I. (eds) *New Zealand: Sociological Perspectives*, pp. 119–141. Dunmore Press, Palmerston North.

Davis, P. (1982b) Health and Health Care. In Spoonley, P., Pearson, D. and Shirley, I. (eds) *New Zealand: Sociological Perspectives*, pp. 217–237. Dunmore Press, Palmerston North.

Davis, P. (ed.). (1992) *For Health or Profit? Medicine, the Pharmaceutical Industry, and the State in New Zealand.* Oxford University Press, Auckland.

Delphy, C. and Leonard, D. (1992) *Familiar Exploitation: A New Analysis of Marriage in Contemporary Western Societies.* Polity Press, Cambridge.

Department of Social Welfare. (1998) *Discussion Document – Code of Social and Family Responsibility.* Wellington.

Donaldson, A. (1991) Oestrogen ... the Menopause Miracle. *New Zealand Women's Day*, 20 February: 28–29.

Doyal, L. and Pennell, I. (1979) *The Political Economy of Health.* Pluto Press, London.

Du Plessis, R. (1994) Gender. In Spoonley, P., Pearson, D. and Shirley, I. (eds) *New Zealand Society: A Sociological Introduction*, 2nd ed., pp. 98–112. Dunmore Press, Palmerston North.

Dunning, E. and Rojek, C. (eds). (1992) *Sport and Leisure in the Civilising Process: Critique and Counter-Critique*. Macmillan, Basingstoke.

Dunstall, G. (1981) The Social Pattern. In Oliver, W. (ed.) *The Oxford History of New Zealand*, pp. 396–429. Oxford University Press, Wellington.

Dupuis, A. (1997) Housing Wealth and Inheritance: A Theoretical and Empirical Exploration. PhD Thesis. University of Canterbury, Christchurch.

Dupuis, A. and Thorns, D.C. (1997) Regional Variations in Housing Wealth. *Urban Policy and Research, 15*(3): 189–202.

Durie, M. (1994) *Whaiora: Maori Health Development*. Oxford University Press, Auckland.

Durie-Hall, D. (1993) Whanau, Hapu, Iwi. In Coney, S. (ed.) *Standing in the Sunshine*, pp. 68–69. Penguin Books, Auckland.

Durkheim, E. (1961) *Moral Education: A Study in the Theory and Application of the Sociology of Education*. Free Press, Glencoe.

Easton, B. (1995) Poverty in New Zealand: 1981–1993. *New Zealand Sociology, 10*(2): 182–213.

Elizabeth, V. (1997) Something Old, Something Borrowed, Something New: Heterosexual Cohabitation as Marriage Resistance? – A Feminist Deconstruction. PhD Thesis. University of Canterbury, Aotearoa/New Zealand.

Engels, F. (1884) *The Origins of the Family, Private Property and the State*. International, New York.

Fanon, F. (1970) *Black Skin, White Masks*. Paladin, London.

Farquhar, C. (1991) The Facts and Fallacies of Hormone Replacement Review of The Menopause Industry. *New Zealand Doctor*, 21 October: 40.

Featherstone, M. (1987) Leisure, Symbolic Power and the Life Course. In Horne, J. (ed.) *Sport, Leisure and Social Relations*. Routledge, London.

Ferguson, G. (1994) *Building the New Zealand Dream*. Dunmore Press, Palmerston North.

Field, F. (1997) The Underclass of 97. *New Statesman, 17*: 30–31. January.

Filion, P. (1991) The Gentrification-Social Structure Dialectic: A Toronto Case Study. *International Journal of Urban and Regional Research, 15*(4): 553–574.

Fiske, J. (1998) Surveilling the City. Whiteness, the Black Man and Democratic Totalitarianism. *Theory, Culture and Society, 15*(2): 67–88.

Fleming, R. (1997) *The Common Purse: Income Sharing in New Zealand Families*. Auckland University Press/Bridget Williams Books, Auckland.

Fleming, R. and Kell Easting, S. (1994) *Couples, Households and Money: Report of the Pakeha Component of the Intra Family Income Study.* Intra Family Income Project, Wellington.

Foucault, M. (1977) *Discipline and Punish.* Allen Lane, London.

Fougere, G. (1989) Sport, Culture and Identity: the Case of Rugby Football. In Novitz, D. and Wilmott, B. (eds) *Culture and Identity in New Zealand,* pp. 110–122. GP Books, Wellington.

Fougere, G. (1994) Health. In Spoonley, P., Pearson, D. and Shirley, I. (eds) *New Zealand Society: A Sociological Introduction,* 2nd ed., pp. 146–160. Dunmore Press, Palmerston North.

Frey, J. (1986) Labor Issues in the Gaming Industry. *Nevada Public Affairs Review, 2:* 32–37.

Gale, D. (1979) Middle Class Resettlement in Older Urban Neighborhoods. *Journal of the American Planning Association,* 45: 293–304.

Gamson, W. (1992) *Talking Politics.* Cambridge University Press. Cambridge.

Garber, M. (1992) *Vested Interests: Cross-Dressing and Cultural Anxiety.* Routledge, New York.

Giddens, A. (ed.). (1992) *Human Societies: An Introductory Reader in Sociology.* Polity Press, Cambridge.

Giddens, A. (1993) *Sociology,* 2nd ed. Polity Press, London.

Giddens, A. (1997) *Sociology,* 3rd ed. Polity Press, London.

Giddens, A. (1999a) Lecture One: Globalisation. http://news.bbc.co.uk/hi/english/static/events/reith_99/week1/lecture1.htm

Giddens, A. (1999b) Runaway World. http://news.bbc.co.uk/hi/english/static/events/reith_99/default.htm

Gidlow, B. (1993) The Sociology of Leisure. In Perkins, H. and Cushman, G. (eds) *Leisure, Recreation and Tourism,* pp. 157–170. Longman Paul, Auckland.

Gilroy, P. (1990) One Nation Under a Groove: The Cultural Politics of 'Race' and Racism in Britain. In Goldberg, D.T. (ed.) *Anatomy of Racism,* pp. 263–282. University of Minnesota Press, Minneapolis.

Glass, R. (1964) *London: Aspects of Change.* MacGibbon, London.

Glennerster, H. (1998) Priorities for Welfare. *The Times Higher Education Supplement,* 7 August.

Glezer, H. and Mills, E. (1991) Controlling the Purse Strings. *Family Matters, 29:* 35–36.

Goffman, E. (1967) Where the Action Is. In *Interaction Ritual: Essays on Face-to-Face Behaviour.* Penguin, Harmondsworth.

Goldberg, D.T. (1993) *Racist Culture.* Blackwell, Oxford.

Gooding-Williams, R. (ed.). (1993) *Reading Rodney King/Reading Urban Uprising.* Routledge, New York.

Goodman, R. (1995) *The Luck Business: The Devastating Consequences and Broken Promises of America's Gambling Explosion.* Free Press, New York.

Gray, J. (1998a) Triumph of the West. *New Statesman,* 1 May: 54–55.

Gray, J. (1998b) *False Dawn: The Delusions of Global Capitalism.* Granta, London.

Green, E., Hebron, S. and Woodward, D. (1990) *Women's Leisure, What Leisure?* Macmillan, Basingstoke.

Hall, S. (1995) New Ethnicities. In Ashcroft, B., Griffiths, G. and Tiffen, H. (eds.) *The Post-Colonial Studies Reader,* pp. 223–227. Routledge, London.

Hamnett, C. and Randolph, B. (1986) Tenurial Transformation and the Flat Break-up Market in London: The British Condo Experience. In Smith, N. and Williams, P. (eds) *Gentrification of the City,* pp. 121–152. Unwin Hyman, Boston.

Hamnett, C., Harmer, M. and Williams, P. (1990) *Safe as Houses: Housing Inheritance in Britain.* Paul Chapman, London.

Hannigan, J. A. (1995a) Introduction: Postmodernism and Contemporary Society. *Current Sociology,* 43(1): 155–164.

Hannigan, J.A. (1995a) The Postmodern City. *Current Sociology,* 43(1): 165–224.

Haralambos, M., Van Kriekan, R., Smith, P., and Holborn, M. (1996) *Sociology: Themes and Perspectives,* Australian ed. Longman, Melbourne.

Harvey, D. (1973) *Social Justice and the City.* Blackwell, Oxford.

Harvey, D. (1978) The Urban Process under Capitalism. A Framework for Analysis. *International Journal of Urban and Regional Research,* 2(1): 101–132.

Harvey, D. (1982) *The Limits to Capital.* Basil Blackwell, Oxford.

Harvey, L. and MacDonald, M. (1993) *Doing Sociology: A Practical Introduction.* Macmillan, Basingstoke.

Heidensohn, F. (1985) *Women and Crime.* Macmillan, London.

Henderson, H. (1978) *Creating Alternative Futures.* Perigee, New York.

Henderson, H. (1988) *The Politics of the Solar Age.* Knowledge Systems Inc., Indiana.

Hunt, S., Benford, R. and Snow, D. (1994) Identity Fields: Framing Processes and the Social Construction of Movement Identities. In Johnston, H. and Gusfield, J. (eds) *New Social Movements: From Ideology to Identity,* pp. 185–208. Temple University Press, Philadelphia.

Illich, I. (1971) *Deschooling Society.* Harper and Row, New York.

Illich, I. (1975) *Limits to Medicine.* Calder and Boyars, London.

Jacobs, J. (1961) *The Death and Life of Great American Cities.* Penguin, Harmondsworth.

James, B. and Saville-Smith, K. (1989) *Gender, Culture and Power: Challenging New Zealand's Gendered Culture.* Oxford University Press, Auckland.

Jasper, J. (1997) *The Art of Moral Protest: Culture, Biography and Creativity in Social Movements.* University of Chicago Press, Chicago.

Jelliffe, D. and Jelliffe, E. (1977) The Infant Food Industry and International Child Health. *International Journal of Health Services, 72*: 249–250.

Jencks. (1996) The City That Never Sleeps. *New Statesman,* 28 June: 26–28.

Jensen, A. (1971) *Educational Differences.* Methuen, London.

Johnson, P. (1996) Poor are Poor Because They are Stupid. *Sunday Star-Times,* 28 January.

Jones, A. (1991) Is Madonna a Feminist Folk-hero? Is Ruth Richardson a Woman? Postmodern Feminism and Dilemmas of Difference. *Sites 23*: 84–100.

Joseph Rowntree Foundation. (1995) *Inquiry into Income and Wealth.* Joseph Rowntree Foundation, York.

Karier, C. (1976) Testing for Order and Control in the Corporate Liberal State. In Dale, R., Esland, G. and McDonald, M. (eds) *Schooling and Capitalism.* Routledge and Kegan Paul.

Keck, M. and Sikkink, K. (1998) *Activists Beyond Borders: Transnational Advocacy Networks in International Politics.* Cornell University Press, Ithaca, New York.

Kelsey, J. (1995) *The New Zealand Experiment.* Auckland University Press/ Bridget Williams Books, Auckland.

King, A.D. (1991) *Global Cities.* Routledge, London.

King, M. (1985) *Being Pakeha.* Hodder Stoughton, Auckland.

Kitschelt, H. (1991) Resource Mobilization Theory: A Critique. In Rucht, D. (ed.) *Research on Social Movements: The State of the Art in Western Europe and the USA,* pp. 323–347. Campus Verlag/Westview Press, Frankfurt/Boulder, Colorado.

Lafferty, G. and McMillen, J. (1989) Labouring for Leisure: Work and Industrial Relations in the Tourism Industry: Case Studies of Casinos. *Labour and Industry, 2*(2): 32–59.

Larana, E., Johnston, H. and Gusfield, J. (eds). (1994) *New Social Movements: From Ideology to Identity.* Temple University Press, Philadelphia.

Lauder, H. and Hughes, D. (1990) Social Origins, Destinations and Educational Inequality. In Codd, J., Harker, R. and Nash, R. (eds) *Political Issues in New Zealand Education,* pp. 43–60. Dunmore Press, Palmerston North.

Lorenz, K. (1987) *The Waning of Humaneness.* Urwin Paperbacks, London.

Lupton, D. and Barclay, L. (1997) *Constructing Fatherhood: Discourses and Experiences.* Sage, London.

Lyman, S. (ed.). (1995) *Social Movements: Critiques, Concepts and Case Studies.* Macmillan, London.

Macionis, J.J. (1993) *Sociology,* 4th ed. Prentice Hall, New Jersey.

Macionis, J.J. and Plumner, K. (1998) *Sociology: A Global Introduction.* Prentice Hall, New Jersey.

Maharey, S. (1990) Understanding the Mass Media. In Spoonley, P. and Hirsch, W. *Between the Lines: Racism and the New Zealand Media*, pp. 13–25. Heinemann Reed, Auckland.

Malik, K. (1996) *The Meaning of Race, Race, History and Culture in Western Society.* Macmillan, Basingstoke

Marshall, G. (1990) *In Praise of Sociology.* Unwin Hyman, London.

Martin, W. (1995) *The Global Information Society.* Aslib Gower, Aldershot.

McAdam, D. (1982) *Political Process and the Development of Black Insurgency, 1930–1970.* University of Chicago Press, Chicago.

McAdam, D. (1994) Culture and Social Movements. In Larana, E., Johnston, H. and Gusfield, J. (eds) *New Social Movements: From Ideology to Identity*, pp. 36–57. Temple University Press, Philadelphia.

McCormick, J. and Oppenheim, C. (1996) Options for Change. *New Statesman and Society*, 26 January: 18–21.

McGrew, A. (1992) A Global Society? In Hall, S. et al. (eds) *Modernity and its Futures*, pp. 91–116. Polity Press. Cambridge.

McKeown, T. (1976) *The Role of Medicine: Dream, Mirage or Nemesis?* Nuffield Provincial Hospitals Trust, London.

McLennan, G., Held, D. and Hall, S. (eds). (1984) *The Idea of the Modern State.* Open University Press, Milton Keynes.

McMahon, M. (1995) *Engendering Motherhood: Identity and Self-transformation in Women's Lives.* Guilford Press, New York.

Meek, R. (1976) *Social Science and the Ignoble Savage.* Cambridge University Press, Cambridge.

Melucci, A. (1985) The Symbolic Challenge of Contemporary Movements. *Social Research, 54*(4): 789–815.

Messner, M.A. and Sabo, D.F. (1994) *Sex, Violence and Power in Sports: Rethinking Masculinity.* The Crossing Press, Freedom, Ca.

Mills, C.W. (1959) *The Sociological Imagination.* Oxford University Press. Oxford.

Milne, K. (1996) Tough on Criminologists. *New Statesman*, 22 November: 26–27.

Mitchell, A. (1972) *The Half Gallon, Quarter Acre, Pavlova Paradise.* Whitcombe and Tombs, Christchurch.

Morrison, P. (1995) Inner City Housing in Historical Perspective. Paper presented at the New Zealand Geographical Society Anniversary Conference. University of Canterbury. August.

Mullins, P. (1991) Tourism Urbanization. *International Journal of Urban and Regional Research, 15*(3): 326–342.

Multiple Risk Factor Intervention Trial Group. (1982) The Multiple Intervention Risk Factor Intervention Trial – Risk Factor Changes and Mortality Results. *Journal of the American Medical Association, 248*: 1465–1476.

Murdock, G. (1949) *Social Structure.* Macmillan, New York.

Nash, R. (1997) *Inequality/Difference: A Sociology of Education.* ERDC Press, Massey University, Palmerston North.

Navarro, V. (1978) *Class Struggle, the State and Medicine.* Martin Robertson, London.

Nettleton, S. (1995) *The Sociology of Health and Illness.* Polity Press, Cambridge.

Newbold, G. (1992) *Crime and Deviance.* Oxford University Press, Auckland.

Oakley, A. (1974) *The Sociology of Housework.* Martin Robertson, London.

Offe, C. (1985) New Social Movements: Challenging the Boundaries of Institutional Politics. *Social Research, 52*(4): 817–867.

O'Leary, E. and Roberts, N. (1985) Bad track record. *NZ Listener,* June 15.

Pagnucco, R. and Atwood, D. (1994) Global Strategies for Peace and Justice. *Peace Review, 6*: 411–418.

Pahl, J. (1989) *Money and Marriage.* MacMillan Education, Basingstoke.

Pahl, R.E. (1975) *Whose City?* Penguin, Harmondsworth.

Pakulski, J. (1991) *Social Movements: The Politics of Moral Protest.* Longman Cheshire, Melbourne.

Papadakis, E. (1984) *The Green Movement in West Germany.* Croom and Helm, London.

Parkin, S. (1984) *Green Parties: An International Guide.* Heretic Books, London.

Parsons, T. (1951) *The Social System.* Free Press, Glencoe.

Parsons, T. (1959) The School Class as a Social System: Some of its Functions in American Society. *Harvard Educational Review, 29*: 297–318.

Paxman, J. (1998) *The English.* Michael Joseph, London.

Pearson, D. and Sissons, J. (1997) Pakeha and Never Pakeha. *Sites 35*: 64–80.

Pere, R. (1984) Te Oranga o te Whanau: The Health of the Family. In *Hui Whakaoranga Maori Health Planning Workshop.* Department of Health, Wellington.

Perkins, H.C. and Cushman, G. (eds). (1993) *Leisure, Recreation and Tourism.* Longman Paul, Auckland.

Petersen, A. (1994) *In a Critical Condition: Health and Power Relations in Australia.* Allen and Unwin, Sydney.

Pool, I. (1991) *Te Iwi Maori: A New Zealand Population Past, Present and Projected*. Auckland University Press, Auckland.

Population Division of the Department of Economic and Social Affairs of the United Nations Secretariat. (1999) *The World at Six Billion*. (ESA/P/WP.154, 12 October 1999.)
http://www.undp.org/popin/wdtrends/urb/urb/urbpcf.htm

Porrit, J. (1989) *Seeing Green: The Politics of Ecology Explained*. Basil Blackwell, Oxford.

Porrit, J. and Winner, D. (1988) *The Coming of the Greens*. Fontana Collins, Glasgow.

Powles, J. (1971) On the Limitations of Modern Medicine. *Science, Medicine and Man, 1*: 1–30.

Pratt, J. (1994) Crime, Deviance and Punishment. In Spoonley, P., Pearson, D. and Shirley, I. (eds) *New Zealand Society: A Sociological Introduction*, 2nd ed., pp. 213–236. Dunmore Press, Palmerston North.

Rainbow, S. (1989) New Zealand's Values Party: The Rise and Fall of the First National Green Party. In Hay, P., Eckersley, R. and Holloway, G. (eds) *Environmental Politics in Australia and New Zealand*. Centre for Environmental Studies, Tasmania.

Rainbow, S. (1991) The Greens and the 1990 New Zealand General Election, *Sites, 22*: 87–95.

Rainbow, S. (1993) *Green Politics*. Oxford University Press, Auckland.

Rex, J. and Moore, R. (1967) *Race, Community and Conflict*. Oxford University Press, London.

Ritzer, G. (1993) *The McDonaldisation of Society: An Investigation into the Changing Character of Contemporary Social Life*. Pine Forge Press, Thousand Oaks.

Rodger, J. (1996) *Family Life and Social Control: A Sociological Perspective*. Macmillan, Handsmill, Basingstoke.

Rojek, C. (1993) *Ways of Escape: Modern Transformations in Leisure and Travel*. Macmillan, Basingstoke.

Rose, D. (1988) A Feminist Perspective on Employment Restructuring and Gentrification: The Case of Montreal. In Dear, M. and Wolch, J. (eds) *The Power of Geography*, pp. 118–138. Unwin Hyman, Boston.

Rudig, W. and Lowe, P. (1986) The Withered 'Greening' of British Politics: A Study of the Ecology Party. *Political Studies, XXXIV*: 262–284.

Saegert, S. (1980) Masculine Cities and Feminine Suburbs: Polarized Ideas, Contradictory Realities. *Signs: Journal of Women in Culture and Society, 5*(3): S96–S111.

Sassen, S. (1991) *The Global City: New York, London, Tokyo*. Princeton University Press, Princeton.

Saunders, P. (1990) *A Nation of Home Owners*. Allen and Unwin, London.

Savage, M. and Warde, A. (1993) *Urban Sociology, Capitalism and Modernity.* Macmillan, London.

Scott, A. (1990) *Ideology and the New Social Movements.* Unwin Hyman, London.

Scott, J.W. (1988) Deconstructing Equality-Versus-Difference: Or, The Uses of Poststructuralist Theory For Feminism. *Feminist Studies 14*(1): 33–50.

Scull, A.T. (1992) The Social Control of the Mad. In Giddens, A. (ed.) *Human Societies. An Introductory Reader in Sociology.* Polity Press, Cambridge.

Seabrook, J. (1982) *Unemployment.* Quartet Books, London.

Seabrook, J. (1995) Of Human Bondage. *New Statesman and Society,* 19 May: 22–23.

Short, J.R. (1996) *The Urban Order. An Introduction to Cities, Culture and Power.* Blackwell, Oxford.

Skolnick, J. (1978) *House of Cards: Legalisation and the Control of Casino Gambling.* Little, Brown and Company, Boston.

Smart, C. (1976) *Women, Crime and Criminology.* Routledge, London.

Smelser, N. (1962) *Theory of Collective Behaviour.* Routledge and Kegan Paul, London.

Smelser, N. (1994) *Sociology.* Blackwell, Oxford.

Smith, M.P. and Tardanico, R. (1996) Urban Theory Reconsidered: Production, Reproduction and Collective Action. In Smith, M.P. and Feagin, J.R. (eds) *The Capitalist Society, Global Restructuring and Community Politics,* pp. 87–110. Basil Blackwell, Oxford.

Smith, N. (1987) On Yuppies and Housing: Gentrification, Social Restructuring and the Urban Dream. *Environment and Planning D, Society and Space, 5*(2): 151–172.

Smith, N. and Williams, P. (eds). (1986) *Gentrification of the City.* Unwin Hyman, Boston.

Spector, M. and Kitsuse, J. (1987) *Constructing Social Problems.* Aldine de Gruter, New York.

Spoonley, P., Pearson, D. and Shirley, I. (eds). (1994) *New Zealand Society: A Sociological Introduction.* Dunmore Press, Palmerston North.

Spretnak, C. (1986) *The Spiritual Dimension of Green Politics.* Bear and Company, Santa Fe.

Statistics New Zealand. (1999) *New Zealand Now: Women.* Statistics New Zealand, Wellington.

Stilwell, F. (1993) *Reshaping Australia: Urban Problems and Policies.* Pluto Press, Leichhart, NSW.

Swift, R. (1987) What if the Greens Achieved Power? *New Internationalist,* May.

Tarrow, S. (1998) *Power in Movement: Social Movements and Contentious Politics*, 2nd ed. Cambridge University Press, Cambridge.

The Press (1990, 16 June) Greens Politicos Have Opportunity to be Groundswell Alternative?

Thompson, W. and Hickey, J. (1994) *Society in Focus: An Introduction to Sociology.* Harper Collins, New York.

Thorns, D. (1973) *Suburbia.* Paladin, St. Albans, Herts.

Thorns, D. (1992) *Fragmenting Societies?* Routledge, London.

Thorns, D. (1994) Urban. In Spoonley, P., Pearson, D. and Shirley, I. (eds) *New Zealand Society: A Sociological Introduction*, 2nd ed., pp. 39–54. Dunmore Press, Palmerston North.

Thorns, D. (1997) The Global Meets the Local: Tourism and the Representation of the New Zealand City. *Urban Affairs Review*, 33(2): 189–208. November.

Tietjens Meyers, D. (1997) *Feminist Social Thought: A Reader.* Routledge, London.

Tokar, B. (1987) *The Green Alternative: Creating an Ecological Future.* R.E. Miles Publishing, San Pedro.

Tokar, B. (1991) Eco-apocalyptics. *New Internationalist*, August.

Touraine, A. (1971) *The Post-Industrial Society.* Translated by Leonard Mayhem. Random House, New York.

Touraine, A. (1981) *The Voice and the Eye: An Analysis of Social Movements.* Cambridge University Press, New York.

Townsend, P. (1979) *Poverty in the United Kingdom: A Survey of Household Resources and Standards of Living.* Penguin, Harmondsworth.

United Nations Population Division – *see* Population Division of …

Valentine, G. (1989) Women s Fear and the Design of Public Space. *Built Environment*, 16(4): 288–303.

Vance, C. (1989) Social Construction Theory: Problems in the History of Sexuality. In *Homosexuality, Which Homosexuality?* pp. 13–34. GMP Publishers, London.

Wacjman, J. (1994) Technology as Masculine Culture. In *The Polity Reader in Gender Studies*, pp. 216–225. Polity Press, Cambridge.

Walby, S. (1994) Towards a Theory of Patriarchy. In *The Polity Reader in Gender Studies*. Polity Press, Cambridge.

Walzer, S. (1996) Thinking About the Baby: Gender and Division of Infant Care. *Social Problems*, 43(2): 219–234.

Waring, M. (1988) *Counting for Nothing: What Men Value and What Women are Worth.* Allen and Unwin, Wellington.

Wekerle, G.R. (1980) Women in the Urban Environment Signs. *Journal of Woman in Culture and Society*, 5(3): S188–S214.

Whittier, N. (1995) *Feminist Generations: The Persistence of the Radical Women's Movement.* Temple University Press, Philadelphia.

Wilkes, C. (1994) Class. In Spoonley, P., Pearson, D. and Shirley, I. (eds) *New Zealand Society: A Sociological Introduction,* 2nd ed., pp. 66–80. Dunmore Press, Palmerston North.

Wilkinson, R. (1996) *Unhealthy Societies: The Afflictions of Inequality.* Routledge, London and New York.

Williams, P. (1986) Class Constitution Through Spatial Reconstruction? A Re-evaluation of Gentrification in Australia, Britain and the United States. In Smith, N. and Williams, P. (eds) *Gentrification of the City,* pp. 56–77. Unwin Hyman, Boston.

Williams, R. (1983) Concepts of Health: An Analysis of Lay Logic. *Sociology,* 17: 185–204.

Willis, E. (1994) *Illness and Social Relations: Issues in the Sociology of Health Care.* Allen and Unwin, Sydney.

Willis, E. (1999) *The Sociological Quest: An Introduction to the Study of Social Life,* 3rd ed. Allen and Unwin, St. Leonards.

Winstanley, A. (1995) Women's Experiences of Gentrification in Mount Victoria, Wellington (New Zealand), MA Thesis. University of Canterbury.

World Health Organisation. (1985) *Targets for Health for All.* W.H.O. Regional Office for Europe.

Zaretski, E. (1976) *Capitalism, the Family and Personal Life.* Harper and Row, New York.

Zimbardo, P. (1990) Pathology of Imprisonment. In Anderson, J. and Ticci, M. (eds) *Society and Social Science: A Reader.* The Open University, Milton Keynes.

Zukin, S. (1987) Gentrification: Culture and Capital in the Urban Core. *Annual Review of Sociology,* 13: 129–147.

Zukin, S. (1991) *Landscapes of Power: From Detroit to Disney World.* University of California Press, Berkeley.

Index

absolutism, 55
abstentionism, 36
abstracting, 15, 31
accountability, 35
achievement
motivation, 80
school, 101–10
Acker, Sandra, 100
Addams, Jane, 45
affective individualism, 83
affluent society, 49, 153
diseases of, 217
age
and employment, 132–3, 150
and leisure pursuits, 279
agricultural society, 22, 23
AIDS, 225–6, 230
Alexander, Jeffrey, 56
alienation, 29–30
anarchic capitalism, 153
ancient, or slave, mode of production, 28
anomie, 40, 295
Australian Time Use Survey, 86–7
Austrin, Terry, 127–30
Awatere, Donna, *Maori Sovereignty*, 197

baby boomers, 132–3
Backett, Kathryn, 81–2
Bahro, Rudolf, 268
Banton, Michael, 205
Baudrillard, Jean, 287
Bauman, Z., 236, 248
Becker, Howard, 240
Bedggood, David, *Rich and Poor in New Zealand*, 142
behaviouralism, 218
The Bell Curve, 195

biculturalism, 197, 201, 202–4
Big Brother, 157–8, 163
Binet, Alfred, 102
biological reductionism, 213
biomedical model, 213–14
blue-collar crime, 238, 239, 241
body beautiful, 73–5
Bourdieu, Pierre, 56, 105, 280
bourgeoisie, 295
Bowles and Gintis, *Schooling in Capitalist America*, 99
Brazilianization, 150
bureaucratic rationality, 35, 36, 38, 297–8
Burke, Edmund, 22

calculability, 35, 297
Campbell, Ann, 248
capitalism, 26, 29–31, 34–5, 39, 42, 45, 46, 49,
51, 117, 119, 131, 163, 293–5
anarchic, 153
and cities, 188–9
and class, 29, 30, 51, 131, 140–2
and crime, 238, 239, 241
disorganised, 123
and education, 99
and the family, 80–1, 82, 92
and health, 219
Capra, Fritjof, 268
careers in sociology, 2
casino dealers, 127–30
Castells, Manual, 188–9
casual labour, 119, 125, 126, 131, 132, 151,
152, 272, 295
cervical cancer, 226
Chambliss, William, 238
change, *see* social change
Chicago school era of sociology, 43–5

childbirth, medicalisation of, 227
children, 81, 82, 84
    and crime, 248, 249
Chinese Box model of systems and sub-systems, 47–8
Chodorow, Nancy, 84
choice, *see* rational choice
cities, 172–90
    global influence and local problems, 176–7
    safety in, 178–81, 189
    theorising, 187–9
    see also gentrification; suburbs; urbanisation
citizenship, 198–204
citizenship movements, 252, 253–4
civil rights, 197, 205, 252, 258
class, 28, 30, 35, 51, 137–55, 297
    housing classes, 205
    New Zealand, 141–4
    and sport and leisure, 275, 280–1
    see also middle class; working class
class conflict/struggle, 30, 51, 131, 140, 188
class consciousness, 28
class inequalities, 131, 137–55
    education, 99, 104–110
    health status, 217–18
classlessness, 141–2, 143–4
classrooms without walls, 112
Code of Social and Family Responsibility, 93–4
coherence, 25
collective action, 252–5
    semi-rational, 255, 256
collective consciousness, 32–3
collective identities, 262–4
collectivism, 30, 32–3, 34, 41, 45, 49, 51–2
colonialism, 21, 50, 142, 194, 195–7, 299, 300
    and health, 216–17
commodification, 112
communism, 26, 30, 295
community solidarity, 178–80
compensatory education, 105
competition, 29, 84, 152, 294
complexity, 25, 26, 35, 56, 256
computers, 111–15, 152, 292
Comte, Auguste, 23–6, 26

concepts, 15
    interpretative, 18
Coney, Sandra, 226, 227–8
conflict theory, 50–1
consciousness, 39, 51, 60
consumption, 7–8, 40, 82, 143, 144–7
    and cities, 182, 183, 186, 188
    passive, 98–9
content analysis, 13
control, *see* social control
Cooley, Charles, 43
Cooper, Anna Julia, 41–2
correspondence principle, 99
crime, 232–50
    blue-collar, 238–9, 241
    in cities, 180, 185, 187
    levels, 234, 237–9
    Maori, 232, 241
    Pacific Islanders, 232, 241
    white-collar, 239–41, 243–6
croissantisation of society, 184, 185
cultural capital, 105–6, 109
cultural construction of protest, 256, 258–9
cultural deprivation theories, 104–5
cultural diversity, 56, 57, 193, 291
    of cities, 174, 183
cultural hybridity, 291
cultural identity, 192–5, 198–204
cultural norms and values, *see* norms; values
cultural revolution, 19–21, 22, 40
cultural transfer, 165
culture, 39, 51, 52
    and individualism, 6
    postmodern, 291
culture of consumption, 7–8

Davidson, Carl, 265–9
Davis, Peter, 143
decolonisation, 197, 202, 203–4, 207, 208–9, 216, 300
deconstruction, 55–6
de-differentiation, 277–8
de-industrialisation, 120, 132, 152, 153, 175, 206, 207
democracy, 159, 161–4, 167, 168–9, 170, 300–1
determinism, 26
    technological, 114–15

Index 321

deviance, 232–50
    definition, 233
Dew, Kevin, 220–23
dialectic materialism, 30
differences and divisions, 9–10, 290
    cultural capital and the reproduction
      of class inequalities, 104
    defining the deviant other, 239–42
    domestic labour and control of
      household income, 86–92
    health status, 214–23
    ideological conflict in social
      movements, 264–9
    inner city and outer suburbs, 184–7
    men, women and violence, 70–3
    a racist society?, 205–7
    significance of class, 140–7
    sport and leisure, 278–85
    theorising democracy, 161–4
    theorising racism and ethnicity, 207–9
    theorising the city, 187–9
    work and inequality, 130–4
differently abled people, sporting profile,
    278–9
differentiation
    medicine and religion, 227
    see also de-differentiation
digitisation of data, 111, 113
dioxin, 220–23
disciplinary power, 228–9
discrimination, 10, 192
Disneyland, 287
disorganised capitalism, 123
division of labour, 32, 119
    household, 81, 86–7, 121–2, 132, 298
doctor–patient interactions, 224–6
documentary sources, 12
domestic labour, 81, 86–7, 117, 121–2, 132,
    298
domestic violence, 81, 82, 241, 248, 249
drug offences, 237
dual labour market, 131–2
Du Bois, W.E.B., 41–2
Dupuis, Ann, 181–4
Durie-Hall, Donna, 78
Durkheim, Emile, 27, 31–4, 40, 47, 54, 97, 117,
    119, 178, 233, 240, 295–7, 301

eating disorders, 74–5
economic life, 116–35
economic ownership and production, 119,
    122–30, 151
    see also mode of production;
      production
economic rationalism, 93, 123, 148, 154, 199,
    236
    and crime rates, 236–9
    see also market economy
economy, 119
    informal, 121
    political, 173
    weightless, 152
education, 96–115, 303
    compensatory programmes, 105
    gender differences in, 99–100, 114–15
    inequalities in, 99–100, 104–11, 114–15
    and the information society, 111–15
    Maori, 102, 103, 106, 150–1
    Pacific Islanders, 106–10
efficiency, 35, 297
Elias, Norbert, 286
Elizabeth, Vivienne, 88–91
embourgeoisement, 153
emotion, 56
empirical facts, 33
empiricism, 20, 45, 49
employment, *see* paid work
Engels, F., 81
Enlightenment, 19–21, 22, 40
environment, 294
environmental movement, 261–2, 264–9
epistemology, 28, 30, 35, 36
Equiticorp, 244, 245
essentialism, 55
ethnic conflict, 196
ethnic revival, 200, 205
ethnicity, 41–2, 191–210
    and health status, 216, 217–18, 219
    and inequality, 138, 139, 143, 144
    New Zealand statistics, 193
    and poverty, 150–1
    and sport and leisure interests, 275,
      279–80
ethnography, 13
ethnomethodology, 54

Europe/Eurocentrism, 20–1, 26, 46, 140, 293–9, 300
evolution, 25, 26–7
  see also social evolutionism
exchange theory, 51–2

facism, 196
factual questions, 14
Fahey, Jacqueline, 180
family, 77–95
  definitions, 77, 79
  nuclear, 41, 80, 81, 92
  relationship between society and, 80
  relationships in, 82–5
  responsibility, and the state, 92–4
  roles, 81–2
  violence in, 81, 82, 241, 248, 249
Fanon, Franz, 197, 205
fashion, 40
fathers, 84–5
femininity, 61, 85, 284, 285
feminism, 21, 40–1, 45, 51, 52–3, 71, 144, 252, 253–4, 298, 302–3
  criminology, 248–9
  and education, 98, 99–100
  and family, 80, 81
  and safety in cities, 180–1
  theories of state, 163–4
Ferguson, Adam, 22–3
feudal mode of production, 28, 83
fibre optics, 111
figurational analysis, 286
fin de siècle, 40, 56–7
Fordism, 122, 135, 142, 177
Foucault, Michel, 228–30, 242
fragmentation, 99
framing collective identities, 262–4
fraud, see white-collar crime
free market, 123, 151, 169–70, 267–8, 301
French revolution, 18, 19, 23, 252

Galton, Francis, 101
gambling, 274
Gamson, William, Talking Politics, 258–9
Garfinkel, Harold, 61
gay communities, 175, 179

gay men, 9–10, 63–6, 67–70, 182, 225–6, 230, 278
families, 80
  see also homosexuality
Gemeinschaft, 178
gender, see also men; women
  and inequality, 71, 77, 81, 84, 86–92, 95, 131–2, 138, 139, 143, 144, 163–4, 298
gender assignment, 60–1
gender differences, 60–76
  education, 99–100, 114–15
  health status, 218, 219
  housework, 81, 86–7, 121–2, 132
  personal safety, 247–9
  sport and leisure, 281–5
  technology use, 114–15
gender identity, 63, 84–5
gender role, 63
gender socialisation, 63
gendered culture, 122
gentrification, 175, 181–4, 185–7
Gesellschaft, 178
ghettoes, 187–8
Giddens, Anthony, 3, 56, 71, 75, 111, 113, 138, 254
Gilman, Charlotte Perkins, 40–1, 298
glass ceilings, 132
global information society, 111–15
globalisation, 7, 56, 75, 113, 164–5, 169–70
  and cities, 174, 176–7, 189
  criminal activities, 237–9
  leisure, 277–8
  medical power, 226–30
  production, 124–5, 151, 153, 207–8
  rhetoric, 261–2
  transnational social movements, 259–62
  see also information society; labour migration
Goffman, Erving, 54
Gough, Kathleen, 79
Gramsci, Antonio, 167, 208
Green movement, 261–2, 264–9
Greenpeace, 260, 261
Gronfors, Marti, 241
groups, 51–2, 162, 254–5
  see also social movements; stratification

habitus, 105–6
Hall, Stuart, 208
hapu, 78
Harvey, David, 188
health, 211–31
    biomedical model, 213–14
    definition, 212–13
    differences and divisions in health
      status, 214–23
    holistic model, 212–13
    Maori, 206, 212–13, 216, 230
    women, 71, 217, 226, 227–9, 230
Hegel, Georg W.F., 30
hegemony, 167, 168, 208
Heidensohn, Frances, 248
heterosexuality, 9–10, 26, 63, 67–70
hidden curriculum, 98, 99
historical materialism, 29, 30
Hobsbawm, Eric, 18
holistic model of health, 213–13
holocaust, 196
home ownership, 144–7
homosexual law reform, 65–6, 247
homosexuality, 9–10, 63–6, 67–70, 80
hormone replacement therapy, 227–29
household income, management of, 87–91
households, 78, 79
housework, 81, 86–7, 117, 132, 298
housing classes, 205
human rights, 205
Hume, David, 19
hunter-gatherer stage of society, 22, 23
hyper-reality, 287, 290, 299
hypotheses, 14–15

ideas, 19
identity
    collective, 262–4
    gay, 68
    gender, 63, 84–5
    Maori, 197, 199–201
    national, 156–71, 275–6
    Pakeha, 201–4
    personal, 5, 42, 60, 84–5
    sexual, 68
    social, 290

ideological conflict in social movements,
    264–9
ideology, 36, 67
Illich, Ivan, 227
    Deschooling Society, 98–9
illness, 211–31
    see also health
imagination, 3
immigrants, 194, 197–8, 207–8
income, 121, 133, 148–9
    disposable, 272
    from home ownership, 145–7
    New Zealand, 148–9, 153, 154
    see also wages and salaries
independence, 80
independent money management (IMM), 87,
    88–91
individualism, 6, 23, 24, 34, 35, 43, 47, 52,
    138, 148, 218, 295–6
    affective, 83
    and family relationships, 82–5, 94
industrial revolution, 18–19, 120, 252
industrial society, 22, 23, 24, 25, 80, 92, 99,
    120
inequality/ies
    class, 104–110, 137–55
    and crime, 239, 241
    in education, 99–100, 104–11
    health status, 214–23
    Maori, 10
    and power, 157
    women, 71, 77, 81, 84, 86–92, 95,
      131–2, 138, 139, 143, 144, 163–4, 298
    work, 71, 81, 84, 86–92, 95, 130–4
inevitabilism, 26, 27
infant mortality rate, 214, 216
informal economy, 121, 152, 272
information poverty, 114
information society, 111–15, 126, 259–60,
    289–90, 292
inheritance, 81, 145–7
inner cities, 175, 181–4, 185–7
institutional racism, 197
institutions, 64
intellectual order, 23
intelligence, 101–4
interconnection, 6

interdependence, 94
interest groups, 162, 254–5
international law, 164
Internet, 111–14, 290
interpretation, 2, 3, 14, 18
intimacy and inequality, 77, 82–5, 86, 95
iwi, 78

Jackson, Moana, 241
Jacobs, Jane, *The Death and Life of Great American Cities*, 180
James, William, 43
Japan, 123, 134
Jasper, James, 252–3, 258, 261, 263
Jones, Alison, 106–10
just-in-time production system, 123

Kant, Immanuel, 36
Kelsey, Jane, 166–70, 267
Keynesianism, 122–3
King, Michael, *Being Pakeha*, 201
kinship, 78
Kirkman, Allison, 63–6
knowledge, 112
Kohanga Reo, 106
Kura Kaupapa, 106

labelling, 240–2
labour market, 83–4, 131, 144, 150, 151–2
    deregulation, 133
labour migration, 197–8, 207–8
Labour Party, 142, 153, 166, 167, 168–9, 290
labour power, 29–30
language, 15
    as a symbolic medium, 43
    as a system of meanings, 54–5
Lasch, Christopher, 92
laws, 233–4
Left Realism, 238–9, 241
legal system, 47–8
leisure, 8, 117, 271–88
    as 'not work', 272–4, 280
    theorising, 286–7
Lemert, Edwin, 240
lesbian women, 64–5, 66, 70, 182
    families, 80
    see also homosexuality

liberal democracy, 159
liberalism, 49
    see also neo-liberalism
life chances, 116, 119, 131, 143, 150–1
lifestyles, 143, 273
local vs global society, 6–9, 56
    body beautiful, 73–5
    changing dimensions of stratification and class, 151–4
    classrooms without walls and the global information society, 111–15
    economic decline and growing crime, 236–9
    evolution of economic ownership and production, 122–30
    future of the nation state, 164–70
    global influence and local problems in cities, 176–7
    health care : the globalisation of medical power and local resistance, 226–30
    leisure globalisation, 277–8
    reality of 'race' and the resistance to racism, 195–8
    state, neo-liberalism and family responsibility, 92–4
    transnational social movements, 259–62
'looking-glass selves', 43
Lorenz, Konrad, 267
Los Angeles riots, 1992, 10–15, 185
love, 82, 83, 84
lumpenproletariat, 153

malestream, 41, 52, 298
Maori
    in cities, 188
    and colonisation, 195–6
    crime, 232, 241
    disadvantage, 206–7, *see also* inequalities
    education, 102, 103, 106, 150–1
    health, 206, 212–13, 216, 230
    home ownership, 147
    household income management, 88
    identity, 197, 199–201

incorporation into working class, 142, 206, 241

and IQ tests, 102, 103

kin relations, 78

poverty, 150–1

self-determination, 197, 202, 203–4, 207, 209, 300

social differences from Pakeha, 10

sovereignty movement, 160, 164, 197

sport and leisure activities, 279–80

suicide, 295–6

and work inequality, 132

marginalisation, 42, 106, 198, 207, 239, 241

market economy, 123, 151, 169–70, 245, 267–8, 301

   see also economic rationalism

marriage, 80, 81, 82–4, 122

Marx, Karl, 2, 23, 27–31, 51, 117, 119, 131, 140, 143, 153, 178, 191, 193, 293–5, 302

Marxist view

   of class, 140–2, 153

   of crime, 238

   of education, 98–100

   of the family, 80–1

   of gentrification, 183

   of health, 216

   of leisure, 273, 286

   of ruling class, 162–3

   see also neo-Marxism

masculinity, 61, 67–8, 85

   and sport, 271, 274–6

materialism, 23, 51–2

matrifocal families, 79–80

McAdam, Doug, 258

McDonaldisation of society/work, 7–8, 135, 152, 165, 189, 297

McMahon, Martha, 85

Mead, George Herbert, 43–4

meanings, 36, 54–5, 85, 296

mechanical metaphor, 213

mechanical solidarity, 178

media, 290

   representation of men's and women's bodies, 60, 72

   and women's sport, 282–5

medical gaze, 228–30

medical power, 213–14, 215, 224–30

medicalisation, 227–8

megalopolis, 175, 176

men

   body shape, 73, 75

   Charlotte Perkins Gilman's view, 40–1

   differences between women and, 60–76

   in the Enlightenment, 21

   inheritance of property, 81

   power relations with women, 71–3, 81

   violence, 71–3, 81

   see also fathers; gay men; masculinity

meritocracy, 98, 101–4

metaphysical stage of human development, 24

micro-sociology, 39, 42, 44, 53–4

middle class, 104–10, 142, 143–7, 153–4

   and gentrification, 182–3

   and leisure, 280–1

migration, 197–8, 207–8

Miles, R., 207

militant stage of society, 25

Millar, John, 22–3

Mills, C. Wright, 3–4, 6, 163, 298

mind–body dualism, 213

mob activity, 255

mode of production, 23, 28, 81, 83, 140

   see also production

mode of subsistence, 23, 82, 83

modernity, 18–21, 30, 31, 39, 52, 94, 195, 226, 291, 293, 299

moral authoritarian, 236

mothers, 84–5

multidimensional society, 25

multi-factoral approach, 35

Multiple Risk Factor Intervention Group, 218

Murdock, G., 79

nation-state, 19, 31, 156–71, 236–7, 291, 294–5, 299

   New Zealand Experiment, 166–70

national identity, 156–71

   and sport, 275–6

National Women's Hospital experiments, 226

nationalism, 26, 160, 164

Nayar society, 79
neo-liberalism, 92–3, 161–2
neo-Marxism, 50–1, 53, 142, 154, 188
neo-Weberianism, 143, 154, 188
New Right, 92, 206, 208, 267
new social movements, 252–4, 257
New Zealand Family Planning Association, 66
Newbold, Greg, 240, 243–6, 248
NIABY, 262
NIMBYism, 261
norms, 31, 33, 40, 44, 46, 47, 49, 51–2, 80, 97, 179, 300
    family, 80, 82
    and sexuality, 69
    see also deviance
nuclear family, 41, 80, 81, 92

Oakley, Ann, *The Sociology of Housework*, 86
observation
    of empirical facts, 33
    participant, 13, 106, 108
occupational health, 218–23
older people
leisure pursuits, 279
poverty, 150
ontology, 28, 30, 49
oppressive effect of the state, 157–8
Orwell, George, *Nineteen Eighty-four*, 157–8, 163

Pacific Islanders, 106, 207
    in cities, 188
    crime, 232, 241
    disadvantage, 206
    educational attainment, 106–10
    poverty, 150–1
    sport and leisure activities, 279–80
    work inequality, 132
Pahl, Jan, 87, 188
paid work, 116, 117, 119–22, 144, 151–2
    end of work as we know it, 126
    management control of labour, 126–130, 219
    see also casual labour; labour market; occupational health; part-time work

Pakeha identity, 201–4
parents, 82–5
Parker–Hulme case, 64–5
Parsons, Talcott, 45–9, 50, 51, 52, 53, 56, 80, 97–8, 224, 227
participant observation, 13, 106, 108
part-time work, 119, 126, 131, 133, 152, 272
passive consumption, 98–9
pastoral (shepherd) society, 22, 23
patriarchy/patriarchal relations, 52, 59, 71, 73, 80, 163
Paxman, Jeremy, *The English*, 198
PCP, 220–23
Pearson, David, 201–4
personal identity, 5, 42, 60, 84–5
personal lives, *see* social and personal interface
pessimism, 36, 38
pharmaceutical industry, 230
philosophical underpinnings, 28, 33
pluralism, 56, 162–3, 174, 297
Poincaré, Henri, 14
police prejudice, 241–2
political economy, 173
political opportunity structures, 257–8
political revolution, 18, 19
politics, 36, 156–71
    postmodern, 290–1
Pool, I., 150
Pope, Alexander, 21
Porteous, Stanley, 103
positive stage of human development, 24
positivism, 33–4
post-citizenship movements, 252–4, 257
post-colonialism, 194–5, 208–9, 299–301
post-Fordism, 123, 135, 142
post-industrial
    society, 289–90, 292
    theorists of social movements, 255, 257, 262
postmodernity, 18, 183, 189, 289–93, 299–300
    and leisure, 286–8
post-structuralism, 54, 55–6
post-welfare society, 92
poverty, 133, 148–51
    in cities, 177, 178
power, 156–7

medical, 213–14, 215, 224–30
state, 156–71
power relations, 70–3, 80–81
pragmatism, 43
pre-industrial protests, 252
prejudice, 192, 241–2
primate cities, 173
prisons, 235, 236, 238, 239
privatising, 8
family, 82, 83, 92
production, 23, 28, 40, 81, 123–6, 133
globalisation, 124–5, 133, 151, 153, 207–8
see also mode of production
professions, 34
proletariat, 29–30, 153, 294
see also working class
prostitution, 237
protest movements, 252–70, 278, 302
cultural construction, 256, 258–9
psychoanalysis, 84
public issues, 4–6
see also social and personal interface

questions
factual, 14
theoretical, 14
'what' and 'why', 15
Quinney, Richard, 238

race, 191, 192, 195–8
racialisation, 198
racism, 41–2, 51, 191–210
institutional, 197
rape, 72–3, 248
rational choice, 51–2, 93
rationalisation, 8, 227
rationality, 34–5, 52
bureaucratic, 35, 36, 38, 297–8
rationalism, 20, 21, 24
reductionism, 53
re-integrative shaming, 239
Reith lectures, 113, 138
relationships, 30
relative deprivation, 148
relativism, 20

religion, 33, 34–5, 296
and medicine, 227
rent-gap, 183, 185, 186
representations, 11–12, 159
research, 10–15, 45, 49
resource mobilisation theories, 256–7
retirement, 150
revolutions, 18–21, 29–30
Rex, John and Robert Moore, *Race, Community and Conflict*, 187–8, 205
riots, 255, 256
ritual, 275–6, 286
Ritzer, George, 7–8
romantic love, 82, 83, 84
Ronald McDonald, 8
rural life, 178–80

Saegert, S., *Masculine Cities and Feminine Suburbs*, 180
safety
in the city, 178–81, 189
and gender, 247–9
Said, Edward, 205
Saint-Simon, Henri, 23, 26
salaries and wages, 71, 120–1, 132, 133, 142, 150, 151–2
Sambia society, 67–8
satellite technology, 111, 113
school achievement, 101–10
schooling and society, 96–100
scientific method, 33
scientific realism, 30, 31
Scottish culture/thought and sociology, 22–3, 26
Seabrook, Jeremy, 5–6, 267
secondary labour market, 131–4
secularisation, 227
security surveillance, 189, 235, 242, 249
self-development, 2
self-esteem, 74, 75, 130
selfhood, 43–4, 45, 85, 226
semiotics, 13
semi-rational collective behaviour, 255, 256
separation from parents, 84
Serious Fraud Office, 240, 244, 245
sexual desire, 63, 68
sexual double standard, 71

sexual harassment, 71–2
sexual identity, 68
sexual offending, 72–3, 238, 247–9
sexual practice, 68, 226
sexuality, 56, 63
    social construction of, 67–70
    see also heterosexuality;
      homosexuality
short-termism, 134
Sicherheit, 236, 248
sick role, 224
Simmel, Georg, 39–40, 43
Simpson, Clare, 282–5
Simpson, O.J., 241–2
single-parent families, 150
Smart, Carol, 247, 248
Smelser, Neil, 255, 256
Smith, Dorothy, 56
Smith, Neil, 186
social action, 36, 47
social and personal interface, 4–6, 21, 45
    Big Brother and national 'belonging',
      157–61
    ethnic identity and notions of
      citizenship, 198–204
    familial relationships and identities,
      82–5
    framing collective identities, 262–4
    illness: interaction, identity and
      ideology, 224–6
    intelligence, school achievement and
      meritocracy, 101–4
    personal safety and gender, 247–9
    rituals, masculinity and nationality,
      274–6
    safety in the city, 178–81
    social and economic significance of
      paid work, 119–22
    social construction of sexuality, 67–70
    wealth and poverty, 148–51
social change, 2, 6–7, 24, 25, 27, 36, 49
    Marx's view, 30
social class, *see* class
social closure, 35, 297
social conflict, 49, 50–1
social constructs, 36
    parental relationships, 82–5

sexuality, 67–70
social control, 235–9
    management control of labour,
      126–130, 219
    medical, 229
social differentiation, 32
social dynamics, 24
social evolutionism, 22–7, 32, 41
    see also evolution
social facts, 33
social identity, 290
social integration, 49, 56, 295
social interaction, 39, 43–4, 45, 51, 52, 54, 55
    doctor–patient, 224–6
    family, 81–2
social interdependence, 94
social mobility, 98
social movements, 19, 251–70, 302
    coalitional politics, 262
    ideological conflict in, 264–9
    oppositional nature, 254
    rhetoric, 261–2
    theorising, 255–9
    transnational, 259–62
social order, 23, 53–4
social organism, 25, 26, 33
social problems, 43, 44–5
social psychology, 39
social reality, 6, 35–6
social ritual, 275–6, 286
social roles, 5, 39–40, 44
    family, 81–2
social solidarity, 32, 275, 295–6
    mechanical, 32, 295
    organic, 32, 295
social statics, 24, 32, 82
social status, 35, 119, 121, 131, 297
social stigma, 10, 69, 225–6, 240
social structure, 25, 25–6, 27, 31, 32, 36, 42–3,
    47–9, 52–3
    and crime, 239, 241
    and health status, 218
    see also class; ethnicity; gender;
      inequalities; stratification;
      structural constraints; structural
      functionalism; structuralism

social welfare, 131, 138, 141–2, 150, 151–3, 163–4, 166–9, 294–5
socialisation, 80, 97
socialism, 36
society, 19
sociobiology, 72
socio-economic revolution, 18–19
sociological imagination, 3
sociologist, role of
    professional, 303–4
    revolutionary, 302–3
    scientist, 301–2
sociology, 23–4
    classical period, 27–36
    definition, 3–4
    first *fin de siècle*, 38–42
    from Europe to America, 42–5
    from the past to the post, 289–305
    from the sixties to the nineties, 50–6
    second *fin de siècle*, 56–7
    social evolutionism, 22–7
    Talcott Parsons and the mid-century consensus, 45–9
    as understanding modernity, 18–21
    why study?, 2
solidarity, *see* social solidarity
specialisation, 32, 35
Spencer, Herbert, 23, 24–6, 26, 33, 42, 43
sport, 271–88
state, 19, 31, 156–71, 236–7, 291, 299
    New Zealand Experiment, 166–70, 294–5
state socialism, 46
    see also welfare state
status, 35, 119, 121, 131, 297
stigma, 10, 69, 225–6, 240
strangers, 39
stratification, 137–55
    see also social structure
structural constraints, 42–3
structural functionalism, 25–6, 49, 50, 53
    and education, 100
    and social movements, 255
structuralism, 54–5, 258
    perspectives on the family, 80–1
    see also social structure
subsistence, 23, 82, 83
sub-systems, 24, 25, 275

suburban neurosis, 180
suburbanisation, 175, 184–5
suburbs, 181, 182–3, 184–7
suicide, 34, 295–6
sunbelt cities, 175–6
surveillance, 189, 235, 242, 249
Sutherland, Edwin H., 243
Sutherland, Oliver, 241
symbolic interactionism, 43, 44, 53–4, 77, 240, 262
    perspective on the family, 81–2

Tarrow, Sydney, 254–5, 257–8, 259–60
technological determinism, 114–15
technological imperative, 213
technology and work, 111–15, 151, 152
television watching, 274
terrorism, 237
theological stage of human development, 24
theorising, 1, 14–15
theory, 1, 44, 47
third-world countries, health status, 217
Thorns, David, 143, 144–7
tikanga Maori, 197, 199
tino rangatiratanga, 203, 209
Tonnies, Ferdinand, 178
total action system, 47–9
total institutions, 54
total system of meanings, 54
Touraine, Alain, 257
tourism, 277–8
Townsend, Peter, 148
trade unions, 30, 120, 141, 153, 252
training, 304
transnational advocacy networks, 260–1
transnational social movements, 259–62
Treaty of Waitangi, 195–6, 200, 202, 203
triad, 39

unconscious, 70
underemployment, 126, 237
unemployment, 5, 110, 126, 133, 153, 206, 237, 295
unit act, 47
United Nations, 165
universalism, 20

unpaid work, 116, 117, 121–2
    see also domestic labour
urban recycling, 175
urbanisation, 40, 174, 178, 188
    see also cities
urbanism, 173, 174, 179

values, 47, 49, 51–2, 80, 97, 274–5
    and sexuality, 69
victims, 248
    of white-collar crime, 245
violence, 71, 72–3, 180, 238, 241, 248, 249
virtual reality, 8
voluntary action, 47, 49

wages and salaries, 71, 120–1, 132, 133, 142, 150, 151–2
war, 26
Waring, Marilyn, 122
wealth, 148–51
    distribution, 149, 151
    generation, 145–7
Weber, Max, 8, 27, 34–6, 38–9, 47, 54, 117, 119, 131, 140, 143, 191, 194, 273, 297–8
weightless economy, 152
welfare state, 131, 138, 141–2, 150, 151–3, 163–4, 166–9, 294–5
Western societies, 20–1, 43, 46, 49, 67–8, 73–5, 78, 114, 214, 217, 226, 293, 298–9, 300–1
whanau, 78
white collar crime, 238, 239–41, 243–6
white flight, 175, 183
Wirth, Louis, 178–9
Wollstonecraft, Mary, 21, 40, 298
women
    body shape, 73–5
    Charlotte Perkins Gilman's arguments, 40–1
    Chicago School, 45
    criminals, 248

    differences between men and, 60–76
    as economic resources, 83
    economic and cultural subordination, 41, 52, 81, 86–92
    in the Enlightenment, 21
    exploitation of, 41
    family heads, 79–80
    and gentrification, 183–4
    health, 71, 217, 226, 227–9, 230
    inequalities, 71, 77, 81, 84, 86–92, 95, 131–2, 138, 139, 143, 144, 163–4, 298
    and male power relationships, 71–3, 81
    sport and leisure, 281–5
    violence to, 71, 72–3, 81, 82, 180, 247–9
    see also femininity; lesbian women; mothers
work, 116–35
    definitions, 116–19
    and leisure, 272–4, 280
    separation of home and, 82, 83, 120, 121
    and technology, 111–15, 151, 152
    see also labour market; occupational health; paid work; unemployment; unpaid work
work-rich and work-poor households, 133, 150
working class, 29–30, 131, 140–2, 182, 290
    health, 219, 219–23
    and leisure, 280
    Maori, 142, 206, 241
    and school achievement, 104–10
    see also proletariat
Wright, Eric, 142

Young, Jock, 238

Zaretsky, Eli, 83
Zimbardo, P., 6